Dedication

Few people have had as much impact on Stafford County as Anne Eliza Stribling Moncure. Born on February 4, 1895, she spent her entire lifetime in Stafford. Miss Anne E., as she was known to most people, dedicated over forty years of her life to educating Stafford's children. She served as a first grade teacher and Supervisor of Elementary Education. An elementary school in the northern end of the county was named in her honor.

Miss Anne E. was a strong supporter of Aquia Episcopal Church as were many other members of her family. With her assistance, a considerable amount of restoration was done to this lovely eighteenth-century church.

Miss Anne. E. was an intelligent, strong-willed woman who touched the lives of many of Virginia's leading citizens. She left us all too soon on October 18, 1984 at the age of eighty-nine and her death marked not only the passing of one of Stafford's finest ladies, but also the passing of an era.

I dedicate this to Miss Anne E. Moncure. As I write, I feel her smiling. I hope I can retell Stafford's history with as much love and humor as she put into her stories. Miss Anne E., I love you.

Table Of Contents

Acknowledgements

Mr. and Mrs. William Acree
Mr. Robert Ballance
Mr. and Mrs. Turner Ashby Blackburn
Mr. and Mrs. Harold Buckholz
Mrs. Jane Carr
Mrs. Daniel McCarty Chichester
Mr. and Mrs. Daniel M. Chichester
Mrs. Fontaine Cooke
Miss Sally Fitzhugh
Mrs. Harvey Fleming
Mr. George L. Gordon, Jr.
Mr. William Wallace Gordon, Sr.
Mrs. E. Boyd Graves
Mr. Peter Grover
Dr. Stewart Jones
Mrs. Thena Jones
Colonel and Mrs. Donald Kendall
Miss Mary Cary Kendall
Mrs. Barbara Kirby
Mr. Edgar Marburg
Mr. Rick MacGregor
Mrs. Catherine Miller
Miss Anne E. Moncure
Mrs. Louise S. Moncure
Mr. McCarty Chichester Moncure
Miss Scott Moncure
Mr. Thomas M. Moncure
Mrs. Barbara L. Moody
Mr. N. Richard Mountjoy
Mrs. Elizabeth Wight Osterman
Mrs. Felicia Waller Parlier
Mrs. Richard Pynn
Mr. Walter "Pete" Roberts
Mrs. Lou Silver
Mrs. Nancy Southworth
Mr. and Mrs. George Stevens
Mr. and Mrs. Lenwood Stevens
Mrs. Pat Wiggington
Mr. Ralph Williams

Very special thanks are extended to Miss Mary Cary Kendall of Richland for her time and unselfish assistance with this project and to Mr. George L. Gordon for sharing his incredible knowledge of Stafford County.

JERRILYNN EBY
P.O. Box 301
Garrisonville, VA
22463

Introduction

A very limited amount of research has been done on the history of Stafford County. This puzzled me for quite some time because the county has a wealth of historical sites, has been home to some of the nation's most notable leaders, and was impacted tremendously by the Revolution, War of 1812, and the Civil War. However, reference works on Virginia or on the South rarely, if ever, mention Stafford, though references to other eastern Virginia counties are found in their texts. Stories, handed down from generation to generation, are told by some of the older residents of the county although facts and details sometimes have become sketchy due to the passage of time.

There seem to be several basic reasons for this obvious lack of information. Many county records were lost in courthouse fires and early land grants were rarely surveyed, much less recorded, resulting in a very noticeable lack of information about the county's early years. Add to this some confusion about the names of creeks, tributaries, and places. Also, when Charles II took the throne after the death of Cromwell, he chose to reward those Cavaliers who had supported his father by granting them huge tracts of land despite the fact that much of that same land had already been granted to other colonists years before. This resulted in double grants which took years to settle in the courts. Many of these records are no longer available and those that are often prove quite confusing.

Finally, it is hard to compare the efforts of Giles Brent carving out his little settlement in the wilderness of Aquia with the empires of Robert "King" Carter, Lord Baltimore, or Lord Culpeper, and it is easy to see why historians would so naturally turn instead to a study of these amazing men and the empires they built.

The Stafford settler's day-to-day objective was survival which he accomplished with varying degrees of success. Those who came to Stafford did not come with the wealth of those who settled along the James and York Rivers or to the north and west of the county. To be sure, many fine old Virginia families descended from those early settlers in Stafford, but to study the county is not so much to study wealth and power as it is to marvel at the resourcefulness and tenacity of an amazing group of people.

Those who settled in Stafford were far removed from their wealthy counterparts to the south, both geographically and economically. Lowland planters (those settled along the James and York) controlled the Assembly until the Virginia Constitutional Convention of 1829. In 1748 a newly-appointed burgess wrote, "I have long observed that the lower members disregard and look upon the Northern Neck as a separate interest, tho' under the same laws." Those who lived in the "back country" generally resented the "tuckahoes" claiming they knew nothing of the "back country." Thompson Mason of Stafford County was so deeply prejudiced against the lower Virginia planters that he wrote in his will of 1785 that he "positively directed that neither of my younger sons shall reside on the South side of James River or below Williamsburg before they respectively attain the age of 21, lest they should imbibe more exalted notions of their own importance than I could wish any child of mine to possess." The hardships faced by those tenacious enough to remain in the area produced generations of self-sufficient, hardy individuals.

As I did the research for this project, I had many questions concerning the best way to organize and present the information. Stafford is a large county and a great deal has happened here in nearly four hundred years. Different sections of Stafford developed at different times and each section became a little community unto itself. I decided, therefore, to organize my material geographically and then chronologically, beginning with what is today known as the Widewater area.

I made every effort to confine my writing to the comings and goings in the county prior to about 1900. In some instances, I had to progress beyond that point for the sake of continuity. All of the homes mentioned were built prior to the end of the Civil War which I chose as a cut-off point because almost all activity in Stafford ceased after the close of that dreadful period. With so little to come home to, so little reason to stay, and embittered by five years of upheaval, most of the county's surviving residents moved westward, many to Kentucky. There they made new starts far from the despised Yankees. County historian George

Gordon tells of one of his ancestors who left the county for Kentucky, expressing the feelings of so many of his fellow Staffordians by saying that Stafford was "too close to those damn Yankees."

I make no claim that every detail in this little sketch of Stafford is correct. With so obvious a lack of historically accurate sources the best to be hoped for is that the reader will come away with a feeling for early life in our county.

My original goal was to catalog as many of the old homes as possible, to mark their locations on a county map, and to provide a picture of the home if available. The frighteningly rapid pace of development in Stafford threatens to obliterate the few old building we have left. New residents are flocking to our county and moving into subdivisions and developments. They have no way of knowing what came before them or of the people who lived and died on that land so long ago.

In 1867 John Lewis Peyton wrote of Stony Hill, "It is impossible to wander over the grassy lawns and through the solemn groves of these lovely grounds, where rare and exotic plants fill the air with their perfume, and flourish in wanton and unpruned luxuriance, while far off stretch the dark forests of oak and pine, without solemn and interesting emotions; to pensively muse, in the deep silence which is still reigning in vale and grove, upon the lives of those who once lived here, and the manners and customs of other days, without being a better, wiser, and happier man."

Southerners have always been close to the land. The English settlers brought with them a passion for land and sought to acquire as much as possible. Second only to God, land was the Southerner's end-all and be-all. Land could make him rich or it could make him poor, but without land he was nothing.

Larry Evans, writer for the *Free-Lance Star*, wrote of Sally Fitzhugh of Poplar Grove,

> There is no way one can verbalize the meaning, the importance of that land. It is certainly something that no dollar value can assess. Sally Fitzhugh senses the meaning; she knows what it is just as well as she knows herself, but she doesn't try to analyze it She touches on that complex meaning when she talks

> about the family graveyard which sits beneath an evergreen, and where most of the members of her family have been buried since 1861.
>
> Southern character has its roots in that brooding land, and Southerners as perceptive as Sally Fitzhugh have been taught humility by that land. They have been taught that there is something larger than themselves. Many of the whites and blacks who have lived with that land of the South seem to share that humility...
>
> Sally Fitzhugh, sitting in a chair next to the Singer sewing machine she has used for many years to make clothes for her family, is staring out the window toward the rolling green hills of the farm. Without turning her gaze from that land, she tells me, "My idea of heaven isn't walkin' on golden streets and eatin' bread and honey. I can't imagine nothing more boring. I hope that heaven is just like this farm and I will be able to roam around it as I please."

So many people are unhappy today. I believe that is because we have lost touch with the land. Most people today live crowded in subdivisions or apartments. How many times have we heard them wish for a house "with a little land around it"? How many tiny gardens and flowerbeds do we see tucked into postage stamp-sized yards? We have a need to work the land, to feel the soil in our hands, and to watch things grow.

The old residents of Stafford know the value of the land. But it isn't a dollar value; there is a much deeper value. And the pain they feel as they see the land paved and subdivided is impossible to put into words.

I think the new residents of our county need to know that before their arrival there was much more here than concrete and subdivisions. I believe that despite their distance from the land, they need and want to understand what came before. Now, more than at any other time in our history, people are looking back, desperately seeking their roots. They are searching for the old strengths and values that were inextricably tied to the land and to the sturdy people who worked it.

The early residents of Stafford were a hardy, independent,

and self-sufficient lot. A number of them played well-documented roles in creating our country, among them George Mason, George Washington, and William Fitzhugh. But many of our residents played less obvious, though none the less important roles. To forget James Hunter, John Rowzee Peyton, John Mercer, Giles Brent, Margaret Brent, and John Moncure to name a very few would be a terrible loss. Without the support of individuals like these, the well-known leaders of our country would have had nothing to lead. Because of their dogged determination and insuppressible independence, America was born. Without understanding the past, how can we take pride in the future?

Stafford County Timeline

1608	John Smith explores and maps river and creeks of Stafford
1620	Indians destroy English trading post at Marlborough
1634	Maryland founded as a Catholic colony
1646-47	Giles and Margaret Brent settle at mouth of Aquia Creek
1650	Sandstone quarries open on Aquia Creek
	50 acres set aside for town of Aquia
1651	Samuel Mathews patents land on Chopawamsic Creek
1654	Valentine Peyton granted land on Aquia Creek
1662	Potomac Parish formed from Washington Parish (Westmoreland Co.)
1662-63	Assembly orders road built from Aquia to Passapatanzy
1662-64	Potomac Church built
	Potomac Parish divided into Upper Parish and Lower Parish
1664	First court meets in Stafford
1668	John Waugh becomes rector of parish
	Brent's Mill built
1671	Margaret Brent dies
1672	Giles Brent dies at Retirement
1676	Nathaniel Bacon led planters against Gov. Berkeley and burned Jamestown
1680	Upper Parish becomes known as Stafford Parish
	Act of Parliament establishes Marlborough as official port town
1686-87	George Brent, Nicholas Hayward, Richard Foote, and William Bristow purchase land for Huguenot settlement (now in Prince William County)
1688	John Waugh nearly causes war with Maryland
1690	First court house burns
1692	New courthouse built at Marlborough
1694	William Waller settles on Hope Run
1700	(?) Salvington built
1701	John Waugh removed as rector of Overwharton
1702	Stafford Parish renamed Overwharton Parish
1706	John Waugh dies

1710-11	Alexander Scott settles in Overwharton as rector
1718	Convict laborers begin arriving in Stafford Courthouse at Marlborough burns
1725	Principio Company of Maryland begins mining iron ore on Accakeek Creek
1726	John Mercer arrives at Marlborough
1727	Falmouth incorporated
1728	Accakeek Furnace begins operation
1730	Overwharton Parish divided with largest section being renamed Hamilton Parish (?) Concord built
1736	Clermont built
1738	Augustine Washington moves to Ferry Farm John Moncure becomes rector of Overwharton
1746-48	John Mercer builds manor house at Marlborough
1750	(?) James Hunter begins manufacturing iron products near Falmouth
1752	Boscobel built
1754	Interior of Aquia Church destroyed by fire
1756	Principio abandons Accakeek property
1768	John Mercer dies
1768-71	Chatham built
1775	Patrick Henry addresses Virginia convention (Give me liberty...)
1776	Richland burned by British James Hunter's musket made standard by Revolutionary convention
1777	Present county border established between King George and Stafford Counties
1781	Cornwallis surrenders at Yorktown
1786	Samuel and Basil Gordon settle in Falmouth
1786-87	Gold found in Stafford
1791	Aquia Sandstone quarry purchased for building of new capitol
1798	(?) Windsor Forest built
1800-03	Aquia sandstone quarries close
1803	Louisiana Purchase
1810	Sherwood Forest built
1812	Potomac Church destroyed by British
1813	Potomac Steamboat Company chartered

1819	Chelsea built
1829	Eastwood built
1842	Trains begin running from Aquia Landing
1850	(?) Fleurry's built
1855	(?) Shelkett's Mill built on Aquia Creek
1861	Virginia seceded from Union
1862	McDonald's Union forces take over house at Chatham Battle of Fredericksburg
1893	Financial panic led to 4-year depression
1894	Great train robbery at Aquia Creek
1901	Wright brothers fly
1908	Henry Ford introduces the Model T car
1920	First adequate road opens through Chopawamsic Swamp
1922	Aquia Sandstone temporarily reopened
1943	U.S. Government condemned some 30,000 acres for expansion of Marine Corps base

Chapter 1

Stafford's Earliest Residents

When the earliest English settlers arrived in what is today known as Stafford County, the Native Americans they found living there were not savages roaming the woods eating berries and roots. They were farmers who lived in a highly-developed social structure. At Marlborough Point alone, the Potomac Indians had cleared about one thousand acres by burning, and worked corn with stone tools.

John Smith began exploring the Stafford area and mapped its rivers and creeks as early as 1608. In his journals, Smith distinguished between three Indian groups which he called the Mayaones, Nacothtant, and Taux (or Toags) which we now know as Piscataway, Anacostins, and Doegs. These tribes lived on both shores of the Potomac River and Smith recorded that there were villages at the mouths of all the creeks where cultivable land and fishing were available.

At the beginning of the seventeenth century Virginia's Northern Neck was populated by Algonquins of the Powhatan Confederacy. Their main town was called "Petomek" ("the place where the tribute is brought") and was located on what we now call Marlborough Point. The Potomac Indians lived there in relative peace and autonomy as they were well distanced from Powhatan himself, and the northern and western parts of Stafford provided a buffer between the Potomacs and the hostile Manahoac tribe to the west.

In 1612 Smith explored the Potomac above "Petomek town" and wrote, "Here doth the river divide itself into three or four convenient branches. The greatest of the least is called Quiyough, trending North-West." Quiyough ("the place of the gulls") is now called Aquia Creek. Smith did his exploration and mapping while on hunting trips out of Jamestown, and many of the names he gave to places in the county are still used today. In his journal he wrote of trading with a group of Potomac Indians at Marlborough in 1608. This village included about one hundred thirty warriors, suggesting a settlement of perhaps as many as five hundred inhabitants.

Not all Native American settlements were permanent like that at Marlborough. More frequently, sites were inhabited off and on for many years. When shells, garbage, and other debris mounted up to the point that they could no longer stand living there, the inhabitants would move. Over time nature would purify the area and the tribe would move back.

An abundance of wildlife provided easy hunting and added variety to the diets of these early inhabitants. Acorns, along with other nuts, plus berries, wild plants, and their cultivated corn rounded out the fare.

In 1612 William Strachy wrote of the Native Americans harvesting oysters up to thirteen inches long. The oysters were shucked, and the fleshy meat was threaded on strings and suspended over a fire. Smoked and dried, the meat provided nourishment for winter. From rivers and creeks the Native Americans caught great quantities of fish. They made wooden points with an added barb of bone; attached to long sticks, these points were used to spear fish. Also, catching nets were woven of fine twigs and attached to poles pounded into the creek bed. Fish, crabs, and oysters provided a bountiful supply of food for most of the year. Meat was dried and stored for use during difficult times. Fish were used for food as well as fertilizer. Placing a couple of fish beneath each hill of corn at planting time increased the yield. These early local inhabitants were far better farmers than the Europeans who followed them.

Soon after Smith's explorations, the English established a trading post at Marlborough. They organized expeditions to map and explore the countryside and traded goods with Jamestown. It was at Marlborough that, according to legend, Pocahontas was sold to Captain Samuel Argall for a copper kettle. The trading post remained until about 1620 when an Indian uprising destroyed it.

On the whole, the settlers' early relations with the Native Americans were good. Misunderstandings arose over land boundaries, ownership of hogs, and trading deals. Unfortunately, these misunderstandings sometimes led to bloodshed, especially when an Indian felt he had been cheated. The promise of an Indian was a sacred oath. He, therefore, believed that when a white man gave his word it, too, would be sacred. That wasn't always the case, however, and the whites often cheated on business agreements with the Indians. The Indians believed that if a man broke his sworn promise, then revenge was in order and it should be taken on as many of the liar's kinsmen as possible. Many whites never understood this concept and for them lying was just a way of doing business when it came to dealing with the natives.

In a letter to his father dated August 12, 1774, John Rowzee Peyton of Stony Hill observed of the Native Americans of Kentucky,

> ...The Indians who have come into contact with Europeans, however, are so crafty, suspicious, vindictive and withal so full of courage and duplicity, that the whites do not readily trust to friendly appearances. I mention where they have come in contact with the whites designedly, for it is admitted by all travelers among them, yourself, dear father, among the number, that where uncorrupted by this association, they are kind, hospitable and inspired by just and noble sentiments. They have been so often deceived; treated with such treachery and barbarity, that their souls thirst for revenge, and there is nothing which the savage will neglect to gratify this passion. He has been known to travel 500 miles on foot, through the forest, in the darkness of night, concealing himself by day, to avenge a wrong. This deep-rooted determination to revenge his injuries, has led to his great caution and his rare powers of dissimulation. I must not forget to say, however, what I have discovered from personal observation, that the Indian when a

> friend, is a steady and warm friend. We know this to be true among those in Virginia, and it is confirmed by the whites of those in the west.

Giles Brent founded the first permanent settlement in Stafford. According to his land patent of January 10, 1686, Brent owned "All that entire Tract Territory of parcell of Land scituate Lying and being in America and bounded by and within the Heads of the Rivers Tappahannock and Rappahannock and Quiriough [Aquia] or Potowmack Rivers and Courses of the said Rivers..."

A Catholic who emigrated from Somersetshire and first settled on Kent Island, Maryland in 1637, Brent held various offices in that colony including Commander of Kent Island, Treasurer, Lieutenant Governor, Councilor, Magistrate, Chief Justice, and Chief Captain of the Province of Maryland.

When the Emperor of the Piscataway Indians converted to Christianity, he sent his only child Kittamaquad to Margaret Brent, sister to Giles, to be taught English. The child was about seven when she went to live with Margaret and it was no doubt here that Giles met her. He married Kittamaquad when she was about twelve years old and upon her father's death, Giles claimed ownership to most of Maryland. This claim provoked a furor among both Indians and whites. Piscataway custom allowed the daughter of the Emperor to take control but the Indians were determined their leader wasn't going to be the daughter's white husband. Lord Baltimore was incensed because he believed that he owned most of the land in question. In the end Giles was encouraged to leave Maryland.

About 1650 Giles sailed across the Potomac with his teen-aged wife and landed on the shores of then-Westmoreland County (now Widewater), uninhabited save for the Indians there. He settled on the point between Aquia Creek and the Potomac River. Here, on the north side of the creek, he found broad flat lands on which to start his plantation, which he named Peace.

Giles' naming of Peace was either wishful or optimistic because early life there was far from peaceful. When Lord Baltimore discovered that Giles had settled just across the river, he ordered Governor William Stone to issue land patents in the Northern Neck including "that place where Mr. Giles Brent now

They Called Stafford Home

The Development of
Stafford County, Virginia
from 1600 until 1865

By

Jerrilynn Eby

Heritage Books, Inc.

Original cover art by Robert Ballance.

Published 1997 by

HERITAGE BOOKS, INC.
1540-E Pointer Ridge Place
Bowie, Maryland 20716
1-800-398-7709

ISBN 0-7884-0665-5

resides and called by him Peace." Settlers began arriving on Brent's Point bearing grants with Lord Baltimore's seal. In 1654 Giles petitioned the quarterly court in Jamestown and requested action be taken to protect the residents of the Northern Neck from Lord Baltimore's encroachments. The ensuing investigation brought an end to Maryland patents in Virginia.

In 1680 the Virginia Assembly proposed to found a town near Brent's plantation, calling it Peace Point. Within a few years a settlement developed a little further up the creek and became known as Aquia Village. The neck of land between Aquia Creek and the Potomac River which included the sites of Peace Point and Aquia Village is now known as Brent's Point.

Brent was a Catholic and, like many Englishmen, he left England looking for religious freedom and hoping to make his fortune. Unlike most who settled in the New World, however, Brent was tolerant of other religions and encouraged people to settle in Stafford regardless of their religious beliefs. Giles' nephew, George Brent, continued to encourage people of diverse beliefs to come to Stafford.

Because Brent's wife was a Native American, the Indians of Stafford were, on the whole, friendly toward Brent. At least one unpleasant incident, however, occurred involving Brent, Colonel Fowke, John Lord and George Mason (I). On March 23, 1661/2 Giles Brent charged the King of the Potomac Indians, Wahanganoche, with the murder of an Englishman. The case was referred to a commission in Jamestown which found no evidence against Wahanganoche and he was fully acquitted. The commission then ordered a committee to look into the affair to determine the source of the differences between the English and the Indians. The trouble seems to have been caused by the murder of several Englishmen, quarrels over land bounds, and a dispute over wild hogs. For the "severall injuries and affronts" suffered by the Indian king, it was ordered that Giles Brent "pay the said Wahanganoche two hundred arms length of roanoke; and that collonell fowke, Mr. Lord and captain Mason pay him one hundred arms length a peece." In addition to ordering these fines, the Jamestown committee declared the men ineligible to hold any public office. (This was a period of extremist actions by those both in and out of office and later records indicate that the men's standing in the community was not impaired by the incident.) Unfortunately, Wahanganoche died on his return from Jamestown and over the next few years the Potomac Indians all but vanished.

Soon after Giles Brent settled on the north side of Aquia Creek, the Waller family took over the land on the south side. They called their new home Concord. The Wallers continued to obtain land in the area and their descendants live in the county to this day.

Relations between the whites and Native Americans in colonial Stafford were fairly stable until the late 1600s, when tensions between the two groups led to bloodshed. In 1669-1670 Parson John Waugh nearly caused a war between Maryland and Virginia by claiming that the Catholic Marylanders were conspiring with the Indians to murder the Stafford Protestants (this story related elsewhere). This did nothing to improve relations between the whites and the Indians.

To make matters worse, by then the white settlers had so grown in number that they had taken over much of the land which the Indians had been cultivating. It must be understood that permanent settlements, be they Indian or white, at this time occupied only a thin fringe along the coast of Virginia; the interior of the colony was wilderness and was inhabited by a few Indians tribes who roamed the dense forest and were mortal enemies of the Potomac Indians. This land take-over by the whites, then, left the coastal Potomacs nowhere to go and reduced their means of making a living to scavenging and stealing.

White–Native American relations deteriorated until, in September 1671, the Assembly at Jamestown authorized the building of a fort for defense against Indians at or near the home of John Mathews on the Potomac River. It is unknown exactly where this fort was located, but the Mathews grant followed Chopawamsic Creek and was bounded on the east by the Potomac River. Captain Peter Knight was to have been in charge of the fort with fifty-nine men.

In July 1675, some Doegs and Susquahannocks rowed over from Maryland and stole some hogs from a farmer living near Aquia. The Indians maintained that this Mr. Mathews had cheated them in a deal and, therefore, they were entitled to the hogs. The Indians were followed back to Maryland and the hogs were retrieved. A short time later, the Indians returned to Stafford and killed two of Mr. Mathews' servants and his son.

That same summer another murder in Stafford was blamed on the Doegs (an unfortunate incident which triggered a chain of events leading to Bacon's Rebellion). A group of Englishmen on their way to church found a white man badly beaten, lying in his doorway. When asked who had attacked him, he answered, "Doegs, Doegs," and died. A boy who had hidden under a bed to escape the attack substantiated the story. Colonel Mason and Captain Brent (Giles II), Troop of the Horse of Stafford, quickly gathered about thirty men and went after the Doegs.

Brent and Mason went to Maryland and found two possible paths; each took a few men and followed a path. Brent happened upon a Doeg cabin where the Indians were having a council meeting. Accusing them of the murder—a charge which the Indians denied—Brent and his men shot about twenty-four of them. Mason, having found a gathering of Susquahannocks and hearing Brent's shooting, opened fire on those poor souls. The Susquahannocks had always been friendly with the whites and this was a most unfortunate turn of events.

Very soon afterward, both Maryland and Virginia established armies of about one thousand or so men to protect their citizens and to stop the Indians from crossing the river. The Indians sent four representatives to ask why they were being treated in this manner, whereupon two of the emissaries were killed. The Indians responded with a major uprising, resulting in many deaths on both sides.

The Indians had a fort on Matapoint Creek in Prince George's County, Maryland, and in 1676 the whites attempted to overrun it. They could not gain access to the fort, however, so they kept the fort surrounded in an attempt to starve out the Indians. Undaunted, the Indians escaped during the night, making their way down the Rappahannock and York Rivers, killing every white in their path. They finally came to the head of the James River, where they killed Nathaniel Bacon's overseer and a servant.

The angry Susquahannocks were terrible enemies, preying mercilessly on the Virginia whites. English settlements on the Rappahannock and Potomac Rivers dwindled, shrinking back to Aquia. It was ten years before these settlements began to return.

Bacon, unhappy with Governor Berkeley's inactions toward the Indian problem, took about two hundred men into the field and almost decimated the Susquahannocks. By 1677 there were very few Susquahannocks or Doegs left. Most of the remaining Susquahannocks fled into Pennsylvania and the Doegs scattered and were absorbed into other tribes.

In addition to his anger over the Indian raids, Bacon also carried a grudge against the now elderly Berkeley. He maintained (with some truth) that the Cavalier Berkeley had been granting political favors to his friends and the friends of Charles II. Bacon used the Indian uprising as an opportunity to run Berkeley out of Virginia and to burn Jamestown, an event which came to be known as Bacon's Rebellion.

After his disastrous trip to Maryland, Giles Brent organized a group of men to help Bacon with his actions against the Indians. Brent was an ardent Indian fighter but he was not willing to support Bacon's defiance of the royal Governor of Virginia; neither were his volunteers. When Berkeley's soldiers began advancing on Brent's men, they all fled, leaving Giles to fend for himself. Giles was arrested but because he laid down his arms, he was not hanged (the fate of many of Bacon's followers).

Giles' life continued its downward spiral. The year after his arrest, in 1677, his wife, Mary (also his first cousin), procured a judicial separation from her husband (only the second recorded separation in Virginia) on the grounds of extreme cruelty. Disgusted, Giles moved to Middlesex County and died there at the age of twenty-seven.

There is no surviving will or record of Brent's estate beyond two grants for 1,800 acres taken out in his name by his father. Giles (I) understood the lucrative possibilities of trading with the Indians and the land he patented for his son was adjacent to the town of the Piscataway (present-day Alexandria). Giles (II) left two sons, Giles (III) and William.

The white population in Virginia was drastically reduced as a result of the Indian massacres but settlers continued to come. In time the population recovered and then exceeded what it had been prior to the massacres. With that growth came towns, businesses, and industries. The Indians gradually disappeared and the colony prospered until the Revolution.

Chapter 2

County Boundary Changes

Stafford has undergone a number of boundary changes since those earliest days of European settlement. To understand the changes one must first understand how counties evolved from parishes. When an area was first seated or settled, parishes were designated and these were often enormous in size. Due to an absence of roads, early settlement began along rivers and creeks and population tended to spread in a north-south orientation. Due to the importance of shipping and transportation, land along the Rappahannock River was very valuable and so was carefully surveyed, the lines running straight from the river east to the ridge on which State Route 218 (White Oak Road) was later built. Present-day tax maps show that many of those old dividing lines survive today. In fact, State Route 601 follows one of those lines very nearly to State Route 218. Land to the west was inhabited only by scattered groups of hostile Indians; settlers and surveyors alike were reluctant to venture in that direction. For this reason, the parishes usually had north and south boundaries but rarely western boundaries.

As the numbers of people increased and new population centers formed, smaller parishes would be cut from the larger original. Later, these new parishes became counties as increases in population required the establishment of courts and other governing bodies.

Stafford County began in 1662 as Potomac Parish, which was the upper portion of Washington Parish of Westmoreland County. The act creating Westmoreland County in 1653 specified a northern boundary at the falls of the Potomac River near present-day Anacostia. There was no western boundary and Westmoreland included everything between modern Westmoreland and Anacostia.

Sometime between 1662 and 1664 Potomac Parish was divided into an Upper Parish and a Lower Parish. According to *Hening's Statutes,* the earliest recorded meeting of a court in Stafford was in 1664, and it is assumed that Stafford County and Potomac Parish were one and the same.

Although the exact date of the dividing of Potomac Parish into the Upper and Lower Parishes is unknown, the division left the greatest part of what was then known as Stafford in the Upper Parish. In fact, this parish contained all of present-day Stafford, Prince William, Fairfax, Loudoun, and Arlington Counties as well as the part of Fauquier that drained into the Potomac River. It is important to note here that the parish and county lines were coterminous and all of this area made up what was then called Stafford County. Overwharton Parish contained all land west of Passapatanzy Creek which drained into the Potomac (a line that roughly followed State Route 218). George Gordon described the boundary as follows:

> In the White Oak section the White Oak Road (Route 218) itself is the dividing line between the two watersheds and the old land grants in the county would come up either from the Potomac River to the White Oak Road or from the Rappahannock River to the White Oak Road. Especially on the Rappahannock River side those old land grant lines are very plain. After the line went northwest to Crane's Corner (U.S. 1 and State Route 627) and west into the wilderness it tended to get lost. In those days that area was sparsely settled and nobody cared very much, but lines were still determined by whether the water flowed to the Rappahannock or to the Potomac.

At that time all the land between the Rappahannock and the dividing line described above was part of King George County. That put most of what we today call the south end of Stafford in King George.

In 1680 reference was made to the Upper Parish as Stafford Parish and the Lower Parish as Choatank Parish. An official list of parishes in 1702 indicates that Choatank was renamed St. Paul's Parish and Stafford Parish became Overwharton Parish (probably named for Parson John Waugh's plantation by the same name). The boundary between the two was Passapatanzy Creek (now in King George).

Increases in population required a division in Overwharton in 1730. Hamilton Parish, formed from the northern and western portions of Overwharton, took by far the greatest part of then-enormous Stafford County. By the mid-1700s Overwharton contained a much reduced Stafford County and a small portion of land along the Potomac which is today part of King George.

The dividing line between Hamilton and Overwharton was the north branch of Chopawamsic Creek to its head and then southwest almost to the Rappahannock near the area known as Beach on State Route 616. These lines remain as the boundaries between Stafford and Prince William and Stafford and Fauquier Counties.

A redrawing of the Stafford–King George boundary line in 1777 placed all land north of the Rappahannock in Stafford.

Chapter 3

Seventeenth-Century Homes

When the phrase "colonial Virginia" is mentioned, most people think of the lifestyle represented by the restoration of Colonial Williamsburg. Quaint villages, great plantations, and cozy cottages create a fantasy image of life in the New World. Unlike their lower Virginia counterparts, the seventeenth-century Northern Neck planters lived in the utmost simplicity. Typically, a new settler in Stafford cut down trees with an ax, thereby opening land for cultivation and providing building materials for a very simple log house. If the man survived such difficulties as starvation, disease, fires, accidents, hungry animals, and disputes with local Indians, and managed to establish himself, he would make improvements to his little house. These improvements included adding clapboard to the outside and, perhaps, an addition on one end. Sometimes it took several generations to accomplish this.

In 1691 an "established" planter, Edward Mason, left the following to his widow: "one Bed and Covering, one small Chest and Box, one small Case, one old brass Candlestick, one old Warming Pan, one Pestle, one old iron box, one pair of Bellows, one old Frying pan, Two dishes, Two plates, one old Bason, one old Pewter Pott, and three Trayes." Clearly, life was not as idyllic as might be imagined.

A Huguenot gentleman traveling through the area in 1686 described the early plantations:

> People are well lodged in this country. The houses are all of wood. The roofs are made of oak

shingles, and the walls of clapboard. Those who are even tolerably well off ceil them on the inside with mortar made of oyster shell lime, which leaves the walls as white as snow. However mean these houses may appear on the outside, for one sees nothing but wood, within they are most agreeable, well glazed and well ventilated. They make plenty of bricks and I have seen several houses of which the walls were entirely of brick. Whatever their condition may be, for what reason I do not know, they build their houses of two rooms only and several closets, all on the ground floor, with but one or two prophets chambers above; but if they need them, they build several such houses. They have also a separate kitchen, a separate house for the Christian servants and a separate house for the negro slaves, and several houses in which to cure tobacco. So it is that arriving at the residence of a person of some consideration, you would think that you were entering a village. Few ever lock the doors of their houses, because stealing is almost unknown....There are no stables for they never house their cattle, but let them run in the woods. The only risk is of wolves.

Chapter 4

The Development of Estates

The English brought with them a passion for land. Land was cheap, readily available, and there were any number of ways an individual could obtain it. Upon initially arriving in Virginia, a man was granted a tract of land. If he sponsored more colonists from England, he would receive an additional fifty acres for each person sponsored. Some farms were relatively small but others, whose owners had been early arrivals, covered miles along great stretches of riverbanks. The rivers provided transportation for people as well as goods, principally tobacco.

Tobacco, introduced to the Europeans by the Native Americans, grew well along the Potomac River. England wanted all of the plant she could get and the colonists grew it, smoked it, and used it in place of cash. Tobacco warehouses and inspection stations were established on the creeks and rivers, at which the tobacco was transferred from wagons to ships for export to England.

The first tobacco warehouse in Stafford County was at Marlborough, though it was soon replaced by a new warehouse at Aquia, the town cut from George Brent's Woodstock plantation on Aquia Creek. By the late eighteenth century, this warehouse had been closed and three others had taken its place. Two of these, the Falmouth and Dixon warehouses, were located in Falmouth. Cave's Warehouse was on Potomac Creek. Planters brought their hogsheads of tobacco to these warehouses and from here it was shipped all over the world.

Tobacco inspectors were appointed by the court for a term of one year. This was a very important job, for it was the responsibility of the inspectors to check the quality of the tobacco and set a value upon it. Since tobacco was used as legal currency, the economy of Virginia depended upon the quality and, therefore, the value of the tobacco brought to the warehouses. English and Spanish coins circulated only for use as "pocket money" leaving tobacco to be used for trading and major business deals. Each September, the inspectors would report to the court the number of hogsheads of tobacco remaining in the warehouses. The court would set a price per hundredweight and order the sheriff to sell whatever tobacco had not already been exported. According to county court records of 1790-1793, the price ranged from ten to twenty shillings per hundredweight.

Not everyone made fortunes with tobacco, for not everyone had thousands of acres on which to plant the crop. There were only a few individuals who owned huge tracts of land in Stafford, namely the Fitzhugh, Brent, and Carter families. In Stafford, most of the planters were working small tracts of land (a few hundred acres or less), but tobacco was still a major crop and nearly every square inch of open land was planted with it.

The early log cabins gave way to large structures, often of brick made from local clay. The more land one had, the more tobacco one could grow, and the larger a house one could build. Without question, the early economy of Virginia was based upon tobacco.

From about 1700 until the Revolution, Stafford prospered. In addition to successful agricultural production, numerous small goldmines opened along the Rappahannock River and sandstone was being quarried along Aquia Creek. The iron industry also was thriving and, overall, most of the residents were prosperous.

Major plantations along the Potomac usually had their own wharves, warehouses, and inspection stations. Smaller planters or inland planters hauled their tobacco to these plantations where it was inspected, loaded on board the sailing ships, and exported, usually to England.

Planters usually did not get into the ship-building business, nor were they normally sailors. A few, such as Travers Daniel and John Mercer, did own their own ships and many owned shares in shipping companies.

For a good many years, the people of the Potomac grew tobacco on every inch of ground they could clear. Corn was grown only for domestic consumption and the waters were fished only for local needs. Manufacturing was almost totally non-existent except for the making of items necessary for the growing, harvesting, processing, and shipping of tobacco.

During the heyday of the Virginia plantations, then, tobacco was the chief crop. Every inch of available cultivable soil was planted in tobacco; the planting of wheat, corn, barley, and vegetables was restricted to only what was absolutely necessary for survival. Tobacco was grown for domestic use and for exportation to Europe, where it was in great demand.

Plantations grew so much tobacco that at times they flooded the market, causing serious economic problems. Planters would sometimes sneak into their neighbors' fields and cut down the crop when it was young—their method of price control. Laws were passed regulating every aspect of tobacco production, from the planting of suckers to the number of leaves allowed on any one plant, to even the planting times. A law enacted in 1657 forbade the planting of tobacco after July 10 (for tobacco is a slow-growing crop, and late planting would result in an inferior-quality product, which affected the plant's value and, therefore, the region's economy). Those convicted of late planting could be fined 10,000 pounds of tobacco, one-half of which was given to the informer and one-half to the county in which the offense was committed. George Gordon speaks of one of his eighteenth-century ancestors who lived at Crow's Nest on Potomac Creek. He was found guilty of late planting and, therefore, devaluing the currency.

Tobacco was extremely hard on the soil. After two or three seasons of planting in the same location, there would be a noticeable reduction in quantity and quality of the tobacco. The planter might then plant the field in wheat or corn, but, in all likelihood, the field would be abandoned and a new one cleared. The seemingly endless supply of land discouraged planters from careful soil management.

This poor farm management initiated a chain of events which brought great changes to the area. Land that is overworked and then abandoned will suffer major erosion problems. Topsoil is carried away by run-off which, lacking plant growth to slow the flow, causes flooding, resulting in yet more erosion. Rivers silt up, affecting fish and oyster populations, drainage of bottomland, and the depths of harbors and channels. Since most early ports were as far inland as possible to lessen the length of overland transport of goods, they were the most affected by the heavy silting. The average life of these inland ports was about fifty years. They quickly turned into mud flats and the towns that might have become great cities or ports were killed by the very industry that created them.

Prosperity and poverty took their turns in Stafford, with the periods of prosperity being short-lived. Then, the Revolution was an economic disaster for the county. Gone were the English markets for Stafford goods as well as English investment in business and industry. Investment money had slowed during the few years preceding the Revolution, but now was totally gone. Soil depletion added to the problems and many residents moved west to settle on free, fresh land.

After the Revolution, the economy of the county soured. The downturn continued through the early 1800s and was largely a result of poor farming methods and the exhaustion of mineral deposits. The population declined steadily as people left the county.

By the mid-1800s, however, the region's population was on the rise again. The land had been fallow for many years and improvements in farming techniques created a strong agricultural base. Residents were also operating numerous profitable fisheries along the Potomac and lumbering became an industry. Fish were caught both for local use and for shipment to distant locations, and logs were hauled to Coal Landing from where they were sent to Washington and Baltimore. Another boost to the economy was the completion of the Richmond, Fredericksburg, and Potomac Railroad through the county, which provided rapid transportation for the first time.

Unfortunately, this era of prosperity was soon ended with the onset of the Civil War. Although actual fighting occurred only at Aquia Landing and near Hartwood Church, the county economy was decimated and did not recover until well into the twentieth century. After the war, the population dropped below what it had been in the 1790s and life all but halted.

Chapter 5

Labor

During the very earliest days of Stafford's history, the colonist provided his own labor. Ill-prepared for physical labor, having led a somewhat pampered lifestyle in Europe, many of these early settlers depended heavily upon friendly Native Americans to show them how to clear land and plant. (The Indians had discovered slash and burn techniques years before and had applied them freely over great areas west of Virginia. In Kentucky, for example, they cleared vast tracts which attracted bison and other large game.)

By the 1660s indentured servants from England were easily available and the Stafford planters began relying on them to fill their labor needs. Two government policies in England contributed to the great number of indentured servants who arrived in Virginia. First, an act passed during Elizabeth's reign required individuals who wished to be employed in the arts or trades to pass through a regulated apprenticeship. There were few of these positions available in England and by 1662 there were a great many unemployed, able-bodied people in that country.

Another act required each parish to take care of its needy. As the population of unemployed people grew, a greater and greater burden was placed on the parishes. Taxes were raised to feed the poor, resulting in open public resentment of them. The best solution to the problem seemed to be to send these people, who were willing to work, to the colonies. There, they could find work—and, at the same time, their labor efforts there would increase the amount of goods sent back to the Mother Country, helping to free England from her dependence on European imports.

Indentured servants, both men and women, agreed to work for a period of years after which time they would be set free. They could be sold while their indenture was still in effect. When their indenture expired, the employer was required to provide them with certain necessities. The "Act concerning servants and slaves" of 1705 regulated the responsibilities of masters and slaves and servants. Masters were to provide wholesome diet, clothing, and lodging, and were prohibited from administering "immoderate correction" and, specifically, from whipping a Christian servant naked without an order from a justice of the peace. At the end of a servant's indenture, his employer was required to set up the now-free person as a potential planter, giving him "freedom dues" consisting of "10 bushels of Indian corn, 30 shillings in money or the value thereof in goods and 1 well fixed musket or fuzee of the value of 20 shillings at least."

England sent many indentured servants to the colonies, solving much of the unemployment problem in her parishes. She had found a convenient dumping ground for her less desirables and she next turned to relieving the overcrowding in her prisons.

In 1718 an Act of Parliament was issued which provided for the transportation of convicts to the colonies. By 1722 convicts were arriving and being bought as indentured servants; they would work on a plantation for seven years and then be given their freedom. The slave trade was still in its infancy and planters of Stafford, poorer than the lower Virginia planters, found it cheaper to use the convicts as a labor source than to purchase slaves.

Virginia repeatedly protested the sending of convicts from England. Having the opportunity for a new life had no effect upon the anti-social behavior of these individuals and they quickly began causing problems in Virginia. After serving their indentures, many began stealing and murdering to support themselves. Crime was rampant in the colony and the Assembly sought to do something about it.

In 1722 the Assembly recorded that "Whereas of late years many persons convicted of felonies and other notorious crimes in Great Britain, have, according to Act of Parliament made in the fourth year of the Reign of our Sovereign Lord King George, been transported into this Colony, and not only great frauds have been committed here by such Convicted persons, whereby the lives and estates of his Magesties subjects are in great danger."

One idea put forth in the Assembly was to put all the convicts in one area with overseers to watch over them. They would grow and cultivate hemp and flax. This area would be called Hempshire and the rope produced would be used to supply the royal navy. This plan never materialized.

An act passed by the Assembly in 1722 required planters to register any convicts they bought and record their names and the offenses for which the servants had been transported. The Privy Council of the King, however, disallowed the act on the grounds that it imposed such difficulties on the importers as to put them out of business. Of course, this was exactly the result the Virginians had had in mind.

Convicts continued to pour into the colony. Crime, especially arson, became so rampant in the Northern Neck area that in 1730 the Assembly increased the punishment for arson, declaring that severe penalties were necessary "in a country which is so much crowded with convicts, who after they have committed a crime may easily be concealed by their abettors until they find means to escape into another government."

The arson continued, with losses including Mount Pleasant Plantation and tobacco warehouses in Northumberland, Lancaster, and Falmouth, all burned in March 1732. The following June, Spotsylvania lost the new parish church of St. Mark. The climax came in 1746 with the burning of the colony's Capitol at Williamsburg.

Finally, in May of 1740 the Assembly recorded that the King had ordered the lieutenant governor of each colony to raise soldiers to fight against the Spaniards in America. "There are in every county within this colony able bodied persons fit to serve his magesty who follow no lawful calling of employment." The county courts were ordered to impress any person except those "who hath any vote in the election of a burgess or burgesses to serve in the general assembly of this colony or who is or shall be an indented or bought servant." Through the process of elimination, this left only the convicts. And so the Northern Neck area was temporarily purged of many of its less desirable citizens.

This simple solution worked so well that not only was the quota of Virginia troops easily met in 1740, but the drafting of the convicts set a precedent soon to be followed by other colonies. In fact, the supply of convicts available to the military was soon exhausted for that year.

Yet more convicts came with each succeeding year. Northern Neck planters were not as wealthy as the lowland planters and the convicts provided a cheap source of labor, cheaper than slaves, of which they owned relatively few. The problem of the freed convicts, likewise, normally affected only the Northern Neck area and not the lowland residents, an important fact when it came to trying to solve the crime problem.

The "Act concerning servants and slaves" of 1705 also protected and provided for the convicts once their indenture was completed, a sore point among many in this part of the colony. During the Assembly of 1748, a proposal was made to rewrite the Act of 1705 to include a more severe rule to deal with convict servants. The burgesses from this area claimed that the convicts had been sent to Virginia for punishment and that they should not be entitled to the same privileges as servants. The lowland planters, who controlled the Assembly and who were not directly affected by the problem, however, disagreed. They argued that as long as England insisted on sending the convicts, it was better to at least try to set them up as productive citizens than to do nothing at all for them. They also felt that the convicts might be encouraged to move to the westernmost frontier and so provide a buffer between hostile Native Americans and the rest of the colony. The lowland planters won the vote and even increased the freedom dues to "3 pounds, ten shillings, current money."

Dinwiddie, upon becoming Governor, proclaimed the Act of 1748 void and in 1753 the act was rewritten to exclude convicts from all "humanitarian" provisions and became law.

Despite this, more convicts were imported due to what Beverley described as the "greedy planter" anxious for cheap labor. In fact, importation continued even after the Revolution when Virginia could have been free to stop. It continued until Congress finally called a halt to it in 1788.

Blacks first came to Virginia in 1619. By 1660 they were being bought and sold as slaves. They continued to be brought to the colony throughout the eighteenth century and, in many parts of Virginia, replaced indentured servants. By 1756 there were an estimated 120,000 slaves in Virginia. Most of the farms in Stafford were not owned by wealthy land barons, however, and there were never the great numbers of slaves in the county that there were in other parts of the colony. There were a few extremely wealthy people in the county (the Fitzhughs and Mercers, for example) who owned a great many slaves, but the majority of the planters had from one to five slaves and many farms had none.

William Fitzhugh used slaves for the growing and handling of tobacco. Because few slave ships came to Stafford, Fitzhugh had to send to York and Gloucester to purchase slaves.

John Mercer of Marlborough was also a slave owner. In 1730 he bought a black woman named Margaret for forty-three pounds of tobacco. By 1736 he owned more than a dozen slaves. Fourteen years later he owned sixty-six, an unusually high number for this area.

Many whites did not own slaves and those who did rarely owned more than five. The care and feeding of slaves was costly. A person owning ten slaves was considered to be rather well off. Mercer described the cost of keeping a slave as "enormous" and estimated that care to run five pounds per year.

Some slave ships did come in to Falmouth, but because this was the last stop on a circuitous route, there were complaints that the slaves still on board were picked over. A Scot merchant in Falmouth, William Allason, was an importer and exporter and also dealt in slaves. He only handled American-born blacks, however, as African-born were often rebellious and could not speak English. Allason served as a slave agent for Lord Fairfax, a Virginia proprietor.

Whites who did not own slaves would often hire one from another owner or hire a free black. Slaves owned by the French family of Poplar Grove were hired out in Richmond and given annual leave to visit Stafford.

The use of indentured servants declined in favor of slaves for several reason. First, there was a constant quest for the cheapest labor possible. Both servant and slave carried an initial purchase price. The slave, however, did not have to be periodically replaced with a substitute who was expensive to purchase. Both servant and slave had to be fed, clothed, and housed, but once the servant completed his term of indenture, he had to be freed and provided with the costly allowances already mentioned.

Indentured servants were more expensive over the long run because the cost of transportation was high, their term too short, and the chances of sickness or desertion too great. One owned the slave for his entire lifetime. If the slave produced a child, that was increasing the valuable labor force. The slave had to be provided for in his old age, but even old slaves could perform some tasks.

Many poorer planters bought a few slaves. If the cost of an adult was too high, a child could be bought which would grow into a valuable asset. The initial outlay for the slave was greater than that for the indentured servant, but planters could secure their purchase by pledging their farms and crops, and the investment usually paid handsome dividends.

Widewater

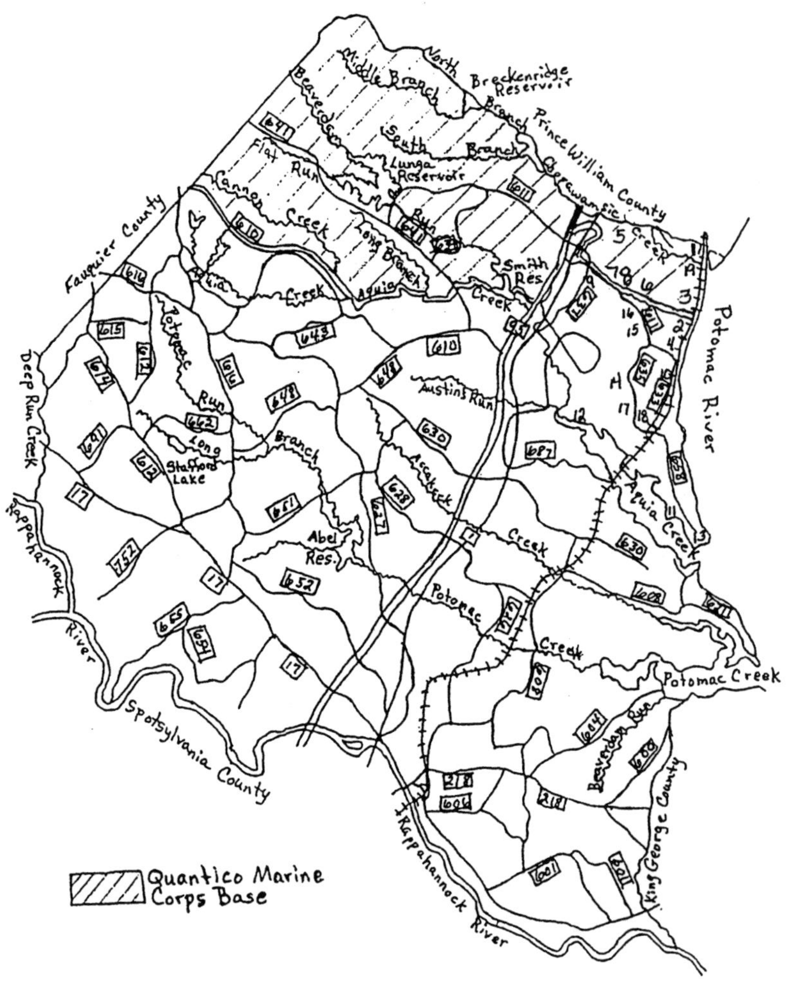

1 .. Dipple
2 .. Clifton
3 .. West Farm
4 .. Richland
5 .. Clermont
6 .. Somerset
7 .. Chelsea
8 .. Rectory
9 .. Bloomington
10 .. Arkendale
11 .. Myrtle Grove
12 .. Rock Ramore
13 .. Peace
14 .. Palace Green
15 .. Brent's Mill
16 .. Clifton Chapel
17 .. Edge Hill
18 .. Westwood
19 .. St. Mary's

Chapter 6

Widewater

Folks visiting Widewater today blink and ask, "Well, where is it?" There is little evidence remaining to indicate that Widewater was once one of the busiest areas in the entire county. Here the largest colonial commercial fishing industry operated. Boats sailed in and out of the creek hauling hundreds of tons of cordwood, fish, and sandstone which were quarried nearby. During the Civil War, a railroad terminal across the creek at Aquia Landing (now Aquapo) served as a primary supply route for the South. Today, we use the name Widewater to refer to the land between Chopawamsic Creek and Aquia Creek although the name Widewater didn't come into popular use until early in the twentieth century.

There were numerous farms in Widewater which raised tobacco and grains. Brent's Mill once stood next to the little stream that flows behind Widewater Grocery, and ground quantities of corn and wheat. The Brents also operated a store, distillery, and blacksmith shop nearby.

The Brents (Stafford's first English colonists), Wallers, and Lees owned large tracts of land and built fine homes on their estates. The oldest home remaining is Richland (built by the Brent family), the rest falling victim to fire and neglect and vandalism by Union troops.

Peace was Stafford's first homestead and the home of Giles Brent after he left Maryland in 1652. This simple log building was built on the little point where Aquia Creek converges with the Potomac River, and was part of Westmoreland County. Shortly after establishing himself, Giles moved inland and built a second home which he called Retirement. He died there in 1672, having opened the wilderness of what would become Stafford to people of all religious beliefs.

Through the centuries there were a number of fine old houses built in Widewater, most of which are gone now. In 1942 the government condemned some 30,000 acres to expand the Quantico Marine Corps Base. Much of that area was made up of large farms in the Widewater-Chopawamsic area. The residents were paid small sums for their land and given two weeks to pack up their families, livestock, and belongings and find new homes. The old places they left behind were used by the Marines for experiments or target practice. Consequently, they were soon leveled. Among those lost were Somerset, Clermont, Rectory, Dipple, and Laurel View. At least an effort was made to move identifiable graves from the family cemeteries to the graveyard at Aquia Church. The federal government hired men to move the graves and the project was monitored by a descendant of the Moncure family.

Dipple

Dipple was located about five and one-half miles from the town of Triangle in Prince William County on Chopawamsic Creek (today, on the airfield at Quantico). Little is known about the house except that it was a two and one-half story brick home built on land that was originally part of the 5,211-acre Samuel Mathews grant. Alexander Scott purchased the property from Mathews' grandson in 1724 and named it Dipple after his native parish in Scotland. The first house on the site was most likely built of wood. The brick house, which survived until the expansion of Quantico in 1942, may have been a second or third structure.

Alexander Scott was born in Dipple Parish, Scotland on July 20, 1686. Scott arrived in America in 1701 but returned to England to be ordained in 1710. Upon returning to America, he settled in Stafford and accepted the position of minister of Overwharton Parish.

A glebe was a farm owned by a parish. The glebe was

used by the parish minister and formed part of his legal stipend. By law, the vestry of the parish had to supply the glebe with at least two hundred acres, a house, kitchen, dairy, meathouse, cornhouse, barn, and fenced garden plot. In addition, the rector was to be paid 16,000 pounds of tobacco per year. Rarely, however, were the parishes able to make such a payment and the tobacco that was offered was often of the poorest grade.

If the glebe was larger than the rector needed to provide for his family, then parish-owned slaves were used to work the fields, the profits being used to support orphans and the needy. After the Revolution, the Episcopal (Church of England) churches lost their glebe lands. By 1802 many had been sold for the benefit of the public treasury.

At the time Alexander Scott took the position of minister, the glebe for Overwharton Parish was in the south end of the county (now Waugh Point, King George County), and was inconvenient because the parish then included half of present-day Stafford, Fauquier, and King George Counties, as well as all of Prince William, Fairfax, Arlington, and Loudoun Counties.

Scott married Sarah Gibbons Brent, widow of William Brent of Richland (1677-1709). William had returned to England from Aquia to claim his family estates of Stoke and Admington; while there he married Sarah Gibbons of Wiltshire, in 1709. Unfortunately, he died soon after, leaving her with child. Some time after the birth of her son, William (1710-1742), Sarah sailed to Virginia. In 1717 she married the Reverend Alexander Scott. They had no children; William inherited his father's property, including the Richland tract.

After Sarah's death in 1733, Alexander invited his younger brother, the Reverend James Scott, to live with him at Dipple. Alexander died on April 1, 1738, leaving the plantation to his brother. James Scott and his family lived at Dipple until 1745, when James left to serve in Dettingen Parish in Prince William County, a position he held for thirty-seven years. His five eldest children were born at Dipple.

Alexander Scott served as minister of Overwharton Parish for twenty-eight years, preaching at both Aquia and Potomac Churches. His will provided thirty pounds sterling for the purchase of "a silver pottle flaggon, a silver pattin and good substantial silver pint chalice and cover for the communion service in the said church and each to them to have engraved these words, Given by the Revd. Alexander Scott, A.M. late minister of this Parish and the date when given..." Scott was followed by the Reverend Mr. John Moncure, also from Scotland.

Dipple was one of the fine old farms lost to the Quantico Marine Base in 1942. An interesting feature of the Dipple house was a double chimney on one end. The graves from the cemetery were moved to Aquia Church.

Chopawamsic Island, just to the east of Dipple, is part of Stafford County. Many maps show this island as belonging to Prince William or to Quantico. Actually, it did not become an island until Quantico engineers diverted Chopawamsic Creek and filled the adjoining swampy area to build the airfield. Prior to these activities, the ground between Dipple house and the river was low and wet but not underwater.

Clifton

From Boswell's Corner at U.S. Route 1, Clifton was .6 mile southeast on State Route 637, 3.2 miles east on State Route 611, and then .5 mile north on a private road. Clifton's early history is somewhat vague but it is likely that the first house on the site was built in the late 1600s. The property seems to have belonged to Margaret Brent, sister of Giles. Clifton has been the home of the Cliftons and Wallers since that time. Today, the property is owned by Mrs. Elizabeth Wight Osterman, whose mother was a Waller.

Clifton probably took its name from the Clifton family who lived there in the seventeenth and eighteenth centuries. Because of their close proximity to the Brents of Richland, it is quite possible that the Clifton family were Catholic. This is further supported by the fact that no mention of the family name, Clifton, appears in the Register of Overwharton Parish—had they been Protestants, they should have been listed.

While Giles Brent was establishing his settlement (and living on or near the present-day Richland property), his niece Anne Brent married a James Clifton in England. James came to Virginia but returned to England with his wife. He died there in 1714, outliving all of his children except one daughter. His principle heir was nephew Thomas Clifton to whom he left his lands in Virginia. Thomas visited Virginia in 1700 but, like his uncle, didn't stay. His grandson, William, inherited the Virginia property. While we are not certain of the exact location of the Clifton property, it seems likely that the present Clifton home is a part of it.

Anne Brent was a sister to George Brent of Woodstock. Court records of September 27, 1671 show the settlement of a land dispute between James Clifton and Giles Brent. The parcel in question had been assigned to Clifton by Margaret Brent as a dower for his wife, Anne. The court ordered Giles to deliver the land or the value of it to Clifton plus pay damages and costs.

It is unknown how long the property stayed in the possession of the Cliftons. An insurance policy of 1806 shows the home as belonging to the Clifton family. Hannah Waller of Concord married B. (Burditt?) Clifton. They had no children and at their deaths the property was inherited by the Waller family.

During the Civil War, the farm was used as a camp by both Northern and Southern troops due to its strategic location in relation to the rail head at Aquia Landing, which was directly across the mouth of Aquia Creek from Clifton. The house miraculously survived shelling by Union forces; during some

Clifton

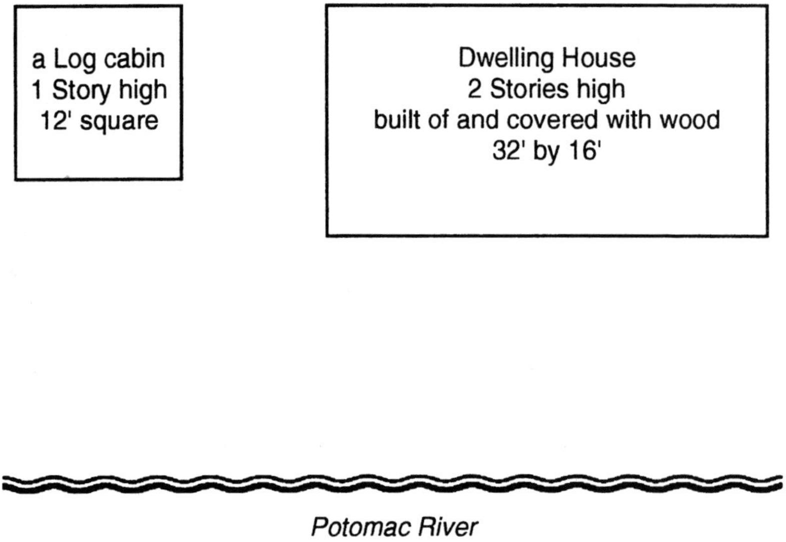

a Log cabin
1 Story high
12' square

Dwelling House
2 Stories high
built of and covered with wood
32' by 16'

Potomac River

From an 1816 Mutual Assurance policy

twentieth-century repair work, shell remnants were found in the walls.

According to one story, the day that war was declared gunboats sailed down from Washington to shell the rail head at Aquia Landing. Mistaking the cluster of buildings at Clifton for the rail head, the boats commenced shelling. Mrs. Waller ran for her life with her infant, Kate, and hid in a ditch all day until, by darkness, she was able to sneak back to the house.

While Clifton was most noted for the huge seine fishery to be discussed later, the property may also have been one of the first duck hunting establishments in the United States. It was extremely well-known for its excellent hunting and the ducks came there by the thousands. Presidents Cleveland and Harrison came regularly to hunt as did many other people. Theodore Roosevelt also came once or twice but not as frequently as Cleveland and Harrison.

The large frame house on the Clifton property was lost in a tragic fire on Christmas Day, 1945. After opening their packages, the family put the wrapping paper into the wood stove and left for dinner at Richland. Apparently, the chimney caught fire and by the time the family returned home, the entire back section was in flames. They were able to save the silver and a few pieces of furniture, but the rest was lost. A new home was built near the old foundation, and some of the sandstone from the old chimneys and foundation was salvaged and used in the walls of the new house.

Clifton Chapel

Tiny Clifton Chapel was built in the mid-1800s on two acres of land given from the Clifton estate by Withers Waller. Because county roads were so bad, many Widewater residents were unable to attend Aquia Church and the chapel provided them with a convenient place to worship. There are no known records which provide the exact building date for Clifton Chapel. For many years it was believed that it had been built sometime after the Civil War. An 1856 diary entry, however, proves that the church had been built and services were being held much earlier.

Clifton Chapel

Mrs. Chester Pierce, a descendant of the Edringtons of Myrtle Grove, wrote about attending services there and commented on the sermon.

During the Civil War, Clifton Chapel played an important role in the defense of the Potomac River, Aquia and Chopawamsic Creeks. On May 28, 1861, *The Fredericksburg News* reported that the Lacy Rifles were forming. The company formed at Lancaster court house under Captain Samuel P. Gresham. They sailed up the Rappahannock to Fredericksburg, moved by train to Brooke, and marched to Clifton Chapel where they became Company F, 47th Virginia Infantry.

Colonel George W. Richardson assumed command of the 47th in July 1861. He established his headquarters at Clifton Chapel, what he described as "an extreme outpost on the Potomac." Richardson and his 47th Virginia Infantry were charged with the defense of some ten miles of coast between Aquia and Chopawamsic Creeks. The ridge on which stood Clifton Chapel was strategically located to provide troops with a clear view of the mouth of Aquia Creek and the rail head on the opposite shore. Soldiers from "Camp Clifton" and two other Confederate camps on the banks of Aquia Creek defended the rail head at Aquia Landing, the primary north-south supply route. In late March 1862 Colonel Richardson marched the 47th to Richmond to help defend the Confederate capital.

In 1869 Mrs. Sydney Smith Lee, sister-in-law of Robert E. Lee, wrote to her son in the Northern Neck saying that she would be unable to send a contribution to help restore his church as her money would have to go towards repairing Clifton Chapel. It is unclear whether Clifton had suffered damage from the war or simply from several years of neglect.

Clifton Chapel was only used intermittently after 1940. Today it stands in a sad state of disrepair although the parishioners of Aquia Church hope to restore it soon.

The Waller Fishing Shore

Stafford has had a number of industries since its beginning, and one of the most impressive and longest-operating was the Waller Fishing Shore at Clifton. Quite a bit of fishing was done along the Potomac and its tributaries in the eighteenth century. Fishing was primarily carried out at "fisheries," each described legally as a "regularly-hauled fishing landing"—normally a length of privately-owned shoreline that had been cleared of obstructions. The land owner might fish it or he might rent the area to someone else, thus providing some extra income.

At Clifton, net fishing followed the seine method. The nets used in the seine operation were huge—often several miles long. The nets—each called a seine—had large blocks of cork floaters attached at intervals along the top edge and pieces of lead sinkers attached along the lower edge. The seine would "hang" vetically in the water; when its ends were pulled together, it would encircle and thus capture fish. The width of the net was determined by the depth of the water; the cork needed to remain floating on the water's surface and not be pulled under by the weight of the lead. Had the top of the net submerged, fish could have escaped over the top.

Fish caught at Clifton were of such incredible number and variety that Andrew Burnaby made the following observation in 1759:

> Sturgeon and shad are in such prodigious numbers that one day with the space of two miles only, some gentlemen in canoes caught above six hundred of the former with hooks, which they let down to the bottom and drew up a venture when they perceived them to rub against a fish; and of the latter above five thousand have been caught at one single haul of the sein.

Now, I'm not sure how two men in canoes ever made it back to shore with over six hundred sturgeon, but it is clear that the waters teemed with fish.

During the early-to-mid-eighteenth century, one of the major problems confronting the commercial fishermen was the unpredictable availability of salt, a great deal of which was needed for the preservation of the fish. England reduced the amount of high-quality Portuguese salt being sent to America and, instead, forced the colonies to use an inferior quality English salt. By the end of the eighteenth century, however, the salt issue had been resolved and the Potomac fishing industry was stable and providing good income for those people involved.

While the price offered for fish was low and remained so throughout the eighteenth and nineteenth centuries, the quantities caught were so huge that a good profit could be made.

A letter from John Mercer to Richard Sprigg describes the preserving process:

> April 19, 1779. To cure the fish properly requires two days in the brine before packing and they can only lie packed with safety in dry weather. These circumstances joined with the heading and drawing will show that no time was lost—only 9 days elapsed from his arrival here to his completing his load of 15,000 herrings, a time beyond which many wagons have waited on these shores for 4,000 uncured fish and many have been obliged to return without one, after coming 40 and 50 miles and offering 2 and 5 dollars a thousand. Several indeed from my own shore and six who want 36,000 herring will, I believe, quit this night

> without a fish, after waiting all this storm on the shore at Marlborough Point five days.

Fish were taken in such numbers that as early as 1815 concern about over-fishing was observed. A notice placed in the Washington newspaper *The National Intelligencer* remarked on "the destructive effects of tide or Gill Nets, which have been unlawfully set in our waters and have within the last three seasons so greatly lessened the number of Shad and Herrings taken out at the best landings."

In 1835 an article appeared in the *Gazetteer of Virginia* stating that "one haul is 4000 and upward, and of herrings from 100,000 to 300,000. In the spring of 1832 there were taken in one seine, at one draught, a few more than 950,000, accurately counted."

Prices for the fish varied with the quantity and the species. Fresh herring in 1832 sold for about 25¢ per thousand, while shad, a delicacy, brought $1.50 per hundred. At times, though, the herring could be bought for as much as $1.50 per thousand and shad for $3 to $4 per hundred. The *Gazetteer* further stated that "In the height of the season, a single shad, weighing from six to seven pounds is sold in the markets of the District for 6 cents." During the heaviest years for herring, they were often just thrown away or spread on the fields as fertilizer for want of a buyer. Salt herring were a standard for feeding slaves and workers and were often stored for use by everyone during hard times. George Washington issued twenty salt herring per head per month at Mount Vernon.

The 1835 *Gazetteer* also notes that along the Potomac there were one hundred fifty-eight fisheries employing 6,550 laborers, and 450 boats operated by 1,350 navigators. The sex-week shad harvest yielded some 22.5 million shad. That same year 750 million herring were caught, requiring 995,000 pounds of salt and a great many packing barrels to hold the finished product. While these figures seem astronomical, the catches after the Civil War were even greater. Fishing all but stopped during the war, allowing the fish to recover from the over-fishing, since in Stafford there was no one left to operate the fisheries.

Fishing in Widewater dates back to the earliest settlement of the area, for it was fish and corn that formed the diet of the residents for many generations. Somewhere along the way, however, the Waller family of Clifton developed fishing into an industry. This happened well before the Civil War because Withers Waller, who was operating the business at the time of the war, had been taught by his father and even at that time no one was certain when the business actually began.

At Clifton, the fishing operation was carried out on the shore just below the house. Close by were cottages for the workers and buildings for packing, salting, and storing hundreds of barrels of fish. A barn provided shelter for the mules who walked countless circles around the great turnstile used to haul in the nets.

The Potomac is about five miles wide at Clifton and the seine was as long. Setting the net required two boats and careful timing. The first, a net boat, held the bulk of the net which was folded accordian-style and poled on the stern of the boat. This boat stayed close to the shore while a second boat occupied by a captain, steersman, and twelve rowers took the end of the net and headed out into the river, describing a semi-circle. The boats then returned to shore. The mule-powered turnstile helped to draw in the net, heavy with tons of fish.

The Potomac has always been blessed by an inconceivable abundance of fish. A typical single haul from the Wallers' seine yielded between 75,000 and 135,000 fish. The net would contain so many fish, in fact, that it could not be drawn in all at one time and some of the workers would wade out and dip the fish into the boats, where they were cleaned. From Clifton, fish were sent up and down the east coast and as far west as Chicago.

During the Civil War, the Wallers—as well as most Stafford residents—left the county, and business came to a halt. Withers enlisted in the Confederate Army to fight for the Southern cause and his family left Stafford to avoid the invasion of Northern troops. After the war, some of the people returned. The area was so desolate, though, that many people who came home decided not to stay. The Wallers, however, returned to the life that had supported them for generations and within a few years the fishing business began to pick up and was soon thriving again.

In 1868 Henry Moore, partner with Withers Waller, filed suit in Stafford County Circuit Court charging Waller with selling fishing equipment belonging to the partnership without sharing the profits. Moore claimed that in 1861 when "hostilities commenced between the Southern States and the United States Government" put an end to fishing operations at Clifton, he was forced to return home to Maryland. Left at the fishery were three to four hundred barrels of herring worth about $6 per barrel, along with "a complete and extensive outfit for fishing consisting of seine, Boats, barrels, etc amounting in value to eight or ten thousand dollars." Moore returned to Clifton in 1865 and found that Waller had disposed of the fish and equipment and had failed to make any settlement with his partner.

Waller replied to Moore's suit stating that at the end of the 1861 fishing season, he realized the fishing equipment would "be greatly exposed to pillage, depredation and loss from the violence and spoilation incident to military operations." The fish were sent to Fredericksburg to be sold and the proceeds from the sale deposited in a bank there. After the war the Confederate accounts were worthless.

Waller remained at Clifton while Confederate forces were in control of the area. In the spring of 1862 he, "seeing the great peril in which said seine and rope etc were, caused them to be removed to a farm of a relation situate some seven miles (in the Forest) from the Potomac, in Stafford County, and store them in a house on said farm [probably Woodstock]...Fortunately during all the campaigning and Military movement conducted in said region in 1862 and 1863 no harm happened to said seine etc.

"Said Seine etc lay at said House of said relative until May 1864 when the Confederate authorities were making active search for and proceeding to impress all Fishing outfits belonging to private individuals." Waller realized he would lose the equipment through impressment and he chose, instead, to take the equipment to Richmond and sell it. There he received a contract for the seine and ropes, $10 per pound for the nets and $5 per pound for the ropes. Unfortunately, he was paid in Confederate currency which was soon as worthless as that he had deposited in the Fredericksburg bank. Despite his efforts, Waller had no profits to share with Henry Moore.

Clifton was not the only fishery operating along the river, though it was unquestionably the largest. Just above Clifton was St. Mary's Fishery at Dipple on the point of land where the

Marine Corps air strip was later built. South of Clifton and Richland was the Arkendale fishery, and on Aquia Creek, just around the end of Brent's Point, was the Edrington fishery. As a general rule, fishing was quite profitable, the rivers teemed with fish, and most people who owned shorelines operated their own fishery or leased the land to someone else to fish.

The West Farm

Just north of Clifton was the West Farm, probably named for the West family who patented land in this area in the seventeenth century. Little is known about the house or farm and the only illustration known remaining is a drawing from an 1806 Mutual Assurance Society of Virginia policy. This drawing shows a large frame house with a porch on both long sides, a barn, a school house, and a stone kitchen. The house was valued at $2,500, the kitchen, school house, and barn at $150 each. Compared to other insured homes at the time, this seems to have been a fine house.

Colonel John Cooke (1755-1819) may well have built the house. He served as a justice for Stafford in 1781 and his name appears in the 1785 and 1786 personal property tax records as owning 26 slaves, 8 horses, and 18 cattle.

Colonel Cooke's daughter Elizabeth inherited West Farm and seems to have been a notable manager in her own right. She inherited several plantations in Stafford from her own family prior to her father's death, which she managed with some measure of success. In 1768 she was taxed on 2,324 acres in her own name. After the colonel's death, she apparently did not marry but continued to operate her plantations and ferry.

The West Farm is perhaps best known for the ferry that operated there for many years and provided transportation between Stafford and southern Maryland (just across the Potomac River). In November 1766 the Assembly ordered the establishment of several new ferries on the Potomac, one of which was to operate "from the land of Elizabeth Cooke, in Stafford county, below the mouth of Chopawamsic creek, across the river Patowmack, to the land of Clement Kennedy in Maryland, the price for a man two shillings, and for a horse the same; and for the

West Farm

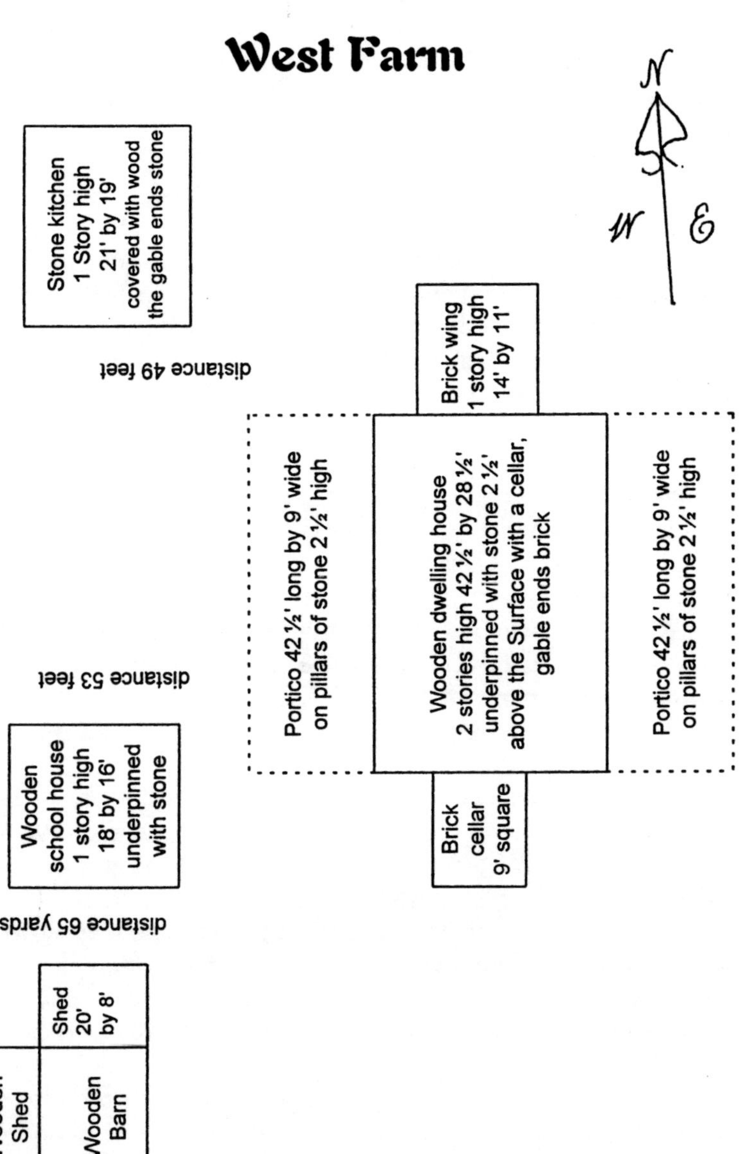

From an 1806 Mutual Assurance policy

transportation of wheel-carriages, tobacco, cattle, and other beasts" the prices were specified.

It is interesting to note that at this same meeting of the Assembly, the Burgesses turned down a request by James Scott, brother of Alexander, to establish a ferry from Dipple to Cedar Point, Maryland.

In October 1791 the Burgesses again authorized a ferry "from the land of Gustavus Scott whereon Hawkins Stone liveth, in the county of Stafford, across Patowmack river, to the lands of Clement Kennedy, in the state of Maryland." It seems likely that this was a continuation of the earlier license to Elizabeth Cooke.

At this point a bit of genealogy is appropriate. John Cooke (d.1733) married Elizabeth Travers. Their son, Travers Cooke (c.1730-1759), married Mary Doniphan (1737-1781), daughter of Mott Doniphan, Vestryman of Aquia Church. Mary Doniphan married secondly Colonel William Bronough (1730-1800) and had numerous children. The only child to survive from Mary's first marriage was Colonel John Cooke (1755-1819) who married Mary Thomson Mason. Colonel Cooke acquired the very handsome Marlborough estate from the Mercers, to whom Mary Mason was related. John Cooke also owned the Aquia quarry in partnership with Daniel Carroll Brent (1760-1815). At the time of the insurance policy mentioned above, a Mr. John Bronough was residing at Marlborough, most likely a son of Mary Doniphan's second marriage.

In 1825 Withers Waller bought West Farm from the estate of John Cooke. Family letters reveal that, prior to the Civil War, Mr. and Mrs. Waller considered leaving Clifton house and moving into the home of West Farm because it was much grander than Clifton. Their plans were interrupted by the war, however, and after the war there was no money for renovation of the then run-down building. The house remained vacant for years, providing shelter for occasional vagrants. It finally burned early in this century.

The above-mentioned John Cooke was fairly well to do by Stafford standards. This was reflected by his inventory, as recorded in county court records upon his death. The inventory included:

10 slaves	2 heifers	20 hogs
2 horses	2 steers	12 sheep

2 cows
1 walnut table
1 pine table
2 sets of drawers
1 cupboard and safe
2 spinning wheels
1 loom
12 chairs
4 chests
2 saddles and saddlebags
2 looking glasses
18 empty barrels
1 crosscut and 3 hand saws
9 pewter basins
4 pewter plates
1 coffee mill
1 spice mortar
2 flat irons
4 iron pots
2 covered skillets
1 grid iron
3 pot racks
1 flesh fork and griddle
2 ladles
3 beds and furniture
1 frying pan, fencer, and hooks
1 tongue shovel
2 iron forks and drawing knife
4 hoes
2 spades
4 wedges
3 grubbing hoes
3 augers
1 cart and gear

The appraisers valued his personal property at $2,046.70, a substantial sum of money.

The origin of the name of this property is uncertain. Originally it was part of Margaret Brent's grants. In 1688 Parson John Waugh became involved in some political unrest which included one Ignatius West, who apparently lived in or near this part of the county. It is possible that the West family may have obtained the property from the Brents. Due to missing records, however, it seems unlikely we will ever know for sure.

Richland

One of my favorite homes in all of Stafford is Richland. From Boswell's Corner and U.S. Route 1, Richland is six-tenths of a mile southeast on State Route 637, 3.6 miles east on State Route 611, and then two-tenths of a mile north on a private road.

By some miracle this exquisite home has survived the War of 1812, the Civil War, threats of vandalism and fire, and the ravages of time. The land which makes up this farm was part of a huge grant owned by Margaret Brent. In 1668 the Brents built a grist mill on Brent's Mill Branch (also known as Meadow Branch). This was located very near to what is now Widewater Grocery.

Richland

We don't know when the first Richland was built. The 1742 Quit Rent Rolls charged William Brent's executors for 7,452 acres. This William (1710-1742) was the son of William Brent (died c.1709) and Sarah Gibbons, who later married Alexander Scott of Dipple. It was this second William's son, William Brent (1733-1782) of Richland, who married Eleanor, the second daughter of the Carrolls of Marlborough, Maryland. This William paid taxes on 6,952 acres, according to the Quit Rent Rolls for 1773-1776. He served as a justice for Stafford in 1781 and was listed in 1785 as owning 56 slaves, 30 horses, and 50 cattle.

It was to Richland that Father John Carroll sailed from England, landing at Aquia on June 26, 1774. His was reputed to be the last vessel to leave an English port bound for America prior to the outbreak of the Revolution. Father Carroll preached to his Catholic parishioners at Widewater, then moved to Rock Creek where his mother lived. He often returned to visit and preach at Richland.

The original Richland house did not survive the Revolution. One of the last British acts in Virginia during the Revolution was the burning of Richland. Some 300 members of the Stafford militia were camped at Richland when Lord

Dunmore and Captain Andrew Hamond arrived with their small fleet. The Virginians taunted the English from shore and accounts of what followed vary somewhat. Hamond wrote:

> [We landed] about 100 men at Noon day, under cover of a Tender & the Row Galley, beat the Enemy off (which was double that number, and very advantageously posted) set fire to the house and all the buildings: when we returned to our Ships without the loss of a single Man and only 1 officer & 5 Men wounded.

A letter written by John Parke Custis to his step-father, George Washington (August 8, 1776), also describes the activities that evening:

> You have no doubt heard of the Men of War coming up Potowmack as far as Mr. Brent's whose House they burnt with several outhouses and some Stacks of Wheat. A Capt. James with the Militia were stationed there who all got drunk, and kept challenging the Men of War to come ashore, and upbraiding Them with Cowardice. Hammond sent 150 Men who landed about 10 oclock under cover of a Gondola Tender, the Militia were asleep after their drinking Frolick and did not discover the Enemy untill they landed and their vessels began to Fire. Capt. James desired his Men to shift for Themselves and ran off without firing a Gun. A Young Man by Name Combs stayd untill he killd three of the Enemy. Col. Grayson appearing with 30 Prince William Volunteers, the Enemy thought it proper to retire to their ships. Capt. James is to be held for Cowardice—The Fleet after performing this Exploit, returned down the River to George's Island, from whence they have been drove off by Major Price with some losses. They are gone down the Bay in a most sickly Condition. I have not heard where they have stopt, before they left

Richland

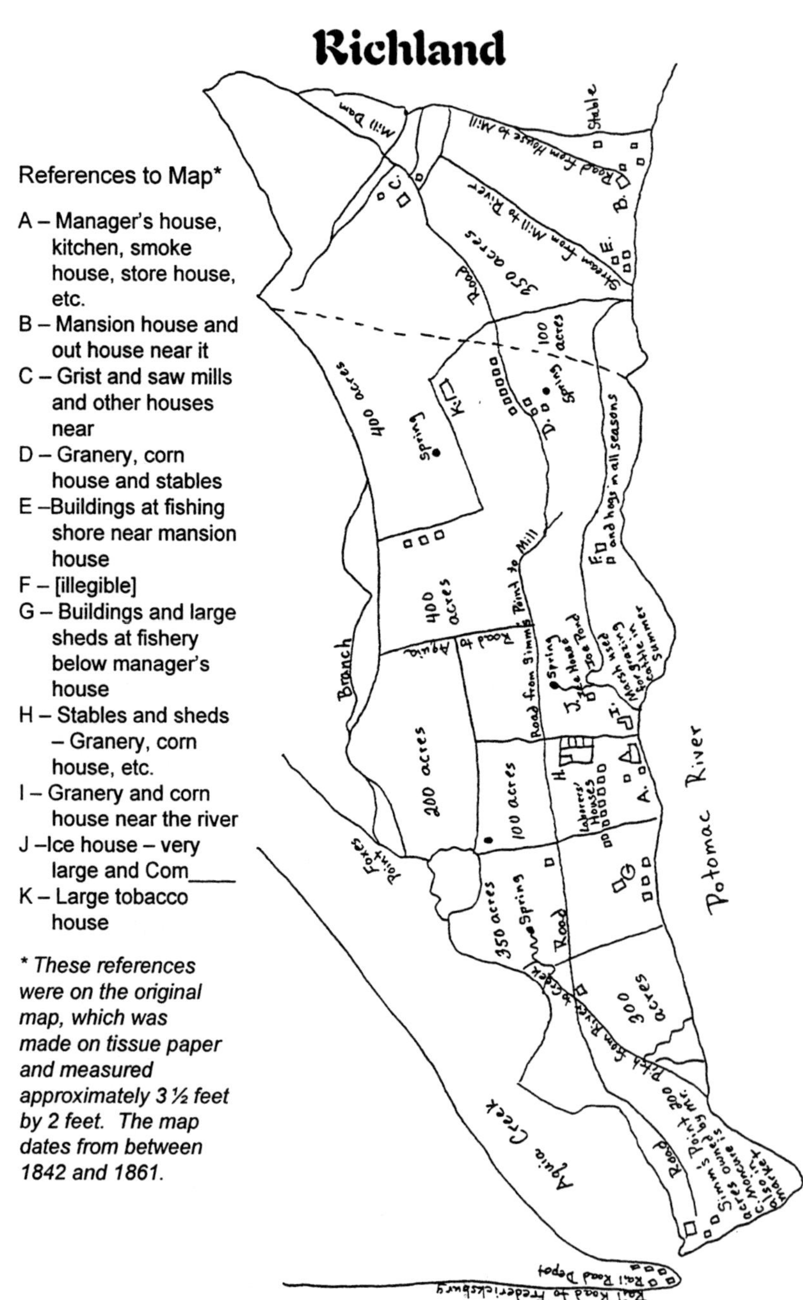

References to Map*

A – Manager's house, kitchen, smoke house, store house, etc.
B – Mansion house and out house near it
C – Grist and saw mills and other houses near
D – Granery, corn house and stables
E –Buildings at fishing shore near mansion house
F – [illegible]
G – Buildings and large sheds at fishery below manager's house
H – Stables and sheds – Granery, corn house, etc.
I – Granery and corn house near the river
J –Ice house – very large and Com____
K – Large tobacco house

** These references were on the original map, which was made on tissue paper and measured approximately 3 ½ feet by 2 feet. The map dates from between 1842 and 1861.*

From a map in the possession of Miss Mary Cary Kendall

> the Island they burnt several Vessels, and I hear that two Sloops belonging to them have fallen into Capt. Boucher's hands.

An article appearing in *The Virginia Gazette* on September 6, 1776 describes the damage wrought by the English troops:

> Since our last, we have certain advice that lord Dunmore, with his motley band of pirates and renegadoes, have burnt the elegant brick house of William Brent, esq; at the mouth of Aquia creek, in Stafford county, as also two other houses lower down Potowmack river, the property of widow ladies, with several ferry boats; that on Tuesday fe'nnight he relanded on St. George's island, but was beat off by 1200 Marylanders; that he had burnt eight of his vessels, and was seen standing down the bay the Thursday after with all his fleet.

The Stafford militia had fled the scene, Hamond's men had burned the buildings within close proximity to the house and were on their way up the hill to burn the mill, when the Prince William militia arrived. William Brent, a major landholder in both counties, was captain of the Prince William militia, though it is unknown if he was with them that day.

Captain James of the Stafford militia was blamed for the disaster at Richland and was court-martialed on September 20, 1776. The trial was held at Stafford court house and the county justices listened to the depositions of several witnesses. A report of the proceedings was published in *The Virginia Gazette* of September 27, 1776. Interestingly, the justices concluded that the destruction was "owing to the militia's not being better armed and disciplined." According to witnesses, Capt. James held his ground until all but fifteen of his men had fled, despite several attempts to rally them. The British forces "approached under a constant fire of cannon and swivels from a gondala, two sloops, and nine boats." The decision of the court was "that capt. James [was not] deficient in spirit as has been frequently alledged."

The date of the rebuilding of Richland is unknown,

although a journal entry by Lucinda Lee mentions that her sister Anne Fenton Lee and Daniel Carroll Brent were living there in 1787. The new house was built on the same foundation but built of wood rather than brick. This structure remains today.

Colonel William Brent (1733-1782), like most gentlemen of his day, had a passion for horse racing. He owned several racehorses and had a race course just below the house. Known through the years as "the racetrack field," it was located on the west side of present-day State Route 633, across the branch and just a couple of hundred yards down the road. Today, the land is heavily wooded.

When William H. Fitzhugh bought the house and 1,906 acres in the early 1820s, the estate left the Brent family. From 1860 to 1865, Mr. and Mrs. George Washington Carlisle Whiting rented Richland (with an option to buy). On June 23, 1863, Mrs. Whiting wrote to her daughter describing their difficulties,

> We lost heavily by the Northern Army but in some way our losses have been made up. Our hay was all taken, and the stock in consequence would have starved had not a large vessel laden with hay caught on fire and all its contents were deposited on our shore. We had enough for ourselves and several of the neighbors. Our horses were all taken when the Yankees left, by mismanage nearly one hundred good horses were mired in the marsh and left there to perish. The neighbors saved nearly all of them...The Confederates have taken possession of all but six, if we manage to keep them we shall be very fortunate.

Mr. and Mrs. Whiting did not buy Richland. Soon after they moved in, Mr. Whiting became very ill and was unable to ever work the farm. Without the help of neighbors, the Whitings and their young children would have starved.

After the war, Mrs. William H. Fitzhugh allowed Robert E. Lee's brother, Sidney Smith Lee, to live at Richland. He had been head of the Confederate Navy and, like most Southerners, had lost everything. Mrs. Fitzhugh, who owned the property at the time, invited the Lee family to live there so they might make a fresh start. Sidney Smith Lee died at Richland in 1869. Mrs. Fitzhugh left the house and 1,175 acres to her godson, General Fitzhugh Lee, who lived there until he was elected governor of Virginia in 1886. In 1893 the house was purchased as a wedding gift for Alfred K. Pyke, who married Mary Cary Waller of Clifton. They built a chapel in the house where priests from Fredericksburg could come to hold Mass. This was the first known Mass in Stafford since the days of the Brent settlement when priests secretly crossed the Potomac River from St. Mary's, Maryland and held Mass in various homes.

Richland has been sold only twice in more than three hundred years. The letter below was written by William Brent Jr. to William H. Fitzhugh, Esq. of Ravensworth, Jefferson County, Virginia. Mr. Fitzhugh was the grandson of William Fitzhugh of Chatham near Fredericksburg. He and Mr. Brent were law partners and Mr. Brent was desirous of selling the Richland property after the death of his father.

> Richland near Aquia
> July 31st 1820
>
> Dear Sir.
> I regret that my reply to your favour of the 22nd has been unavoidably delayed, until now.
>
> In addition to the information, contained in my advertisement I inform you, that the flats lay in a regular, and compact body, from Aquia creek to Potomac river, a considerable portion of them, having been cleared, and in cultivation many years, and from 300, to 400 acres within a few years back, and a portion of that thus cleared never has been grubbed or put into cultivation. The growth originally was red, white oak, and hickory. They lie uncommonly well, improve most rapidly from deep plouging, and very accurate experiment has proven their adaptation to plaister. My brother in law _____ Simms is now shewing the value of these lands by a rapid improvement of a small farm originally a part of this tract, and of similar character. They partake of the general character of the Potomac

lowgrounds being somewhat Stiff, adapted to corn, tobacco, and Small grain—Since my father's death, I have rented them with great ease to persons in the neighbourhood, and even under their management they may be considered certain land and for four Blls of corn to the acre, and from 7, to 10 Bush. of wheat to the Bushel seeded in corn land. From my own experience, on these lands before my fathers death, after a food fallow they would yield from 20 to 25 Bush of wheat to the acre.—

The neighbourhood tole of the mill, is from 20, to 25 Bush of corn per week and as I have remarked, in my advertisement, the stream is singularly constant.—This has been recently proven, by what is considered here as a drought more severe than the drought of 1806: in which year this mill never ground less than 40 Bushels per day, and during the present drought not less than 35. For the LAST eight weeks until Friday last we have not had a rain to lay the dust.—No notice is here taken of the wheat mill which depends on the quantity of wheat purchased. The mill is situated about 1 mile from the River. There is an overproportion of wood on these tracks if they are marked by one person.—

These lands at the late revaluation, and reassessment of lands in this state are rated at 40 Dolers per acre. I will take 20 $ round for the whole as mentioned in my advertisement. I mention to you the price without hesitation, with a request that you will not mention it to any person, an _____, which I feel well assured will be complied with.

I think were you to see the lands, we might agree on something mutually advantageous. In any opinion it would be most adviseable for you to ride over, and view the lands: and I need not, I am sure, assure you they it will give me much pleasure to see you here as soon as you

> conveniently can. Having communicated to you my price, I suggest to you whether my coming to Alexandria would expedite this transaction.
>
> —I remain ______ very
> respectfully your abl sert.
> Wm: Brent Jr.

As a result of this offer, the transaction was made. Thus, William Fitzhugh bought Richland and William Brent moved to Sully near Manassas.

Richland was the hub of the community in Widewater. As mentioned earlier, the Brents operated a grist mill, lumber mill, store, blacksmith shop, and distillery. Ledger books recording activities in the mill and store between 1804 and 1806 survive, and from these one gets a vivid picture of the busy life in Widewater.

The mill ground great quantities of corn, wheat, and rye. Customers purchased all manner of goods from the store and Mr. Brent kept running accounts for them. These accounts were paid in cash, goods taken in trade, or grain which was then ground and sold in the store as flour or meal. The ledger books reveal that the goods sold in the store included:

"sundries"	shad	lead
tea	butter	tallow
rum	midlings	knives
whiskey	caster oil	forks
brandy	tobacco	chalk
wine	calico	"plaister paris"
crackers	muslin	sand
pork	linen	hay
flour	cotton	harnesses
bran	flannel	gun powder
molasses	bagging	shot
sugar	needles	lime
salt	thread	paper
ginger	shoes	combs
coffee	stockings	candles
rice	indigo	snuff
potatoes	shawls	playing cards
cheese	buttons	nails
catfish	soap	hardware

scythe blades oil for putty locks

For a fee Mr. Brent would also provide a laborer to cut and deliver wood. For those who preferred to do it themselves but needed a means of hauling, Mr. Brent would rent a team of oxen for $2.50 per day.

The records indicate that a large number of people had accounts with the store. Below is a partial listing:

Benjamin Adie
Betsy Adie
Aquia Quarry
Robert Ashby
John Beagle
Blacksmith Shop
Daniel C. Brent
William Brent
Bailey Bridgeward
John Burroughs
John Carter
Fielding Combs
Thomas Conneway
Colonel John Cooke
John Dunbar
John Edrington
William Fairfax
John Fox
Alexander Gaddis
Samuel Gallyhorn
Soloman Gallyhorn
Moses Garretson
Mrs. Green
Benjamin Guy
Joseph Guy
Captain Harris
Peyton Harrison
Thomas Harrison
Elias Hore
Daniel King
Christopher Knight
Gusty Knight
Jeremiah Knight
John Lowe
Thomas Millburn
William Millburn
John Mitchel
Eustace Moncure
John Moncure
Valentine Pates
Valentine Peyton
Hezekiah Posey
Adam Rains
Burditt Ratliff
Rickets Newton & Co.
James M. Robertson
William Rolls
William Shacklett
John Simonton
William Starke
William Steward
Dr. Hawkins Stone
Richard Stone
Robert Swan
Benjamin Truslow
Bailey Washington
Mark Waters
Henry Woodrow

(Robert Swan became a partner in the business in 1804.)

The Aquia Quarry purchased supplies for the laborers including bran, corn, meal, whiskey, coffee, sugar, molasses, tea, pepper, and candles. They also rented Mr. Brent's team of oxen.

The blacksmith's shop purchased paper, coffee, ginger, nails, corn, sugar, whiskey, flour, and brandy. They also rented the team of oxen for hauling. It is interesting to note that the shop purchased nails from Mr. Brent instead of making them. By this time, nails were no longer hand-made one by one. Instead, workers in a forge rolled out strips of iron and cut the strips with a device resembling a cookie cutter. The result was similar to a comb, the teeth of the comb being nails all joined together at the top. If someone needed nails for building he would buy several of these strips and take them to a blacksmith who would cut apart the nails and put heads on them.

Wood for the blacksmith's shop was bought from Mr. Brent; the shop also paid for a laborer to cut the wood—including his room and board while he was cutting and splitting—and paid to have the wood hauled by Mr. Brent's oxen.

Next to flour and meal, the most frequently sold products in the store were whiskey, brandy, wine, and rum. Mr. Brent had his own distillery, where he doubtless made some of what he sold. These products could be purchased by the quart, gallon, or barrel.

Brent's Mill

Brent's Mill, which operated from the mid-1600s until about 1900, was larger and more elaborate than most Stafford mills although it served the same function as other mills by being the center of the surrounding community. Because early development in Stafford tended to be in pockets, each community was fairly self-sufficient. Each had its own mill, store, and small industries that served the needs of the local residents. Few ledgers of the county's other mills survive for comparison but mention of them in historical records indicates that they, too, provided nearly everything their customers could afford to buy.

In 1816 Mr. Brent took out an insurance policy with the Mutual Assurance Society of Virginia. He insured what he described as a "manufacturing mill" two stories high, built of stone with a wooden roof. He valued the building at $6,000, a sizable sum in those days. That can be compared to Tackett's Mill which, in the same year, was valued at a little more that $3,000.

Clermont

Owners:

1727 Reverend John Moncure (1710-1764) immigrated from Scotland, acquired the property, and built the house

1786 Inherited by John Moncure II
1796 John Moncure II willed Clermont to his son, John Moncure III
1800 Inherited by Edwin Moncure
George C. Glascock inherited the property by marriage to Agatha Moncure, daughter of Edwin
c.1886 Sold to George Middleton of Philadelphia
1920 Purchased by Frank Hill
1940 House burned
1941 New house built on site
1942 Property became part of Quantico Marine Base

This unusual brick house was built about 1736 on a high hill overlooking the Potomac River on the east side and Chopawamsic Creek on the north. Clermont was unique in design among the early Stafford homes. The illustration shows the unusual roof line which is similar to Patrick Henry's Scotchtown in Ashland, Virginia. The wing and porch were probably later additions, but they complement the design of the house. The brickwork in this house was exceptionally attractive. Glazed headers were interspersed with the plain bricks, creating a checkerboard effect. Another interesting feature of the house is the lack of exterior shutters. Like many brick homes, Clermont had shutters mounted on the insides of the windows. The shutters could be pushed back into the thick walls surrounding the windows, giving the impression of paneling. From the outside, the shutters were invisible unless closed.

The Reverend Mr. John Moncure was born in the parish of Kinoff, County Mearns, Scotland about 1714. He was very well educated and had made a study of medicine. He came to America about 1733 and served as a private tutor in Northumberland for two years. While a tutor, he studied divinity and at the beginning of his third year in Virginia, he sailed to England to be ordained. He returned to Virginia in 1738 and became minister of Overwharton Parish. It was during his ministry that the present Aquia Church was built.

The Clermont property adjoined the eastern side of Chopawamsic Farm, home of George Mason (II) and (III). The Moncures and Masons were close family friends and on March 12, 1764 George Mason (IV) of Gunston Hall wrote to Mrs. Moncure

Clermont

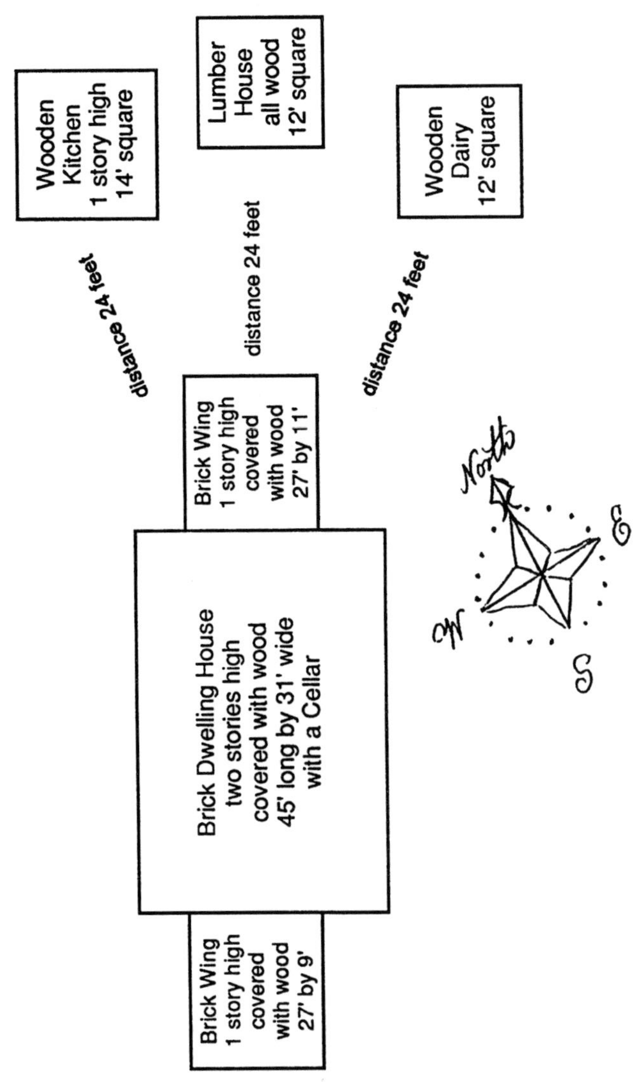

From an 1805 Mutual Assurance policy

regarding funeral arrangements for her husband. Ill at the time, Mason wrote that he needed crutches to walk and suffered from "such a cold as greatly to increase my disorder."

Clermont was an exceptionally fine house compared to most Stafford homes of the eighteenth and nineteenth centuries. County tax records of 1861 listed the assessed value of Clermont as $2,000 (the average house at that time was valued from $300 to $600). A Mutual Assurance Society of Virginia policy of 1803 shows the house, a kitchen, dairy, and smokehouse. At that time the house was valued at $1,200, the kitchen $100, the dairy $30, and the smokehouse $20.

The original brick structure burned in 1940. A simple frame farmhouse was built upon the old foundation but the government took the property in 1942 and the house was destroyed.

The property also contained a Moncure and Glascock cemetery. The following are inscriptions from gravestones that were still readable in 1936:

> Here lies the body of Agatha A.C. wife of George G. Glascock and daughter of Edwin G. and Elinor Moncure, who departed this life August 13, 1859, 44 years, 4 months, and 19 days.
>
> To the memory of Edwin G. Moncure, who departed this life on the 19th day of August, 1815, in the 35th year of his age. An affectionate husband, a fond father, a good neighbor and kinder hearts never left this earth than his and those which gave him birth.

Somerset

Owners:

1727 Somerset was part of Clermont and owned by John Moncure

1736 Separated from Clermont but still owned by John Moncure
1853 Inherited by William Edwin Moncure
1898 Left to heirs of William Edwin Moncure
1942 Became part of Quantico Marine Corps Base

From Boswell's Corner and U.S. Route 1, Somerset was six-tenths of a mile southeast on State Route 637, 2.1 miles east on State Route 611, and then one-tenth of a mile north on a private road. The original house built by John Moncure was a summer home and was called Summer Seat. Most of the homes of that day were built on the water, boats being the only reasonable source of transportation. Malaria was quite a problem, however, and those who could afford to have a summer house back from the water and mosquitoes did so.

An 1805 insurance policy described the house as a "Brick Dwelling House two Stories high covered with wood, 45 feet long, by 31 feet wide with a Cellar." The drawing on the bottom of the policy indicates that there were brick wings (27′ by 11′) on each end of the house which were valued at $1,200.

This brick home burned at some point and a frame house was built on the site in 1853. This was a rectangular, two-story frame structure very similar to Bloomington (another nearby Moncure home discussed later in this chapter) in that it had a wing on one side and a porch over the front door. The roof was gabled and covered with cedar shingles which were later replaced with tin. A brick chimney was built on each end of the main structure. Above the fireplace were inscribed the name "Monceur" and the coat of arms of the Moncure family.

Somerset was typical of most Stafford farmhouses of the day, though perhaps just a bit finer. The rooms were quite large, and fourteen windows in the main section on the house provided plenty of light. The walls were plastered and the mantels plain.

Somerset was built with slave labor; Mr. Moncure was a major slave owner in the county. The last of those slaves was Jim Hedgeman who died in the mid-1930s at the age of eighty-five.

To the south of the house was a lovely boxwood garden planted by the first John Moncure, who was said to have brought the plant from Sir Walter Scott's home in England.

Somerset's most famous resident was Evalina Gree. Born a slave there in 1836, Evalina left the farm with her family when

Emancipation was announced. She walked to the end of the lane leading from the house and turned back, choosing to stay with the Moncure family. There she remained, nursing three generations of Moncures until her death in 1926 at the age of ninety. She was buried in the Somerset cemetery.

Chelsea

Owners:

1720 G. M. Cooke
1750 Purchased by John Moncure
1890 Willed to George V. Moncure
1920 Purchased by a Mr. Raffman from Pennsylvania
1926 Purchased by George Herring (Mr. Herring and Mr. Pyke managed the fishing shore at Clifton)
1930 Purchased by Michael Wandrick

From Boswell's Corner and U.S. Route 1, Chelsea is .6 mile southeast on State Route 637 and 1.5 miles east on State Route 611. The house stands on the north side of the road.

This once lovely old home was built in 1819, the date of

construction carved in a stone in the chimney. John Moncure acquired a considerable amount of land in the Widewater area including this property, Somerset, and Clermont.

After the Civil War, recovery in Stafford County was painfully slow. The land had not been worked for several years. Union troops had taken and destroyed nearly every fence rail and tree in their never-ending search for firewood. Most barns had either been dismantled for firewood or burned out of sheer spite. The Stafford families who returned to their homes after the war had to rebuild their lives from the soil up.

In the Widewater area, the land owners joined together and formed the "Stafford Agricultural Society." Members included George V. Moncure of Chelsea, Withers Waller of Clifton, Major John M. Lee of Arkendale, J. B. T. Suttle of The Fluerry's, Nathaniel Waller Ford of Woodstock, and others. The members of the society met at different farms, inspected them, and made suggestions for improvements. Members took turns leading discussions on the newest, most economical, and most promising farming techniques. After the inspection and business meeting, the members feasted on hearty meals from what was produced on the host farm.

The society provided its members with opportunities to socialize and helped maintain high spirits during difficult times. George V. Moncure described the harsh reality of the times when he wrote about cultivating corn:

> Before the War, when we owned our labor, all of us cultivated corn at double the expense that we do now, which was mostly owing to the process of hoeing. It is all important now, in our impoverished condition with the heavy burden of taxation, and the large amount of produce that is brought from the richer lands of the West, and the little that is made by agriculture in this county, that we should study economy in the conduct of all our farming operations, especially the corn crop as it is one essentially necessary and attended with considerable expense, when cultivated in the most approved manner.

The Stafford Agricultural Society and informal associations in other communities helped bind together the war-battered residents as they struggled to eke out a living in what remained of Stafford County.

The Chelsea house was known for its beautiful interior woodwork: it housed a staircase of walnut, and some of its rooms were paneled. Many years ago the woodwork was stripped out for other purposes. Today, unfortunately, the house is on the verge of collapse, having been neglected for many years.

The Rectory

From Boswell's Corner and U.S. Route 1, The Rectory was .6 mile southeast on State Route 637, and 1.3 miles east on State Route 611; it stood on the hill on the north side of State Route 611.

The Rectory began as a small log home built sometime during the eighteenth century. It was also known as the Meredith home because it was owned by the Reverend Mr. Jaquelin Marshall Meredith (1833-1920), who preached at Clifton Chapel and Aquia Church from 1864 to 1880. In May 1862, Rev. Meredith was appointed chaplain of the 47th Virginia Infantry. He resigned from that position in May 1864. He was married to Ellen Bankhead.

Mr. Meredith was rector of Aquia Church during very difficult times. The vestry and parishioners were scattered as a result of the Civil War, and the church had suffered considerable damage at the hands of marauding Union troops. From his own funds Mr. Meredith spent $90 for repairs to the church after the Union forces had withdrawn. Vestry minutes of May 1866 reported his salary to be $200 per annum; in September 1868 the treasurer, George V. Moncure, reported that the church had paid Mr. Meredith only $100 to date. The rector's dedication to his calling and to Aquia Church are admirable.

The Rectory house grew through the years, succeeding generations adding a wing here and a room there. The drive approached the front of the house which sat on a pretty knoll overlooking the present-day road into Widewater. Below the house and across a dirt road was the Rectory Post Office, which burned in 1987.

The Rectory was yet another home taken by the government in 1942. The last people to live in the house were Mr. and Mrs. George Vowell Moncure III and their two children. Mrs. Moncure recalls that the house was huge—her smallest room was twenty feet square! Not shown in the picture was a porch that ran almost the entire length of the back of the house. Nothing remains today but the foundation and thousands of yellow daffodils that bloom in the spring.

Bloomington

From Boswell's Corner and U.S. Route 1, Bloomington was .6 mile southeast on State Route 637, .8 mile east on State Route 611, and then .3 mile south on a private road. There was an earlier house on this site, but the last one was built in 1854 by the Adie family. James Waller bought the farm in 1856 which was also home to the Fords and Moncures.

The house was a two-story frame structure over an English basement. There were three bedrooms, two attic rooms, and a large center hall. Once kitchens became a part of a house proper, a small wing was added to one end to serve that purpose. There was a bedroom upstairs. The cellar had two rooms.

The Adies came from England and settled at Bloomington. An ancient pear tree in the garden was planted by the Adie family and was known for many generations thereafter as the "old time sugar pear."

A private school about twenty steps from the main house operated on the farm. This was a simple log cabin which housed students from neighboring farms.

The house was struck by lightning and burned in the 1970s. It was unoccupied at the time.

Arkendale

Arkendale, one of the Lee estates, was located on the neck between Aquia Creek and the Potomac River and included most of the lower peninsula between Aquia Creek and the river. The original house was built of sandstone quarried from the deposits on the creek. The house was destroyed during the Civil War.

Life was very busy around Arkendale. Ships were constantly coming and going, bringing goods from Alexandria and Washington and off-loading at the wharves nearby. These goods were then transferred to small boats and sent up the creek.

The Arkendale property had once been part of the Brent grants and was later included in the some 4,000 acres that made up Richland. At some point well before the Civil War, 2,348 acres of Richland came into the possession of the Lees, and the estate was named Arkendale. The property ran from present-day State Route 611 south along the neck of land towards but not including Brent's Point. It was bounded east by the Potomac River and west by Bozey's (now Boar's) Run. At that time Arkendale Road followed the run.

In the 1880s, 1,779 acres of the Lee tract was divided between four Lee brothers. From the south end, Smith Lee received 541 acres, Henry Lee received 541 acres (which included the huge building for the fishery as well as the fishery itself), Daniel M. Lee received 535 acres, and John M. Lee received 162 acres at the north end of the property. Daniel Lee called his part of the farm The Anchorage. The plat showing the division of Arkendale does not indicate any buildings other than the fish house given to Daniel.

Myrtle Grove

Myrtle Grove, the home of the Edrington family, was another commercial center in the Widewater area. The Edringtons established themselves in Stafford sometime during the early years of the eighteenth century and became major landholders in the county. At the time of the Civil War, Myrtle Grove consisted of some 440 acres. Near the end of the peninsula between Aquia Creek and the Potomac River, the Edringtons built a large frame house high upon a hill overlooking the creek. Below the house was a beach that was used as a fishing shore similar to that at Clifton, but not nearly as extensive.

Also associated with the Myrtle Grove farm was a store called Edrington and Moncure. An account book dated 1834-1872 in the possession of the Virginia Historical Society provides a good picture of the activities in the area. Not only did these two men, John Catesby Edrington and William A. Moncure, operate a store and fishery, they also ran one of the small quarries on the creek.

The establishment of Edrington and Moncure did not offer as extensive a variety of items as Brent's store. The two best-selling items were salted herrings and whiskey. Herrings could be bought by the pound or by the barrel. Whiskey could be purchased by the pint, quart, gallon, or barrel. Also available were:

molasses	turnips	socks
sugar	lamb	shirts
loaf sugar	beans	pants
brown sugar	salted pork and	shoes
coffee	beef	calico
potatoes	bacon	brown linen
pepper	corn	tallow
salt	rye	candles
lard	wheat	saw files
flour	oats	quires of paper
meal	tobacco	etc.

The company also did hauling for $3 per day. For fifty cents a pair, shoes would be resoled.

Some of the local people who had accounts with the store included Mary, Alfred, and Rowzee Colvin; Hugh Adie; John F. Bell; George Brent Daggs; Barney and Lewis Whorton; James Edrington; John King; Samuel S. Brooke; William Anderson; John H. Suttle; William H. Fitzhugh; Enos Hord; George Lewis; Lemuel Chadwell; John Moncure; and the shipyard that was located on the creek.

Captain John Catesby Edrington was born in 1806. He married Elizabeth Hawkins Stone (1810-1891), the daughter of his grandmother's third husband (by a previous marriage). He inherited Myrtle Grove from his father, John Catesby Edrington, and amassed a considerable estate, his businesses obviously paying well.

When Captain Edrington died in 1879, his personal

property was sold. The listing of this sale fills some four pages in the Stafford County Deed Book in which it is recorded. Among the items sold were

- three dozen plates
- two sets of Chincy ware
- a set of Chincy cups and saucers
- two sets of silver teaspoons
- a set of silver tablespoons
- four sets of bedroom furniture
- two dressing glasses
- one small scow
- one large scow
- 1,000 pounds of pork
- 130 pounds of beef
- a barrel of wool
- a barrel of soap
- two barrels of apples
- seventy-eight barrels of corn
- twenty-nine pigs
- thirty-five sheep
- eighteen head of cattle
- eight horses
- one still

Rock Ramore

Located at the end of Quarry Road is another old farm, Rock Ramore. Local pronunciation of the name varies from Rock Rimmon to Rock Ramer to Rock Raymond.

During the eighteenth century, the property was owned by the Conways who operated one of several sandstone quarries along Aquia Creek. Thomas Barrett Conway (died 1825) owned this farm and another near Richmond. In his will, he refers to the Stafford property as Rock Ramore. Conway's daughter, Susan Newton Conway (1814-1864) married Edward Waller of Grafton when she was just sixteen. Conway's sister, Catherine, married Withers Waller of Clifton.

The quarry at Rock Ramore was one of the major quarries in the county and, according to George Gordon, continued operating until the 1920s. At that time, the operation was known as the George Washington Quarry. There was a wharf down the creek from which the blocks of stone were loaded onto boats and taken north to Washington and Alexandria. In later years, the quarries used mechanical stone cutting equipment and booms for handling the heavy blocks.

In later years, the farm was owned by the Harper family, who called it Mount Pleasant. Today, all that remains of Rock Ramore is a cemetery. Below are inscriptions from three of the stones:

In memory of
Katrina Miller
The Wife of
Robert Miller
Who Departed This Life
January 20—1794
To The Great Grief of Her
Husband and Children
Aged 48 Years
(Katrina Miller was Thomas B. Conway's mother.)

Sacred
to the memory of
Thomas B. Conway
who was born on the 16th
September 1779 and
departed this life on the
1st day of December 1825.
Aged 46 years 2 months
& 15 days.
None knew him but to love him
None named him but to praise

To the memory of
WITHERS WALLER.
The devoted Husband,
The fond, affectionate
Parent, the sincere &
Generous friend.
He died at Clifton his residence
on the 5th day of August 1827
in the 43rd year of his age.
This stone is raised by his
Forlorn and afflicted Wife.

Palace Green

This beautiful old farm is located on the north side of State Route 661 and is one of Stafford's most picturesque homeplaces. Very little information is available about the farm except that during the eighteenth century it was home to the Carter family.

Additional sites

Edge Hill—also known as the Norman tract, adjoined Rock Ramore on the north east side.

Providence—adjoined Bloomington. At the time of the Civil War, the property was owned by James E. and Nathaniel Waller Ford. After the war, Jaquelin Meredith bought it. Later taken during the expansion of Quantico.

St. Mary's—probably part of Dipple.

Westwood—home of Nanny Lee. The house was on the east side of State Route 658 and north of Arkendale Crossing.

Aquia & Chopawamsic Creeks

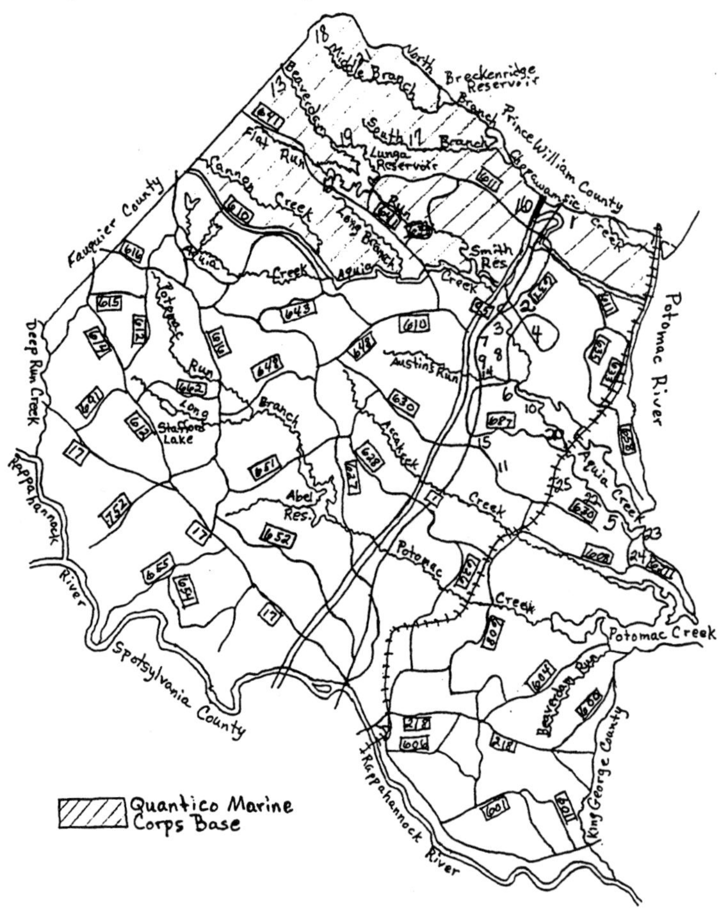

1 ... Chopawamsic Farm
2 ... Woodstock
3 ... Catholic Cemetery
4 ... Stony Hill
5 ... Aquia Landing
6 ... Coal Landing
7 ... Aquia Church
8 ... Peyton's Ordinary
9 ... The Fleurry's
10 ... Concord
11 ... Spring Hill
12 ... Laurel View
13 ... Stafford Springs
14 ... Grape Hill
15 ... Garrard's Ordinary
16 ... Mount Experiment
17 ... Chopawamsic Baptist Church
18 ... Red Oak Level
19 ... Stafford Shore
20 ... Hope House
21 ... Black Rock
22 ... Cole Trips
23 ... Tump
24 ... Rose Hill
25 ... Orchard Field

Chapter 7

Aquia and Chopawamsic Creeks

❧ ☙

Chopawamsic Creek

Chopawamsic Creek forms the northern border of the area we call Widewater today and extends northwestwardly along Stafford's present boundary with Prince William County. Now overgrown with heavy timber and brush, it is difficult to imagine that the area around Chopawamsic Creek was once quite populated and busy. All of the old homes are gone and long forgotten, their foundations totally concealed beneath the layers of dense undergrowth. The mills and other businesses which operated beside the creek have long been silent. And yet, prior to the 1930s, there was a great deal of activity here. Chopawamsic is an Indian word meaning "by the separation of the inlet" and the area was named after a nearby Algonquin Indian village. White settlement here began in 1651 when Samuel Mathews patented land along the creek and in 1659 started a small settlement.

Mathews' father, Samuel, had immigrated to Newport News in 1622. There he became a successful businessman, operating a tannery and producing flax, beef, pork, and grains on his plantation. Samuel Jr. inherited his father's business and became one of the wealthiest men in Virginia. He served for two years (1656-1658) as Virginia's governor and had land holdings all over the colony. A 1702 deed recorded in Stafford County gave power to Nicholas Brent of Woodstock to sell any part of Mathews' 5,211 acres in Stafford County.

Soon after Mathews began his early settlement in Stafford, a sandstone quarry began operating about three-quarters of a mile upstream from the mouth of the creek. The Missouri Mills were built there in the late eighteenth century to grind grain and by 1871 there were several landings along the creek—Moncure's Landing (at the fall line) and Griffin and Cedar Landings. Colonial records indicate that most of the flour from the Missouri Mills was shipped to South American ports. It is difficult to look at shallow Chopawamsic Creek today and imagine that not so long ago, ocean-going vessels docked and loaded goods along its banks.

Bellfair Mill, another large commercial mill like the Missouri Mills, was also built on the creek and survived the Civil War. Oddly, while most people left the area after the war, Bellfair was repaired in 1865 and continued to operate. A receipt for these repairs survives today: $235 was spent, including Andrew Parson's bill for twenty days' work ("19.50 in Yankee Money"). More repairs were done in 1873, including work on the wheel and building. The owners must have given up shortly thereafter, however, as a picture taken about 1920 shows only the ruins of the building with the undershot wheel still in place.

The famous George Masons of Virginia had a large tract of land along the creek also. Tax records indicate that by the time George Mason (III) died in 1735 he owned 20,875 acres in Stafford alone. The first George Mason to leave England for the New World settled on Potomac Creek. His son, George, acquired land on Chopawamsic Creek and called his plantation Chopawamsic Farm. This property was situated on the east side of present-day U.S. Route 1 and ran from the creek south to about Boswell's Corner and east to the Moncure property (Clermont). It was George Mason (IV) who moved north to Fairfax County and built Gunston Hall; he wrote the Bill of Rights.

Much of the area along Chopawamsic Creek was taken over by the government for the creation of the Quantico Marine Corps Base in 1942. Much of the land near the mouth of Chopawamsic Creek was swampy. This land was filled after the government takeover and is now used for housing developments and airfields.

Wherever you have groups of people, you will find churches. While the majority of people in early Stafford were members of the Church of England (later the Episcopal Church), there were little pockets of other denominations scattered about the county. Prior to the Revolution, the only officially recognized church was the Church of Virginia which, of course, was closely aligned with the Church of England. Dissenting voices were becoming increasingly worrisome by 1760-1770 however and, after the Revolution, numbers of people broke away from the Church of Virginia to establish a wide variety of denominations.

On November 22, 1766 a group of Baptists from the Baptist Church at Broad Run, Fauquier County, established the Chopawamsic Baptist Church. Robert and Keziah Million were among the early dissenters in Overwharton and their names appear as subscribers to the Covenant of Chopawamsic Baptist Church.

The Fristoe family was long associated with Chopawamsic Creek and, later, with the Baptist church there. On April 4, 1770 William Fristoe was ordained at Chopawamsic Baptist Church and was elected to serve as minister; he was the son of Richard and Grace Fristoe and had been born on Chopawamsic Creek. William appears several times in the old records. In 1776 he signed the legislative petition requesting a change in the Stafford–King George County boundary. He was also listed in the 1784-1789 personal property tax records and does not appear to have been a slave owner, with the exception of 1788 when he had one slave.

In 1772, William's brother Daniel (1739-1774) was also ordained at Chopawamsic. Daniel was listed in the 1768 and 1773 Quit Rents as owning 100 acres.

Eighteenth-century vestry records indicate that the church played a central role in the lives of its parishioners. A normal worship service consisted of a religious service followed by a business meeting, at which time the affairs of the church as well as those of its parishioners were discussed. Disputes between members were settled by the church as recorded in official church records:

> *August 10, 1772*
>
> *Agreed, that our Sister Milly Cristy do return the cloth she took away from Sister Threlkeld, and receive Ten Shillings or keep so many of the cloths as shall amount to that sum as they can agree, and that*

> *Sister Milly be debard communion untill she give Satisfaction to the Church.*

Sister Milly obviously did not take the church's advice, for she appears in the records again.

> *September 16, 1772*
>
> *Resolved that Milly Criste be called the first opportunity for crimes stated above and rejecting the counsil of the church.*
>
> *January 6, 1773*
>
> *Resolved that Mr. Ignatious West be debard communion for misusing his wife and threatening to shook a man for a very frivolous cause and other things.*
>
> *April 7th, 1773*
>
> *Brother Ignatious West was present to justify his conduct but it being defective, still remained under cinsure.*
>
> *May 3rd, 1775*
>
> *Resd. that Ignatious West be debard communion for his obstinate continuance in his former disapprd. practice and judgment.*

For those members who would not follow the rules of the church, there was no alternative but excommunication.

> *May 29, 1790*
>
> *Resd. to excommunicate Joshua Carney and Mary his wife for their wrangling and fighting—as well as neglect of the worship of God at home and abroad.*

Members could be excommunicated for numerous reasons, among them:

- Not attending worship services
- Marital discord

- Drunkenness
- Profanity
- Playing cards
- Adultery
- Encouraging horse racing
- Irreligious conduct
- Allowing a borrowed slave too much liberty amongst family members
- Stealing

Members who were excommunicated could be restored to good standing upon proving themselves repentant.

> *June 30, 1822*
>
> *The Church proceeded to examine the list of the Black members. In ____ to ascertain the conduct and managing of them. When Cillars, a Black member who had been Excommunicated came forward and gave satisfactory signs of Repentance where upon the church agreed to restore him to fellowship.*

Less serious breaches could result in being refused communion. These might include:

- Getting angry and refusing to settle a dispute
- Refusing to follow the advice of the church
- Drinking too much
- Being connected with a Mormon in an unlawful way

A number of blacks were members of Chopawamsic Baptist and problems among them were also dealt with by the church; the same rules governed their behavior. There is very little mention of blacks in the record books until May 4, 1816. Apparently, there had been problems with some of the black members and a recommendation was made "to set off the Black members and appoint some of the Brothers to take the oversight of them to keep order amongst them and to allow them to commune with us so long as they conduct orderly."

It was also decided to establish a separate membership book in which the names of the blacks would be kept. Prior to this time, the names of all members were listed together. Interestingly, a count of members prepared in August 1834 listed sixty-nine white members and one hundred twenty-two black members, a total of one hundred ninety-one.

A number of slaves belonging to a Mr. Moncure were church members. Among familiar family names of Stafford were Shelkett, Weedon, Cloe, Starke, Fritter, Lewis, West, Tolson, and Gallahan. The church also drew members from Prince William County, among them the families of Keys, Mountjoy, and Cato.

After the Civil War, the records list only forty-seven white members and five black members. Membership dwindled steadily until 1919. The church records end with an entry for June 14, 1919. Six members attended the last service and the church doors were closed for the next twenty years.

When the government decided to expand the Marine Corps base, they used the old church building as a meeting hall. On November 6, 1943 an article appeared in *The Free Lance-Star* announcing the government's intention to condemn some 30,000 acres of land along Chopawamsic Creek which included the church. For most people, this was the first they had heard of such a plan. Government representatives held meetings at Chopawamsic Church and informed property owners that they had to be out of their homes by November 21. Residents were assured that they would receive immediate compensation for their property (which didn't happen as the court cases were not closed until the 1960s). As if this were not enough, heavy rains were causing severe flooding and making it horribly difficult to move wagons and trucks. Many people had no place to go and were forced for the first times in their lives to go to banks to borrow money. While we take this choice for granted today, many of these poor souls found it shameful and frightening.

The government was paying only for acres and didn't care about true property value. A man who had a fine substantial home was paid the same as a man with a cottage, and there was no recourse for those involved.

After everyone moved away the Chopawamsic Baptist Church was forgotten. Unfortunately, the government never saw fit to move any of the graves in the church cemetery and they remain there today.

Chopawamsic Farm

On April 12, 1709 Bryant Folio, Stafford County planter, and his wife, Mary, sold to George Mason (II) for 5,000 pounds "good Tobo and twenty shillings Sterling" a tract of land along both sides of Chopawamsic Creek, "being part of a patent of 2,066 acres formerly granted to John Mathews the grandfather of the said Mary." This property ran from about Boswell's Corner on the west to John Moncure's Clermont on the east.

On this property George Mason built a large home using blocks of local sandstone, although it is likely that there was an earlier residence there. He planted a large orchard and opened great fields on which to graze sheep and cattle.

Mason lived at Chopawamsic for an unknown period of time. Like his father, he amassed tremendous land holdings in Stafford, Prince William, Fauquier, and Fairfax Counties. We do know that he leased the Chopawamsic property and was living in Fairfax County when he drowned in the Potomac in 1735.

On July 10, 1728 a deed between George Mason (III) and John Peyton was recorded in Stafford for "land lying on Acquia Run in Overwharton Parish where the said George Mason now dwells: 150 acres being part of 1,000 acres patented to Valentine Peyton on June 6, 1654 who conveyed to Henry Peyton on May 26, 1657 who conveyed to George Mason (II) on July 8, 1694 and was inherited by George Mason (III)." Obviously, Mason felt at home at Chopawamsic for he added to the end of the deed, "Before signing the aforesaid George Mason doth reserve to himself twenty foot square of land in the Orchard for a burying place exclusive of fruit trees."

After the death of her husband in 1735, Ann Thomson Mason moved back to Chopawamsic to raise her three children. She never remarried. Ann deeded the farm to her son, Thomson, "One hundred and fifty acres of Land part of the said Tract of five hundred acres of Land to be laid [out] as the said Ann Mason shall think proper so as to include the houses and plantation known by the name of the Ordinary." This is the only known reference to the property by this name and it probably indicates that it had, at one time, been used as an ordinary.

Chopawamsic Farm

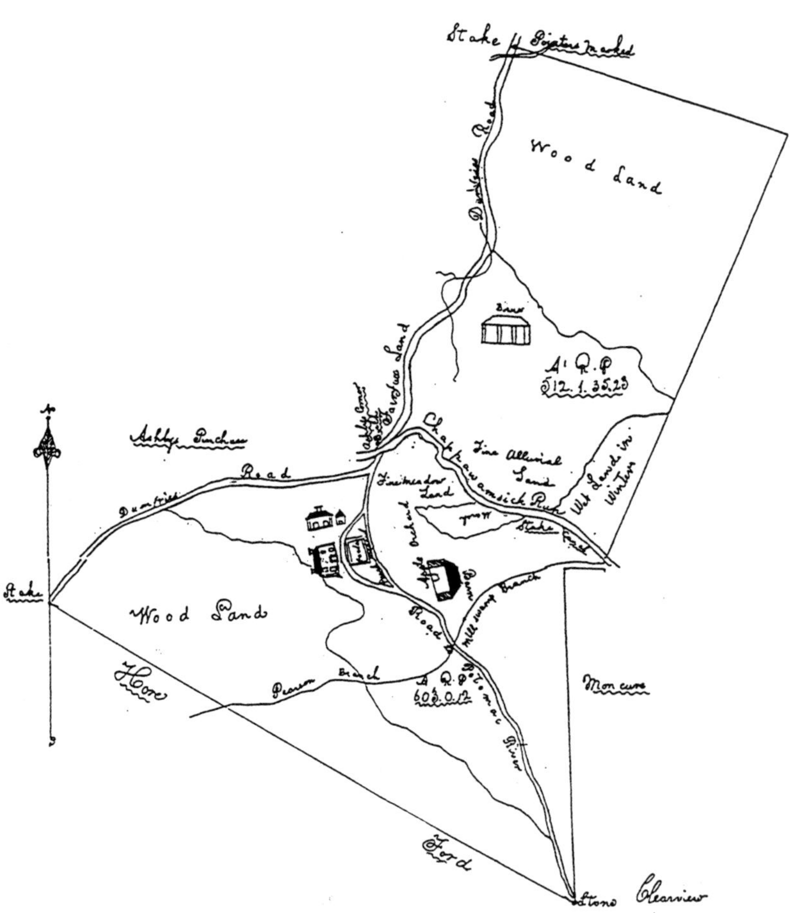

An 1850 survey plat of Chopawamsic Farm.

Apparently, Thomson Mason had financial difficulties later in life for he twice advertised the sale of Chopawamsic Farm, although he never actually sold it.

The first advertisement for the sale of Chopawamsic appeared in *The Alexandria Gazette* on September 11, 1769: "Choppawamsick. In order to satisfy the subscriber's debts will be SOLD, to the highest bidder...on Monday the 4th day of December, the house and 38 slaves." The farm was not sold at this time, and another ad appeared in *The Virginia Gazette* in May 1773 describing 2,600 acres in Prince William and Stafford situated four miles above Aquia Warehouse. The property included a mill seat with a "large and never failing stream...There is a great appearance of iron ore and a large quantity of white oak and pine timber, a tolerable commodious dwellinghouse, a great number of convenient outhouses, good orchards, and several tenements in order for cropping." The ad continued, stating that if Mason could amass twice the value of the property, he would not have to sell it.

Mason never sold Chopawamsic for in his will, proved in 1785, he left it to his wife, Elizabeth, for her lifetime and then to his son.

In 1850 Major William H. Fitzhugh purchased and surveyed Chopawamsic Farm. The accompanying plat is beautifully detailed and shows the orchard mentioned by Mason as well as the house, two barns, various outbuildings, a garden forests, pastures, and marsh. This is a small map which encompasses a tremendous amount of acreage. The Dumfries Road marked on the plat is the present-day Mason Road just north of Boswell's Corner (U.S. Route 1). Today this old road dead-ends but it originally ran through Chopawamsic Farm, Clermont, Richland, and on to the Potomac River. The Moncure property on the east side of the farm was Clermont and the Ford property was Bloomington.

It is unknown what became of the early stone house. In all likelihood it was abandoned after the Civil War and the stone probably ended up in the foundations of nearby buildings. It is also possible that the stone was sold to the builders of the National Cathedral, a fate of numerous other stone buildings in Stafford. By the time of the Quantico expansion, however, the house site was occupied by a basic white frame farmhouse.

Woodstock

In the early days of this country, in the backwoods of Stafford, fate brought together an extraordinary group of men—Giles and George Brent, William Fitzhugh, George Mason, and John Mercer. Together they formulated ideas startlingly new to their era, ideas which became the foundation for the Bill of Rights, the United States Constitution, and the Virginia Constitution. All were Protestants except the Brents, who were remarkable in that as staunch Catholics they held numerous important military and civil positions in a Protestant colony. Without doubt the association of the Brents with the Mason family and John Mercer defined the concept of freedom of religion that later became incorporated in primary national documents.

There were two Brent estates in Stafford, Richland and Woodstock. The latter was not only a plantation but also a briefly thriving community which grew around the Brent plantation home and the tobacco warehouse built there in 1734-35.

The first Woodstock house was built in the wide flat bottom land along Aquia Creek (now part of Aquia Harbor Development). Homes of first-generation colonists were usually built right on the water due to the region's dense forestation and lack of any transport routes save water. Mosquitoes and malaria quickly drove settlers to higher elevations; later Woodstock houses were built upon the hill overlooking the creek, tobacco warehouse, and wharves.

Stafford's first George Brent (c.1640-1699) was the son of George Brent and Marianna Peyton. He was sent from England to his uncle Giles in Virginia "to learn how to live." He quickly acquired land by means of the headright system (individuals received fifty acres of land for each new colonist they sponsored) and by buying up other tracts. At the time of George's death in 1699 he described Woodstock as consisting of 500 acres bought from Giles (II), 300 acres from Henry Peyton, 200 acres from Mary Rinit, and "900 acres adjoining John Guin's land."

George was initially trained as a surveyor but changed his profession to law and for many years he was one of the most active lawyers in the northern part of the colony. During his time in Virginia he held the offices of Commander of the Potomac Garrison, Receiver General north of the Rappahannock River, Burgess of Westmoreland County, and King's Attorney General, and with William Fitzhugh was an agent for Lord Fairfax and Lady Culpeper, Proprietors of the Northern Neck. This latter position gave him authority over all rentals and the settlement of all lands within the Northern Neck. His actions as agent for the Proprietors were apparently high-handed and earned him a public scolding by Robert Carter in the House of Burgesses. Carter accused Brent of threatening to double rents of people who displeased him. Undaunted, Brent remained an agent of the Proprietors until his death.

During the 1680s George and his brother, Robert (who joined him in Virginia in 1686), enjoyed an extensive law practice in the courts of Stafford, Westmoreland, and several other counties. Court records of 1689-1693 indicate George and Robert were the most prominent lawyers acting in cases before the very justices who should have been fining them for their Catholicism.

With the ascent of Catholic James II to the throne in 1685, even greater opportunities were opened to Catholics. George was elected to the Assembly and was appointed to several committees. During this service he helped draft two addresses to the Governor and presented a bill to the Council. In general, he left his mark as a prominent and respected member of the Assembly.

The Brents were well-respected and enjoyed relative freedom in Protestant Virginia despite their religion. There are several reasons for this, not the least of which was the fact that they were living in a sparsely-occupied wilderness where there were few people to take notice. Further, the Brents proved very useful in their community by holding military offices and providing legal services. Finally, they were wealthy enough to forge friendships and associations with powerful Protestant landholders who were willing to come to their aid when needed.

The Brents were only occasionally challenged over their religion. In 1681 when George was serving as Captain of the Stafford Rangers assigned to guard the northern frontier, his men refused to ride with a Papist. This difficulty must have been overcome, however, as Brent continued to command the troop and draw pay for himself and his men until 1684. During this time he received public thanks as a frontier defender from the

Assembly, and the minutes of the House of Burgesses commended him for assisting Captain Jones in putting down a Seneca uprising. They further rewarded his with 1,000 pounds of tobacco.

The most serious threat to the Brents involved the wild accusations of Parson John Waugh in 1688-89. Stafford politics had long been marked by a bitter feud between the Tories led by William Fitzhugh and the Whigs of George Mason (II) and John Waugh. Waugh enraged local farmers by preaching that Maryland Catholics were conspiring with the Seneca Indians (who were allegedly under the direction of George Brent) to murder the Protestants in Stafford. Armed and vengeful, Waugh's band headed for Woodstock with plans to kill Brent and burn his property. Members of the council, sensing political motives, intervened and ordered Brent to report to William Fitzhugh's house for protection. Three Councilors arrested Waugh and his co-conspirators, Burr Harrison and John West, and transported them to Jamestown to answer charges. Simultaneously, they suspended George Mason from his command of the county militia. In the end, Waugh had to apologize for his dangerous misconduct but he still claimed a partial victory. Although he had advanced the Whig cause in Stafford his efforts had not driven out William Fitzhugh or destroyed George Brent. The Council drew its membership from the landed gentry who had been friends and associates of the Brents for forty years, and they were not likely to allow his future or fortune to be ruined without cause.

George Brent lived for ten years after Waugh's uprising. Twice in those years there were attempts to subject him to anti-Catholic restrictions. In 1691 Richard Gibson, a frequent opponent of the Brent brothers in the Stafford Court, petitioned the Court to require George and Robert to swear to the oaths of allegiance and supremacy if they intended to continue to practice law. The justices seem to have simply ignored Gibson for no formal action was taken. The Brents continued to practice, and Robert even served in 1692 as attorney for his family's great enemy, John Waugh. Gibson didn't relent in his efforts to destroy the Brents. Due to his continued complaints to the court, in December of that year a Stafford grand jury asked to present George and Robert "for several wicked crimes" and for recusancy.

Once again, nothing happened. In May 1693 Richard Gibson again appeared before the Court complaining of these two instances in which no notice had been taken of his charges. Insulted, the justices made him apologize but they did call the brothers to court and read them Gibson's complaint. The Brents answered that as they had not been legally summoned to court they should not be expected to respond to the charges until the next court meeting. The Stafford justices declined their request for a postponement but did allow them to appeal their case to the General Court (the Governor and Council) who dismissed it.

The death of George Brent in 1699 closed a period in which the Brents held important military and civil offices. The Aquia region was no longer a wild frontier. Lands around the Brent estates were settled, and organized church and political life was established. Yet another reason for the decline in the Brents' influence was the rapid succession of Woodstock owners over a twenty-year period following George's death. George Brent (II) survived his father by just one year, dying in 1700. His brother Nicholas died in 1711, aged about thirty-four. The third brother, Robert, inherited Woodstock but died c.1721, aged about forty. His son George succeeded to the estate as a minor. Woodstock farm finally left the Brent family through its sale by Robert Carroll Brent to the Ford family in 1832.

Like his uncle Giles, George was always careful not to display offensive evidence of his religion. He even began his will with the customary Protestant phrases but, like Giles, ordered that 2,000 pounds of tobacco be devoted to "Pious uses" and he asked that Masses be offered for the repose of his soul.

The Catholic Brents of Stafford, in the century and a half preceding the Revolution, enjoyed practical toleration despite anti-Catholic laws. Secured initially by isolation in the wilderness, their services as guardians of the frontier, and inconspicuous religious practices, the Brents were further safeguarded by long-standing friendships and association with fellow gentry. Tolerance was on several occasions severely tested but it survived because in each instance colonial authority so willed it.

The Town of Woodstock

At the heart of the colonial economy was tobacco; tobacco warehouses were the equivalent of banks in today's society. Tobacco warehouses were established by order of the Burgesses, who also approved local court appointments of official tobacco inspectors. It was their responsibility to monitor the quality and quantity of tobacco stored in the warehouses. The first official warehouse in Stafford was at Marlborough. By August 1734 the Burgesses had ordered that the Marlborough warehouse be discontinued and a new one built "at or near the head of Acquia" on the Woodstock property. The change in location of the official tobacco warehouse was due to a shift in the population concentration from Potomac Creek to Aquia Creek. The establishment of a warehouse frequently spawned the creation of new businesses to serve the many people who came to the warehouse. Thus, a town developed at Woodstock which was also called Woodstock or Woodstock Town.

In February 1772 the Burgesses appointed commissioners to report on damaged tobacco at the Aquia warehouse. These commissioners included Thomas Ludwell Lee, Thomas Blackburne, Henry Lee, John Fitzhugh, Samuel Selden, and William Alexander. The commissioners determined that the tobacco had been damaged by rain and floodwater. Twenty-three hogsheads were affected amounting to 18,282 pounds damaged or ruined. The owners of the tobacco were due compensation and the Burgesses ordered the county treasurer to pay the inspectors eighteen shillings per hundredweight so they could in turn pay the owners.

In October 1792 the Assembly ordered the establishment of a town on fifty acres of George Brent's (1760-1804) land. Tax records indicate that the loss of fifty acres was far from a hardship for Brent; in 1776 he paid taxes on 1,700 acres. By 1792 the Woodstock house had been built on the hill overlooking the flats of Aquia Creek. Eighty-one slaves did the day-to-day work on the plantation. The Aquia tobacco warehouse attracted people and businesses to the wharves built for ships hauling the tobacco, and the town grew up in the low, swampy flats. The trustees named for the new town of Aquia were Travers Daniel Jr., Bailey Washington, John Cooke, Daniel Carroll Brent, John R. Peyton, Valentine Peyton, John Murray, Robert Brent, Thomas Mountjoy, John Mountjoy, Elijah Threlkeld, and Nathaniel Fox. The land was surveyed into one-half-acre lots and sold at public auction. For a time the community thrived; tobacco and other goods passed across its wharves en route to distant ports.

Like so many of these port towns, however, Woodstock's prosperity was short-lived. A number of factors contributed to the demise of the town. The low wet flats were still infested with the mosquitoes that had forced the removal of the original Woodstock house, and malaria was epidemic during the warm months. Since early port towns were always built as far upstream as possible (to reduce land transportation distances), they quickly silted as a result of poor agricultural techniques and became unnavigable; the town of Woodstock was no exception. Finally, population centers were constantly shifting and by the time the creek silted, there were fewer people who needed a town at that location anyway. Woodstock town faded into memory although the Brents continued to own the farm for many more years.

The Woodstock estate suffered terribly at the hands of the Union. Margaret Waller Ford wrote a letter during the war about the Union soldiers who were camped on her farm. She claimed that they raided the Brent family cemetery (behind the Crucifix on U.S. Route 1) and carried the tombstones back to their camps where they made fireplaces from them. This would account for the lack of markers in the Brent cemetery today.

All physical evidence of Woodstock farm and town has vanished with the exception of an abandoned albeit modern silo upon the hill where the last Woodstock house stood. The great rolling fields are now crowded with the houses of Aquia Harbor, as are the low swamp lands which once spawned malaria epidemics. Yet once again there is life like so many generations ago.

Stony Hill

Stony Hill adjoined Woodstock to the south, and would have been part of Giles Brent's seventeenth-century patents. This lovely old farm is now a part of the Aquia Harbor community. Stony Hill was described by John Lewis Peyton (b.1824, discussed later) in his book *The Adventures of My Grandfather* as "built, after the style of an English country mansion of the Inigo Jones architectural school, of brick brought from England, in combination with the native sand stone, and surrounded with extensive grounds, improved after the manner of the parks, for which the mother country is so famous; was the home of taste, refinement, and luxury..."

Stony Hill was the home of the Moncures and Peytons and the property was part of the original Valentine-Peyton tract. An old family story says that Judge Richard Cassius Lee Moncure of Stony Hill decided the case of a poor black man charged with stealing a pig from a local farmer. Judge Moncure knew that the man had indeed stolen the pig but realized that he had done so to feed his family, and the owner of the pig was a wealthy man who could well afford the loss of the one animal. He told the accused man to go home and cut the pig exactly in half from snout to tail and hang half of it in the Stony Hill meat house. When the hearing came around, Mr. Moncure listened to all arguments and finally said to the farmer, "I've listened to all sides and I've decided that this man has no more of your pig than I have. Case dismissed."

John Peyton of Stony Hill (1691-1760) was a leading citizen of Stafford County. The Peyton family is an ancient one, tracing its ancestry back to the 800s. John was a vestryman of Overwharton Parish during which time the present Aquia Church was built, possibly on part of his Stony Hill tract. He served as a Burgess for the county in 1736 and again from 1757-58 and was a justice from 1745 until his death. He seems, also, to have been one of Governor Spottswood's Knights of the Golden Horseshoe who in 1716 searched for a passage through the Blue Ridge. He was a landowner, holding plantations in several counties as well as property in Alexandria. The 1742 Quit Rent rolls charged John for

2,291 acres; by the time he died he owned 5,159 acres in Stafford. His executors were charged for the taxes on that acreage in 1773 but a notation was made in the records that the executors "will not make any payments as they say they are uncertain whether they have any land untill the present dispute with G. Britain is settled." The 1776 tax records indicate that the executors were still in arrears at that time. John Peyton was buried at Stony Hill but was later moved to the Aquia Church cemetery. He willed the 350-acre Stony Hill tract to his son Yelverton (1735-1794/5), who operated an ordinary nearby.

John Rowzee Peyton (1754-1799), son of Yelverton, led a fascinating, albeit short, life. He was an ardent letter writer and, fortunately, many of his letters survived to be compiled by his grandson John Lewis Peyton. These letters were published in 1867 in a book he called *The Adventures of My Grandfather*, and they chronicle the years between 1768 and 1774.

In May of 1773 John Rowzee's father sent him to the West Indies to attend to business matters. After completing his father's business in the islands, John sailed to New Orleans on the first leg of his journey home. Upon leaving New Orleans on the return trip, John's ship was boarded by hostile pirates who took hostage the entire crew and passengers and accused them of being French enemies. They were bound and suffered terribly at the hands of their captors. After landing at Rio Del Norte, they were forced to march, shackled, to Santa Fe, a journey of eighty-nine days. Upon arriving in Santa Fe (a number of the group perished along the way), they were imprisoned in barbarous conditions for over five months. John, his servant Charles Lucas, and the jailer's daughter, Annette, made a daring escape. John spent the next ten months wandering through the wilderness to get home to Stony Hill. During this time, John met his old friend, Major Charles Lewis of Augusta County. Major Lewis had brought an army to the Appalachian Mountains in anticipation of an Indian uprising. John agreed to take command of one of the companies. He fought in the day-long bloody Battle of Point Pleasants in which he suffered a wound that would eventually prove fatal.

John Rowzee Peyton had fallen in love with Anne Howe while in Jamaica attending to his father's business. Anne and her mother were only temporary residents of the island, their permanent home being on the Occoquan River. John married

Anne in Virginia in 1777, a year after his father's death, and the couple moved to Stony Hill. (John had by this time inherited Stony Hill and was in residence there.) John's health steadily deteriorated over the next twenty-one years, the bullet he took at Point Pleasants having damaged his spine. He died at the early age of forty-four and was buried at Stony Hill next to his father.

Stony Hill was destroyed by Union troops during the Civil War.

Sandstone Industry

Just up the creek from Aquia Landing was one of Stafford's major industries—the sandstone quarries. Located on what is now Aquia Harbor property, the quarries operated off and on from the 1650s until the 1930s and provided building stone for some of the most important buildings in the nation, the White House and Capitol among them.

In 1652 the Governor of Virginia set aside fifty acres for the town of Aquia, about three miles up the creek from Brent's Point. The Aquia warehouse and tobacco inspection stations were built but, soon after, the sandstone was discovered and the tobacco business was all but forgotten. One of the earliest uses of the stone was in grave markers; the earliest surviving of these markers, which dates back to 1681, can be found in the Brent family cemetery.

This stone was used for the foundations and chimneys of many houses in the area, including Woodstock. Some buildings, such as Aquia Church, were built of brick and trimmed with sandstone. Christ Church in Alexandria was also trimmed with Aquia stone. The windows, doors, and corners of the building were all decorated with sandstone.

Gunston Hall, home of George Mason (IV), also combined brick and stone. Mason's great-grandfather had settled in Stafford after leaving England, and his father had operated an ordinary at Marlborough.

Long known as the best building stone in the Potomac River and Chesapeake Bay region, Aquia sandstone was used in many fine buildings including Gunston Hall (1754), Fort

Aquia Mill

The wheel runs in this part, which is built of stone, one Story high and not covered, 12' by 30'	Manufacturing Mill two stories high, one of stone, the other wood, covered with wood, 40 feet long by 30 feet wide

From an 1807 Mutual Assurance policy

Washington (1808), and Mount Vernon (1743). Even the nation's White House and Capitol were built of Aquia stone. During the War of 1812, both of these buildings were burned. The stone was cleaned and repaired and the exterior of the President's home was painted white.

Most of the Aquia stone, called "freestone" by the colonists, was a reddish color. In 1822, a "white stone" with a greyish hue was discovered at Aquia and this was used to build the Old Patent Office Building in Washington.

Aquia produced a fine stone ranging in color from cream to reddish-brown. Large particles of quartz and feldspars caused the stone to appear mottled. The stone was easy to work owing to the fact that unlike most sandstone, the matrix of the Aquia stone was harder than the crystals and not brittle. The demand for this stone continued until after the Civil War when architectural preferences called for a stone of solid color.

While there were a number of small quarries along Aquia Creek, much of the stone came from Wiggington Island. Also known as Government Island or Brent's Island, it is separated from the mainland by a marshy bog near the marina at Aquia Harbor. On December 2, 1791, George Brent of Woodstock sold eleven of the island's twelve acres to architect Pierre L'Enfant who had been sent to find stone for the new city of Washington[1] which he had been contracted to design (one acre had earlier been sold to Robert Stuart, a stone mason from Baltimore). Brent received £1800, equivalent to about $6000. L'Enfant also arranged to rent another quarry on the creek belonging to John Gibson of Dumfries (Gibson had bought the quarry from Brent). A canal was dug between the two facilities and buildings erected to house twenty workers at each site.

Local slave owners, anxious to make some extra money, hired out their slaves to work the quarries to provide stone for the

---

[1] Washington was laid out as a square, each of its four corners oriented to the four cardinal points on a compass. Lines were marked by boundary stones quarried at Aquia. Each stone was one foot square with a pyramidal top. Each bore the name of the state it faced on one side and "District of Columbia" on the other. George Washington set the first stone at Jones Point on April 15, 1791.

nation's new capital. The wages were paid to the masters while the government provided food and shelter for the workers.

Skilled stonemasons were difficult to come by, however; after advertising in the eastern states failed to bring a response, the city planners advertised in Europe and finally had to agree to pay transportation costs for the men and their wives and guarantee their social standing upon their arrival. Hence, stone cutters were finally hired from Scotland, Holland, Germany, and France.

To cut the stone, the workers marked off blocks with chalk. Then, using a pick, they chipped along the chalk line to a depth of eight to sixteen inches. Wedges were finally pounded in until the blocks broke free. The blocks were then moved by block and tackle to waiting boats on which they were shipped to Washington.

The plans for the presidential mansion called for the walls to be made of stone, which required a tremendous amount of stone to be cut at a far faster pace than was being done at the time. The commissioners in charge of planning directed that each worker be given one half-pint of whiskey each day in hopes of increasing production. When this failed, they authorized the hiring of twenty-five more slaves. Production, however, was still not great enough, so the planners decided to build the mansion of brick and use the stone as a facing only.

By 1800 the President's house and the north wing of the Capitol were in use. Sometime between 1800 and 1803, however, the Aquia quarries had to close down because the workers were unable to find any more "fine" stone. The project's new architect, Henry Latrobe, believed there was more usable stone in the quarry and it was reopened. By 1807 another wing had been added to the Capitol. When the British arrived in Washington in 1812, the Capitol consisted of just these two wings joined together by a wooden walk. The British set fire to many of the public buildings and had it not been for a rain storm that night, the damage might have been unrepairable.

After that war, the Aquia quarries were again closed, reopening only when needed. During the 1820s and 1830s, stone for the central portion of the Capitol was quarried as well as stone for the eastern portion of the Treasury.

Aquia Creek was navigable at low tide for large ships, making transport of the stone relatively simple, although hauling stone by ship was risky due to the incredible weight. The stone was transported by longboat close to its building site, then placed on flatbed train cars and rolled on a track to its final destination. The first lighthouse built in America was located at Cape May, Virginia and was built of Aquia stone.

Architects from Boston to Jacksonville specified this stone in their buildings until after the Civil War when architectural changes demanded a solid color stone. The warm-colored stone then fell from favor and the quarries were abandoned. Trees grew up in the quarry, obliterating its presence. It was almost totally forgotten until, in 1891, an attempt was made to revive the use of Aquia stone. The Aquia Creek Stone Corporation was chartered but operated for only a short time before closing.

Because preferences in stone colors and architectural design change almost as rapidly as tastes in clothing style, the quarry was again opened in 1922, this time by the George Washington Stone Corporation of Virginia. Aquia stone was again being requested by architects in the northern cities. In 1923 the company purchased the Marine Railway and Coal Company Shipyard in Alexandria, making it one of the largest stone-cutting businesses on the east coast. Facilities at Alexandria included a 250-foot pier, cranes, saws, rubbers, and the like for handling the stone. Six railroad trunk lines came into the plant at Alexandria, providing rail transport all over the country. At Aquia, a short railroad and derricks were constructed on the four-acre quarry site. The silted creek was dredged, a loading wharf built, and a tug and barges purchased. All this effort was in hope of obtaining a contract to supply the building stone for the new Masonic Temple in Alexandria. That contract did not materialize, however, but the stone did again become popular. "Colonial Freestone," as it became known, was used in buildings at Yale University, the New York Gallery of Fine Arts, and many other notable buildings in Boston, Philadelphia, Baltimore, and Washington. Financial problems during the Depression caused the sale of the properties to the Ford Motor Company. Ford doesn't seem to have done anything with the quarries. The property was sold to the Aquia Colonial Freestone Company and they cut a little more stone from the quarries.

In 1936 one last effort was made to operate the quarry. Aquia Colonial Freestone Quarries of Washington cut stone there for about four years. Finally, the quarry which had provided stone for some of the finest structures on the east coast closed permanently.

Not only was the stone used in public buildings, it was also popular for use in many fine homes. Lord Baltimore, Lord Fairfax, Thomas Jefferson, the Masons, Tylers, Lees, and Washingtons all used this excellent building material in their homes.

There were numerous other stone quarries around the county. It is difficult to find information about operations at these other sites because, unlike the Aquia quarry which became a major government operation, most of the quarrying was done sporadically. A little stone would be cut for use in or around a new house, maybe a few blocks would be cut and sold by individuals, etc. Only two other quarries seem to have operated with any consistency. The Conway quarry was also located on Aquia Creek (see "Rock Ramore" in Chapter 6) and Robertson's was next to Rocky Run a mile or so behind the court house.

Aquia Landing

Aquia Creek would have so many tales to tell if only that were possible. The creek has been a vital part of the development of the county since Giles Brent established his home there in the late 1640s.

Development along the Atlantic coast during the nineteenth century required adequate rail service for the transportation of people and goods. By the early 1800s travel between north and south was accomplished by jumping from rail to stage to boat and back again. Stage passengers reaching Aquia Creek in 1815 boarded the 186-ton New York-made side paddle steamer *Washington*, in order to journey elsewhere along the Atlantic coast.

In 1837 passengers traveling north rode the train from Petersburg to Fredericksburg. They then boarded a stage that carried them as far as the mouth of Potomac Creek, where there was a steamboat landing. Just three miles north was another steamboat landing at the mouth of Aquia Creek (now Aquapo). Because the water in Aquia Creek was much deeper than the water in Potomac Creek (allowing for connections with large steamboats), the decision was made in 1837 to extend the train tracks to that point. Aquia Creek became the northern terminus of the Richmond, Fredericksburg, and Potomac Railroad. Thus, trains began running in and out of Aquia Landing in 1842.

Travel by steamboat had, prior to this time, been difficult during the winter months due to the ice in the river. By the time R, F, & P reached Aquia, however, new steamboats, called "ice boats," had been developed that could break through the heavy ice on the river, even in the coldest weather.

On April 17, 1861, Virginia seceded from the Union. Almost immediately, the four steamboats forming the connection between Aquia and Washington were seized in Washington and converted into armored gunboats. Realizing that the railhead at Aquia would be a prime target for Union occupation, steps were taken to fortify the terminal. General Daniel Ruggles was assigned to protect the terminal. Under his direction gun pits were dug into the hill at the mouth of the creek. On May 31 five Union gunboats appeared on the river and attempted to take the terminal. They were repelled by Ruggles' troops. These were the first shots fired by the United States Navy during the Civil War. The next day, a second attempt was made and this, too, was repelled. A letter tells of the Union troops shelling the fortifications on the hill above the terminal for two days, killing nothing but someone's old white mule.

Union forces made a third unsuccessful attempt to take the railhead. In response, the Confederates fastened an explosive charge to two empty wooden barrels, lit the fuse, and sent it out into the creek. A soldier on one of the gunboats spotted the barrels floating in his direction. Fortunately or unfortunately, the fuse had gotten wet and gone out. This was the first attempted use of a torpedo.

In April 1862, however, Union forces were dangerously close to a takeover of the entire R, F, & P system. In an attempt to protect the crucial rail link between the southern states, Major T. H. Holmes burned the wharf and buildings at Aquia and destroyed the bridges at Accakeek Creek, Potomac Creek, and the

Rappahannock River. Due to the lack of a bridge, McDowell's Union forces were forced to stop at the edge of the Rappahannock and could only look at Fredericksburg. Without a supply line, McDowell and his men could go no further.

Herman Haupt, an engineering genius, was chosen by Union forces to make the necessary repairs to restore rail service from Aquia to Fredericksburg. Not only had Holmes burned almost one acre of wharf at Aquia, he had completely removed about three miles of track south of the terminal and had burned the ties. The bridge over the gorge at Potomac Creek had been totally destroyed. To cross there required a bridge four hundred feet long and eighty feet high, and the original structure had taken R, F, & P almost one year to build.

Haupt was made a colonel and superintendent of the Construction Corps of the United States Military Railroad. Actually, there was no such thing. Haupt was provided with a handful of experienced railroad men and three companies of soldiers. By working in twenty-four hour shifts, the crew laid three miles of track in three days. Upon reaching Accakeek Creek, Haupt had a bridge one hundred fifty feet long and thirty feet high built in sixteen hours. With only crude hand tools and unskilled labor the crew took on the gorge at Potomac Creek. Twelve days later, a train crossed the bridge. In another four days, trains were running from Aquia to Fredericksburg. The stone abutments may still be seen next to the present-day R, F, & P bridge. Abraham Lincoln, who was touring the area, remarked, "I have seen the most remarkable structure human eyes ever rested upon. That man Haupt has built a bridge across Potomac Creek four hundred feet long and nearly one hundred feet high, over which loaded trains are running every hour and, upon my word, there is nothing in it but beanpoles and cornstalks." Tom Moncure, clerk of the circuit court and local historian, feels certain that the bricks and stones from Potomac Church were also used in this bridge. Although the bridge appeared rickety, it actually contained almost two million feet of lumber, most of which had not even been stripped of bark. Haupt's crew had rebuilt the northern section of the railroad in less than one month. By restoring the supply line, Union forces were then able to push into the South.

After a series of Union losses ending with the Battle of Manassas, there was concern that the Confederates might try to take Washington. Burnside's troops, stationed at Aquia Landing, burned the wharves and facilities at Aquia as well as Haupt's three bridges over the Rappahannock River and Potomac and Accakeek Creeks. It turned out that Confederate forces were stopped at Antietam, and Haupt was ordered to replace what had needlessly been destroyed. Haupt replied to McClellan,

> The destruction of this road was an unfortunate piece of vandalism on the part of our troops. I reported to General Halleck that the destruction of this road was unnecessary and highly censurable. The Potomac Creek bridge was nearly eighty feet high and four hundred feet long. Nearly all available timber within reach was used in its construction. The bridge was blown down, then burned. [The] wharf at Aquia Creek was very complete covering 1 1/2 acres with double track and commodious buildings. Will take four months to rebuilt. Sixty cars all destroyed.

While facilities at Aquia were being improvised, Haupt was in Alexandria creating a prefabricated truss bridge that could be towed to its destination on barges. The landing and railroad formed the primary supply line for Union forces pushing south and, thus, had to remain open.

In June of 1863 Confederate General Robert E. Lee set out for Pennsylvania. Aquia Landing was heavily populated with Union forces and camp followers, and they had to be quickly evacuated to Washington. Once again, the facilities were destroyed, on June 22.

As a result of Lee's advancements, Union forces had been ordered to retreat from Falmouth and Aquia Creek. In their wake Confederate Major C. R. Collins burned all the buildings and tracks at the landing. The following day Mrs. George Whiting of Richland (diagonally across the mouth of the creek from the landing) wrote to her daughter describing the incidents of the night before: "The Northern troops have again left Aquia Creek, last night all their fine buildings and the bridge were destroyed.

The illumination was magnificent—there were sixty new buildings burnt to the ground."

One final restoration of the lines between Aquia and Fredericksburg was undertaken in May 1864. By the end of the war, however, the tracks were in horrible condition. Most of the bridges were down, the facilities at Aquia were destroyed and what cars were left were damaged or worn out. The facilities at Aquia Landing were never rebuilt. It was not practical to have to unload the trains at Aquia and transfer to a boat to get to Washington. A new line was opened between Fredericksburg and Quantico and began operating on May 1, 1872. The old ten-mile stretch between Brooke and Aquia became State Route 608.

An event which took place after the war brought national attention to Widewater. On the night of October 12, 1894, two armed men climbed onto an R, F, & P train as it slowed to cross the drawbridge over Aquia Creek. To give the impression to passengers and crew that this was a large gang, the men ran back and forth along the train, firing their guns into the air. The train was brought to a stop and the engineer was forced to detach the locomotive. The robbers blew the door off of the express car and took about $150,000 in money and valuables. *The New York Herald* reported, "The 'hold-up' of a train at Aquia Creek, Virginia, forty-one miles from Washington, on the Richmond, Fredericksburg and Potomac Railroad, and the robbery of a sum estimated at one hundred and fifty thousand dollars from the Adams express car, is bringing train robbery a little too near home."

R, F, & P put up $1000 for the capture of the robbers. The governor added another $1000, and the two men were quickly apprehended.

Potomac Steamboat Company

In the earliest days of the county, practically all transportation was by water, roads being all but nonexistent. The Virginia Assembly, however, was determined to create a simple network of roads which would not only connect the widely scattered communities, but also encourage settlement inland from the creeks and rivers. They were successful to some degree and transportation of people and goods by road became common, despite the dreadful conditions of the roads in bad weather.

The Potomac Steamboat Company was chartered in 1813 and made its first run from Washington to Potomac Creek in just eight hours, half the time required to make the same trip by stage. The roads, however, remained the principle means of transport even though, at times, they were next to impassable. With the heavy traffic of stages, carts, wagons, and horses the ruts on Potomac Path grew deeper and more menacing. During severe weather or heavy frost, the steamboats did not run at all. In 1836 Joseph Martin described the condition of the road and, especially, the terrors of Chopawamsic Swamp:

> During the freeze in the winter when the steamboat between the city of Washington and Potomac Creek is obstructed by ice the great northern and southern mail from Washington City to New Orleans is carried through Dumfries. The road in its neighborhood between Fredericksburg and Alexandria is utterly impassable at times that the mail cannot travel, this road being the principal source of the irregularity of the mail to the South.

In 1837 the Richmond, Fredericksburg, and Potomac Railroad was extended to connect with the steamboat at Aquia. Although the line between Fredericksburg and Washington was not completed until after the Civil War, its connection with the Washington steamboat all but eliminated through stage traffic on Potomac Path.

Coal Landing

By 1900 the forests had recovered sufficiently from the ravages of the Civil War to support a lumber business again. Long boats sailed from Coal Landing to Aquia Creek, up the Potomac and on to Baltimore.

Between 1890 and World War I, wood provided one of the few available cash incomes in Stafford. The locals would cut what timber they could and haul it to Coal Landing by wagon or boat to sell for pulpwood. The stacks of logs waiting at the docks were often forty feet high. Because the docks at Coal Landing were fairly extensive, there were a number of fishing boats that worked out of here, also. An 1872 U.S. Engineers' report provides us with a glimpse of the activities around Aquia Creek. The report cites the presence of "6 steam saw mills, 10 grist mills, 24 farms, 33 sailing vessels, 4 steamers, and 2 tugs with barges daily to Washington 12 months a year carrying immense quantities of wood, barrel staves, stone, corn, wheat, rye. The boat building yard at Coal Landing builds steamboats for the excursion trade from D.C."

During this time, one of the largest general stores in the county was at Coal Landing. The store was built in the early 1800s and was first owned by a Captain Thomas Towson. It served for many years as a fishermen's store. Thomas Towson owned well over 1,000 acres in Stafford County when he died in 1867, including Coal Landing, the quarries at Rock Ramore, and the Robertson tract. Thomas' son, James, inherited his father's property and Coal Landing was sold at public auction on December 16, 1896. The poster announcing the auction described Coal Landing as "a valuable piece of Wharf Property, containing one-quarter of an acre, more or less."

In 1936 the store was owned by Captain Wesley Knight (then 91) who gave a description of activity around Coal Landing when he was a young man. According to Captain Knight, the landing was a very busy place during those days. Thirty to forty cords of wood were shipped by boat each day; it was common to see as much as two thousand cords of wood stacked in the yard awaiting shipment.

Knight was an accomplished captain and operated many vessels on the Potomac during his sailing days. For many years he hauled lumber from Coal Landing to Alexandria on his schooner *Ipsawasson*. Knight commented on the warming of the winters on the Potomac since his childhood, saying that in the late 1800s it was normal for ice on the river to be eight or nine inches thick.

> Now, it stays warm all the year around, or the winters are not as cold as they were. One December, more than fifty years ago, I can recall setting sail with some friends for Alexandria. So fiercely did the wind spring up we were forced to anchor for the night in Chichamaxen Creek on the Maryland side of the river, opposite Quantico. By morning, the river was frozen solid. Our ship was completely ice-bound, the whole party had to walk back over the ice. Not until March did a warm spell release the vessel from its prison.

Knight was a small boy when the Civil War broke out but he recalled the Union troops coming onto his family's farm and shooting the guineas, turkeys, chickens, sheep, and cattle. The family finally begged some of the soldiers to camp there to prevent total ruin.

Economic depression in the 1930s brought an end to most activity at Coal Landing as well as in the rest of the county.

Importance Of Churches In Colonial Life

Churches were the center of colonial life. They were, of course, places for people to gather to worship and thank their God, but they served a much greater function as well.

Prior to the Revolution, the church and the county were practically one. In fact, the parish lines were the county lines and county government was nearly synonymous with the parish vestry. Membership in the vestry was made up of the most influential landholders of each county and it was not unusual for these same men to also be Justices and/or Burgesses.

Throughout the eighteenth century, vestries were self-perpetuating; that is, they could select their own replacements to fill vacancies. When the House of Burgesses ordered the division of an existing parish, it usually authorized the election of a new vestry as well. Once elected, however, a vestryman retained his title until he either died or chose to step down. Throughout the century many petitions were submitted to the House requesting new elections or the dissolutions of existing vestries; few of these petitions were granted.

The vestry hired ministers and negotiated their salaries; bought, sold, or rented glebe lands and slaves; and determined when and where to build new churches and manses. Vestries were further responsible for maintaining roads, and in counties divided by rivers were required to operate ferries. Beyond these civil duties, the vestries also cared for the poor, whether sick, aged, widowed, orphaned, disabled, or born out of wedlock. Relief might come in the form of direct payments to indigent persons or their caretakers, or poor folk might be hired to work on some parish project. These functions were paid for through poll taxes levied by the vestry.

As a result of this combination of civil and ecclesiastical duties, vestries had considerable power over the wealth of their constituents, a fact which led to fiery disputes between those in power and those paying the bills. Parishioners resented being taxed by men who did not have to stand for election, though they rarely had recourse. Despite many recorded petitions to the House to set aside vestry decisions or to dissolve entire vestries, little was done to limit their power until late in the eighteenth century. This change was triggered not only by an increased desire to separate the powers of church and state but also by the rapid decline in the authority of the Episcopal Church after the Revolution. After the war, membership in the Episcopal Church was drastically reduced as people were free to join the denominations of their choice.

Beyond its obvious ecclesiastical and civil roles, the church had another function. In the early days of the colonies, there were no newspapers (and many people couldn't read), so one of the chief ways to keep up with the news was by going to church. Day-to-day survival left little time for socializing and one of the only opportunities for people to gather with their neighbors and socialize was at church. For most, church was what held them together as a community.

Stafford, unlike much of the New World that proclaimed to honor religious freedom while actively limiting the religious practices of the residents, actually welcomed people of varying beliefs. Prior to the Revolution, the official church was Anglican and while the greatest number of residents belonged to the Church of England, there were also groups of Catholics, Baptists, Methodists, and even a small settlement of Quakers in Roseville. The Aquia area was settled by a Catholic family and a small Catholic settlement prospered there. After the Revolution, the variety of denominations in Stafford increased. There were Methodists along the Warrenton Road and Presbyterians in Hartwood. Chopawamsic Baptist Church served the area around Chopawamsic Creek, including what is now Dumfries.

Aquia Church

Overwharton Parish was created out of giant Potomac Parish sometime before 1680 and was known as the Upper Parish for a while, then called Stafford Parish and finally, by about 1700, Overwharton Parish. The name Overwharton is said to have originated with an early settler, Colonel Henry Meese, who named his plantation after his native parish in North Oxfordshire. This plantation, presently in King George County, eventually came into the hands of one of Stafford's rectors, the infamous John Waugh, and is now known as Waugh Point.

The first major church in Stafford was Potomac Church, located just southeast of the present court house. Potomac Church was built in the mid-1600s and was apparently still in good condition when it was decided to build a second major parish church (the reason for this remains unclear).

Upon the chosen site was another old church that some in the parish thought should be repaired rather than replaced. While it is unknown how many buildings preceded the present brick structure, it is believed that divine worship has been held on or near this site since shortly after the formation of the county. Records indicate that in 1667 there were two places of worship and by 1724 there were two chapels and one church. What few county records exist are extremely vague. In fact, the first deed to Aquia does not appear until 1850.

In 1745 Lawrence Washington, brother of George and manager of Accakeek Iron Works, petitioned the House of Burgesses to dissolve the vestry, who had agreed to pay for a new brick church. Washington claimed that the parishioners would "labour under great Hardships" to pay the levy and asked the Burgesses to give "such Relief as to this House shall seem meet." The House rejected the petition, saying that adequate public notice had been given for the parishioners to speak their opinions. According to their investigation, few bothered to attend the public meetings and the vestry was within its power to build the church if it saw fit.

The vestry contracted with "one William Walker, an Undertaker" to build "a new brick Church, Sixty Feet Square" for 153,920 pounds of tobacco. Another petition by "sundry Inhabitants" also protested the cost of the building, but the House found that the price for the church was fair and the petition was rejected.

Few of the politicians in Williamsburg (home of the House of Burgesses) had ever set foot in Stafford, and they did not realize that Potomac Church was so near the proposed building site for the new church. Also, residents in the extreme northern end of the county did not have to travel the extra few miles to Potomac if they found the way difficult, as there was Dettingen Church close by on Quantico Creek. Despite these things, the

House approved the vestry's plans, causing a furor amongst the Stafford residents who found it ludicrous to pay for two major parish churches.

The building of Aquia was delayed for several years as the residents repeatedly petitioned the Burgesses to dissolve the vestry of Overwharton. Each petition was reviewed by committees in the House and each was denied. In the end, the residents were taxed and Aquia Church was built.

Determined to build their new church, the vestry placed a notice in the *Virginia Gazette* of June 6, 1751, stating, "The Vestry of Overwharton Parish, in the County of Stafford, having come to a Resolution to build a large brick Church, of about 3000 Square Feet in the Clear, near the Head of Aquia Creek, where the old Church now stands. Notice is hereby given, That the Vestry will meet at the said Place, to let the same, on Thursday the 5th Day of September next; if fair, if not the next fair Day. All persons inclinable to undertake it are desired to come then, and give in their Plans & Proposals." William Walker had either tired of waiting to begin building or died, because Mourning Richards became the undertaker or contractor for the church.

By 1752 or 1753 the church was almost finished. A fire, however, destroyed the little frame church and the church house to the north of the present structure. Contemporary newspaper accounts say that the fire occurred on March 17, 1754. That same fire also consumed the inside of the nearly completed new brick building.

There is no recorded explanation for the fire, but it is intriguing that arson committed by English convict laborers had become such a problem that by 1730 the Assembly stiffened the penalty for such a crime. Records indicate that convicts were responsible for the burning of numerous homes, warehouses, and public buildings in the surrounding area. In February 1752 Nathaniel Harrison and Hugh Adie were to be paid for their work in a new court house on Potomac Creek which "some evil disposed person or persons feloniously burned" prior to its completion. There seems a strong possibility that the chapel and church at Aquia were also victims of arsonists.

Mourning Richards, however, had a problem. He had no funds with which to rebuild the inside of the church. On June 2, 1757, a bill was submitted to the House "to impower the Vestry of the Parish of Overwharton, in the County of Stafford, to levy for Mourning Richards a reasonable Satisfaction for rebuilding a Church at Acquia." After some deliberation, financial arrangements were made and the church was completed.

Due to the difficulties of travel in the early days, the parish church and the court house were built near the center of the heaviest population. Smaller chapels were often built in outlying areas and a single minister would be assigned to the parish. By 1730 population shifts had led to the carving of Prince William County from Stafford. Although both Potomac and Aquia Churches operated concurrently, the greater shift in population near Aquia in 1757 established it as the parish church while Potomac drifted into obscurity.

The walls of Aquia Church are double. There is a brick wall on the outside which is complete in itself. Then there is another complete brick wall on the inside. The space between the two is filled with rubble. Because of this double-walled construction, only the inside of the building was destroyed by the 1754 fire.

The inside walls of the church are plastered and painted white. The woodwork, now a cream color, was originally guinea grey, a grey which had a slight blue tint.

The chancel, copied after English design, was painted heavenly blue. Above the altar hang arched wooden tablets upon which are lettered the Ten Commandments, the Lord's Prayer, and the Nicene Creed. In the eighteenth century there were no prayer books; those people who knew how to read could read from the tablets above the altar. Only one or two other surviving churches of this period have such tablets.

Virginia was an English colony and her residents, therefore, were expected to attend and support the Church of England. At the time Aquia was built, the records indicate that there were about one thousand communicants. After the Revolution, however, people were free to choose and they began breaking off and joining other denominations. This, of course, reduced both membership and money available to Aquia as churches could no longer tax their parishioners to obtain funds. Aquia survived quite well, though, despite the losses, until the Civil War.

Beautiful Aquia Church suffered horribly during the war, yet somehow avoided the complete devastation wrought on so many colonial buildings in Stafford. From 1861 to 1865 the church grounds were used as a campground for Union troops involved in the various skirmishes over the rail head at Aquia Landing. The building served as a stable and hospital. The lovely box pews became stalls and the horses chewed the wooden walls of the pews, destroying them. The wooden floors were ruined by manure, horses' hooves, and blood from the hospital, and were later removed and replaced with concrete.

Various Union units camped at Aquia during the war, including the Seventeenth Pennsylvania Volunteer Regiment. The names of some of the occupiers and their regiments are carved in the sandstone trim of the building and written on the interior walls of the tower. During this horrible time, the masses of Union soldiers who camped in Stafford were little more than common vandals. Unoccupied buildings were burned or dismantled. Aquia survived purely because it served as a hospital and, according to legend, a stable. After the troops finally left, the building stood deserted, the floors damaged beyond repair, pew backs destroyed. Soon vegetation took hold, and bushes and small trees grew up inside the once magnificent structure.

After the Civil War, the church continued to suffer, as a result of poverty and of the mass exodus of the old families who had worshipped there and cared for the building for generations. A few families did return to the area and they began rebuilding their beloved Aquia. Horses had chewed on the tall pews, and so the pews had to be cut off to a uniform height. The lovely raised wooden pew floors had rotted from neglect and had to be removed. Somehow, however, the beautiful three-level pulpit survived the war.

Most of the money and effort to put the church back together came from the Moncure family. The Moncures were descendants of the first minister of Aquia and had supported the church for well over one hundred years.

Rev. Jaquelin M. Meredith, whose cousin Anne Eliza Stribling had married Withers Waller of Clifton, became rector of Aquia in 1864. Through dedication, hard work, and personal sacrifice (he worked for over a year without receiving a salary and contributed $90 of his own money for renovation), Aquia gradually recovered from the war. Throughout his tenure at Aquia, Mr. Meredith never received a regular salary as the church was too poor to pay him. In 1868 the treasurer, George V. Moncure, told the vestry that they had only paid Mr. Meredith $100 to date. When Mr. Meredith accepted the position as rector of Aquia there were only seven communicants. By the time he resigned in the 1870s to become rector of Bruton Parish in Williamsburg, the church had ninety communicants. Had it not been for the efforts of Jaquelin Meredith, Aquia might well have succumbed after the war and collapsed from disuse and neglect. Most colonial churches were not so fortunate; Aquia's is one of only two surviving.

The three-level pulpit clearly illustrates the hierarchy of the early church. The lowest level was for the clerk, pronounced "clark." He was in charge of the business affairs of the church and led the singing and the service. Because there were no hymnals (few people could read them anyway) the hymns were interlines. The clerk used a little pitch pipe to get everyone on the same key. He would then sing a line of the hymn and the congregation would repeat the line. And so it went.

The second level of the pulpit was for the lay reader. The parish had only one minister and he was responsible for several churches. The lay reader could do everything except give the sermon. The service would continue until the minister arrived (he might be an hour or so late). He would go up to the third level, preach his sermon, and leave immediately. He was traveling by horseback from church to church and didn't have time to stay for an entire service.

Below the first level of the pulpit was the Singing Pew. The best voices in the church were placed there to help lead the singing.

Unlike the rows of benches so often seen today, the pews at Aquia are box-like. Each pew belonged to a family who would use that pew generation after generation. The sides were originally very high so that the occupants could see only the pulpit when sitting. This not only helped keep their minds on the service (and off of what so-and-so was wearing), but also cut down on drafts. There was no heat of any kind in the early days and the services were often three to four hours long. People covered the wood pew floors with rugs brought from home, wrapped themselves in blankets, and brought hot bricks to warm their feet. It was even permissible to bring light refreshments to keep up one's strength during the service.

The bricks for the church were fired on the site. Brick-making at Aquia was carried out to the southwest of the present building. While preparing a site for two little buildings from The Fleurry's (an old Stafford home discussed later in this chapter), many bricks and burned soil were excavated. Those buildings now rest upon the brick-making site.

The report on Aquia Church issued by the Virginia Historic Landmarks Commission notes, "As it stands today, Aquia Church is one of the most elaborate, as well as one of the best preserved of Virginia's colonial churches. It ranks as one of the more important examples of colonial ecclesiastical architecture in the nation. Its rich interior appointments are among the finest in the state; the magnificent triple-tiered pulpit is unique in Virginia."

Aquia Church was conceived in controversy and suffered through political struggles, fire, enemy occupation, and neglect. Yet it remains today, standing tall upon its commanding hill, a symbol of the tenacity and fortitude of those who built, loved, and restored it.

Roads

For all of the negative impact of the twentieth century, one blessing of progress has been the improvements in roads in Stafford County. When white settlers first began arriving in Stafford there were no roads to traverse by horses or wagons. There were a few Indian trails but they were of little value to the settlers, who had little need to wander through the wilderness. The earliest transportation, then, was by water and the first settlers to arrive quickly claimed the best shoreline property. As more people came, inland property was settled, necessitating the opening of roads.

One of the earliest roads in northern Virginia was the Creekside Road (now State Route 218). This was originally an Indian trail running along the ridge between the Rappahannock

County Roads c.1820

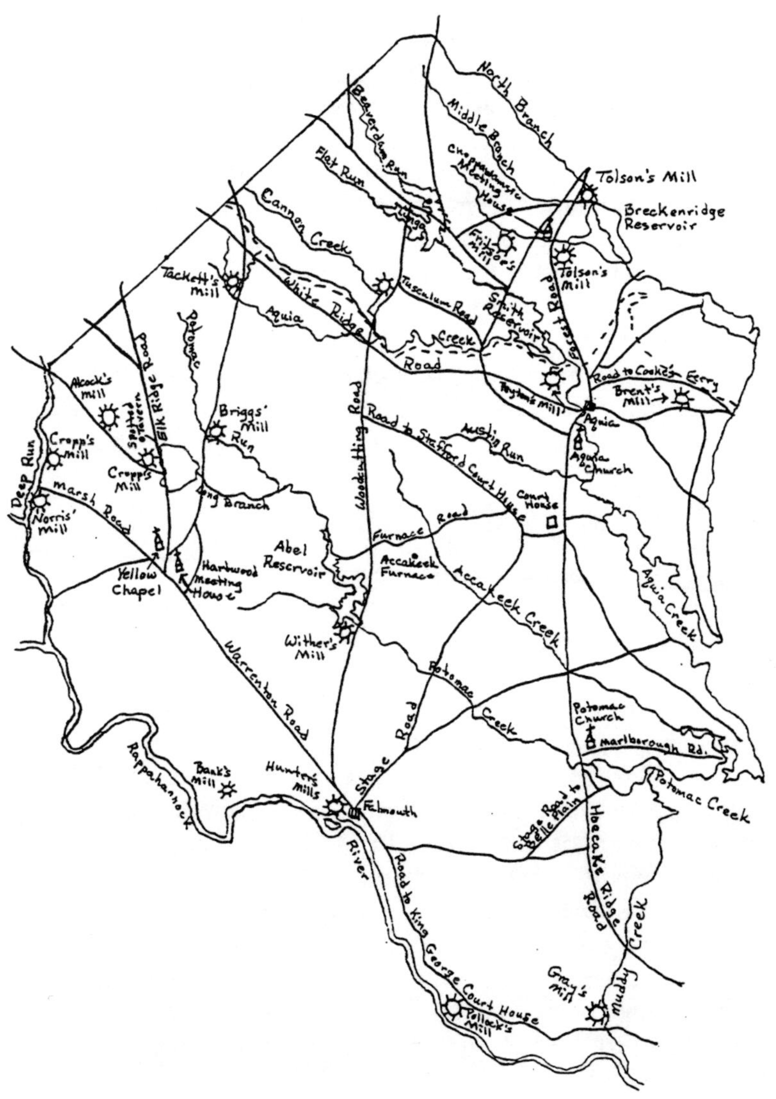

and Potomac Rivers. Early English settlers preferred to travel by water as they built their homes on the creeks and rivers. They did, however, even from the beginning, try to keep open this primitive trail. By 1662 the Assembly had enacted a road law requiring each county to appoint road surveyors to "lay out the most convenient wayes to Church, to the Court, to James Town and Potomac Path from "Capt. Alexander's to Pasbytanzy," "from Pasbytanzy to Head of Potomac," and "from Head of Potomac to Capt. Brent's." In 1666 another extension was ordered "from Aquia to Chopawamsic." In 1667 the road extended "from the frontier inhabitants down to the head and ferry at Aquia." These "frontier inhabitants" were probably those located towards the middle of the present border between Stafford and Prince William Counties—now part of the Marine Corps base.

This was still not a very good road, however, and travel by water was often much easier. Making a road usually meant little more than cutting a path through the trees and brush. During wet weather, these "roads" flooded; wagons, horses, mules, and oxen would become mired in massive ruts. Travelers trying to get from lower tidewater to the northern colonies usually avoided the frontier of Stafford by going via water around southern Maryland to Bohemia Manor at the head of the Chesapeake Bay. Fairfax Harrison notes that Lord Howard traveled in this manner in 1687 and Cuthbert Potter did it as late as 1690, carrying messages from Governor Nicholson to Boston.

By 1820 Stafford boasted a number of roads, though it must be noted that most of these roads were nearly to totally impassable much of the time. The map accompanying this chapter illustrates the major roads during the early-to-mid nineteenth century. The Stage Road from Falmouth to the court house corresponds to modern U.S. Route 1, but the hill just south of today's State Route 628 (Eskimo Hill) was so steep that it was nearly impossible to get a wagon to the top.

During this time, the major north–south route through the county was the Woodcutting Road (State Route 627). People living in the northern part of the county who wished to go to Fredericksburg turned east towards Potomac Church (on what is today the dirt road leading to Marion Manor Nursing Home) or traveled west towards Mountain View and used the Woodcutting Road.

Many of the old roads are still used today. White Ridge Road is now State Route 610. The Warrenton/Marsh Road is now U.S. Route 17. To get to Warrenton most travelers did not continue into Fauquier County by way of the Marsh Road because there was no bridge over Deep Run and the water was too deep to ford safely. Instead, they turned north at Hartwood Meeting House and used Elk Ridge Road (now State Route 614).

Another road still in use today is the road to King George Court House, now known as State Route 3 east. Many roads were named for the places they led to, court houses being popular designations.

The Woodcutting Road also bears mentioning. The area in the center of the county (all around Ramoth Church) was known from at least the eighteenth century as "The Woodcutting." Even the tax records make use of this name when referring to the locations of various pieces of property. Throughout the nineteenth century lumbering was a common employment among Stafford residents; the logs were hauled out of The Woodcutting to Coal Landing, loaded onto barges and taken to Washington and Baltimore. After the Civil War, there was no more wood left to cut and the name was largely forgotten.

Peyton's Ordinary

Inns or ordinaries were centers of social activity in the colonies. They were usually built along the roads at about fifteen-mile intervals and catered to the needs of early travelers. Visitors not only received a hot meal and a place to sleep, but they could also hear and share the latest news. Ordinaries often served as post offices as well. Travelers were usually willing to carry a letter to their next stop.

Peyton's Ordinary on Aquia Creek was quite busy from at least the 1760s until the mid-nineteenth century. According to county court records, Yelverton Peyton (1735-1794/5), son of John Peyton (I) of Stony Hill, was granted a license to keep an ordinary in 1768. He married Elizabeth Heath, who survived him and continued to operate the ordinary. This was one of only two licensed ordinaries in the county at that time and served the many people coming and going from the docks and warehouse at Woodstock. Yelverton was a Stafford justice in 1769. He was also a member of the "Committee of Stafford" who prepared the address to the "Inhabitants of Staff'd" expressing sympathy with the people of Boston and the justices' intention to not meet again until the conflict was resolved. During the Revolution, he served in the Virginia Line. In 1790 he was Deputy Sheriff in Prince William County.

On March 6, 1769, George Washington dined at Peyton's Ordinary. He also spent the night there on October 31, 1769, on his way to the House of Burgesses and again on September 14, 1772. General Rochambeau's army, marching north from Williamsburg, camped there in 1782.

Operators of ordinaries were men of some importance in their communities. Thomas Peyton was a lawyer as well as an innkeeper. In August 1792 he was also appointed to the position of Inspector of Tobacco for the Aquia warehouse.

We are unsure as to the exact location of the ordinary. During the eighteenth century, the main road did not run north and south as it does today but east and west, passing in front of The Fleurry's (now Shoney's on the east side of U.S. Route 1) and leading traffic down to Aquia Village. To the east of The Fleurry's and Aquia Church are a ridge and a walled spring. The wall around the spring was built sometime during the nineteenth century, but a spring would have been an absolute necessity for an ordinary and there is a strong likelihood that Peyton's stood nearby.

The Fleurry's

The Fleurry's has been our latest loss to the developers in Stafford County. While not as grand as some of the old homes, The Fleurry's was a landmark and was certainly witness to some of the most important people and events throughout much of the county's history. It seems cruelly ironic that it should be replaced by a nondescript strip shopping center. The beautiful old trees, boxwood bushes, and rolling fields are now a slab of flat,

The Fleurry's

impersonal parking lot. What a tragedy that we allow this to happen to the few historical sites that remain in our county.

The original house was built in the late eighteenth century on a one-hundred-acre tract of land that extended from Woodstock to the present site of Anne E. Moncure Elementary School. The land at this time belonged to Elizabeth Harrison (daughter of Peyton Harrison) who married Gabriel Green; the place was home to the Greens, Suttles, Fleurrys, and Moncures. This little house was very typical of the homes built in Stafford at this time. It was a simple two room, one and one-half story frame cottage. If one had viewed the house in the illustration from the side, the eighteenth-century portion would have been in the middle, sandwiched between the "front" which was added around the mid-nineteenth century and the old kitchen which had been moved up and attached to the old part. The eighteenth-century structure as well as the kitchen were saved from the developer's bulldozer and moved to Aquia Church where they now serve as a vestry house.

The newer front part of The Fleurry's was build about 1850 by Miss Anne E. Moncure's father, Robert Ambler Moncure. The old county road had originally run east and west in front of the old cottage, and travelers rode by The Fleurry's on their way to Aquia Village. The road was later changed to run north and south (U.S. Route 1) and, therefore, Mr. Moncure's addition was built facing the new road. A porch was added to the front and was built of several huge slabs of Aquia sandstone. From this porch the first War Bonds were sold during World War II.

The Moncures operated a thriving nursery business for many years and there was a nice little greenhouse in the field to the south of the house. It was during this time that hundreds of American and English boxwood bushes were planted around the house. There were also daffodils by the thousands as well as a great variety of trees and shrubs.

Using existing tax records, we can trace the house back to 1832. Earlier records do not mention a house, but the original structure was built using handmade nails and pegs. Machine-made nails were used after 1800, which indicates that the house was built prior to 1800. In style, it is typical of homes built in Stafford during the latter part of the eighteenth century.

The old part of the house was covered with beaded siding. People who had a little extra money often used beaded siding to add some fanciness to their homes. Today the bead is added to the siding by machine, but in those days it had to be done by hand. The kitchen was covered with plain siding. The floors in both buildings appear to have been replaced along the way because they were laid using machine-made nails. We do not know the age of the kitchen; kitchens burned frequently and were rebuilt. We also do not know when the kitchen was moved from the yard and added to the back of the house.

Court Houses and Jails

There has been a long succession of court houses in Stafford. It seems that every time a new one was built it soon burned. Stafford was not unique when it came to this problem—for many colonial court houses fell victim to fire—but Stafford seems to have suffered more losses and more frequent fires than most counties. Roughly two-thirds of the deeds and wills written before 1860 have been lost to court house fires. For this reason it is difficult if not impossible to carry out complete title searches on most properties in the county. Many wills are missing, as are court orders and other legal records.

The first court met in September 1664 at the home of Robert Townsend in Chotank, not in present-day Stafford. On December 9, 1665, Captain John Alexander's workmen were ordered to build a court house on the south side of Potomac Creek. This building was completed and records show that divine services were held there. It is likely that Potomac Church was either not built or not completed by the time the court house could be occupied.

In 1690 the court met at the home of Thomas Elsey (or Elsoy), but we do not know where he lived. On November 14 of that year it was stated that the court would continue to meet there until the new court house was built. Sampson Darrell and Ambrose Bayley were ordered to build a new court house in the town of Marlborough. According to the contract between the justices and Darrell and Bayley, the contractors were to build a court house at Marlborough in exchange for 40,000 pounds of tobacco apiece. The building was to be thirty feet long by twenty feet wide and constructed of English frame "mortus and tennant" with locust sills twelve inches square. The outside was to be covered with clapboard. The new court house was to have a "large fair door" with a gable. It was also to have "a Couple of large Fair Winddowes" with shutters. Finally, the contractors were ordered to build the furniture for use in the building, including three tables, each five feet long by three feet wide, and handsome benches for the justices.

Court records list levies paid to John Withers for stocks and a pillory. George Mason was paid for the building of a prison. Thomas Watts was paid for mending court benches and rails, and Edward Watts received payment for work done on the court and prison. Francis Waddington was paid for "trouble in his house" and entertaining the court (he was apparently an inn keeper), and Malachi Peale was paid for a prison keeper.

During an early session in the new court house, a small riot took place led by the infamous John Waugh. On this occasion the Reverend Mr. Waugh called William Fitzhugh, the presiding magistrate, a Papist. The result of this disturbance was a ban on the sale of liquor on court days. One is left to wonder if the good rector had, perhaps, imbibed too much.

This court house was built but burned very soon after completion, probably around 1718. As activity around Marlborough had ebbed and no new lots were being sold, the justices ordered that the replacement court house be built closer to the center of population. A court house was once again built on the south side of Potomac Creek, this time just upstream from Belle Plain and very close to Cave's Warehouse. This building burned in 1730 or 1731 and the justices ordered it rebuilt in the same place.

It may be assumed that this new building also burned, because in February 1752 Nathaniel Harrison and Hugh Adie were "to be paid for work on a new court house which some evil disposed person...feloniously burned" before it was finished. This occurred at a time when convict laborers were setting many public buildings on fire.

Upon the redrawing of the Stafford boundaries in 1779, which divided King George and Stafford from Rappahannock and Potomac Counties, the magistrates moved from the old court house on Potomac Creek to the home of William Garrard, a place more convenient to most of the county's inhabitants. At the last meeting of the court in August 1778, only nine of the thirty justices had been able to attend as the court house was not centrally located. Garrard lived just north of today's court house complex, probably about where the old Stafford Middle School now stands. The justices then ordered a commission of the peace to find the center of the county, proposing to build a new court house at that location. The commission found that the center was in a deep valley with no access to water or level ground for general musters. The magistrates then chose a place between the ordinaries of William Garrard and Moses Phillips, "a high and dry situation of equal distance from Potomack and Rappahannock rivers." Bailey Washington stated that he believed the new location was between four and five miles from the center of the county. The magistrates recommended, however, that due to the current high taxes the building of a new court house and jail be postponed until better times. When Travers Daniel surveyed the proposed site, it could not be determined if the land belonged to William Garrard or William Fitzhugh. Both were willing to convey and both signed the deed in March 1780. The land was sold for £5, "two acres of land for the use of building a Court House." The new court house, jail, and clerk's office were built in 1783.

1783 Court House ↑

↓ 1783 Jail

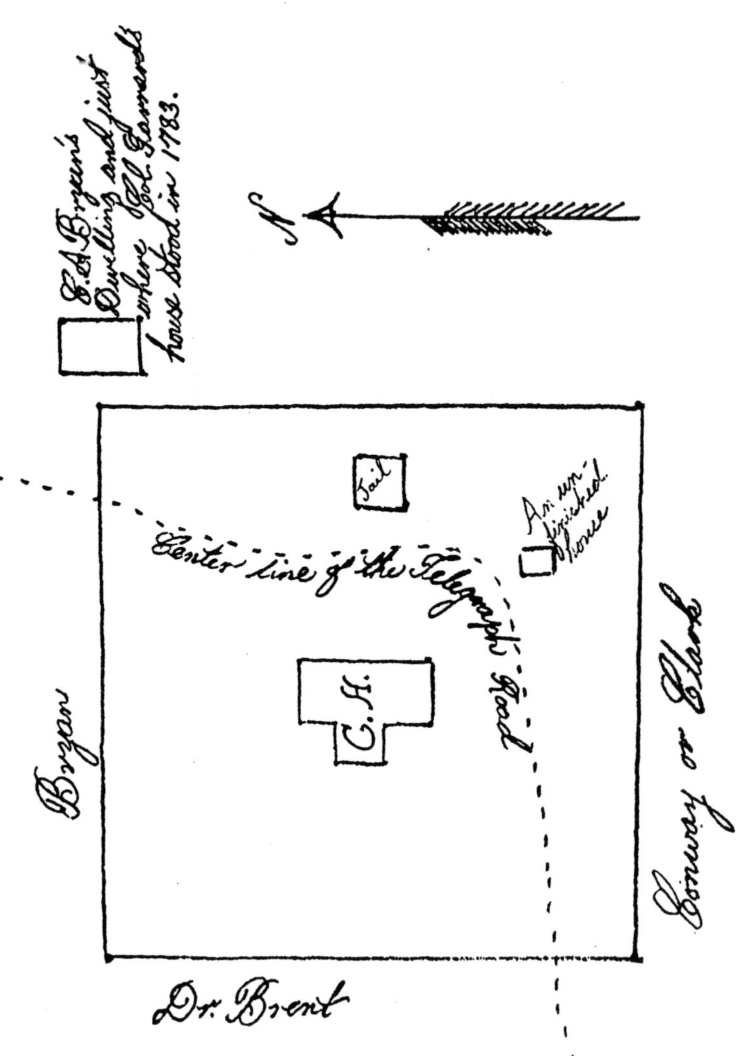

The 1783 court house lot was resurveyed in 1893 as there was some question as to the exact bounds of the property. Interestingly, while the court house, jail, and C. A. Bryan's home were shown, the clerk's office was not. That building was standing at the time of this survey but for some reason was omitted from the drawing. The Telegraph Road marked on the survey roughly follows today's U.S. Route 1 and State Route 630.

In 1787 an advertisement appeared in *The Virginia Independent Chronicle* of Richmond announcing the sale of property in Stafford. "William Garrard, executor, advertises for sale 620 acres in Stafford County [described as] belonging to the estate of William Garrard, deceased. On it stands the court house of the county with a tavern (which rents for £50) where the stages regularly stop once every day."

The court house foundation was covered by the building of the present old court house. Not shown in the illustration was a substantial brick wing on the back of the building. The court house was about fifty feet long by about eighteen feet wide and was covered with stucco and painted white, most likely in the nineteenth century.

The clerk's office was built on the north side of the court house and at a right angle to it. This building was approximately thirty-six feet long by twenty feet wide and twelve feet high. Like the court house, it was trimmed with sandstone and was built upon a sandstone foundation. The court house and clerk's office stood at right angles to one another, and the front corner of the court house was no more that about twenty feet from the back corner of the clerk's office.

The court house was modernized in 1898. A contract was issued authorizing a contractor to fireproof the building by pouring a cement floor and replacing the two wooden windows in the jury room with iron windows and iron shutters. The door to the jury room was to be replaced with a standard iron vault door, all at a cost of $1,200.

The jail was built in the middle of what is now U.S. Route 1, just in front of the present old part of the court house and next to the old well on the corner of U.S. Route 1 and State Route 630. It was about twenty feet square and two stories high, and probably had one large room on each floor. When the jail was torn down to build the new highway in the 1920s, some of the sandstone blocks were used to build the retaining wall along the south side of the court house. The large block that had been the jail doorsill was buried during the new expansion. George Gordon remembers seeing the jail when he was a boy. He recalls that there was only one prisoner and on warm summer evenings the man would sit at the top of the stairs, enjoying the air.

Conditions in the Stafford jail were no better than in other jails of the period. On June 14, 1775, Peter Hansborough petitioned the House of Burgesses asking to be paid for a slave who had died in the Stafford jail. According to Hansborough, "a negro man Slave of the Petitioner, named Sharper, was committed to the Gaol of the County of Stafford, charged with an attempt to poison one of his Master's family, where he remained five months, as no Court was held for the trial of him, there being no Sherif in the County by which means the said Slave was frost bitten so that he died; and therefore praying, that the Petitioner may be allowed the value of the said Slave, to be paid by the Public." The petition was referred to the Commissioners of Public Claims but it is unknown if a resolution was reached.

Hansborough also petitioned the Stafford Court claiming that the slave had been well and healthy when incarcerated, "but had got frost bitten insomuch that he lost one of his feet and several bones out of the other, so that he was entirely disabled and in about three months after died."

By 1920 the jail was in a state of disrepair and far from secure. Court records state, "It appearing to the Court that the Jail of Stafford County is unsafe for the detention of prisoners therein; it is ordered that all persons who are subjects to confinement in said jail be, by the sheriff or other officers of this county delivered to the jail of the City of Fredericksburg to be by the jailer of said jail held therein as provided by law, this order being effective until the further order of this Court, and the Clerk of this Court is directed to certify this order to the Sergeant of the City of Fredericksburg."

The present old court house was built in 1922 upon the foundation of the 1783 building.

Hope Grant

For years the ancient Hope Grant has been something of a mystery for Stafford historians. While surveys of adjoining tracts frequently mentioned "Hope Land," "Hope Line," or "Hope Spring," little was known about the original grant or who patented it. For years it was suggested that the owner of the property wished to remain anonymous, perhaps for political reasons. In truth, the mystery seems to have resulted from the scarcity of county records.

What we know today as the Hope Grant is actually only a portion or the seventeenth-century patent. A deed describes the boundaries as beginning at the mouth of Hope Creek (Willow Landing) and running westward to Jackson's Branch, northward on Jackson's Branch to Austin's Run, eastward to Aquia Creek, and back to Hope Creek. Jackson's Branch is the little stream which runs through the old Wayside Park between the divided U.S. Route 1 north of the court house. The name of the missing grant was discovered recently when a deed was located detailing the early history of the property. On May 9, 1780, Alexander Doyle and his wife Eliza sold to William Hewitt for 25,000 pounds of tobacco "a certain tract of Land called the Hope, situate on Acquia River supposed to contain 500 acres, and bounded as in said deed being part of a Patent for 600 acres granted to Robert Hubbert the 12th Decr. 1654." Hubbert had sold the property to Solomon Day and Daniel Matheny on March 10, 1684, the deed having been duly recorded in the Stafford court:

> Solomon Day and Daniel Matheny by their Deed of Partition...did divide the said track of 500 acres in manner following Vizt. That Daniel Matheny and heirs, should hold 300 acres to begin at the upper end of the said Tract, and to extend to the back line, and along the back line...thence parallel with the first side line North east down to Acquia river up river to the beginning, the said 300 acres, and that Solomon Day and heirs, should hold the lower part of the said track, being the residue of the same, supposed to contain 200 acres and whereas the 200 acres, Solomon Day's divident, by several Descents and Conveyances, descended and came to be vested in Cleam Slye of the State of Maryland in fee simple. Who sold the same (as well as another tract of land in County of Stafford) by deed...and afterwards surrendered to Alexander Doyle by Deed of Surrender...

Once the name of the grantee was determined, it was a simple matter to locate the grant in the patent books. On December 12, 1654, Hubbert received a 1,600-acre patent in Westmoreland County "on the south Side of Potomac River beginning at a branch of Ocquia River extending west along the line of Capt. Mason." (The Doyle deed states that Hubbert's patent contained 600 acres while the patent book lists 1,600. The difference is likely an error in transcription from the earlier document.) From this description it is impossible to determine the exact boundaries of the grant. According to the Doyle deed, Hubbert sold 500 acres of the property to Henry Peyton and John Fossaker on March 17, 1683. By the time Day and Matheny became involved with the property, the original 1,600 acres had been broken into several large chucks and sold to different parties.

The Day-Matheny division of 1684 left Daniel Matheny with the northern half of the land, including at least part of Concord and Coal Landing. Solomon Day received the southern portion, which now includes Hope Spring and present day Willow Landing Marina.

Court records of February 11, 1691/2 provide evidence of a family squabble as Sarah Matheny, widow of Daniel, charged her eldest son, William, with taking all of her land. On June 10, 1691, Sarah was ordered to bring to court all papers relative to "The Hope Land, being 500 acres formerly purchased by Daniel Matheny and Solomon Day." Daniel and Solomon had purchased the land in common from Henry Peyton and Richard Fossaker (note difference in first name) on March 17, 1683. The result of the dispute is unknown but the will of William Matheny, proved in the Stafford County Court in 1705, left his eldest son, Daniel, 300 acres, "the land I now live on."

William Hewitt purchased and settled on the Day portion of the Hope Land in 1780. He became prominent in local politics, being appointed in 1784 to serve with Bailey Washington Sr., John Brown, Gerrard Banks, Harris Hooe, Thomas Fitzhugh, Daniel Triplett, William Phillips, Charles Carter, Arthur Morson, William Fitzhugh, William Garrard, John Pollard, Thomas Mountjoy, John Rowzee Peyton, and William Alexander as a justice for the county. By 1790 he was acting as High Sheriff. Hewitt was one of the signers of the 1779 legislative petition to the House of

Delegates to move the court house to a central location in the county. He was also listed in the 1787 tax records as owning 28 slaves, 8 horses, and 20 cattle.

The locations of dwelling houses on the Hope Land are uncertain. There was a small house built right on the banks of Aquia Creek very close to the present Willow Landing Marina. The close proximity of the house to the water indicates that it was built in the seventeenth century, very shortly after the land was granted. Nearby are Hope Spring, which still flows, and Hope Creek, which opens into Aquia Creek on the other side of the marina. Later dwellings would have been built on higher ground to escape the mosquitoes, probably on the ridge that parallels the creek.

Concord

The house at Concord is one of the oldest buildings still standing in Stafford. This quaint little house is attributed to the Waller family, early settlers who played important roles in county history. The Concord property was part of the old Hope Grant. A very early house was built right on the bank of Aquia Creek. This site, with its sandstone-cased spring and old stone chimney, was destroyed in the 1960s when sand was removed for the building of Interstate 95. The beach made a perfect boat landing but the mosquitoes were a perpetual problem, and the family eventually moved up to the bluff above the beach and built the house that still stands today.

Across the paved road from the present house is a small sandstone quarry which likely provided stone for the foundation and chimneys of one or both Concord houses. Flowing from a crack in the sandstone is Waller Spring, which is referred to on surveys of the property.

There are three cemeteries near the house, one for the Wallers, one for the Waller slaves, and one for the MacGregors. Suzannah Waller, mother of Edward, was buried at Concord in 1747 and her will survives. Sometime prior to the MacGregors' purchase of the property, the Wallers had three fine marble headstones made for their deceased ancestors, William Jr. (died

January 3, 1815, age forty-nine), William Sr. (died August 4, 1817, age seventy-six), and Ursula. The stones had been stacked in the yard near the cemetery but never placed and the Wallers never returned to do so. Over time the exact locations of the gravesites disappeared and the MacGregors were left with a pile of marble stones. They finally dragged the stones out of the yard and used them for steps into and out of the house.

At the corner of the yard stands a small sandstone grave marker inscribed "Mary Lam." Mary was a Waller slave and her husband was a stone cutter who made the stone after his wife's death. This is one of the few slave graves in the state to have a stone marker.

Interestingly, the name Waller does not appear in relation to this land until 1859 when Concord was sold to the MacGregor family. Speculation about the Wallers' desire to live incognito is probably unfounded. Edward Waller, Suzannah's husband, is credited with building the present Concord house. His son, Edward, appears frequently in county court records and his will was recorded in 1784 and contested in 1785. Most likely, the deed to the property was lost, or possibly never even drawn. In 1792 William Hewitt was ordered "to view and examine the state of the records of this County and make a report thereof to the Court." Records management at the court house was less than adequate.

Concord was a simple, unpretentious farmhouse typical of the period. The present one and one half story house, which stands on the ridge overlooking the creek, was built of native oak and poplar. It was standing by at least 1730. The post and beam construction was exposed on the interior walls, indicating very early construction methods. The original windows were tiny; glass was an expensive luxury. Initially, the 28′ by 16′ house had two rooms downstairs and two rooms upstairs. Doors in the center of each long side provided ventilation but there was no center hall. A narrow stairway led to the rooms upstairs. Originally the north door had a small overhang to protect it. By the time the MacGregors came to Concord, there were porches on the north and south sides of the house. On the north side the left half of the porch had been enclosed to form a room. The other half remained an open porch, which was later enclosed to form another room.

In 1859 Nathaniel Mortimer MacGregor bought Concord as a wedding present for his daughter, Mary Eliza. Family tradition says that Nathaniel was much put out by the fact that Mary Eliza had married her first cousin, John Ridout MacGregor. Perhaps as a reflection of his opinion of his son-in-law, Nathaniel stated in his will that Concord was free of all debts of Mary Eliza's husband.

At about the time Concord was transferred from the Wallers to the MacGregors, major renovations were made to the building. Dormer windows were added to the steeply pitched roof, larger windows were installed, and the exposed interior beams were either removed or plastered over.

Concord survived the Civil War because the MacGregors continued to live there. In March 1863, the 4th Artillery, Battery F was camped at the court house. In need of fuel and food, they stripped Concord of much of its cordwood, livestock, and even the fence rails. First Lieutenant E. D. Mulenburg, who was in charge of the battalion, was thoughtful enough to write receipts for all of the supplies his men took, and he promised that the MacGregors would be paid for the items. A copy of a receipt still in the possession of Rick MacGregor lists "170 cords oak wood at $8.00 a cord, 203 cords pine wood at $6.00 a cord, and 2,700 white oak and [pine?] rails making over 150 cords at $7.00 a cord" for a total of $3,628.00 for wood alone. Part of the receipt is missing and may well have contained an itemized list of the livestock known to have been taken by the soldiers. According to Rick MacGregor's grandfather, the Union soldiers gathered up every animal they could find except one pig which John MacGregor put in the cellar. He told the soldiers that he would shoot anyone who dared try to take the pig as it was the last animal left on the place. John MacGregor was so affected by the looting of his property that he became ill and never recovered. He died soon after.

In 1900 the MacGregor family attempted to make a claim against the U.S. government for the items taken during the war. The receipts were turned over to a lawyer in Washington but, despite his efforts, the government refused to pay the MacGregors for their losses. Between 1900 and 1924 several attempts were made to claim reimbursement, but to no avail. The MacGregors' claim was part of some $34 million due to Southern property owners, little of which was ever paid.

A chimney fire in the early 1900s necessitated more restoration. Fortunately for the house, a man was outside chopping wood when the fire broke out. He rushed inside and hacked frantically at the burning wall. The children ran outside and gathered buckets of snow, and even the contents of the chamber pot were used to extinguish the blaze. The burning section of wall was cut free from the house and pushed out into the yard. As a result of the fire, the chimney was pulled down and the hole was covered over with weatherboarding.

Concord is presently owned by Rick MacGregor, who has spent years restoring his family home. Ravaged by age and termites, much of the structural woodwork has required replacement. Mr. MacGregor has cut, hand-hewn, and installed most of the new beams and trusses himself. The weatherboarding has been cut from local trees, planed, and hand-beaded. Mr. MacGregor also hand cut and shaped every cypress shingle. Displeased with the appearance of modern nails, he bought cut nails and had an uncle put heads on them. Of the original woodwork, the upstairs floors remain as do all but one of the interior steps. Wood for the downstairs floors came from large pine trees in Widewater. Mr. MacGregor cut the trees and used his own mill to cut the heart from the trees to make floorboards nearly identical to the originals. With this level of dedication and love, Concord will once again stand as a reminder of the proud, sturdy people who called Stafford home.

Spring Hill

In 1669 Gerrard Masters and William Waller emigrated from England and settled on 800 acres "on the south west side of Ocquia Creek...adjoining Mr. Richard Fossiker, near the head of Hope Creek, on a Ridge, along the Hope line &c." The grant was in payment for the transportation of sixteen new settlers. Part of this land became known as Spring Hill. The house was built on top of the ridge and was home to many generations of the Waller family.

The house was a comfortable farmhouse, not a mansion. Typical of Stafford homes of the period, it was a two-story frame building. An unusual feature of the house is that it was built upon a basement walled with cut sandstone blocks. Early houses rarely had basements because of the extra effort and time required to dig the hole; most houses were built on the ground and had a separate root cellar nearby. The presence of the stone-walled basement, however, indicates that the Waller family was better off than most others in the area.

While the owners of Spring Hill and Concord shared the same last name, there is a possibility that they were not directly related. There is no evidence in the public records which indicates any relationship between the two families other than as neighbors.

The Spring Hill house fell into disrepair after the Civil War and by the 1960s had all but rotted away. The old family cemetery, including several very old tombstones, was bulldozed in the 1980s to make way for Vestavia Woods subdivision.

Laurel View

This very attractive farmhouse was built around 1840 and was home to the Starke and Cloe families whose ties with Stafford County go back to about 1755, when James Cloe and his wife,

Mary, arrived from Scotland. James Starke (born 1665 in Glasgow, Scotland) first settled in New Hampshire, married Elizabeth Thornton, and then moved to Stafford sometime shortly after 1716.

Like most of the farms in Stafford, Laurel View was impacted severely by the Civil War. Union troops camped on the property and an elderly great-uncle in the Starke family who was a boy during the war remembered the troops forcing his mother to cook for them. Belt buckles, bullets, buttons, and other war debris were found on the property for years afterward. The house was abandoned for a period of time following the Civil War and fell into a state of disrepair.

In 1923 William Weedon Cloe purchased the property from the Starke heirs. He and his wife effected many repairs, replaced dilapidated outbuildings, and improved and modernized the house. They opened a dairy which later became a Grade A Retail Permit operation. Some of the modernizations included the installation of running water (courtesy of a gasoline-powered pump), a carbide gas lighting system, and a battery-operated telephone system carried on the barbed wire fence between Laurel View and the adjoining farm.

An interesting architectural feature at Laurel View is the use of two front doors. These opened into the same room, so there was little reason for the two doors except to balance visually with the upstairs windows. The house was one room deep, and the Cloes added a one and a half story wing in the mid-1930s which served as a kitchen and extra bedroom. A partially enclosed porch ran along the back of the house.

At the time of the Quantico expansion in 1942 the farm consisted of approximately 160 acres. Most of the farm was inundated by Lunga Reservoir about 1945.

Stafford Springs

Owners:

pre-1782	Thomas Blackburn
1809	William Fitzhugh
1813	Lewis and Catharine Dickinson

1828	sold to Burnaby Cannon
1833	sold to Bazil Brawner
1840– at least 1861	Elias King
1942	Property condemned for expansion of Quantico.

Stafford Springs is perhaps one of the least known farms in the county. Now a part of Quantico Marine Corps Base, Stafford Springs was, even in its heyday, in a remote corner of Stafford. Nonetheless, the farm played an important role in county history.

Located on the northern edge of Stafford near the Prince William and Fauquier County lines, the property contained several sulfur and iron mineral springs. Lewis and Catharine Dickinson operated a resort at Stafford Springs. During the nineteenth century, it was considered quite fashionable to "go to the waters" and drink and bathe in the mineral springs. Maps of 1820 and 1836 also indicate that Stafford Springs was a stage coach stop on the stage road leading to Manassas and Centerville.

In 1828 Lewis Dickinson sold Stafford Springs to Burnaby Cannon. Five years later, it was sold at public auction at Stafford Court House to satisfy a deed of trust between Lewis Dickinson and Burnaby Cannon, deceased. On that day Bazil Brawner paid $710 for the property, subject to dower rights of Catharine Dickinson, widow of Lewis. Stafford Springs sold again in 1840 to Elias King. At this point the farm consisted of 525 acres, and by 1865 King had transferred 215 acres to his son, George W. King. The property remained in the King family until 1943, when the U.S. government condemned some 30,000 acres for the expansion of Quantico Marine Corps Base.

From 1840 to 1942 the King family farmed at Stafford Springs and operated a woodworking and cabinet business, where they made furniture, coffins, wagon components, and performed general carpentry until the death of George W. King in 1914. After this time Stafford Springs continued as a farm. Mrs. King also rented rooms to travelers needing a place to spend the night. She had a regular guest in Mr. W. D. Reamy, county treasurer, who always spent the night at Stafford Springs when he came around in his horse and buggy collecting taxes.

During the Civil War, people were concerned more with survival than bathing in a spring, but activities on the farm did not cease. It became the headquarters for Confederate spy operations in the area. The property was ideally located for this purpose, as the surrounding area was quite desolate and there were few roads traversing that part of the county. The farm was very close to the county line, thus providing the Confederates with easy access to Union troops in Prince William and Fauquier Counties. Their missions completed, the Southern spies would disappear into the forests and make their way back to their secluded headquarters.

It is unknown how long the Confederates used Stafford Springs as a headquarters. The Kings were secretive about the activity there and spoke of it very little, even amongst themselves. When George Gordon talked to some of the older members of the family many years ago, they were reluctant to divulge information though the war was long over.

The old house at Stafford Springs dated from the eighteenth century and was a simple two-story frame building. Around 1900 a new house was built next to the old one. By 1936 all that remained of the original house was the huge chimney. Gone also were the five slave cottages and tenant house from the east lawn.

Additional Sites

Adallum—on Aquia Run. This was an old Griffis family farm.

Bell's Hill—just north of the court house on the west side of Bell's Hill Road (State Route 631). Prior to the Civil War, this farm was home to John H. Daniel and the Taliaferro family.

Black Rock—known for the large dark rock protruding from the ground.

Clover Hill—on Aquia Run, home of the Payne, Barger, and Mason families. Lost to the expansion of Quantico.

Cole Trips—now a Boy Scout camp on the north side of State Route 630 east. There has always been uncertainty about the spelling of Coal (Cole) Landing and Cole (Coal) Trips. There was very little coal hauled through the county, and there was a family on Aquia Creek named Cole, but no records seem to exist to connect the Coles to either of these properties. Both spellings are used in the land tax records. Between Cole Trips and Aquia Landing was built Fort McLean, a Confederate gun emplacement built to guard the rail head on the creek. This site is one of the best preserved Confederate forts in the South.

Eastern View—near the court house.

Ebenezer United Methodist Church—located at the intersection of Onville Road (State Route 641) and Ebenezer Church Road (State Route 696). This church was built in 1856. The building was designed by Thomas Towson, who operated the stone quarry between Garrisonville Road (State Route 610) and Court House Road (State Route 630) (see "Old Stone House" in Chapter 8). Bricks for the building were made in the field adjacent to the church. Prior to the construction of the brick church, the congregation met in a log building called the Woods Church. During the Civil War, Union soldiers burned the floors, broke the windows, and used the building as a stable. Repairs were made after the war and the church continues in use today.

Edgefield—a Williams and Hore family home on the south branch of Chopawamsic Run. At the time of the Civil War, it was owned by Thomas Norman. It was taken during the expansion of Quantico.

Forest Home—Powers family farm. This property adjoined Laurel View west of U.S. Route 1, on the north side of modern State Route 637. The farm originally included land on both sides of Route 1, including what is now "The Keep" and "Zum Rheingarten" restaurants. The dwelling was a comfortable though unpretentious white frame farmhouse. During the Civil War, Sydney Powers was a member of Company A of the 9th Virginia Cavalry. After the war, he and his wife, Mary Ann, gave each of their eleven children an equal portion of the farm as they came of age. The Powerses were farmers, businessmen, and teachers who made substantial, though quiet, contributions to their community.

Garrard's Ordinary—on the site of the old Stafford Middle School, corner of U.S. Route 1 and State Route 687. Owned by Colonel William Garrard, who served in the Revolution and was much involved in Stafford politics, including serving as justice in 1781 and helping to choose the site for the 1783 court house. He was listed in the 1768-1776 Quit Rent Rolls as owner of 200 acres. In 1785 he was taxed on 23 slaves, 7 horses, and 28 cattle.

Grape Hill—an old Moncure home which adjoined Stony Hill (Aquia Harbor) and bordered on Austin's Run. The new post office and Food Lion grocery store are built on the farm. There may have been a mill on Austin's Run associated with the farm.

Highlands—on Aquia Run.

Laurel Spring—part of the Burroughs property (a substantial tract north of Beaverdam Run that appears on Civil War maps) west of U.S. Route 1 and north of State Route 637. It was purchased by William S. Cloe around 1863, who built a home on it the following year. The house burned in 1942 just prior to the government takeover.

Locust Grove—home of the Gaines and Alexander families. Located near Bellfair Mills, the house may have dated from the first half of the eighteenth century. It was built upon the hill overlooking Stafford Run, the dividing line between Stafford and Prince William Counties. The house consisted of two rooms downstairs, two rooms upstairs, and an attic. There was a large chimney on each end of the house. Crops were planted in expansive fields in the lowlands below the dwelling, and a beautiful spring supplied water to the occupants through generations. Not far from the house stood the slave quarters and, in later years, a large orchard. A Gaines family cemetery was located near the house. The property remained in the hands of the Alexanders and their descendants until the Quantico expansion of 1942.

Marble Hill—on the north bank of Beaverdam Run. Lost to the expansion of Quantico.

Marlow—lost to the expansion of Quantico.

Millview—This old home was located at Bellfair Mills and belonged to John Clark until about 1871, when it was purchased by his son-in-law, George Milton Weedon, who lived there until his death in 1902. His heirs sold Millview to Charles Taliaferro in 1916, who used it as a residence until the government takeover in 1942. The house was probably built around 1800.

Mount Experiment—a Perry family home. It owes its interesting name to the fact that it was built in an attempt to avoid the malaria so prevalent in the lowlands near the river. It was located on the first high ground west of the Potomac and across a great expanse of forest from the river. From the house, only the tips of the tallest masts on the sailing vessels could be seen.

Mount Olive—in 1859 this farm was owned by Hannah Stone's heirs. Lost to the expansion of Quantico.

Oak Hill—on Chopawamsic Creek. At the time of the Civil War, this was owned by John Bell.

Orchard Field

Plum Field—near Mount Post Office, west of Boswell's Corner (U.S. Route 1) on State Route 637. Prior to the Civil War, this farm was owned by John and then Thornton Mountjoy. Lost to the Quantico expansion.

Red Oak Level—in the far northwestern corner of the county. By the 1930s this farm was long abandoned.

Rose Hill—occupied land in the split between State Route 608 and State Route 621.

Spring Dale—so named because of numerous springs on the property. This farm originally belonged to the Downman family. Later, it was owned by James Tolson, who married Ann Hickerson of Auburn. Tolson and his wife lived at Spring Dale until he died in 1864, leaving his wife and four children. The farm remained in the family until the Quantico expansion.

Springfield—lost to expansion of Quantico.

Stafford Store—the "hub" of the north Stafford community. The site may now be under Lunga Reservoir.

Traveler's Rest—lost to expansion of Quantico.

Tump—Camelot subdivision is today built on the property. Tump was probably part of the Mason tract.

Williamsville—west of Boswell's Corner (U.S. Route 1) on State Route 637. The hill on the west side of the intersection of Routes 1 and 637 is known as "Williamsville Hill."

The following churches were lost to the expansion of Quantico in 1942:

Bellehaven Missionary Baptist Church
Church of the United Brethren in Christ
Massadonia Baptist Church
Mt. Zion Baptist Church
Providence Church
Stafford Store Baptist Church

Garrisonville Area

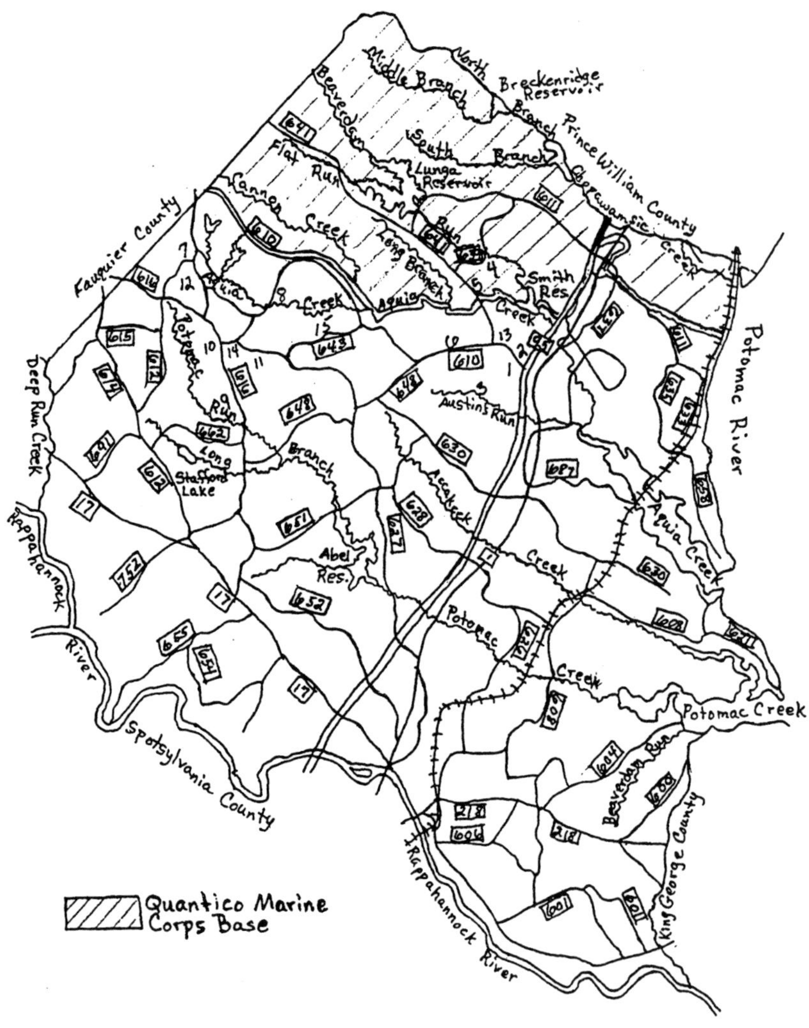

1 .. Patterson's Place
2 .. Wayside
3 .. Old Stone House
4 .. Tusculum
5 .. Windsor Forest
6 .. Woodford
7 .. Tackett's Mill
8 .. Shelkett's Mill
9 .. Hampstead
10 .. Poplar Grove
11 .. Rosedale
12 .. Eustace Farm
13 .. Grafton
14 .. Concord
15 .. Rose Hill

Chapter 8

Garrisonville and Roseville Areas

Patterson's Place

Owners:

1730-1760	Ralls family
1800	Purchased by Bill and Ned West
1830	Purchased by a Mr. Patterson

Though it is difficult to imagine today, during the eighteenth century the northern part of Stafford was quite a wilderness. Development was along Aquia and Potomac Creeks, and the area which today is boundless subdivision was then forbidding forest.

The first house built on the Ralls tract—in 1730—was of logs. The Ralls were careful to build their house on a hill as this allowed more warning in the case of an Indian attack. Like most log buildings, this house burned. The West brothers obtained the property and built another log house and, about 1860, it also burned. When the Patterson family moved onto the property they tore down the old log barn. They used the barn logs to build a third house on the site. Typical of Stafford farmhouses, the interior walls were white-washed. Wide planks were used for flooring. Directly across the road was Wayside Farm.

Federal troops camped on the farm during the time that the Pattersons owned it. Today, the Frank's Hardware and Crafts store stands where the old house used to be.

As of the Works Progress Administration Report, there was one gravestone in the garden near the house. It is a sandstone marker inscribed:

1751
July 24, departed this life, Sarah,
the wife of Edward Ralls

(Edward Ralls was a minor property owner in the county. The 1783 Personal Property Tax Records list him as owning three slaves, five horses, and fourteen cattle.)

Wayside

In its heyday Wayside was a sizable farm, its southern boundary being the Aquia Road (today, State Route 610) and going as far north as the flats on the north side of Aquia Creek (where the go-cart park is located on U.S. Route 1). This low flood plain was known as the barley patch. To the east of Wayside was Grafton. In recent years part of this property was used for Anne E. Moncure Elementary School. Wayside and Grafton were both cut from the enormous Peyton grant.

The home on Wayside was a typical rambling white frame farmhouse which had been home to the Waller family for several generations. The house was surrounded by giant oak trees, and in the spring the lawn came alive with thousands of yellow daffodils. A planting of wisteria gone wild covered acres of trees with a lavender blanket. Although the house is now gone, the daffodils and wisteria still offer a springtime show.

The house was abandoned many years ago, the family members having moved away to live elsewhere. Wayside fell into a state of disrepair and vandals finally set fire to it on July 4, 1983.

One of the Waller men, nicknamed "Johnny Reb" Waller, who lived at Wayside around the turn of the twentieth century was a bit of a character who stuttered. He owned a mule, and a man from Garrisonville was interested in purchasing it. The man asked Waller if it was a young mule and Waller answered, "Y-Y-Yes."

"Well, is he trained to pull a plow?"

"Of c-c-course," stuttered Waller.

The man from Garrisonville bought the mule without inspecting him and Waller delivered the animal to his new owner's farm.

The next day, the man came back with a stick and the intention of clobbering Waller. "Why didn't you tell me that mule was blind?" demanded the irate man.

"W-W-Well," said Waller, scratching his head, "The m-m-man I b-bought him from didn't tell m-m-me, so I thought it was a s-s-secret."

Wayside provided land for the westbound ramp of southbound Interstate 95, and for a number of years has been eyed by developers as an ideal location for a shopping mall.

The Old Stone House

For many years, one of my joys was going horseback riding over a large tract of land between State Routes 610 and 630. One of my favorite spots in this immense woodland was a long-deserted house that sat high on the hill overlooking Rocky Run. The house had been owned by the Robertson family, who had operated a sandstone quarry on the other side of the run. There were a number of quarries around the county, but this one was a fairly large and profitable operation, the stone from which was used to build the Capitol in Washington (see "Sandstone Industry" in Chapter 7).

In the late 1700s William Robertson purchased the land known as the Valentine tract for use as a quarry. At the time he lived about three miles away, which he felt was too far to commute. He selected a wooded knoll next to the quarry and, according to Benjamin Henry Latrobe, "true to Virginia fashion," cleared the trees from the top of a hill, forming an open circle about 150 yards in diameter. He used the cleared wood to build himself a house, kitchen, stable, hen house, meathouse, smith shop, and tool house which were randomly arranged over his hill. The house was a simple affair, 24 feet long by 18 feet wide, one and one-half or two stories high, each floor divided into two small rooms. In his journal Latrobe drew a sketch of the hill shortly after all the buildings were completed. The entire hill was dotted with tree stumps and painfully similar to twentieth-century strip clearing.

Latrobe, an architect, had come to the back woods of Stafford in August 1806 in search of sandstone for the new buildings in Washington, and once arrived he had no choice but to spend the night, owing to the remoteness of the Robertson quarry. Mrs. Suttle, the quarry manager's wife (John Suttle managed the quarry for Robertson), warned Latrobe of the rats which lived in the house. She said that while they were prodigious in number they were quite harmless but "would make no small noise" in the night.

After supper, Latrobe retired to his room on the ground floor. The room was so small that the bed occupied fully one-half of the floor space, the rest of which contained a chair and small chest. He had little trouble falling asleep but was suddenly awakened from a sound sleep by a terrific clatter in his room. As he came to consciousness, he realized that he was hearing the frantic scrambling of animals, and most of the noise was coming from under his bed. Remembering Mrs. Suttle's warning about the rats, Latrobe violently shook his bedstead and rocked the chair next to the bed. The commotion eased for a moment or two and then quickly resumed. Realizing that there was nothing he could do about the rats, he turned over and resolved to go back to sleep. Very soon, however, he noticed that the racket in his room had ceased but had commenced anew above his head. Suddenly, he heard the sound of a girl crying, a terrific crash, and gales of laughter coming from a woman upstairs. Not until morning did he determine the course of events of that evening.

The rats had started their evening frolic in Latrobe's room and had discovered a basket of chicken eggs which had been pushed under the bed. They ripped off the cloth covering the basket and fought mightily over the contents, leaving the entire floor strewn with little bits of egg shell. After finishing that feast, the rats ran upstairs, where one of them discovered that the little servant girl had fallen asleep with a piece of hoecake in her hand. This lucky rat grabbed the hoecake and dashed off with the rest of the pack in rapid pursuit. In their haste to get their share of the bread, the pack of rats galloped across the child's body, awakening her in a terror and causing her to cry out. The rat with the hoecake, determined not to share it, leaped into the open drawer of a writing desk which had been left on the edge of a table. The weight of the rat and hoecake toppled the writing desk which crashed to the floor. By now Mr. Robertson was awake and he entered the room, groping about in the dark for his desk. Upon finding it, he set it upright on the table whereupon the drawer slid open and the indignant rat bit him on the finger. Mrs. Suttle, who had come into the child's room to investigate the commotion, erupted into gales of laughter. After thoroughly cussing the rats, Mr. Robertson descended the stairs and went outside for a smoke. That was the end of sleep for the night.

By the time of Latrobe's visit to Robertson's quarry, a great deal of stone had already been taken from the quarries on Aquia Creek, most of which was used for the White House. During his 1806 visit to Robertson's, Latrobe wrote of the Aquia quarry, "The strata of Stone in this quarry is become so thin and the cope so deep that it is not worth working. Otherwise the stone is exceedingly good and free from Iron ore and clay holes. Mr. Robertson's quarry is now the best in Work."

This part of Stafford was crisscrossed with old county and logging roads, which seemed to wind forever through absolutely breathtaking woodland. Meandering through this beautiful setting was Rocky Run, which had an interesting history of its own.

Prior to the twentieth century, the roads in Stafford were atrocious. For a large part of the year the roads were pocked with holes and awash in a sea of mud. The roads around the Stone House were no different. Rocky Run, however, offered a solution, for it flowed over a sandstone bed which provided a solid "road" for the ox carts. The county road incorporated the run in numerous places for just this reason, and it was often easier to travel in the run than across the land. Sandstone from Robertson's quarry was hauled out of this remote area by oxcarts traveling considerable distances right down the middle of Rocky Run. In some places in the run, deep ruts from the cart wheels are still visible. This road also passed by Woodbourne.

William Robertson died around 1816 or 1818 and was buried at Aquia Church. Missing court records from this time prevent us from determining the exact sequence of events, but the property next came into the hands of Thomas Towson of Maryland. Towson bought his first Stafford property from Basil Gordon of Falmouth, then spent the next forty years buying every piece of Stafford real estate he could. By the time he died in 1867, he owned well over 1,000 acres all across the county. This included Coal Landing and Rock Ramore quarry on Aquia Creek. At his death his property was sold, and stone ceased to be hauled from the quarry at about this time.

Like many Stafford homeplaces, Union soldiers used the Old Stone house and grounds for encampments.

It was Thomas Towson who built the beautiful stone house that still stands on the hill. As we approached from Rocky Run, there was a wooden wing on the right side of the house. This wing had the same dimensions as Robertson's log house and was probably just clapboarded over when the stone portion was built around 1820. A Virginia State Historical Survey was done on the property and it was determined that the house had been two and one-half stories tall. The blocks of sandstone were eighteen inches thick and the house measured 36′ 6″ long by 21′ 8″ wide. There was a stone chimney on one end. Both the wing and stone portions were built above a basement. There were numerous windows and plastered walls; the interior of the house must have been quite light and airy. The last family to live in the house was named Barlowe, but there is little information about what they did there. By the time I began riding in that part of Stafford in the 1970s, the house was only a shell. Its roof and floors were gone and the frame wing was nearly collapsed. Some of the woodwork had been removed in the early 1970s and had been installed in the Wells' house in Fredericksburg. Despite this, a trip to the Stone House was always a treat.

To get to the house, we rode for several miles through magnificent woodland. At that time we rode from a farm just north of State Route 630, although today the site is more easily accessible from Mine Road off of State Route 610. The road followed along the edge of the run until it came to the bottom of the hill on which was built the house. To approach the house, we had to ride through the run and follow a driveway that wound its way up the hill to the house. The entire hillside was covered in periwinkle; springtime was a magical time to visit this lovely retreat because the periwinkle was a mass of little blue blooms. Scattered among the thousands of blue flowers were yellow and white daffodils and lilies-of-the-valley. The flowers, coupled with an infinite range of shades of green, created the perfect fairyland. The ruins of this grand old house stood proudly on the hill overlooking all this splendor, so far away from humanity that the only sounds were the breezes blowing through the massive old trees and the birds singing.

Behind the house had been a lovely little park. While it was a bit overgrown when I was last there (in the early 1980s), the old sandstone seats were still grouped together under the huge trees and the flowers bloomed there in abundance. There was a peaceful feeling in this place that is difficult to describe.

Civilization is rapidly encroaching on this wonderland. Already, much of the woodland between State Routes 610 and 630 has been cut for lumber. More and more houses are being built and soon this, like so many of the very special places in Stafford, will be forever lost.

Tusculum

Tusculum was a little-known estate near Aquia Creek, Beaverdam Run, and present-day Camp Barrett. The road into the old farm was on the right side of Onville Road past Ebenezer Church. Nearly all records containing information about Tusculum have vanished but it was undoubtedly one of the earliest homes in the county and one of the finest. George Gordon remembers that as a child the farm was often referred to as "old Tusculum," and Charles Tackett, Clerk of the Court of Stafford during the 1840s, said that Tusculum was built long before Valentine Peyton inherited it in the mid-eighteenth century.

Various members of the Peyton family patented land all along Aquia Creek in the seventeenth century. In 1654 the first Peyton grant was made to Colonel Valentine Peyton (1629-1665), who received a grant of 1,000 acres for transport of twenty persons to the New World. In 1662 Lieutenant-Colonel Valentine Peyton received 1,600 acres on Aquia Creek. This tract was "adjoining Captain Brent's land" (Woodstock). Henry (1630-1659), Valentine, and Philip Peyton were all granted land along Aquia Creek and it is difficult to determine exactly where one grant stopped and another began. The descriptions of the grant locations are vague at best.

It is known that John Peyton (1691-1760) of Stony Hill owned Tusculum, and it was most likely John who built the house. John Peyton's will lists Tusculum as containing 800 acres.

Dr. Valentine Peyton inherited Tusculum from his father, John of Stony Hill. The sketchy surviving descriptions of the house say only that it was large and contained sixteen rooms.

Dr. Peyton studied medicine at the University of Glasgow in Scotland in 1754 and served as a surgeon in the American Revolution. After the Revolution, he seems to have maintained a school for young men at Tusculum while he continued to practice medicine. He also served as a verstryman of Overwharton Parish. In 1787 he owned 24 slaves, 4 horses, 7 cattle, and a four-wheeled carriage.

About 1780 Valentine Peyton married Mary Butler Washington, daughter of Bailey and Catherine (Storke)

Washington. Bailey Washington owned nearby Windsor Hill, and it is possible that that property was originally a part of the Peyton tract.

Bailey Washington was listed as owner of Tusculum in the 1812 Land Tax Records, and it appears from these records that there were still substantial buildings on the farm. By 1860, however, the property was owned by Kenerick E. Combs and the value of the buildings was only $300.

A picture of the house taken around 1920 shows a very dilapidated two-story frame structure built over a stone English basement. School was taught in the basement and from time to time dances were held there, no doubt a highlight in the lives of local residents who had little in the way of recreational activities. On each end of the house was a chimney, the lower half built of stone and the upper half of brick. Fine dental molding accented the eaves.

Windsor Forest

Although this property was owned by a number of people over the years, it was known primarily as a home to the Bailey Washington and Moncure families. Around 1798 or 1800 a house was built on the property by William Moncure. It is likely that this was a replacement for an earlier structure, as Windsor Forest seems to have been cut from Tusculum and should have been lived upon much earlier. William Moncure died at Windsor Forest in 1833 and the property was conveyed to the Donovan family, then to John English, and then to several others before being taken by the government for the expansion of Quantico in 1943.

The home was very large with a brick-walled cellar, an extravagance at a time when basements had to be dug by hand. There were very large chimneys on the east and west ends. On the east side of the lawn was a tenant house and five slave cabins. The lane leading to the house was flanked by large cedar trees. A forest fire in the early 1930s destroyed the house, tenant house, and five slave cottages.

Bailey Washington Sr. (1731-1807) was a Justice of Stafford in 1769. He was also known as Colonel Bailey Washington. The 1768 Quit Rent Rolls listed him as owner of 1,200 acres, and in 1786 he paid taxes on 16 slaves, 10 horses, and 43 cattle.

Bailey Washington Jr. (1753-1814) was a delegate from Stafford from 1780-1787. His wife wrote that General George Washington visited them at Windsor Forest. The Quit Rent Rolls of 1773 and 1776 credit him with 1,200 acres. In 1783 he owned 35 slaves, 20 horses, and 40 cattle. By 1785 Windsor Forest had one dwelling house and eleven outbuildings.

Like many other farms in Stafford, Windsor Forest was used as a Federal camp.

The Moncures kept slaves, but like most Stafford slave owners, they had only a few. Apparently the slaves were well-treated, as two of them remained with the family until their deaths. One slave, Sully Watson, was born on the farm in 1780 and had no intention of remaining there. He was light-skinned, and had blue or green eyes and other Caucasian features. Determined to escape slavery, he worked for seven years to buy his freedom.

By 1834, Watson was married and free and he moved his family to Ohio and later to Wisconsin. There he supported his family as a whitewasher and bricklayer. He began purchasing property in Milwaukee and by the time of his death at the age of 82 in 1862, he owned four lots and had an estate valued at $5,000.

Sully Watson's descendants played important roles in Milwaukee history well into the twentieth century. William, his eldest son, was a leader in the black community, and his great-granddaughter, Mabel Raimey, became the first female black attorney in the state of Wisconsin.

Woodford

Woodford was located on the north side of what is now State Route 610, about 1.9 miles west of U.S. Route 1. Today, Stafford Home and Garden and a subdivision occupy the old fields.

This farm was first owned by Hugh Adie and the house was surrounded by a grove of locust trees. Woodford had the distinction of being one of the longest houses in the county; the original structure was sixty-four feet long. A sixteen-foot section was eventually removed. The building was rectangular, two-storied, and of frame construction. Within, there were twenty-eight windows, two large brick chimneys, seven rooms, and two halls. The interior walls were plastered and accented with chair rails.

The Adie family came from England to Maryland, and then moved to Stafford. The Adies first appear in the Stafford public record in 1742 when Hugh Adie was listed in the Quit Rent Roll for that year. In 1749 Adie and Nathaniel Harrison were appointed contractors, or undertakers, for a new court house near Belle Plain on Potomac Creek. Mr. Adie's mother was a Waller from Grafton. He was a foreman for the Aquia sandstone quarry and was an exceptional cabinet maker.

During the Civil War, Mr. Adie served in the Ninth Virginia Cavalry. Federal troops camped at Woodford but did not do extensive damage.

Mills and Milling in Stafford

Mills were a part of Stafford County from the beginning, when the Brent family built their watermill on Meadow Branch in Widewater. This mill and others across the county provided the "glue" that held together small communities. Farmers brought their grain to the mills to be ground. While there, they shared news and information and perhaps purchased a few necessary items from the little stores that were often associated with the mills.

The earliest mill in Virginia was on the falls of the James River, but it was a windmill not a watermill. In 1621 Governor Yeardley had this windmill built on his plantation and for at least four years it seems to have been the only mill in the New World.

While it seems as though building mills for the grinding of corn and wheat should have been a prime colonial priority upon arrival in the New World, such was not the case. There were several reasons for this. First, colonists of the early seventeenth century were far more concerned with protecting themselves from local natives and with day-to-day survival; they just didn't get around to planting much grain early on. Secondly, once the colonists had established themselves in Virginia, they almost immediately began planting tobacco, the plant which controlled the region's early economy for generations. Settlers planted corn and other small grains for their own consumption, but it was not until the Revolution that flour and meal were being exported in sufficient quantities to make commercial or "merchant" milling a profitable business.

The members of the House of Burgesses recognized the danger inherent in limiting the planting of grains for the sake of tobacco. By 1667 the members had enacted a law to encourage the building of mills, saying that "mills [should be] erected at convenient places, which diverse persons would willingly doe, if not obstructed by the perverseness of some persons not permitting others, though not willing themselves to promote soe publique a good." In order to operate a mill on a stream with limited water flow, it was necessary to build a mill dam above the mill site. The water could thus be impounded over a period of time and then released when the miller needed it. The perverse individuals referred to in the act were those who would not allow dams to extend across to their side of the stream. The law allowed the mill builder to condemn one acre of land belonging to someone else, so long as the dam did not damage dwellings or orchards.

In 1705 a law was passed limiting the number of mills on any one stream. No new mill could be built within one mile below or upstream from an established mill without permission from the county court. This same law also defined the toll, or fee, that could be legally charged by the miller for grinding. According to law, the miller could take no more than one-eighth part of the wheat he ground or one-sixth part of "Indian corn."

By 1745 the law encouraging the building of mills had been modified and a person desiring to build a mill had to petition the county court, whether he owned the land on both sides of the stream or not. If it was necessary to build a dam across to someone else's property, a committee was appointed by the court to determine the impact of the dam on the adjoining property.

Mill Lots

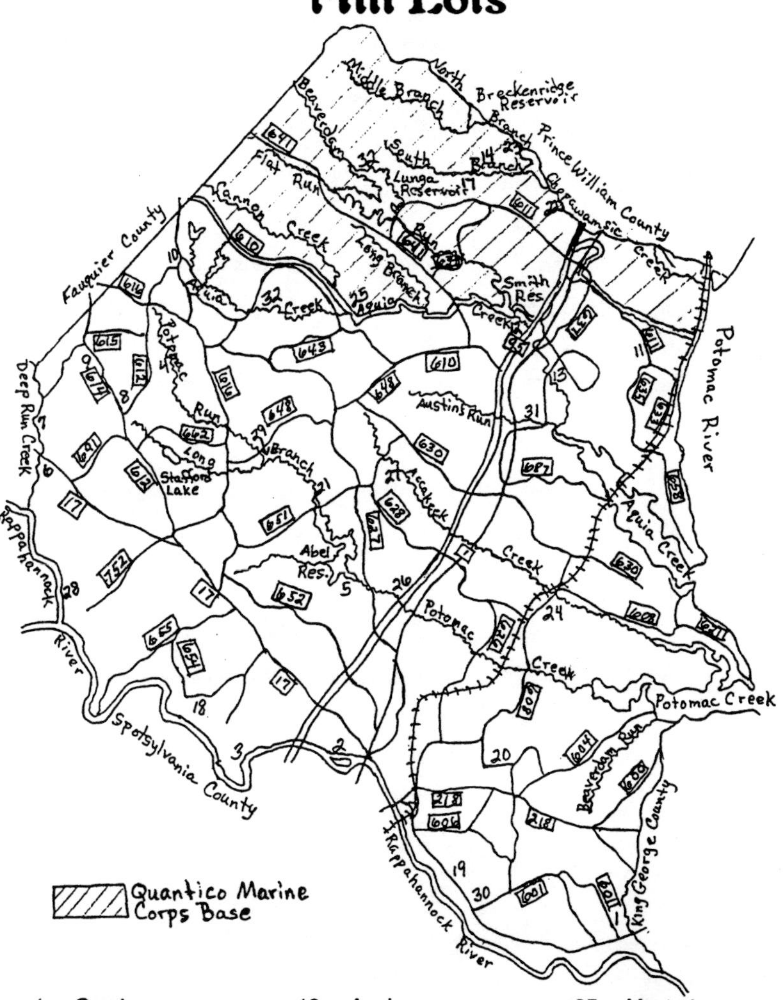

1 .. Gray's
2 .. Forge (Hunter's)
3 .. Banks'
4 .. Briggs'
5 .. Withers'
6 .. Norris'
7 .. Cropp's
8 ... Cropp's
9 .. Alcock's
10 .. Tackett's
11 .. Brent's
12 .. Stone's
13 .. Aquia
14 .. Tolson's
15 .. Poplar Grove
16 .. Kendall's
17 .. Fristoe's
18 .. Benson's
19 .. Pollock's
20 .. Boscobel
21 .. Kellogg's
22 .. Missouri
23 .. Bellfair
24 .. Brooke's
25 .. Master's
26 .. Ravenswood
27 .. Accakeek Furnace
28 .. Strother's
29 .. Wiggington's
30 .. Little Falls
31 .. Grape Hill
32 .. Shelkett's
? .. Unknown on Cannon Creek

Mills by Other Names

No.	Common Name	1820s Name	1864 Name	Other Names	Comments
1	Gray's				
2	Forge	Forge		Hunter's	saw mill, grist mill, forge mill, commercial mill
3	Banks'	Banks'	Scott's	Greenbank Mill	grist mill
4	Briggs'	Briggs'		Bridges'	grist mill & cotton gin
5	Withers'	Withers'			saw & grist mill, built of stone
6	Norris'	Norris'	Embrey's		
7	Cropp's	Cropp's	Hansbury's		grist mill
8	Cropp's	Cropp's			also known as Cropp's Tavern (1864)
9	Alcock's	Alcock's		Thompson's	
10	Tackett's	Tackett's	Goolrick's	Skinner's, Master's	saw, grist, & commercial mill, commercial mill built of stone
11	Brent's	Brent's	Fitzhugh's	Baker's, Richland	built of stone
12	Peyton's	Peyton's		Stone's, Withers', Meredith's	built of stone
13	Aquia	Aquia			
14	Tolson's	Tolson's		Ford's	
15	Poplar Grove			Jones'	grist mill
16	Kendall's	Kendall's		Wigginton's, Harding's, Holloway's	grist mill
17	Fristoe's	Fristoe's		Tolson's	grist & saw mill
18	Benson's		Benson's		
19	Pollock's	Gray's	Pollock's	Little Falls, Watson's, Newton's	grist mill, built of stone

Mills by Other Names (continued)

No.	Common Name	1820s Name	1864 Name	Other Names	Comments
20	Boscobel			Fitzhugh's	
21	Kellogg's	Holloway's	Kellogg's	Wigginton's, Meyer's, Embrey's Marquiss'	saw & grist mill
22	Missouri			Bohannon's	commercial grist
23	Bellfair			Tolson's, Callahan's	commercial grist
24	Brooke's			Mountjoy's	undershot, built of stone
25	Master's			Wiggington's, Benson's	grist & saw mill
26	Ravenswood				built of stone
27	Accakeek Furnace				forge mill
28	Strother's				grist mill
29	Wiggington's				
30	Unknown on Cannon Creek				
31	Grape Hill			Knight's	grist mill
32	Shelkett's				grist mill
33	Roach's			Chatham, Fitzhugh's	commercial mill for Fredericksburg 1709-1889
34	Unknown on Deep Run & Green Branch				

Large mills were often built by wealthy colonial officials or by syndicates of local plantation owners. Many small mills, however, were built for private use and then frequently were expanded to small-scale commercial operations to produce income for the owners. In Stafford, little communities frequently grew up near a mill, and the mill often included a little store where necessities could be purchased. In *The Virginia Gazette*, ads for the sale of property frequently mentioned that the land was "convenient to church and mills."

These mills would grind grain for the mill owners as well as for nearby farmers. In payment for the milling the farmer would give the mill owner a quantity of the finished product. William Fitzhugh said of his grist mill, "[the] tole I find sufficient to feed my own family with wheat and Indian corn for our necessitys and occasions." (Fitzhugh used the word "family" to mean not only his wife and children, but his indentured servants and twenty-nine slaves as well.)

The distinguishing feature of a grist mill was, of course, its great wooden mill wheel, the turning of which powered the gears that rotated the millstones that ground the meal. Mill wheels were of two basic designs, overshot and undershot.

The overshot wheel was far more powerful than the undershot and was necessary if the mill was used for sawing lumber as well as for grinding meal. A mill with an overshot wheel was built at the base of a hill. A nearby stream was dammed and a mill race, usually lined with stone, channeled the water towards the mill; a wooden flume was built to carry the water from the race to the top of the huge wheel. In most cases the wheel did not turn continuously. Most small streams did not flow heavily enough to turn the wheel. Only by damming the water in a pond and then releasing it could the necessary flow be created, which meant that most mills operated for only a few hours per day.

The wheel had many small buckets built into it and the water flow was controlled so that only seven or eight of the buckets were filled at a time. The weight of the water in the buckets turned the wheel and created a greater torque or power than could be produced from a stream of water merely flowing beneath the wheel. This latter arrangement was known as an undershot wheel and was normally only used in flat areas where a mill pond could not be built above the level of the mill building. An undershot wheel could turn no faster than the water flowing beneath it and, therefore, was not as powerful as an overshot wheel. Most of the mills in Stafford had overshot wheels.

The system of damming the water and controlling the release was normally used for the undershot mills as well. Water flowing under a wheel did not produce nearly as much energy and the wheel turned slowly, making it suitable for grinding only meal.

The inner workings of the mill were carefully crafted of wood, including gears and pulleys which controlled the energy produced by the mill wheel, and were replaced by the miller when they wore out. Mill stones were cut from blocks of local sandstone and averaged four feet in diameter. A pattern of straight lines was cut into each stone, each groove being cut at a precise angle and depth. Grain, which was fed from a hopper to the stones via a chute, was ground into meal which dropped into the cut grooves in the bottom stone and then flowed out into another hopper.

Mill stones operated in pairs set vertically and the distance between the stones could be adjusted by means of a large screw. By adjusting the screw, the miller could grind the meal as fine or as course as desired. An important part of the grinding process was to watch for the last bit of meal to exit the stones and then crank the stones apart to prevent their grinding against each other and becoming damaged.

Despite precautions, however, over time the stones wore down and had to be sharpened. To accomplish this the miller had to remove the stones and lay them flat on the mill floor. He then used a tool called a mill pick to regrind the grooves to the correct angle and depth.

With the exception of the windmill built by John Mercer of Marlborough, Stafford mills were all watermills. Brent's Mill was built in the late 1600s; at about the same time Tackett's Mill was built on Aquia Creek. Not long after that two mills were built at Aquia Town. Later in the eighteenth century, Falmouth boasted several merchant mills. The Lists of Mill Lots from the Stafford County Tax Records for 1841, 1851, and 1861 show a steady growth in the number of mills in the county during those years. In 1841 there were ten mills listed but by 1861 the number had increased to sixteen. By the late nineteenth century, commercial milling had largely eliminated the need for small local mills and many fell into disrepair.

Water-powered mills were often seriously affected by drought conditions, which reduced or eliminated the flow of water used to turn the wheel. By the early twentieth century, many mill owners had converted to gasoline engines to turn the mill stones. At first, some mill patrons complained of the meal smelling of gasoline fumes but they eventually accepted modern technology and were thankful for the dependable supply of meal and flour.

Prior to the advent of steam, kerosene, and gasoline engines, there seem to have been only four sawmills in the county. Brent's Mill in Widewater had a sawmill, as did Withers' Mill (located near the dam at Abel Reservoir), Tackett's Mill on Aquia Creek, and one of the mills at Hunter's Iron Works. Four sawmills were probably adequate to meet the needs of county residents.

Most of the mills in Stafford were of frame construction over a stone foundation. We know that Brent's and Brooke's Mills and the mill at Ravenswood were built of sandstone, and there is a strong possibility that the original Tackett's Mill was also built of stone.

Two county mills deserve special mention. The mills built at Accakeek Furnace and at Hunter's Iron Works were probably not grist mills, though an 1806 survey of the area around Hunter's shows that there were three mills on that property: a saw mill, grist mill, and "the forge mill." Forge mills were used to operate trip hammers which pounded hot steel into shapes such as bars or strips. A trip hammer was a large hammer head mounted on the end of a shaft. The shaft was attached to a pivot point and the end of the shaft was positioned over a grooved cog. The mill wheel turned the cog, raising the hammer head which then dropped on the steel bar. This hammering process was an integral part of steel-making and such mills were often called naileries since the strips of steel could be cut into nails.

The accompanying map (on page 147) is an attempt to mark the locations of many of the mills that existed in the county. At best it is only a partial account. Names of mills have changed with new owners, fires have consumed old structures, and time has made memories fade. George Gordon is the only person left who knows the locations of many of the old sites; old maps sometimes designated mill lots. The chart of mill names (on pages 148-149) should help clarify some of the confusion over names.

Tackett's Mill

Long-time residents of Stafford, the Tacketts were associated with the milling business for years. Tackett's Mill was one of the earliest mills in the county, built to serve the Huguenot settlement that began forming during the latter part of the seventeenth century.

In 1816 Mr. Tackett renewed an insurance policy on his mill and dwelling on Aquia Creek. An 1817 policy provides us with a diagram of the milling operation. The four buildings included a storage building, a saw mill, a manufacturing mill, and a stone dwelling house. Notes on the diagram specifically describe the mill as a stone building, which is interesting as the mill that survived into the twentieth century was constructed of wood. Either the insurance agent made a mistake on his drawing or the stone building was abandoned or destroyed.

Tackett's Mill had an overshot wheel and for most of its history was powered by water. The mill operation also included a small store, the only store in this part of Stafford from about 1820-1865. George Gordon described Tackett's Mill as "the center of the universe" for the people who lived nearby. Also on the property were a girls' boarding school and two saloons. The girls' school was run by Miss Nanny Tackett and later became a public school.

The mill remained in the Tackett family for many years. After Charles Tackett's death the mill was willed to Lawrence Skinner, who operated it for some time, and in later years was known as Skinner's Mill. By 1851, however, tax records list it as belonging to Peter Goolrick. Apparently, the mill was in poor condition at that time because the tax records value it at only $240. Ten years later the mill is again listed in the tax records but is valued at $1,702.50, a considerable increase. This may indicate

Tackett's Mill

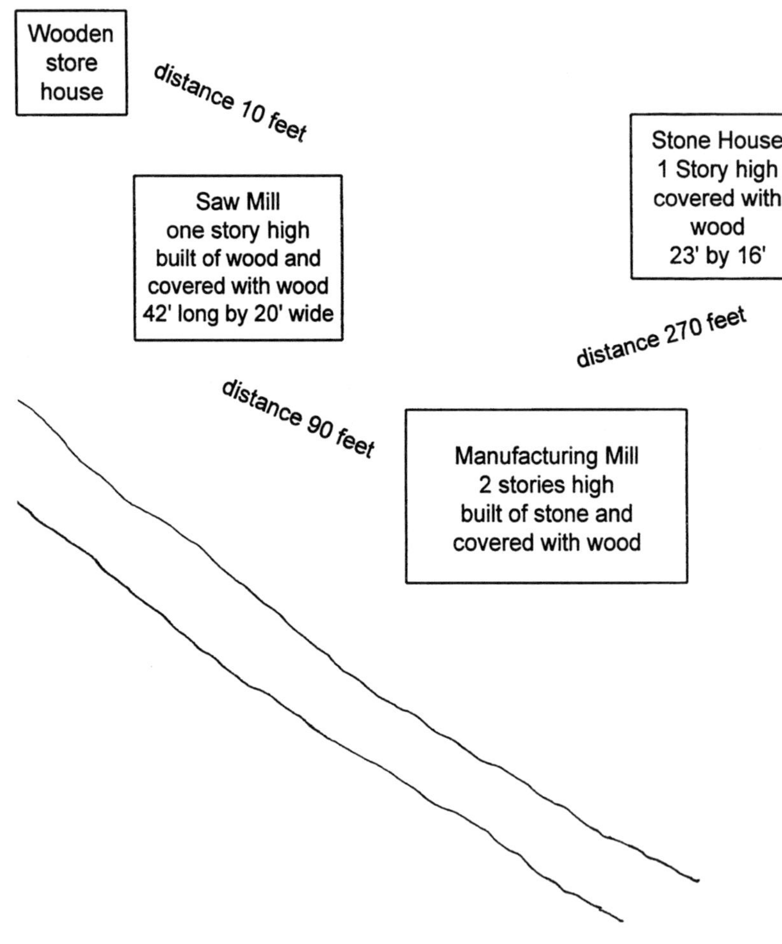

From an 1817 Mutual Assurance policy

the point at which the old stone building was replaced with a frame one.

Rhodie Shelkett House and Mill

This one and one-half story rock and brick house was built around 1700 by the Shelkett family. Each end of the house was flanked by a large chimney. The chimney on the north end was fitted with a crane. The house was torn down sometime after the end of the Civil War.

Rhodie's grandfather, John Shelkett, came from Scotland early in the eighteenth century and settled in a part of Stafford between Aquia and Cannon Creeks on the old Rockhill Road (State Route 644 today).

When John and his brother landed in America, they had no particular plans. They rented a 300-acre farm for $100. Unfortunately, they were not very good farmers and, eventually, John's brother left. John continued to work the farm, making enough money in eight years to buy a 500-acre farm for $600. His son, Rhodie, inherited the property and owned thirty-nine slaves; he built cabins for them near the creek that flowed past the house.

About 1855 the Shelketts built a mill on their property. Constructed of native stone, the structure was located between two hills (three-tenths of a mile west on State Route 644). A stream flowing through the little valley provided the mill with power to grind grain. Unfortunately, the old mill seems to have been abandoned after the Civil War. It was torn down, the stones being used for house foundations around the area.

At the time of the Civil War Rhodie, like most other folks, owned a horse. When he got up one morning and went to the stable, he found his horse missing. Some Federal troops were camped on his farm and he found the captain and asked for his horse. The captain said that they didn't have it but he thought it might be with the troops camped at Bull Run. He gave Rhodie written permission to get his horse, and Rhodie set off walking. Upon arriving at Bull Run he found his horse. He walked up to the animal and ordered the man riding it to get off. The soldier refused to dismount, demanded that Rhodie release the animal's bridle, and asked why he wasn't in the army. Rhodie replied that he didn't have to enlist because he was a miller. He produced the note from the captain in Stafford and the horse was returned to him.

Rhodie Shelkett was Miss Sally Fitzhugh's (Poplar Grove) great-grandfather. She relates a story about his daughter's experience in the war. At the time of the Civil War, she was a young girl. Somehow this child, along with her sister, ended up at the Daffin Place down near Grafton (just north of Falmouth). Union soldiers moved onto that farm and decided to use the house as headquarters. The residents of the house were not allowed to leave the second floor and they spent quite a while confined there. The girls' father, Rhodie Shelkett, wanted his daughters back and so he dressed up as an old man. He was able to cross the Union lines and pick up the children from the house. The girls had been cooped up for so long that they kept hopping out of the buggy on the trip home, picking flowers and running about.

Hampstead

Owners:

1816?-1831	Alexander Fontaine Rose
1831-1893	Edmond Fontaine Rose
1893-1910	Sarah Rose Briggs and Thompson Smith Briggs (of Stony Hill)
1910-1930s	Leonard Alexander Briggs

Hampstead was an exceptionally fine home by Stafford standards. The exact date of its construction is unknown due to the fact that the old records were destroyed. It is known, however, that the house was occupied in 1817 although it was no doubt built long before then.

The earliest owners to appear in surviving records were Alexander Fontaine Rose (1780-1831) and his wife, Sarah Rose (1796-1863). Their first child, Edmond Fontaine Rose (1817-1893), was born at Hampstead. Alexander was an attorney and owned property in Fredericksburg as well as throughout Virginia; he was a descendant of Huguenot immigrants.

The house was built of brick and covered in weatherboard. On each end were massive double chimneys. The parlor and dining room were paneled with beveled wood. Some years ago, some of the interior woodwork from Hampstead was moved to the Kate Doggett house in Fredericksburg. By the late 1800s several additions had been made on the back side of the house, at least doubling the living space. These have not survived to the present.

There were numerous outbuildings on the farm, including a two-room brick building, a kitchen, laundry, and icehouse. Ice was cut from a pond on the farm and stored in a deep hole beneath the icehouse. Blocks of ice were layered between thicknesses of straw. Stored in this manner, the ice would last all summer.

Also on the farm was a large stone barn. It is said that Alexander Rose was a horse breeder and used this building as a stable. The barn disappeared sometime prior to 1900.

This farm is located on State Route 616 next to Poplar Grove. Hampstead remained in the Rose-Briggs family until the Depression. Rather than declare bankruptcy, Mr. Briggs conveyed the farm to W. D. Jones in payment of debts.

Sporadically occupied during the early part of this century, the house has nearly fallen in. The outbuildings have long since disappeared, also. An old family cemetery is located near the house.

Poplar Grove

For a brief period in the early nineteenth century, there was a small settlement of Quakers in Stafford. By 1830 they had moved on to Ohio, but during their stay in the county they built a large stone house on land known as Poplar Grove. This part of the county is squarely on the fall line; rocks have plagued the farmers for generations. In some cases, the rocks were removed from the fields and used to build fences. In the case of Poplar

Grove, the rocks were used in the construction of the dwelling and a spring house.

The old two-story house was built upon a hill, providing a magnificent view of the surrounding fields. The walls were about three feet thick, and the building was similar to a bank barn in that the basement was exposed on one side, making the building three stories high on that side.

There was a large chimney on each end of the house. The north chimney was built within the wall (thereby conserving heat) and the south chimney was on the outside of the wall. The attic was quite large and had dormer widows. Each floor had two rooms, each with a large closet. There was a large center hall with a boxed-in stairway. Unlike most houses in the area which had separate kitchens, Poplar Grove had its kitchen in the basement, according to Quaker custom. When the Quakers moved out of the area, the Curtis family came into possession of the property. Sally Curtis married James French, and they were given as a dowry a slave named Betty and 1,000 acres of land.

The French family had four sons, three of whom were old enough to fight in the Civil War. Hugh joined the Army in 1861 and was stationed at Richmond as a member of the Ninth Virginia Cavalry. He was killed at Richmond and buried there. After his death, his horse and clothes were returned to his mother in Stafford. Mrs. French knew that if the Union soldiers found the clothes or the horse, they would take them. She hid the clothes in the bottom of a basket and the horse in some thick pine woods. The youngest son and a slave would go out daily to feed the horse, going far out of their way so as not to be noticed by the Federals.

After some time, thinking the soldiers had left the area, Mrs. French sent for the horse. No sooner had the slave brought the horse to Mrs. French than some soldiers appeared, seizing the animal and taking it away. A few days later, the soldiers returned to search the house. When the slaves first saw the soldiers coming, they gathered up all the chickens and hid them in the attic. The soldiers searched the house, omitting the attic. Just as they were leaving the house the rooster crowed, giving away the hiding place. The soldiers climbed to the attic and carried away the chickens. Afraid that they would also take her dead son's clothing, Mrs. French gave the basket containing the garments to a slave woman and the soldiers disregarded it.

Another family story tells about a younger brother who, toward the end of the war, became old enough to join the army. His sisters traveled to Alexandria where they bought the material and buttons to make his uniform. To get the fabric back across the Union lines, they had to sew it into the undersides of their dresses. They made it home but the war ended and the boy didn't have to fight. Miss Sally Fitzhugh, their great-granddaughter, still has the buttons.

In the yard of Poplar Grove there is an ancient cedar tree supported by a mass of wisteria. Embedded in the tree is a horseshoe. When James French, by then an old man, heard of Lee's surrender at Appomattox, he hung his horse's bridle reins over the horseshoe and went inside the house. He never came out again. His wife and children planted the wisteria beneath the tree and each year it blooms on the anniversary of the fall of the South.

The war had cost James French everything. His money was Confederate and worthless, he had lost a son, his slaves were free and gone, and there was no one left to work the land. For James French, as for many other Southerners, there was no more reason to live.

Suffering the ravages of time, the original house was torn down by John I. French in about 1900 and was replaced with a similar stone structure. This burned in 1935 and a comfortable frame farmhouse was built on the site. The original Quaker spring house is still standing near the driveway.

Rosedale

1813 bought by William Richards Gordon
1847 bought by William C. Gordon
1867 deeded to Celestine Gordon Montague
After Celestine's death, inherited by Montague Whiting

Rosedale was a comfortable old frame farmhouse that was home to the Gordon and Montague families. It was located behind the old Concord School on the north side of State Route

627 and on the east side of the intersection of State Routes 627 and 644.

In 1813 William Richards Gordon (1780-1855) and his wife, Mary A. M. Gordon (d.1874), bought the property from Falmouth land speculator Benjamin Ficklen. It is likely that William built the house; the style of construction did not suggest that it was built earlier. There they raised their four children.

The house was of frame construction upon a stone foundation; there was no basement. A front porch was graced by a balcony which was draped with climbing roses on both sides, hence the name, Rosedale. There were two rooms downstairs and two upstairs, both floors having a center hall dividing the rooms. Stone chimneys on the east and west ends of the house provided heat. In later years, a 10 foot by 12 foot lean-to addition was built on the east end of the house for use as a kitchen. A very narrow passage led from the kitchen into the adjoining dining room, and food could be passed between the two rooms via a small opening in the shared wall. There was a small porch on the east end of the kitchen. The west downstairs room served as a parlor. Above the second floor was a full attic which ran the length of the house and had wide plank flooring. Two small windows flanked the flues of both fireplaces and provided ventilation to what must have been stifling sleeping quarters for servants.

On the north side of the house were added two rooms, one above the other. The lower room served as a doctor's office and the upper, a nursery. By 1980, the only outbuilding remaining was a pigeon house built by Montague Whiting, a great-grandson of William R. Gordon. A depression to the southeast of the house marked the location of the old ice house. There had been a barn at the foot of the hill east of the house. There was not a well dug on the property until later years. Originally, water was brought to the house from a spring located northeast of the house.

According to county court records, William Richards Gordon borrowed money from Alexander Seddon in 1843 and used Rosedale as security. He was unable to repay the loan and in 1847 the 287-acre farm was sold at public auction at the court house. William's son, William C. Gordon, was able to buy the farm back at that time so that his parents could continue to live there. William C. never lived at Rosedale during his adult life. At some point he moved to St. Louis, Missouri, where he made a profitable living as evidenced by his ability to buy back his parents' farm. After the death of his father in 1855, William C.'s sister, Celestine Louise, lived at Rosedale, possibly with her mother. Although William was the eldest son and rightful heir to Rosedale, he chose to remain in St. Louis rather than return to Virginia to claim his inheritance. In 1867, having no need of the property, he deeded the farm to Celestine.

Sometime shortly after the Civil War, Celestine married Dr. Thadeus Claybrook Montague. The obituary of one of Celestine's sons reveals that Dr. Montague was a member of the Confederate army and had served as surgeon in charge of Emory and Henry Hospital, where he treated soldiers from both sides of the war. A present-day great-grandson still owns a pistol given to Dr. Montague by a dying Union soldier.

Dr. Montague served as Supervisor of Rock Hill District from 1881 to 1887, defeating Lyman Kellogg, owner of Kellogg's Mill just up the road from Rosedale, in 1881 and 1883. Thadeus disappears from the public record in 1887 and although it is unknown when he died, it seems likely to have been at about this time. He was buried across the road from Rosedale in the Gordon/Montague cemetery. The Rosedale house and cemetery remained in the family until the 1980s, when the property was sold. The house was pulled down soon after.

A story involving Rosedale concerned a brother of Celestine Gordon, William Wallace Gordon, who enlisted in the 9th Virginia Cavalry on May 10, 1861 at Stafford Court House. His enlistment record includes a notation that his horse was worth $100 and his equipment, $5. William was involved in the skirmish at Hartwood Church (see Chapter 11), where he was taken prisoner on April 10, 1863. He was taken to Old Capitol Prison in Washington where he remained until he was paroled on May 10 of the same year. The experience apparently unnerved him to such an extent that he remained in Washington until the surrender at Appomattox, at which time he finally returned home. After the war, William studied to become a doctor; he practiced in Richmond and died there in 1888.

Kellogg's Mill

c.1782 mill built by James Holloway
1831 mills and 13 acres conveyed to Samuel Marquiss from the estate of John Holloway
1848 sold to Lyman Kellogg
1897 conveyed to William Wiggington and inherited by his son, Henry
1927 mills abandoned after hurricane destroys main dam

Kellogg's Mill was one of the better-known mills in Stafford and was located upstream of present Abel Lake dam, on the west side of Potomac Run off of State Route 651.

The holder of the original patent on this land is unknown. The first official appearance of the property with reference to the mill appears in a court record of 1782, in which James Holloway petitioned the court to condemn one acre of land, "the property of Samuel Chew whereon the said James Holloway proposes to erect a Mill." The court approved the condemnation and it seems likely that the mill was built shortly thereafter.

Holloway's grist mill was of simple frame construction with a steeply-pitched, shingled roof. Sawmills didn't come into general use until around 1800, at which time a small building was constructed slightly behind the old grist mill for use as a sawmill. There were actually two dams in place on Potomac Creek which provided power for the mills, and the remnants of these may still be seen today though much of the mill lot is covered by Abel Lake.

In 1831 the mills and 13 acres were conveyed to Samuel Marquiss from the estate of John Holloway, likely the son of James. Marquiss operated the mill until his death, at which time his estate was placed in the hands of county commissioners charged with settling his affairs.

In 1848 the property was purchased by Lyman Kellogg (1813-1897) for $300 from those commissioners. Lyman Kellogg was born in Connecticut and settled in Stafford around the 1830s. In addition to operating the mill, Kellogg also sold general merchandise from a horse-drawn wagon. He may also have operated a store at or near the mill, though this cannot be confirmed. It was not unusual for a mill to include a small store (Brent's Mill and Tackett's Mill being local examples).

There was a miller's house near the mill but Kellogg and his wife, Frances (1815-1881), lived nearby, in a home located at the end of a dirt road off of State Route 651 approximately three-fourths of a mile from the intersection of State Routes 651 and 627. Most of the original Kellogg house, barn, and kitchen were still standing in 1985 but are now collapsed. The original part of the house was built of logs and was later weatherboarded. According to the Works Progress Administration Report, the house had an unusual steeply-pointed roof with a very large stone chimney on the south side. There was a cellar below the house, though it was never finished, and a three-flight stairway ran from the cellar to the second story. An old family cemetery and a slave cemetery were located near the house.

Between 1838 and 1895, Lyman Kellogg acquired at least 23 separate tracts of land in Stafford, ranging in size from a few acres to over 400 acres, most of it in the Mountain View area of the county, near his mill.

In addition to his milling and merchandising, Kellogg was also a land speculator, selling property as quickly as he bought it. In 1894 he sold 115 acres of woods adjoining his mill to Charles Byram for $100. In the transaction Kellogg reserved a right of way for a wagon road on the east side of Potomac Run "from a point about opposite the spring from which Wiggington the miller uses water to the point of the backwater at the mill pond; and also reservation is made for the use of stone and dirt in repair of the mill dam."

Lyman Kellogg's most significant contribution to Stafford County was not his milling operation or his selling of general merchandise. He was a tremendous asset to the families of Mountain View after the Civil War as he provided them with work and some income, albeit meager. He was able to make enough profit from his various business ventures to continue to operate his own farm, just slightly more than 400 acres. After the Civil War, there were no slaves to work the fields. Kellogg hired local men, desperate for work, to chop corn, cut wheat, plant and plow the fields. A man would work all day for 50 cents and be grateful for it, as there was no other employer in this part of

Stafford. Without Lyman Kellogg's help, these Stafford residents would have been forced to leave the county after the war in order to support their families. Today, ancestors of many of these families still live in the Mountain View and Rock Hill districts of the county.

Kellogg also held elected political offices for several years. In 1871 he was elected Justice of the Peace for the Rock Hill District. In 1873 he served as Supervisor for Rock Hill, a position he held until 1881 when he lost the election to Dr. Thadeus Montague of Rosedale. Kellogg ran again for Supervisor in 1883 and again lost to Dr. Montague, at which point he retired from public office.

Lyman Kellogg died in 1897 and was buried in the cemetery near his home. He and his wife, Frances, had only one child, Lyman Jr., who seems to have been rather shiftless. As Lyman Jr. was never able to settle to any occupational interest, his father refused to will him either the farm or the mill. Instead, Kellogg left his farm to a faithful employee, Morris Embrey. The mill he conveyed to William Wiggington, his long time miller. William died shortly thereafter and the mill was inherited by his son, Henry. Although the mill continued to operate for many years after Lyman Kellogg's death, the Wiggingtons didn't maintain the mill and it quickly lost value. By 1927 when a hurricane destroyed the upper dam, the mill was abandoned. A sagging national economy on the verge of Depression made it unfeasible to rebuild the dam and continue operations. By the 1950s only the foundations of the mill, the chimney and foundation of the miller's house, and remnants of the two dams remained. The property continues today in the hands of the Embrey and Wiggington descendants.

The Huguenots in Stafford

Throughout the world's history, freedom to practice one's chosen religion has been often denied. In 1598 Henry IV issued the Edict of Nantes, which granted religious toleration to his Protestant subjects. For nearly one hundred years the Protestants and Catholics coexisted on reasonably peaceful terms. Louis XIV, however, did not choose to tolerate Protestants in France; he revoked the Edict in 1685 and the French Protestants were hunted like animals. Some 300,000 Huguenots fled France, making new homes in Prussia, Switzerland, Holland, England, and America. Several shiploads of "French Protestant Refugees" arrived in America in 1700 and the influx continued for several years.

While many colonists settled in America because of religious persecution in their homelands, religious freedom did not truly exist here. One was only free to practice one's chosen faith if that was the chosen faith of those nearby. In Virginia the legally recognized church was the Church of England. Stafford was one of the few areas in the entire colony where people of differing faiths coexisted on reasonably peaceful terms. This was partly because most residents were tolerant and partly because the area was so remote from the mainstream of colonial activities.

The Huguenot religion was Calvinistic in doctrine and Presbyterian in government. Because they were Protestants, the Huguenots were quickly absorbed into the Protestant church in Virginia unlike many other denominations who struggled to follow their chosen faiths.

In Stafford, there were some who viewed the influx of new Huguenot inhabitants as a business opportunity: the new settlers would need a place to establish themselves. On January 11, 1686, George Brent, Richard Foote, Nicholas Hayward, and Robert Bristow obtained a patent on a piece of land from Lord Culpeper. The property became known as Brenton or Brent Town and consisted of some 30,000 acres. Even at the time of its creation, the boundaries of the Brent Town tract were vague. According to the description given in the grant, the property was situated "between the Courses of the said Two Rivers, Rappahannock and Potowmack, backwards at least six miles Distant from the said Main River and from any Land Already seated and inhabited, and upon and Between the Southwest and Northeast Branches of Ocaquan Creek and from thence towards the Mountains." The exact location is uncertain except that it was back from Potomac Path. Today, most of the property is in Fauquier and Prince William Counties, though at the time this area was a part of Stafford. An annual fee of £30 lawful English money was to be paid to Lord Culpeper for the use of the land.

Brent and his partners had great hopes for the Brenton settlement. Brent had even gone so far as to petition James II for a Grant of the Right of Religious Freedom for those who settled on the tract. That grant was issued on February 10, 1686. Brent, himself a Catholic, likely had a dual motive for seeking this grant from the King. Not only did it guarantee that the Huguenots would not be persecuted should they decide to settle at Brenton, but it also allowed Brent to open the tract to anyone else who might like to settle there, specifically, Catholics.

Development at Brenton never quite materialized. The property was on the outskirts of civilization and many authorities viewed settlement there primarily as a buffer between whites and hostile Indians. Also, Brenton was not surveyed until 1737-38, despite an order by the Assembly in 1720 to do so within three years. By this time, the Huguenots had established themselves elsewhere, and the Brenton tract was subdivided amongst the heirs of the original owners. Today, only names such as Bristow Station and Brentsville (in Prince William County) remain to mark the site of this unprofitable venture.

While a major Huguenot settlement in the county never materialized, a number of the French refugees did find homes in Stafford. Productive members of society, they were quickly absorbed into the general population. Most Huguenot names have been lost to intermarriage but some of the original names include Cabel (Cabell), Batie (Patie), Diresubawn, Lebounie, Reinbeau, and Traquette (Tackett). The Tacketts operated a farm, mill, and store in Stafford for many years. Tackett's Mill somehow withstood the ravages of time and war and survived into the twentieth century. Several years ago, the mill was sold and moved to Prince William where it is now the focal point of Lake Ridge Shopping Center.

The 1812 Taxable Property Record

Finding information about Stafford County is a process of gleaning. Contemporary written documentation is sparse at best. Tax records provide statistical evidence about life in the county. The taxable property records list names of landowners, numbers of slaves, horses, mules, and vehicles. From this it becomes clear that although there were nearly twice as many slaves as taxpayers in Stafford, there were very few individuals who owned more than nine slaves. Well over half of the taxpayers had none.

The economy of Stafford was far less developed than the economy of the Northern Neck of Virginia or of other areas in the deep South. Slave ownership was costly: there was the initial purchase price, and then care and feeding were constant expenses. John Mercer of Marlborough estimated the cost of keeping a slave to run about five pounds per year. Stafford, therefore, had no huge estates with hundreds of slaves. The economy simply wouldn't support them. The single largest slave owner in Stafford's history was James Hunter, who operated Hunter's Iron Works (see "The Iron Works" in Chapter 11) near Falmouth, and owned nearly 5,000 acres in the county. In 1783 he paid taxes on 260 slaves. By 1812 the largest slave owner was John Cooke, who lived at West Farm on the Potomac River and Marlborough on Potomac Creek. The second largest slave owner at that time was Daniel Brent of Richland, who owned forty-seven. Mr. Brent was not only farming some three thousand acres, he also had a manufacturing mill, saw mill, and distillery, and a stable of race horses, all of which required a great deal of labor.

This tax record does not list every person in Stafford County. Only those who possessed enough property to be taxed are listed. The majority of residents did not own enough to even be listed.

Another interesting feature of this record is that acreage and real estate tax are also entered for some individuals. When that acreage is added up, it amounts to only 62,529 acres. Today the county contains over 100,000 acres of taxable land—and this area is smaller than it would have been in 1812 because of the Stafford land now part of the Marine Corps Base. Apparently, collecting delinquent taxes was even more difficult then than now!

The following figures illustrate the distribution of slaves in the county, in 1812.

Owners of 16 or More Slaves

owner	*number of slaves*	*plantation*	*acreage*
John T. Brooke	20	Mill Vale	305 ac.
Daniel C. Brent	47	Richland	3184 ac.
John Cooke	53	Marlborough/West Farm	2738 ac.
Travers Daniel Sr.	19	Crow's Nest	2616 ac.
Travers Daniel Jr.	21	Deceased	
Moses Kendall	23	__________	3215 ac.
John Moncure	16	Somerset	1400 ac.
Mrs. Mary Sedden	19	Snowden	1079 ac.
Bailey Washington	19	Tusculum	561 ac.

Owners of 10-15 Slaves

owner	*number of slaves*	*plantation*	*acreage*
Phillip Alexander	13	Potomac Run	500 ac.
Rawleigh W. Downman	14	10 m. west of CH	750 ac.
Benjamin Ficklen	15	Head of Aquia Run	1117 ac.
Thomas Fitzhugh	15	Various tracts	976 ac.
William Mountjoy	12	Accakeek Creek	200 ac.
Richard Morton	15	Near Aquia Creek	468 ac.
Enoch Mason	15	On Chopawamsic Cr.	1967 ac.
Mrs. Anne Peyton	12	Var. tracts on Aquia Cr.	1459 ac.
Valentine Peyton	13	Various tracts	669 ac.
Joel Reddish	10	At Moore's Corner	370 ac.
Ford Suttler	10	Unknown	
John Stern	12	Var. tracts west of CH	798 ac.
Nicholas Voss	10	Unknown	
William Waller Sr.	11	Concord/Pot. Run tract	700 ac.

85 taxpayers owned 4-9 slaves
104 taxpayers owned 1-3 slaves

Tax Rates	
Black tithe	.44
Black over 12 and under 16	.44
Horse or mule	.12
Chariot or coach	5.00
Stage wagon	3.36
Chairs or gigs	.86

Total slaves	1121
Total slave owners	212
Non-owners	359
Total taxpayers	571

37% of taxpayers owned slaves
63% of taxpayers did not own slaves

Of the 571 taxpayers in the county:

- 1.57% owned 16 or more slaves
- 2.45% owned 10-15 slaves
- 14.88% owned 4-9 slaves
- 18.21% owned 1-3 slaves

Also listed on the tax records:

- 1238 Horses/Mules
- 7 Coaches
- 2 Stage wagons or phaetons
- 14 Gigs or carts

Taxes paid to the county:	
Slaves	$493.24
Horses/Mules	148.56
Coaches	35.00
Stage wagons or phaetons	6.72
Gigs or carts	12.04

Additional Sites

Antioch United Methodist Church—This church is located on the south side of State Route 651 and was organized in 1856. Worship services were held in the open for some time before a log building was erected. This structure burned around 1865. A new building was completed around 1891 and then replaced in 1960. Graves in the cemetery dated from as early as 1822.

Concord

Eustace farm—The Eustaces lived just south of Tackett's Mill. Hancock Eustace (1768-1829) was a wealthy county resident during the late eighteenth and early nineteenth centuries. He was the son of Isaac Eustace and Agatha Conway (1740-1826).

Grafton—an old Waller farm that was cut from Wayside. Part of the farm is now occupied by Anne E. Moncure Elementary School.

McDowell's Mill

Rock Hill Baptist Church—located at the intersection of State Routes 644 and 671. This church was organized in 1812 by two men from Chopawamsic Baptist Church (see "Chopawamsic Creek" in Chapter 7) and two from Hartwood Baptist Church. The present building is the second on the site.

Shelbourne—a 647-acre tract sold to Edward Waller of Wayside in 1851. It probably became part of Wayside.

Walnut Hill—on the west side of State Route 644. The house was built around 1814 and was owned by Nathaniel Greaves. The farm was later owned by William and Charles Sterne.

Potomac & Accakeek Creeks

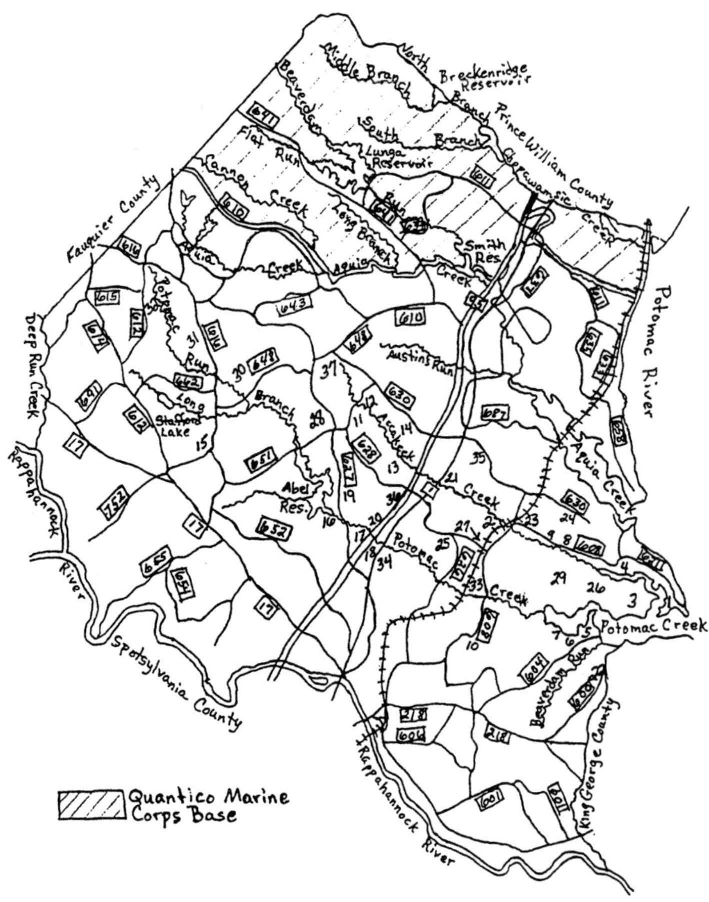

1 .. Marlborough
2 .. Potomac Church
3 .. Crow's Nest
4 .. Accakeek Farm
5 .. Belle Plain
6 .. Cave's Warehouse
7 .. Salvington
8 .. Mill Vale
9 .. Brooke's Mill
10 .. Boscobel
11 .. Woodbourne
12 .. Accakeek Iron Works
13 .. Valley View
14 .. Laurel Wood
15 .. Oakley
16 .. Withers' Mill
17 .. Oakenwold
18 .. Ravenswood
19 .. Chestnut Hill
20 .. Carmora
21 .. Fitzhugh's Accakeek Farm
22 .. Hickory Hill
23 .. Cherry Hill
24 .. Salem
25 .. Ragged and Tough
26 .. Selwood
27 .. Silk Farm
28 .. Woodcutting
29 .. Windsor
30 .. Ludlow
31 .. Fairview
32 .. Park Farm
33 .. Shepherd's Green
34 .. Oakland
35 .. Easternview
36 .. Chadwell
37 .. Potomac Chapel

Chapter 9

Potomac and Accakeek Creeks

An American Legacy

Today, the area between Potomac and Accakeek Creeks is a quiet, perhaps even remote part of the county. The countryside is dotted with individual homes and a few small subdivisions. An occasional train rumbles through the quietude and then disappears in the distance. Driving along Brooke Road (State Route 608) or Marlborough Point Road (State Route 621), one senses something ancient here, be it the Indians who lived along Potomac Creek for centuries before greeting Captain John Smith at Marlborough Point in 1608, or the bustle of the English settlements of the seventeenth and eighteenth centuries which followed Smith's arrival. Nothing solid remains of this period, just a certain presence of souls who lived out their lives here and called this part of Stafford County home.

The earliest white settlement in Stafford County occurred along Aquia Creek in the 1650s. This was quickly followed by settlement along Potomac and Accakeek Creeks. The land here is ideal for farming. High promontories provided beautiful homesites, elevated above swampy areas that were infested with the fearsome mosquitoes that carried malaria. Thousands of acres of fertile bottomland provided rich soil in which to grow crops, primarily tobacco of course, but also grains, fruits, and vegetables necessary to sustain the landowners. Potomac Creek was deep enough to accommodate ocean-going vessels far upstream, Accakeek Creek powered a grist mill, and Aquia Creek was only a couple of miles away. Larger plantations built wharves from which tobacco and other products were shipped overseas. Exotic fineries and mundane supplies arrived at these docks on a regular basis, and fish were caught in abundance from the creeks and the Potomac River. Until the Stafford–King George County boundary changes of 1777, the court house at Marlborough drew people from all over Stafford for regular court days. In the town of Marlborough businesses flourished and vendors sold their wares. Tobacco warehouses at Marlborough and across Potomac Creek at Cave's (see article this chapter) witnessed nearly constant activity and served not only as repositories for the precious leaves, but as banks as well. For nearly all of the eighteenth century, this area was the heart of Stafford County.

There was more taking place here, though, that would have a profound effect on the history of Stafford and on America as well. New ideas about government and personal freedom were evolving in this remote region. Largely cut off from the mainstream of Northern Neck affairs, men such as John Mercer of Marlborough, Thomas Ludwell Lee of Bellview, and George Mason (Mercer's nephew who received his law training in his uncle's library at Marlborough) were forming new ideas about the future of the American colonies. Serving as lawyers, judges, and in the House of Burgesses, they shared these ideas with people such as Patrick Henry, George Washington, and John Adams. The result was a new government unlike anything the world had ever known.

Today, we remember George Washington; some may even be aware that he spent his formative years in Stafford County. We remember the name of George Mason, but how many know that he wrote the Bill of Rights which became a part of our Constitution and served as a model for newly-formed governments in other countries? Mason was a private individual who shunned public life. He is primarily remembered as the builder of Gunston Hall in Fairfax County, but he spent much of his life in Stafford County and it was on Accakeek Creek in Stafford that his grandfather settled. His father lived at Accakeek, also, before moving to Chopawamsic in the northern part of the county.

Throughout its history, Stafford has always been cut off from the mainstream. The region was an inhospitable wilderness when the Brents settled here in the mid-seventeenth century. It continued to be considered as such throughout the eighteenth century, when Williamsburg was flourishing as the heart of colonial Virginia society. Yet, some of the period's finest political minds were at work here, and they created the ideas of religious tolerance, individual rights, and self-sufficiency which formed the ideological foundation of the American nation. As you drive the backroads of Potomac Creek, the spirit of these people is still tangible. Let them never be forgotten.

Marlborough

The neck of land which includes Marlborough Point reaches eastward from the mainland into the Potomac River and is bounded southerly by Potomac Creek. It was here on the point that John Smith ventured in 1608 and wrote of the extensive Potomac Indian town. The Potomacs had built many permanent dwellings and public buildings, and had upwards of 1,000 acres in cultivation. They warmly greeted Smith and his men and traded with them. Could they have had any idea of the implications of this first encounter?

The Potomac settlement continued for another sixty years but as more whites settled in the area, tensions between the cultures led to more frequent confrontations and by about 1662 the Potomacs had all but vanished. It would be thirty years before another town would be built there.

The village which Smith visited was located at the end of Indian Point Road (State Route 681). Today, the site is almost completely eroded into the Potomac River. The remains of an earlier ancestral village, however, survive in an overgrown area several hundred yards back from the river's edge. Thanks to a concerned local citizen (who plans on putting a drain field on the site), archaeological excavations are being carried out there, with fascinating results. To date, several layers of palisades have been discovered as well as post-holes indicating the presence of buildings. The Potomac Indians were careful to maintain a palisaded fortification for defense against other marauding tribes. A palisade would last for ten or twelve years before rotting. When it was time to replace the protective wall, the Indians would build a new layer outside of the old one, thereby never jeopardizing the safety of the village by taking down the old palisade before building the new one.

After the Potomacs were forced from Marlborough Point, white settlement flourished. Rich farmland provided abundant crops and the river yielded fish by the thousands. As more and more people settled in the area, a movement began in Parliament to create official towns which would make government and tax collection more efficient.

Marlborough was one of many towns created by government legislation. Most towns of this period were established by a series of short-lived government orders rather than by necessity. Virginia's "Act for Cohabitation and Encouragement of Trade and Manufacture" of 1680 was responsible for the creation of several towns including Aquia and Dumfries as well as Marlborough. An early town was defined as "Any place where [are] as many houses as are individuals to make a riot, that is twenty as fixed by the Riot Act." Government mandates of 1691 and 1705 provided for the establishment of port towns to serve as central locations for a widely-dispersed population.

The seventeenth-century Virginia economy was totally dependent upon tobacco. Everyone who had a piece of land grew tobacco, and the plant was not only the major export from the colony, it was also used as currency. The Assembly realized that an economy based purely on tobacco was a dangerous situation. A bad growing year or a depressed British market could throw the entire colony into debt. Additionally, tobacco was very hard on the soil, and soil exhaustion led to an ever-widening search for good land, resulting in a widely dispersed population—and it is difficult to govern a population spread thinly over a large area. Realizing this fact as well as the dangers of a tobacco-based economy, the Assembly established a law creating official port towns. These towns were intended to be business and manufacturing centers. If sufficient business and manufacturing could be established, the dependence on tobacco might be lessened. Of course, official ports of entry would also allow for the collection of customs revenues, which often went uncollected when goods changed hands at local wharves.

The first of these laws, enacted in 1662, established a port town in each of the major river valleys. Most of these towns, however, were never built and in 1680 a new act was passed, establishing a port in each county. Here ships were to deliver supplies and pick up tobacco and manufactured goods for their return voyages.

Some of the towns were laid out on fifty-acre tracts of one-half-acre lots. Only nine of the tracts were ever built upon, however. The idea of an official port for each county did not please many planters who would be required to haul their products great distances and pay storage fees in distant warehouses. Many planters had their own storage facilities and wharves at which oceangoing ships could dock and load. The ship captains were also happy with this system, for they too were not anxious to make things any easier for His Majesty's customs collectors.

In Stafford the selected site for the port town was on the neck of land where Accakeek and Potomac Creeks flow into the Potomac River. This piece of property belonged to Giles Brent, son of Stafford's first settler. Malachi Peale, former sheriff of Stafford, held a life-long lease on the property, and on some of the early maps the land is called Peale's Neck. Because he was not yet twenty-one, Giles selected his step-father, Francis Hammersley, as his guardian and administrator of his affairs. Hammersley was paid 13,000 pounds of tobacco for the land. There were fifty-two acres surveyed, the extra two acres being laid out for the court house. For this additional two acres, Hammersley was given 800 pounds of tobacco. Peale was paid 3,450 pounds of tobacco as compensation for the loss of his leasehold.

William Buckland drew up plans for Stafford's port town which included wharves for oceangoing vessels and a court house. The first court house built in Stafford had been located south of Potomac Creek until about 1690 when it apparently burned. The court began meeting in a private home on November 12 of that year. A contract was made with Sampson Darrell for the building of the court house in the new town of Marlborough. The cost of the court house was 40,000 pounds of tobacco. Captain George Mason (II), high sheriff of the county, suggested that a prison be built on the two acres to the east of the court house. These new buildings were to be completed by June 10, 1692.

In 1691 another Act of Ports was passed. Unlike earlier acts which hoped to encourage business and lessen the risk of a tobacco-based economy, this act was purely to ensure that customs revenues were collected on goods. The law required all goods to be imported or exported through the official ports and nowhere else, or risk forfeit of ships, gear, and cargo.

On February 11, 1692, twenty-seven lots in Stafford's new port town were granted to fifteen applicants, among them Parson John Waugh, Robert Alexander, George Andrews, Thomas Ballard, Peter Beach, George and Robert Brent, John Cave, Dr. Edward Maddox, John Withers, and Edward Mountjoy. A Potomac Creek ferry was established and two ordinaries were licensed in 1691 and 1693, but only a limited amount of business seems to have been conducted in the new town. The town does not appear to have been officially named until 1706, when the General Assembly ordered that it be made a port and market town under the name of Marlborough. Merchants and planters, long opposed to the port acts, continued to exert their influence and on March 22, 1693, the act was suspended.

The port acts didn't die easily, however, and in 1705 yet another act was passed. This was basically a repeat of the earlier act but offered substantial incentives for settling in the port towns. Those individuals who actually established themselves in the towns were exempted from poll taxes for fifteen years and relieved from military mustering and marching outside the towns except in the case of war. No goods could be sold within a five-mile radius of the town and ordinaries were not permitted within a ten-mile radius, except at court houses and ferry landings. The new towns were also given names, Stafford's being called Marlborough in honor of John Churchill, Duke of Marlborough. The Duke was one of England's most famous warriors who routed the French-Bavarian army near Blenheim, Bavaria, in 1704. The defeat destroyed French ambitions for dominance in central Europe. While Marlborough never became the metropolis the lawmakers had envisioned, there was a moderate amount of activity there between 1708 and 1710.

In 1710 London again rescinded the Act of Ports. The reason was quite simple—the act provided enticements for the establishment and growth of businesses and manufacturing. There was concern that the success of these ventures would take away from the planting and harvesting of tobacco, thus lessening the colony's dependence upon the Crown. Parliament foresaw grave consequences and could not tolerate the risk of losing tax money.

Interestingly, most of the lot holders in Marlborough were gentlemen rather than craftsmen, and their purchase of the lots may well have been for investment purposes. Only three or four craftsmen and innkeepers settled in the town. The gentlemen who purchased the lots seem to have had little interest in building residences there since they all had established plantations. Among the gentlemen owning lots were the following:

Sampson Darrell—builder of the court house, held two lots but lived on Aquia Creek.

Francis Hammersley—married Giles Brent's widow and lived at Retirement.

George and Robert Brent—nephews of Giles who lived at Woodstock. George was a law partner with William Fitzhugh.

John Waugh—lived on the south side of Potomac Creek in a house owned by Mrs. Anne Meese of London. His failure to pay for that house after eleven years of occupancy led to a court suit. Waugh is best remembered as a political agitator.

Malachi Peale—former lease-holder on the neck of land, owned three lots and may have built there considering that he was already established on the neck.

George Andrews and Peter Beach—less important members of the community and may have been the only full-time residents of the town from the first grantees.

Captain George Mason (II) of Accakeek—also a lot-holder and appears to have built in the town, for in 1691 he petitioned to keep an ordinary there.

The 1705 Act of Ports required the building of a house upon each lot. The minimum requirements for these houses stated that each was to be twenty feet square, one and one-half stories, with a chimney on one end. The ground floor was most likely a single room; the half story was a loft which provided extra sleeping and storage space. The houses at Marlborough would have been no more than the minimum and built of logs or frame. In those early days, even very important people often had rather primitive dwellings.

As mentioned earlier, there were two ordinaries in the town, one run by George Mason (II) and another operated by George Andrews. From Andrews' will we get a picture of typical conditions in a colonial ordinary. There were no bedsteads, although he did have six small feather beds with bolsters and one small flock bed. (A bed was not what we picture today, but rather little more than a mattress. A flock bed was stuffed with bits of wool and cotton.) Andrews also had two pair of curtains with valances. The valances were hung around the bed like a canopy. Curtains hung on rings within the valance and were drawn around the bed for warmth or privacy. Six of the beds had "rugs" or covers. There were four old cane chairs, and an old table with a "carpet" to cover it. Andrews also had one chest of drawers (rare in the seventeenth century), a cupboard to hold dishes and cups, and a pair of tankards. There were also a chest and a "great trunk" for storage. For formal entertaining he had a large punchbowl, punch having recently been introduced from India. A few silver spoons added a touch of elegance.

Despite all the planning and wishing of the Assembly, Marlborough was little more that a crude village with a few primitive dwellings connected by footpaths. There was a boat landing and perhaps a small dock. The rustic wooden court house completed the picture.

Around 1718 the court house burned and all hope for the little town went up in smoke. While there had not been much activity around Marlborough to begin with, by the time the court house burned, the population had already begun moving out of the area. Without the court house, which at least required ferries and ordinaries, and without the Port Act requiring all goods to be shipped from the town docks, there was no future for a town in a society of planters. The court house was not rebuilt on the same site because Marlborough was no longer centrally located with respect to the population. Instead, a new court house was built on the south side of Potomac Creek. Marlborough died quietly and when John Mercer arrived in 1726 to open the next chapter in Marlborough's history, "but one House twenty-feet square was standing."

Mercer was born in Dublin, Ireland on February 6, 1704, and came to the New World in 1720. We don't know what he brought with him, but he does not seem to have been a wealthy man when he arrived. "Except my education I never got a shilling of my fathers or any other relations estate, every penny I ever got has been my own industry and with as much fatigue as most people have undergone."

Mercer was a trader and for several years he employed himself by sailing his sloop up and down the rivers transporting and exchanging goods along the way. During this time, he was also studying law. He began practicing in Maryland and spent several years there before his volatile disposition and outspoken, even rude, behavior put him in trouble with authorities.

Upon arriving in Virginia Mercer became friends with the Mason family; it may have been this friendship that led him to settle at Marlborough close to the Mason plantation. On June 10, 1725, Mercer married Catherine Mason. This was a most advantageous move for Mercer as the Mason family had long been established in Virginia, and thus at the tender age of twenty-one Mercer became a member of Virginia's aristocracy.

Mercer saw a great many possibilities in the failed town, and in the summer of 1726 he settled himself and his wife in the only house left standing in Marlborough. Built by Thomas Ballard in 1708, the house had been inherited by Catherine's uncle, David Waugh, son of John Waugh. Waugh allowed the young couple to live in the house rent-free for a period of three years, after which they would pay a token rent of twelve shillings. Almost immediately, Mercer began buying land both in Marlborough and all around the county. He also began collecting things he would need to set up a plantation, including livestock and servants. He had a new plantation house built in Marlborough, although it in no way compared to the mansion he would later build there. Completed in 1731, this interim house was a simple frame structure, having only two fireplaces in a single chimney. The records do not even indicate if it was painted inside or out.

Mercer had to petition the Assembly for permission to take over the long-dead town of Marlborough. Below is a portion of his lengthy petition requesting that permission, citing the improvements he planned to make.

> To the worshipful, the Speaker of Gentlemen of the House of Burgesses, the Case and Petition of John Mercer, of Marlborough Town, in the County of Stafford, Gent., sheweth:
>
> That by an act of Assembly made in 1691, entitled An Act for Ports and Towns, Fifty Acres of Land where Capt. Malachi Peale then lived, called Potomac Neck, were appointed to be laid off for a Port and Town for Stafford County, which was called Marlborough. That by the said Act the County was to pay the Purchase, and to be reimbursed by the several persons taking up the said lots, pro rata; but every person taking up a lot in the said Town was to build on it a House twenty feet square, in such Time or to forfeit such Lot.
>
> That William Buckner, Surveyor of the said County, having surveyed fifty-two Acres by Order of the said County Court (two of which he says were for a Court-house), and divided the same into ninety-four Lots, the Plat of that Survey was recorded, not only among the Records of the County, but in the Books of Theodorick Bland...

Over the next twenty years, Mercer invested a fortune in Marlborough, buying most of the old town lots, building a mansion for himself, and expanding the town to include the Mercer wharf, a tavern, cider mill, water mill, windmill, brewery, tobacco barns, glass factory, fishing shore, malt house, two granaries, three corn houses, a cooper's shop, Negro cabins, an overseer's house, racetrack, and stables. He owned his own fleet of sailing vessels which carried tobacco from his wharf to England (river charts as late as 1890 still referred to Marlborough Point as Windmill Point because of Mercer's windmill). He also had numerous racehorses which he enjoyed matching with those of his friends. For more than forty years the town thrived, guided by the seemingly boundless energy of this talented and aggressive man. Within just fifteen years of his arrival in the New World, Mercer had established himself as an able planter, superb administrator, and brilliant lawyer.

By 1746 Mercer had begun building his own manor house at Marlborough. He hired David Minitree of Williamsburg to do the brickwork. Minitree would later build Carter's Grove. Mercer hired only the most skilled craftsmen in Virginia to work on his house. He ordered furniture from one of the finest cabinet makers in England. He also bought large quantities of silver. No expense was spared to create his grand manor house.

Catherine Mercer died on June 15, 1750, at the age of forty-three. She was buried in Marlborough and her funeral was preached at Potomac Church four weeks later as was the custom of the day. By this time Mercer had become one of the major landholders in Virginia, though he, like most in his class, was heavily in debt.

Mercer's business kept him in Williamsburg quite a bit and he traveled there shortly after burying his wife. He stayed off and on at a Dr. Roy's and on November 10 he married Ann Roy. The short period of mourning for Catherine showed no lack of love. A manor needed a mistress and his children, who had been in the care of a nurse in Williamsburg, needed a mother.

Maintaining an operation as large as Marlborough required a tremendous investment. Although a brilliant businessman, by the late 1760s Mercer was deeply in debt. His quick temper and caustic outbursts in the courts eventually resulted in his retiring from law practice, and he decided to concentrate his efforts on Marlborough. Always an optimist, he seemed to believe that he would one day be able to pay his debtors. He built a brewery and cooperage and purchased more slaves to grow barley on his farm. Andrew Monroe, grandfather of the future president, was hired to oversee the brewery. The brew, however, was of such poor quality that no one would drink it.

❧ ❧

Mercer was a staunch supporter of the rights of the individual as defined by the Magna Carta and was vehemently opposed to anyone or anything that impinged upon those rights. It mattered little to him whom he offended with his sometimes violent attacks against those who disagreed with him, a fact that caused him no small amount of trouble.

In eighteenth-century society, lawyers were expected to maintain a high standard of decorum toward courts and judges both in court and out. Mercer rarely did so. Prince William justices claimed at the council in Williamsburg that Mercer was dictatorial and presumptuous and frequently impugned their learning and authority. In 1734 the council suspended Mercer's license to practice for six months. The following year Mercer apologized for his behavior, and the council granted him a new license allowing him to practice "in any county Court excepting the County Court of Prince William." A few years later he was once again allowed to practice in Prince William, but was soon before the council again charged with insolent behavior toward the justices. He had not only been disrespectful but had also convinced some of the local citizens that the justices should be condemned.

Mercer's record in the Stafford courts was no better. He was once removed from practice for eighteen months, and a second time he was censured by the council for "intemperate" language and "indecent Treatment of the other Justices." Despite this, Mercer served for a time as chief justice for Stafford.

Some of John Mercer's chief contributions were his legal compilations. He wrote two *Abridgments of the Laws of Virginia*, in 1737 and 1759. During the time Mercer practiced law in Maryland, he wrote *Abridgment of the Laws of Maryland* and *The Compleat Collection of the Laws of Maryland*, and edited *The Laws of Maryland* of 1707 and 1718 (before being asked to leave the colony as a result of his outspoken behavior).

Although he signed his abridgments of 1737 "John Mercer, Gentleman," in truth he had no patience with what he called "gentlemen [who] wore laced jackets" and spent their time at ordinaries, horse races, cock fights, and gaming tables. In fact, he bound his son to an architect and joiner so he would learn a trade rather than a profession. Like Benjamin Franklin, Mercer believed the trades to be equally respectable to professions.

The Stamp Act took effect on November 1, 1765. Although the controversial act would eventually lead to war with England, the initial response of most colonists was disgruntled resignation. Early on, few people were actually in favor of actively opposing the law. Mercer, however, was enraged that Parliament would so much as entertain the thought of implementing an internal tax on the colonies. Among other objections, Mercer was aware that the Stamp Act would drastically increase the cost of legal services, and he felt this would violate the rights of Englishmen to equal justice under the law as written in the Magna Carta. He claimed, "At this Rate, we must not only be obliged to buy, but at such a Price, that not one in a hundred will be able to pay the purchase price for legal counsel."

To impress complacent citizens with the far-reaching implications of the Stamp Act, Mercer created an alphabetical table of Stamp Act levies. To that he attached a flaming cover letter expressing his opinion of the Stamp Act and those who supported it or even those who merely chose to accept it. He submitted his list and letter to the Virginia newspapers for publication, but the governor forbade the printing of the cover letter. Only the list was printed. Although the letter did not make it into the hands of the general public, it did circulate for a month and a half prior to Patrick Henry's introduction of his Virginia Resolves, and copies of it were undoubtedly in the hands of at least some of the Burgesses.

In his controversial letter, Mercer quoted a common English proverb, "Far from Jove, far from Jove's thunderbolts." (The implication being that if one was far from the seat of authority, one was safe from the power of that authority.) He then called for one patriot to defy the false authority of Parliament. Did Patrick Henry answer Mercer's call?

Even civil authorities chose to resist the Stamp Act. Knowing that the act would become effective on November 1, 1765, many county courts closed on October 31 and did not reopen until the act was repealed. Stafford magistrates sent a letter to Governor Fauquier avowing their duty and allegiance to the king but claiming that the Stamp Act was an "unconstitutional Act of Parliament" which would involve them in perjury if they continued to serve. Like most of their peers, the magistrates were deeply in debt and said they had a right to expect indulgences because of "their most universal Poverty" due to the heavy taxes already levied for "supporting the late Glorious war." While they were severely in debt, the justices assured the governor that once their liberties were again secured, they would be able to turn their attention to the production of commodities to pay their "unreasonable British creditors" and supply their mother country with wines and many other goods. Mercer was serving as chief justice at this time, and the letter includes several arguments attributable to him. There is every reason to believe that he wrote the letter. Besides Mercer, signers included Peter Daniel, John Alexander, Travers Daniel, William Bronough, William Brent, Thomas Ludwell Lee, Samuel Selden, Gowry Waugh, Thomas Fitzhugh, and Robert Washington.

Edmund Randolph, a contemporary of Mercer, wrote of his efforts to oppose the act, "It has been stated that Mr. John Mercer was the first in Virginia who distinctly elucidated upon paper the principles which justified the opposition to the Stamp Act. He showed them in manuscript to his friends. They spread rapidly so as to produce a groundwork for and uniformity of popular sentiment." One is left to guess how much influence John Mercer had in regards to the final decision to go to war with England. He died just three years after the Stamp Act took effect, nearly bankrupt.

❧ ❧

Marlborough remained a major shipping port throughout the Revolution. Without Mercer's energy and financial support the town faded. Rind's *Virginia Gazette* of October 14, 1768 gives the following obituary:

> On Friday, the 14th instant, died at his house in Stafford county, John Mercer, Esq., who had practised the law with great success in this colony upwards of forty years. He was a Gentleman of great natural abilities improved by an extensive knowledge, not only in his profession, but in several other branches of polite literature. He was of a humane, generous and chearful disposition a facetious companion, a warm friend, an affectionate husband, a tender parent, and an indulgent master.

Upon his death, Mercer left an extensive library containing some 1,800 volumes, about one-third of which dealt with the law.

His collection was second only to that of William Byrd of Westover.

Marlborough never regained its energy after the Revolution. A new court house was built in 1783 on the other side of Potomac Creek, closer to the center of the county and upon the site of the present building. Mercer's eldest son, George, inherited the Marlborough property. George had been living in England, but in 1765 he returned to Virginia, ironically to take a job as the Collector of Stamps for the Crown. Public sentiment against England was rapidly worsening and the young Mercer received a hostile reception upon his arrival. A mob (directed by Richard Henry Lee) gathered and burned him in effigy. Fearing for his life, George quickly resigned the post and fled back to England never to return. Upon inheriting his father's estate, he turned over the operation of it to his younger brother, James. Unlike George, James seems to have been a permanent Virginia resident and upon inheriting Marlborough, he worked hard to pay off the family debt. However, by 1819 the Mercer family had given up on the endeavor and had abandoned the property.

At this point, the farm came into the hands of Colonel John Cooke. He lived at West Farm, just north of Clifton, but his wife was related to Catherine Mercer. Colonel Cooke's nephew, John Bronough, lived in the house and ran the farm.

In 1806 Cooke took out an insurance policy on the house, which was described as a "Brick Dwelling House one Story high covered with wood 108 feet 8 Inches long by 28 1/2 feet wide, a Cellar under about half the house." Across the length of the house was a "Portico 108 feet 8 Inches by 8 feet 4 Inches." A porch ten by five feet was in front of the portico. Another smaller porch was built on the northeast corner of the house. Cooke died in 1819 and there is no more mention of Mercer's grand house. By the time archeological excavations were begun in 1930, the foundation of the once grand manor house was barely visible under the weeds. Most probably the house burned while unoccupied.

Marlborough

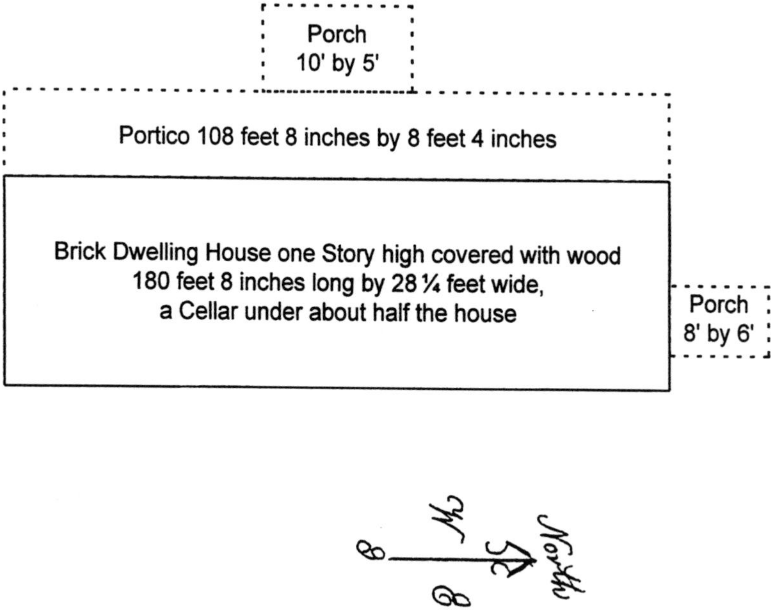

From an 1806 Mutual Assurance policy

John Mercer was an undeniable influence on George Mason (IV). George's father drowned when he was only ten years old and Mercer, already an uncle, became the boy's legal guardian. In 1776 Mason wrote the Virginia Declaration of Rights, the first true bill of rights ever written. Mason's bill of rights influenced the first part of Jefferson's Declaration of Independence and was a model for Madison's Bill of Rights. Hugh Blair Grigsby wrote that it was a miracle that a Virginia planter without any formal education or legal training could have written such a document. No doubt young Mason spent many hours in his uncle's extensive library and had untold opportunities to discuss his readings with Mercer. Throughout Mason's writings one hears the echo of Mercer's beliefs in the undeniable rights of the individual.

❧ ❧

Development and abandon around Marlborough Point have come and gone like the tides in the creek. When whites first visited the point in 1608 there was a huge Indian village there. That settlement died out with the continuing influx of whites, and the area became quiet for a while. The 1705 Act of Ports created a town which flourished briefly before dying. John Mercer gave life back to the town. After his death, however, the point was again all but abandoned. The cordwood business which developed after the Civil War kept the creek teeming with boats up until the 1930s, when the depression brought an end to most activity in the county.

Marlborough Point was an extremely busy area during the nineteenth century. The cordwood operations required a great many longboats up until the 1930s. Additional traffic was produced by mail carriers providing mail service from Washington to Richmond. Also, there were a couple of paddlewheelers, numerous schooners, a ferry, and assorted boats and barges.

The operators of some of the vessels asked Congress for a lighthouse on the shoal due to the many groundings. After studying the problem, however, Congress decided that "The light's usefulness for the generality of vessels navigating Potomac Creek would hardly compensate for the cost of its erection."

Today there are a few houses along the point. Developers are eyeing the area greedily and, no doubt, will soon descend to wreak their havoc on one of Stafford's most picturesque areas.

Potomac Church

Traveling from Fredericksburg to Brooke along State Route 608, one crosses a lovely little creek. On the right-hand side of the road upon a hill once stood Potomac Church, one of the oldest Episcopal churches in the United States. This beautiful house of worship was built on a portion of the ancient Samuel Mathews tract. Thomas Wilkinson bought the parcel from Mathews in 1662, but it is unknown if Wilkinson sold the property to the vestry or if he donated it as a building site.

Potomac was one of the largest colonial churches in Virginia. Built of brick, the building measured 60 feet by 80 feet. Similarities with later Aquia Church included arched windows and the texts of the Law, Lord's Prayer, and Nicene Creed painted upon the walls.

The organization of this church was closely tied to the organization of the county. The church was built possibly as early as 1664 and was a part of St. Paul's Parish. Until the building of Aquia Church in 1751, Potomac Church was the principal place of worship in the area, but the date of its construction is unknown. Few records survive to provide information about Potomac Church. John Waugh was probably the first rector there. John Mercer of Marlborough recorded that his infant daughter, Elizabeth Mason Mercer, was baptized there on Easter Sunday, April 12, 1730, by the Reverend Mr. Alexander Scott. The names of the other rectors are unknown.

Services were held from the church's erection until about 1804, according to widely-known historian George H. S. King. He also noted, "Three wars and the complete exodus of the ancient families in the environs of Potomac Church were the cause of its destruction."

Apparently, Potomac Church was abandoned sometime around 1804. On August 1, 1814, William Brent Jr., Daniel Carroll Brent, John Cooke, John Moncure, Hancock Eustace, and Rowzee

Peyton wrote to the governor asking him to return the Stafford militia to the county immediately as they believed a British invasion was imminent. The militia had been sent to Mattox Bridge in Westmoreland and only thirty men were stationed on Hope Run, four and one-half miles from the mouth of the creek. The men's concern was well-founded, as Potomac Church was burned by British soldiers on their way to Washington. A description by Benjamin J. Lossing who visited Potomac Church in 1848 reveals:

> The plan of the interior is similar to that of Pohick. The roof is supported by square columns, stuccoed and painted in imitation of variegated marble. The windows are in Gothic style. The LAW, the PRAYER, and the CREED were quite well preserved upon the walls, notwithstanding the roof is partly fallen in, and the storms have free passage through the ruined arches. It is surrounded by a thick hedge of thorns, dwarf cedars, and other shrubs, festooned and garlanded with ivy and wild grape, which almost effectually guard the venerable relic from the intrusion of strangers.

By 1855 the building had lost most of its roof. Even then, though, the Lord's Prayer, Creed, and Ten Commandments painted on the interior walls were still well-preserved. The walls, still standing in 1861, were finally destroyed by Union troops. The bricks and stone from those walls may well have been used by Herman Haupt to build the bridge over Potomac Creek during the war (see Chapter 7).

Recently, the surviving foundation was bulldozed and a house built on the site.

Crow's Nest

In 1662 Rawleigh Travers received a patent for 3,650 acres on Potomac Creek. This land had originally been granted to Colonel Gerard Fowke. By 1723 the plantation had been reduced

Crow's Nest

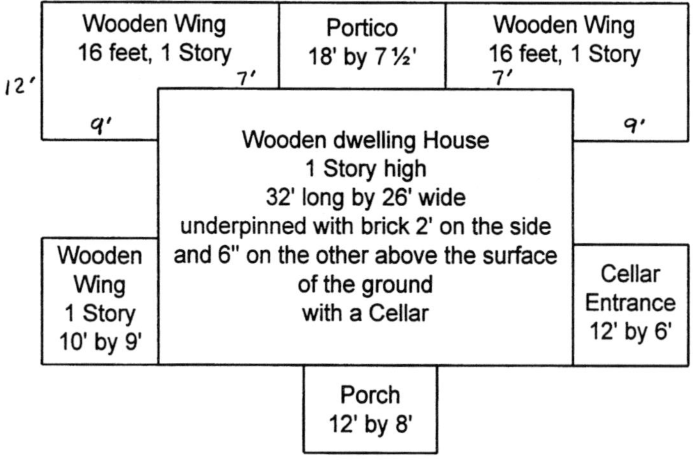

From an 1805 Mutual Assurance policy

to 3,525 acres. This remains a beautiful piece of property, a peninsula extending into the Potomac River, bounded on the north by Accakeek Creek and on the south by Potomac Creek. A high ridge runs parallel to Potomac Creek and it was upon this ridge that a magnificent brick house called Crow's Nest was built late in the eighteenth century.

Peter Daniel (1706-1777) moved to Stafford County from Middlesex as a young man, and married Sarah Travers (171?-1788) of Crow's Nest, daughter of Rawleigh Travers of Stafford. Peter Daniel became one of Stafford's leading citizens, serving as senior presiding justice of the county and a member of the Committee of Safety. Long an advocate for freedom from England, he was the first to sign a protest against the Stamp Act.

Peter and Sarah had three children, Hannah Ball Daniel (1737-1829), Travers Daniel (1741-1824), and Elizabeth Travers Daniel who died an infant. Like his father, Travers was very prominent in county affairs and he was the official county surveyor from 1763 to 1794. Travers was also a Justice for Stafford County and succeeded his father as Presiding Justice. He married Frances Moncure, daughter of the Reverend Mr. John Moncure of Clermont, by whom he had eleven children.

Crow's Nest was originally the home of the Travers family and was named after "The Crow," a black sailing vessel owned by the family. While most planters made use of the services of commercial shipping companies to haul their tobacco, some did own their own ships. Crow's Nest and "The Crow" came to the Daniel family through the marriage of Peter Daniel and Sarah Travers. By having their own ship, the Daniels could transport tobacco and necessary supplies as well as the finest wines and manufactured goods from Europe.

Some plantations were more elaborate than others, and Crow's Nest was one of the largest operations in the area. Crow's Nest was a self-sufficient village. There were cabins for servants, various shops such as blacksmith, tannery, and shoe shops, and a spinning and weaving shop which produced clothing for everyone on the place. A large orchard provided fruit. Grains were grown in great abundance and ground into flour and meal. Many vegetables were grown, and hundreds of pounds of sweet and white potatoes were stored for use through the winter. Pork, sausage, and pickled beef were processed, and tons of fish were seined and smoked or salted to provide for the many people who lived and worked on the farm. Sorghum cane provided molasses, and various types of fowl were raised in addition to herds of sheep and cattle. Hides from butchered livestock provided leather for shoes and harnesses. Beef fat was used to make candles. Numerous herbs were grown for seasoning and home remedies.

Throughout the generations, members of the Daniel family of Crow's Nest held important positions in county, colonial, and later national government. Peter Vivian Daniel (1784-1860) was born at Crow's Nest April 24, 1784. Following the custom of the day for the children of wealthy parents, Peter's early education was by private tutors. He later attended the College of New Jersey (now Princeton) but did not take a degree. He then studied law at the Richmond office of Edmund Randolph. There he met Randolph's daughter, Lucy, whom he married.

Daniel's illustrious legal career began when he was admitted to the Virginia bar in 1808. That same year, he fought a duel with Captain John Seddon (1780-1808), relative of James Alexander Seddon of Snowden. According to *The Virginia Herald* of November 9, 1808,

> Another fatal duel—an affair of honor was, on Saturday last determined in Maryland, between Peter V. Daniel, ESQ and Captain John Seddon, both of Stafford, in this date. The latter received his antagonist's ball in the right side, languished till about 8 o'clock on Monday morning, and died.

At the age of twenty-five Daniel was elected to the Virginia General Assembly representing Stafford County. In 1812 he was elected member of the Privy Council of Virginia, where he served until 1835; and in 1818 he was elected Lieutenant Governor. He was a leader in the Virginia Republican Party and was a supporter of Andrew Jackson and friend of Martin Van Buren. Daniel was asked to serve as Attorney General of the United States but declined the position as he felt the salary was insufficient. He accepted an appointment to the District Court for Eastern Virginia, a position he held for five years.

In 1841 Van Buren appointed Daniel to the United States Supreme Court, the fourth Associate Justice from Virginia. He served as a Justice for eighteen years and was known as an agrarian, populist-oriented, a defender of states' rights, and a proponent of slavery. Peter Vivian Daniel died in 1860 and was the last native Virginian to be appointed to the Supreme Court until Lewis F. Powell Jr. was appointed in 1972.

During Judge Peter Daniel's time, Crow's Nest was beautifully maintained. Daniel even replaced wooden grave markers with stones of marble, granite, and sandstone. Some of the graves were structured into tombs with brick foundations and marble slabs. By 1937 only four inscriptions were readable:

> *Here lies the body of Eliza Travers Daniel, daughter of Travers and Mildred Daniel, who departed this life in her 21 year. October 29, 1825. In the hour of death so strong was her faith in the Savior of the work that her fondest friends administrating what they witnessed. ______ to weep at what they lost, they communed in faith their own hearts and weep not.*

> *To the memory of Mrs. Mildred Daniel, who was born in Charles County, Maryland, February 27, 1772 and died in the county of Stafford, Virginia, October 27, 1837 and was the widow of Travers D. Daniel and the daughter of Mildred Stone of Maryland and of the ____ of independence and ordained minister, lived and died an example of Christian life. Precious in the sight of the Lord is the death of his saints.*

> *Monumental of love and devotion for one who nourished and possessed the veneration and love all whom he was known and faithful and sympathy in every duty of a Christian.*
>
> *Travers Daniel's son*
> *Born March 20, 1741*
> *Died June 28, 1824.*

This marble is erected in the affection of the devoted wife, the tender mother and the humble, pious Christian.

Frances Daniel, Travers Daniel's daughter
Born September 10, 1800
Died in the ________.

A Mutual Assurance Society of Virginia policy for Crow's Nest dated 1805 has a drawing of a large frame house with several additions. At that time, the house was valued at $1,400. The owner also insured his barn for $250. Today, nothing remains of the old house.

The Civil War turned Stafford into a giant campground, and Crow's Nest was not spared the intrusion. Its location high upon a hill made the property a perfect observation point for Union troops watching over activities on Potomac Creek. A pontoon bridge was built from Crow's Nest across Potomac Creek, and the Union's largest supply storage area was just on the other side of the creek at Waugh Point.

After the war, Crow's Nest was largely forgotten and abandoned. Today, the cemetery at Crow's Nest is overgrown with dense woods and underbrush. Tombstones of the once-prominent family have been broken by vandals and roaming livestock, and the elements have destroyed the fragments. The property is presently owned by a developer, who is awaiting approval to build a subdivision there.

Accakeek Farm or Rose Hill

Accakeek Farm was the home of the first George Mason to settle in Virginia. It was located between present-day State Routes 621 and 608. All that remains today is the cemetery, and very little is known about the farm.

In 1653 John Withers patented 150 acres upon the head of a branch of Potomac Creek for his transport of three people to Virginia. This land was sold to Colonel Valentine Peyton, who in 1662 was granted an additional 500 acres contiguous to the 150. This 650 acres was bought by Captain George Mason (I) in 1664.

He probably arrived in Virginia around 1652, landing at Norfolk and traveling up the Potomac River to Accakeek Creek, where he settled. Mason was born in Staffordshire, England, and it is believed that he first named the land cut from Westmoreland County, "Stafford."

Over the years, Mason bought tracts adjoining his farm, gradually increasing its size to some 1,150 acres. The Mason and Waugh families were friends for many years and George Mason added to his landholdings by buying from Alexander Waugh 1,200 acres on Potomac Creek for 16,000 pounds of tobacco. This was part of a 6,300-acre patent taken up by Alexander's father, the Reverend John Waugh.

By 1667 Mason was involved in activities of Potomac Parish, and he is listed in church records as a vestryman along with Colonel Henry Meese, Richard Heabeard, William Townshend, William Heabeard, William Greene, John Wiser, Vincent Young, and David Anderson.

After his father's death in 1686, son George Mason (II) sold 450 acres of his father's Accakeek Farm to Robert Wright, the property including "outhouses, barns, stables, tobacco houses, and all other edifaces." The younger Mason specifically reserved the "tomb of the said Col. George Mason and the burying place in which it stands." Mason had no need of the property as a home for his own family; by this time he was living at Chopawamsic Farm (see Chapter 7). Although Accakeek Farm was known to have been the burial ground for the Mason-Mercer-Hedgman families, the cemetery has long since vanished. (In 1943 Margaret Mauzy Hedgman's grave was moved to Aquia Church; she had died in 1754. As long ago as 1845 the cemetery had disappeared.) Wright died without heirs and the land came to escheat or revert back to the Crown. It was then claimed by William Barber who married Robert Wright's widow.

In 1704 the farm came into the possession of Nathaniel Hedgman, who probably named it Rose Hill. It remained in the Hedgman family until about 1862.

Nathaniel Hedgman (d.1721) came to Stafford as an overseer for Robert "King" Carter's vast land holdings in that part of Virginia. In 1704 Hedgman acquired 450 acres on Accakeek Creek, part of which was the dwelling plantation of George Mason (I). This property was inherited by his son, Major Peter

Hedgman. Nathaniel apparently met a violent death while neglecting the affairs of Colonel Carter. Carter wrote, "I have heard of late he hath been a very great delinquent from my business and lived a loose, rebelling life, which hath brought him to his untimely catastrophe. As for entertaining his son, a wild young lad that hath no experience in the world, I can by no means think proper." Peter wrote to Carter asking to continue in his father's position but was denied. Despite Carter's opinion of him, the young Hedgman rose to a place of some political and social prominence in Stafford County. He died testate in 1765.

The town of Marlborough was laid out in 1691 on the same neck of land which included Accakeek Farm. George Mason (II) became one of the first "feoffees" of the town and was granted a number of lots there. He may have even built upon one or more of his lots as he petitioned to establish an ordinary in the town.

George Mason (II) married three times, first to Mary Fowke, daughter of his father's long-time friend. His second wife was Elizabeth Waugh, daughter of Parson John Waugh with whom Mason had been involved in the rebellion against the Catholics in 1688. His last wife is recorded only as Sarah Mason.

The second, third, and fourth generations of George Masons owned property all over northern Virginia. George Mason (II) purchased a tract of land on Chopawamsic Creek and built a fine stone manor house upon a hill. He called the property Chopawamsic Farm (see "Chopawamsic Farm" in Chapter 7). Part of this property was eventually taken by Quantico. The Masons also owned a farm along the Occoquan River which they called Woodbridge. It was George Mason (IV) who built Gunston Hall.

Dr. Oscar Darter visited Accakeek Farm during the days of the Marlborough excavations in the 1950s. On the edge of the woods, he found what appeared to be the foundation of a house which was built on the high ridge on the north side of the intersection of State Routes 608 and 621. No description or drawing remains of the structure and no excavations have been done there.

Parson John Waugh and the Catholic Rebellion

It is very difficult to understand events or personalities from public records alone; so little of what one does on a day-to-day basis becomes a part of court records, newspapers, or other public records. When dealing with historical figures, only those who left diaries or collections of letters, or those whose lives are reflected in the writings of others, can be understood on a human level. These comprise a relatively small number of people. When trying to reconstruct the lives of historical figures, we often have the added disadvantage of lost records. This is especially true in Stafford County, where there are numerous gaps in the public records as well as the existence of painfully few private letters, diaries, or journals.

Despite the scant surviving records, it is possible to reconstruct part of the life of one of Stafford County's most colorful characters, the Reverend John Waugh (1630-1706). Waugh was the first rector of Overwharton Parish, a position he held from 1668 until he was removed from office in 1701. He lived at Overwharton Plantation, originally part of Westmoreland County. A boundary change later placed the property in lower Stafford County and today it is known as Waugh Point in King George County.

If John Waugh left any personal records, they are long since lost. The only information remaining about this fascinating individual is from public records and from the letters of William Fitzhugh, a long-time adversary. Numerous missing records from the courts at Westmoreland, Stafford, and Jamestown, and lost minutes from the House of Burgesses, make the task of piecing together the life and personality of John Waugh even more difficult. Despite this, the parson appears repeatedly in those remaining public records, and it is obvious that he was an unusual individual; the fact that he appears so frequently and the reasons for his appearances make this plain.

John Waugh was an educated man, but an agitator by nature whose preaching was a mixture of evangelism, Puritanism, and politics. He must have been an inspiring orator. He had the unwavering loyalty of most of his parishioners despite his wild notions and despite the fact that he was forced to make frequent public apologies for his behavior. Perhaps due in part to the remoteness of Stafford County, Parson Waugh seems to have done pretty much as he pleased, getting in trouble with authorities on numerous occasions, but nearly always skirting punishment.

One of Parson Waugh's favorite activities—and one which repeatedly resulted in his being called to Jamestown to answer to authorities—was marrying minors. The law required that an impending marriage be announced publicly from the pulpit and that the couple have a license. Minors had to have permission from parents or guardians to marry. Waugh apparently didn't see a need for such technicalities and on August 26, 1674, he married, "Contrary to Law," Restitute Whetstone and Mathew Steele (possibly a cousin of Waugh's) at the home of William Spence on the Nomini River. Restitute was the orphan daughter of John Whetstone, an early Westmoreland justice, and the granddaughter of Major John Hallowes. The marriage took place despite the objections of her guardian, John Appleton. It seems that not only was Restitute underage, but according to Westmoreland County court records, Steele was "a man of noe estate." The records also claim that Waugh married the two "without any Licence and notwithstanding he was forbidden by Captain John Appleton the Said Orphans Guardian and Others Soe to Doe." The court fined Waugh 10,000 pounds of tobacco, describing him as "being of a very Dangerous Consequence." He was also ordered to "not Hereafter marry any Person whatsoever, unless he be Authorized Soe to Doe by the Right Honourable the Governor and shall pay all Captain Appletons Charges both Attorneys fees and Otherwise."

Waugh felt that the penalty imposed was unreasonable, and he petitioned the governor to restore his powers taken away in the Steele-Whetstone incident: "Therefore your Petitioner being a poore man, sorry for my former offences and promising to endeavor to eshune all offences of that nature [I do] humbly begg your Honour's clemency in passing by my former trespasses in restoring your poore petitioner to your execution of his former function, if it may consist with your Honour's pleasure to release your poore petitioner from the rigor of the punishment in paying the great sum of Tobacco which will be the undoing of your petitioner, wife and family."

Apparently, the governor was impressed with Waugh's petition for he wrote that Waugh's "publique fine is remitted and [he] be restored to the exercise of his Ministry in the parish, where he formerly served, the said Waugh paying all costs."

Waugh's humility was short-lived, for in 1688 he married Mary Hathaway, the nine-year-old daughter of Thomas Hathaway of Aquia, to Mr. William Williams. In a suit filed in 1691, Justices ruled that upon reaching the age of twelve years Mary could "publickly disclaim the said marriage and protest against it, then it is the Judgment of this court the aforesaid marriage...is utterly null and void as if the same had never been had or made." On December 28, 1691, Mary declared her freedom citing "infancy and impuberty as well as force and fraud" at the time of her marriage.

In 1688 Parson Waugh became embroiled in political events that nearly caused a war with Maryland. Relations between Catholics and Protestants had deteriorated to the point of open hostility. Waugh had a deep distrust of "papists" and he frequently made Catholicism the focus of his stirring sermons. His fiery speeches became even more fanatical after the Revolution of 1688 in England, when Catholic King James II fled the country, leaving its rule to Protestants.

Despite his profession, John Waugh was the leader of the Whigs in Stafford. He and long-time friend George Mason (II) were able to incite the parishioners nearly to rebellion against the government of Lord Howard of Effingham. Lord Howard was already unpopular in Virginia because he espoused the views of James II. Crowds flocked to hear Waugh's passionate sermons about the "papists" of Maryland who, according to the parson, were going to attack the Protestants of Virginia. The closest Catholic on whom to vent this fanaticism was Waugh's long-time Tory enemy, George Brent (c.1640-1699) of Aquia. Whether Waugh sought merely to run Brent out of the colony or whether he hoped to see him murdered, we will never know. Fortunately for George Brent, he was wealthy, powerful, and well-respected by most of the leaders in the Virginia colony. As the situation climaxed, Brent very nearly lost his life and property to Waugh's mob.

Parson Waugh spoke to his frightened parishioners and described scenarios in which the Catholics had arranged for Indians to cross the Potomac and murder all of the Protestants they could find; as relations between whites and Indians were already tenuous, the whites believed the natives might easily be incited to such violence. Stafford became an armed camp.

Indian hunting parties had long been crossing the river between Maryland and Virginia. After Waugh's fanatical raving however, all reason was lost by Stafford residents. One of the parson's parishioners, Burr Harrison, saw Indians paddling across the Potomac, remembered the warnings of Parson Waugh, and rushed to warn his neighbors, John West and Ralph Platt. Certain that these were the Indians that their Waugh had warned them about, Harrison reported to the Stafford court. He was told to return home and watch the Indians and report back to the court.

In the meantime, Harrison talked to a Piscataway Indian named Wawoostough who said that he had overheard a conversation at Giles Brent's house about the Indians being sent to kill the Protestants. When cooler heads (William Fitzhugh among them) tried to get to the bottom of the affair, they found Wawoostough conveniently murdered.

William Fitzhugh was a confirmed Tory who strongly disapproved of Mason and Waugh. Fitzhugh was also a close friend and business associate of George Brent. In 1690 Fitzhugh wrote a letter to George Luke, his son-in-law in England. Angry over the Catholic incident, Fitzhugh asked Luke to acquaint Lord Howard with the antics of Waugh and Mason, writing:

> I stood in the gap and kept off an approaching rebellion, to my no small charge and trouble, as you fully know, being sending almost everyday for five months together, and writing with mine own hand above three quires of paper to quash the raised stories and settle the panic fears; having my house most part of the time constantly thronged and in daily expectation of being treacherously murdered; for all which charge and trouble I being out, as you know, above £25 sterling, particularly for messengers sent severally

> up and down, besides the purchasing the powder and shot for our men in arms...

John Waugh agitated the people into such a stir that he became a threat to the entire Virginia colony. With English politics in upheaval, Waugh told his followers that there "being no King in England, there is no Government here" and they should remain armed for their own defense.

Although the threat of danger was purely imaginative and the ensuing panic was the direct responsibility of John Waugh, by the end of the affair the parson was perceived as a hero and Fitzhugh a fool. In his letter Fitzhugh to Luke continued to complain, "for all which I thought at least I deserved thanks, if not retaliation, but...I have missed them both; but to be disregarded, nay, and slighted too, and to see those mischievous, active instruments...Waugh and Mason...the only men in favor grates harder than the non payment for shot and other disbursements."

In the same letter, Fitzhugh asked Luke to give Lord Howard his version of what had happened in Stafford: "I thought good to intimate this to you, that you may give my Lord a particular account of that whole affair (wherin his Lordship as you know from those persons missed not his share of the scandall etc.) and fully set forth to him the wickedness of Waugh and Mason etc., the at present, grand favorites, but I hope upon his Lordship's arivall the scene of affairs may be changed."

William Fitzhugh's political influence in the General Assembly was far greater than John Waugh's, and in the end the true story seems to have been revealed. We are able to discern the outcome of this affair as Fitzhugh writes, "The Conclusion of Parson Waugh's business is, He has made a publick and humble acknowledgement in the General Court, by a set form drawn up by the court and ordered there to be be Recorded, and is appointed to do the same in our County Court, as soon as I come home, with a hearty penitence for his former faults and a promised obedience for the future, which he sincerely prays for the accomplishment of and for the sake of his Coat to do so." This seems to have been the end of the affair as far as the public record is concerned.

Waugh had long mixed politics with religion and it seems only natural that he should have aspired to be a burgess. Just ten years after the embarrassing Catholic incident, Waugh ran for that office and as testimony to his popularity among his parishioners, he was elected. His triumph was short-lived, however, because the House decided to disqualify him from membership due to his profession. At the Assembly of 1698 the minutes read:

> At this session of the assembly a greater number of disputed elections than for many years came up for settlement, and one case involving the qualifications of members. This was the case of Mr. John Waugh, a clergyman, returned a burgess from Stafford County. It was voted by the House that his profession disabled him from serving, and a new election was ordered by the governor.

The law in Virginia did not specify that clergymen were not eligible to membership in the House, but in this action the House followed the English custom and also a Virginia precedent of 1653.

One cannot help but wonder if the House followed that precedent because they knew Parson Waugh all too well. Unfortunately, we will never know. On May 4, 1699, the House ordered that Mr. Waugh be informed that he was ineligible to serve and asked the governor to issue a new writ for the election of a burgess for Stafford. That order was carried out and Rice Hooe was elected.

It was not until 1775 that a resolution was adopted which disqualified clergymen from serving as delegates or sitting or voting in a convention. This was viewed as an effort to separate church and state and reflected the political atmosphere of the time. Prior to the Revolution, it was the custom of the House of Burgesses to refuse membership to a member of the clergy although there was no written precedent for it. Waugh was the second clergyman to be refused membership.

In addition to his other problems, Parson Waugh's credit seems also to have been in doubt. A letter from William Fitzhugh to Nicholas Hayward dated July 10, 1690, refers to John Waugh not paying for the property on which he was living. The land in question belonged to Mrs. Meese, widow of Colonel Henry Meese, first burgess of Stafford County. After Colonel Meese's death, Mrs. Meese decided to return to England. She agreed to sell the Potomac Creek property to John Waugh for £120 sterling, which money he was to send to her in England. Mrs. Meese returned to England but the money was never sent. Waugh had been living on the property for eleven years when Mrs. Meese wrote to Fitzhugh, "Since, Sir, it would yield me some money and if Parson Waugh cannot in all this time pay one penny, there's little hopes he ever will be able, therefore I would have you see to some other body, that should be able to pay me something." Fitzhugh wrote of Waugh, "and the truth of which he is never capable of payment." Fitzhugh directed Hayward to act as his agent to purchase the tract so Mrs. Meese could be paid.

When Waugh discovered that Fitzhugh intended to buy the land, he immediately wrote to Mrs. Meese promising to consign tobacco toward the payment of it. Apparently, Waugh finally paid Mrs. Meese for the property, for there is no more mention of it in Fitzhugh's letters.

Parson Waugh made numerous appearances before the Jamestown authorities during his years in Stafford, and he was finally accused of being a "notorious offender" by the Virginia Council. His career ended, however, not as a result of his political agitation but because he persisted in officiating at the marriages of runaways and minors, despite repeated warnings. Missing records undoubtedly contained more references to his illustrious career for by the time his license was finally revoked in 1701, authorities were very familiar with his activities. They had no doubt grown tired of his frequent and eloquent, though meaningless, apologies. His career ended, he retired to Overwharton, his plantation on Potomac Creek. He died in 1706.

Despite his pleas to the governor in 1674 claiming poverty, Waugh managed to amass a great deal of land, including the first lot to be sold in the new town of Marlborough. On May 9, 1700, shortly before his last marriage, he conveyed 2,246 acres of land to his sons, Joseph and John. Parson Waugh died without a will, and his 6,350 acres along with some other land holdings went to his eldest son, Joseph. The year following his father's death, Joseph divided the 6,350-acre estate into five tracts of approximately 1,200 acres each and gave each of his brothers, John, Alexander, and David, an equal one-fifth part of it. The mansion house tract, part of the 6,350 acres, was equally divided between brothers

Joseph and John, the latter therefore inheriting two-fifths of his father's estate. This tract is in present-day King George County and remains known as Waugh Point.

Parson Waugh never fulfilled his dream of being a burgess but his son John did, and he served several two-year terms. The House of Burgesses records list him as a burgess for the Assembly of 1712-1714 along with Henry Fitzhugh. John, however, seems to have had some of his father's qualities because on two occasions the House ordered that John Waugh "be sent for in custody of the Messinger to Answer [his] defaults in not Attending according to [his] Duty the Service of the House." Apparently related to this incident, John wrote a letter to his "Cossin Steele" (probably the husband from the disputed Whitstone-Steele wedding), "I have business depending at the Court but I am afraid I cannot be there by reason that both my horses be gown out into the woods with a company of wild horses and Cannot be gott therefrom. I entreat if you be at Court humbly to crave reference of the business I have depending there." Waugh was sent for in such a manner on two occasions. Unfortunately, gaps in the public records make it impossible to discern the outcomes of these incidents.

Note: Elizabeth Waugh appears in the records as John's wife from 1674 to 1691. She apparently died in the late 1690s and may not have been the mother of his two eldest sons. His last wife was named Christian.

Belle Plain

Parson John Waugh, local rector and political agitator, owned a great deal of land in what are now King George and Stafford Counties. His home was on present-day Waugh Point in King George, but he owned several thousand acres on the south side of the creek, stretching westward into Stafford County. After the parson's death in 1706, the bulk of his estate was inherited by his son, Joseph (c.1660-1727). Joseph married first Rachel Gowry, the only daughter of John Gowry of Belle Plain, and came into ownership of Belle Plain as a result of that union. John Gowry had taken out two patents (in 1709 and 1719) for the lands that made up Belle Plain. Joseph and Rachel had no male heirs. When Joseph died in 1727, the land passed to the Waugh family.

A house was built on Belle Plain by Gowry Waugh (1734-1783), nephew of Joseph and grandson of Parson John Waugh. Gowry seems to have accumulated the most wealth of any of the Waughs. The Stafford County Rent Roll of 1776 lists him as holding 1,570 acres of land. In 1783, the year in which he died, he paid taxes on 39 slaves, 19 horses, and 57 cattle, indicating that he was quite wealthy.

The land on which the Belle Plain house was built is some of the most beautiful in Stafford. Gently rolling hills sweep back from many acres of flat, rich bottom land along Potomac Creek. Land tax records provide some idea of the grandeur of the home. By 1861, when the 1,395-acre farm was owned by L. J. Huffman, the value of the buildings totaled $19,530. Unfortunately, there do not seem to be any existing photographs of the house, which was destroyed during the Civil War.

Gowry's two bachelor sons, George Lee and Robert Turberville Waugh, inherited Belle Plain and lived there until their deaths. Robert died in 1795 and George Lee in 1796, both intestate. After George Lee's death, the property reverted to his next of kin, maternal and paternal relatives. An official surveyor and representatives from both families met at Belle Plain in 1802 to determine a division of the property. After much haggling a settlement was reached, each side receiving one-half of the land. The death of George Lee Waugh brought to a close the name of Waugh in Stafford County. Other members of the family had previously moved to Orange and Culpeper Counties.

Cave's Warehouse

Tobacco was at the heart of the colonial economy and great care was given to the growing, picking, sorting, inspecting, and storing of this plant. One of the most important positions in county government was that of Tobacco Inspector, a position which had to be approved by the House of Burgesses in Williamsburg. Also determined by those in Williamsburg (following an Act of Parliament) was the establishment of official

Cave's Warehouse

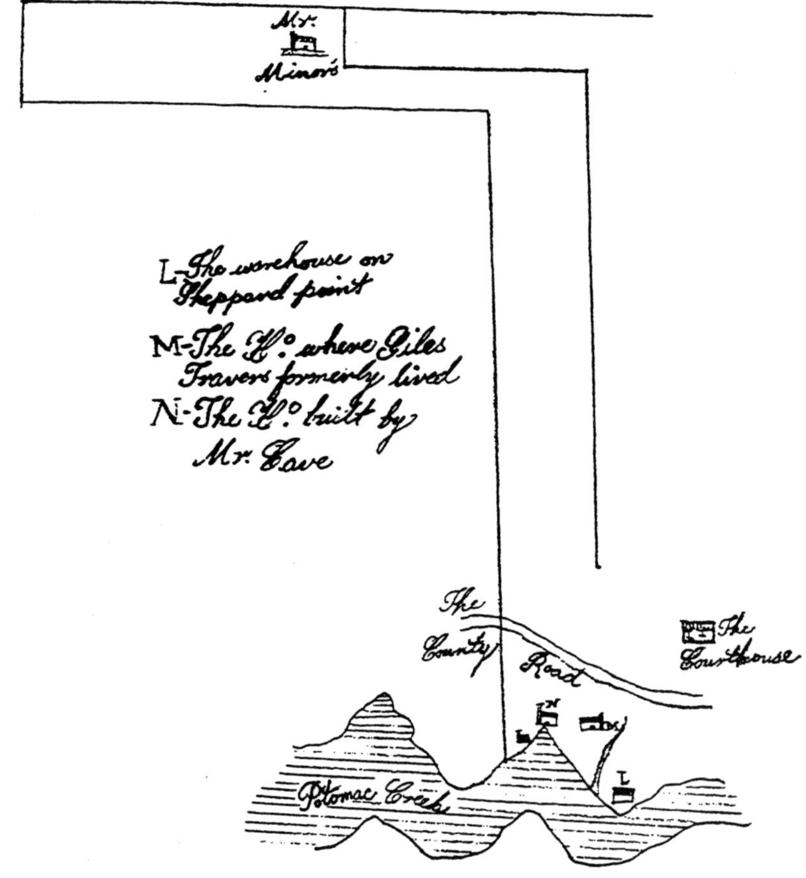

This plat was from a 1743 court case from Fredericksburg and shows not only one of the Potomac Creek court houses but Cave's Warehouse as well.

tobacco warehouses within each county. The purpose of these warehouses was to ensure that the King received his taxes based on the inspections and valuations made by the Tobacco Inspectors. The planter brought his hogsheads of tobacco to the warehouse, where the inspectors checked it thoroughly. If the product met certain well-defined standards, the planter received a receipt for the quantity, and the hogsheads were stored in the warehouse until they were finally exported. At this point the tobacco was considered sold and tobacco receipts circulated as cash, being used to pay for everything from clothing and harnesses to buildings. Receipts often passed through many hands before reaching the merchants who actually exported the tobacco. Dealing in tobacco receipts was not without risk; prices for tobacco were quite steady in times of peace but fluctuated in times of war. The person accepting the receipt during unsettled periods calculated the risks and made his own decisions.

The first official warehouse in Stafford of which we are aware was at Marlborough. This building is mentioned in *Hening's Statutes* in May 1730. By August 1734, due to a shift in the population, the license for that warehouse had been repealed and a new one was ordered built "at or near the head of Acquia...to be settled by the justices of the county." This building was located in present-day Aquia Harbor.

In May 1742 the Burgesses ordered a second warehouse (in addition to the Aquia Warehouse) established on the land of William Cave on Potomac Creek, which came to be known as Cave's Warehouse. This property was located a little upstream from Belle Plain and for many years was a well-known shipping point.

For most of the eighteenth century, Potomac Creek was the population center of Stafford County. The court house was located there as well as businesses, wharves, the tobacco warehouse, and numerous large plantations. The accompanying illustration shows the location of the warehouse in relation to the old court house. Belle Plain is not marked on the plat, but was to the immediate left of Mr. Cave's house. The road marked on the survey was the old "Creekside Road" which followed the south side of Potomac Creek from King George County up the creek towards Brooke and connected Belle Plain, Cave's Warehouse, the court house, and the plantations. Part of that road survives today as an entrance for a small subdivision at Belle Plain. It runs westward from the north side of Belle Plain Road (State Route 604) and is still marked Creekside Road.

On August 5, 1707, John Cave (16??-1721), a carpenter from King and Queen County, had bought 300 acres from Sampson Darrell: "all that 300 acres of land lying on the South side of Potomack Creek in Stafford County bounded...Northerly with Potomac Creek Easterly with the lands of John Gowry, Thomas Gregg & Mr. Waugh southerly & westerly with the land of Giles Travers the 300 acres being one-half of 600 acres formerly sold by Capt. William Heaberd to Capt. John Norgrove by deed dated 6th day March 1667 all which premises are now in the actual possession of John Cave by virtue of one Indenture of Bargain & Sale to him thereof made for the term of one year 120£ Sterling."

John married Elizabeth Travers. In all likelihood, the William Cave mentioned by the 1742 House of Burgesses was the son of John Cave.

Our knowledge of William is sketchy at best. He married Anne Travers, daughter of his neighbor, Giles Travers (16??-1717). Their daughter, Elizabeth, married Keene Withers. William Cave is mentioned in the 1724 tax record as owning one Negro and 1,882 tobacco plants, making him a minor planter. On September 14, 1742, the will of William Cave was presented to the Stafford Court, leaving all his land to his son, James. The 1742 land tax records indicate that his executors paid tax on 800 acres of land.

Cave's Warehouse and Aquia Warehouse were listed in *Hening's Statutes* in October 1748 and October 1765. In October 1776 the Burgesses ordered a naval storehouse built at Cave's Warehouse. This idea met with noticeable resistance from the owner of the surrounding plantation, Andrew Edwards. In 1758 Edwards had married Elizabeth (Cave) Withers, daughter of John Cave. The minutes from the Stafford County Legislative Petitions record that on November 5, 1776,

> Andrew Edwards states that the commissioners for providing for the Navy on Potowmack have thought fit to appoint Cave's as the most convenient place for storing the different commodities for the supplies for the Potowmack

> part of the Navy. This will cause him many inconveniences and impositions.
>
> Cave's is part of the plantation where he and his family lives, and for the conveniency of pasture (being mostly low ground) depends wholly on it for the support of considerable stock, has a valuable orchard on the same ground, which would be under the mercy of lawless and ungovernable people, the men belonging to different ships.
>
> Land must be taken for the building of houses for the reception of commodities purchased, together with a compting house and kitchen. The profit of the rent will not equal the cost of the buildings.

As a final request of the court, he asked that the inspection of tobacco there be stopped.

That same day, James Hunter reported to the court that the Commission of the Navy had contracted with him to store naval supplies and that Cave's would be an excellent location as it was a place not easily accessible by the enemy. He asked permission to use the warehouse there but was rejected.

In October 1778 the Burgesses listed three warehouses in Stafford—Cave's, Aquia, and Falmouth. On November 1, 1779, Andrew Edwards reported to the Stafford Court that the small amount of tobacco brought to Cave's Warehouse for the preceding four years had not exceeded one hundred hogsheads, resulting in the building's being neglected. He asked that inspections be ended there. Mr. Edwards also complained of the public area in the midst of his plantation. A notice appeared the following January in *The Virginia Gazette* announcing that "the inspection established at Cave's warehouse in the county of Stafford shall, from and after the first day of February next be discontinued." What happened to the building after that time is unknown. From that time on, the official warehouses for Stafford County were Aquia and Falmouth.

Salvington

Owners:

pre 1782-1789	Samuel Selden
1790	Samuel Selden's Estate
1796	Ann Selden
1803	Cary Selden
1823	Cary Selden's heirs
1826	Robert O. Grayson
1842	Robert O. Grayson's Estate
1843	Sarah Grayson (Dower)
1850	Samuel Selden Brooke
1854	James M. Scott

Samuel Selden, a lawyer, arrived in Virginia in 1699 and patented a large tract of land located between the junction of Potomac Creek and the Potomac River. High on a hill overlooking the Potomac River he built a fine brick home. This property was inherited by his son, Joseph (died c.1726), who named the farm Salvington after his ancestral home in England. The 1782 tax records show Salvington, then owned by Samuel Selden, probably Joseph's grandson, to have consisted of some 1,700 acres.

This Samuel managed a sizable operation at Salvington as evidenced by the fact that in 1786 he paid taxes on 48 slaves, 17 horses, and 130 cattle. He was also active in county affairs, being appointed in November 1760 sheriff of Stafford and ordered to "collect the Land and pole tax and all other taxes mentioned by law...all Quit Rents, fines, forfeitures, and amerciaments accruing or becoming due to his Majesty...." In 1781 he served as a county justice.

There are very few records remaining to tell about activities at Salvington. After the court house at Marlborough burned, another court house was built on the Salvington property, the foundation of which still exists.

An 1815 insurance policy with the Mutual Assurance Society of Virginia lists the owner of Salvington as Ann Mercer Selden, widow of Samuel Selden (tax records list the owner as

Salvington

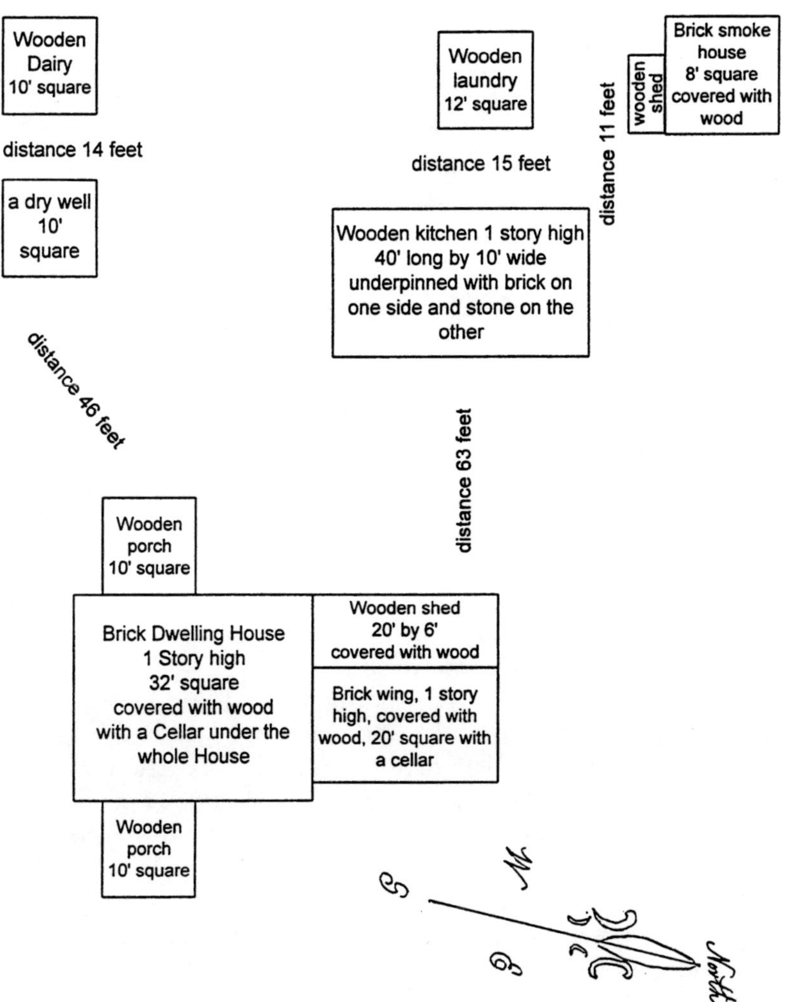

From an 1805 Mutual Assurance policy

Cary Selden). As was the practice of the day, women did not normally own property in their own right. Once widowed, they usually were entitled to a life estate and at the woman's death, the property would be inherited by the eldest son. So it was with Mrs. Selden. She insured two buildings on the farm, the main dwelling house and a kitchen, though from the diagram on the bottom of the policy we know that there were quite a few buildings at Salvington. At the time of the policy, the house was valued at $2,800 and the kitchen at $170.

By the time building values were being listed in the tax records (i.e., in 1817), the house was assessed at $3,000. During the time that Robert and Sarah Grayson owned the property, the house value declined steadily until, by 1841, it was worth only $1,418. This neglect may have been due to the fact that Robert and Sarah do not appear to have lived at Salvington. Robert's place of residence was listed in the records as King George County and Sarah was noted as residing in Alexandria. In 1854 James M. Scott purchased the 814½-acre Salvington farm and made major renovations to the house, increasing its assessed value to $2,500.

Salvington was one of many old houses that did not survive the Civil War. James Scott owned the farm prior to the war, but leased it while living first at Little Whim in Stafford and then at Kenmore in Fredericksburg. Scott was involved in the trading business and had amassed a sizable fortune. He invested most of his money in Confederate bonds; as a result, he lost everything but his land. After the war there was no way to recover the funds and he was destitute.

When Scott's two sons returned to Stafford after the war, they settled at Salvington because there was no house at Pine Grove. All that was left of the house at Salvington was one corner. In an old letter written right after the close of the war, one of the sons described their stretching a canvas across the corner to make a shelter. The once expansive fields were sadly overgrown and they struggled to clear by hand the brush and saplings which had taken over, and plow the root-riddled soil. They finally succeeded in getting a crop in the ground but it was late in the season and the crop didn't have time to mature. With winter coming on and nothing for shelter except their makeshift tent, the Scotts gave up on their plan to reestablish themselves at

Salvington. It was as though all of Stafford had given up and died—crops, people, livestock, even the soil. The Scott brothers tried to sell the property but there were no buyers. As one of the brothers said, he "couldn't get even a nickel an acre for it." Disheartened and poor, the brothers set out for Texas and never returned.

Brooke

The land around the intersection of State Routes 629 and 608 is known as Brooke. This area was named after Captain John Taliaferro Brooke and his descendants, who lived at Mill Vale plantation from the late eighteenth century until shortly after the Civil War. Brooke operated the old Mountjoy's grist mill on Accakeek Creek, which ran through his property. The mill no longer exists but was located just beyond the railroad overpass and in the level area behind the little market called The Trading Post on the north side of State Route 608. Like several other stone buildings in the county, Brooke's (or Mountjoy's) Mill was dismantled earlier in this century and the stone hauled to Washington, D.C., for the building of the National Cathedral.

There has been a railroad station at Brooke since the 1840s, and the presence of the railroad brought a great deal of activity during the Civil War. This stretch of the Richmond, Fredericksburg, and Potomac Railroad formed the main supply route for the Union army for almost four years and there was a Union fortification near Mill Vale to protect it. Defending Confederate batteries were located along Aquia Creek, closer to the terminus of the line at Aquia Landing. During the course of the war, the railroad changed hands between the North and the South some five times and was destroyed and rebuilt each time. In fact, had the Union been unable to control the railhead at Aquia Landing and the line through to Fredericksburg, it is doubtful that they could have overpowered the South.

After the war, the decision was made to extend the tracks northward through Brooke and build a bridge across Aquia Creek to route the trains into Quantico and beyond. Prior to the war, people and goods bound for northern destinations had to

Brooke's Mill

terminate their journey at Aquia Landing and proceed northward on the Potomac River via steamship to Alexandria, Washington, or Baltimore. By moving the line to the north and building a bridge over Aquia Creek, north–south rail travel was uninterrupted. Today, State Route 608 is conspicuously straight because it was built upon the old railroad bed that used to lead to Aquia Landing.

After the Civil War, economic recovery in Stafford was painfully slow. By the turn of the century, however, Brooke boasted tomato and pickle canning factories, three lumber mills, a grain elevator, and several stores. The Depression brought all this to an end, and activities ceased at Brooke as well as in the rest of the county. Not until the 1970s did Brooke, or for that matter the county as a whole, begin to recover from that terrible period of destruction and deprivation caused by the Civil War.

Locust Hill

The Mountjoy family was actively involved in Stafford County government and politics from at least 1686 to about 1792, yet relatively little research on the family has been published.

In the late seventeenth century, four Mountjoy brothers, Thomas from Bristol, England, and John, Edward, and Alvin from St. Peters, Bideston, Wiltshire, immigrated to Virginia and settled in Westmoreland County. Thomas returned to England, John and Edward moved to Stafford, and Alvin established a plantation in Richmond County.

The Mountjoys first appear in Stafford records in 1686 when Edward (d.1712) was given a power of attorney. He appears in county records frequently thereafter, listed as an estate appraiser and in various land transactions. By 1703 he was listed in the militia roll as a captain and also as a Colonial War veteran. His descendants went on to become lawyers, sheriffs, and justices in the county as well as major land owners during the eighteenth century. Most of their land was along Accakeek and Potomac Creeks.

In 1703 Edward Mountjoy patented 940 acres along Accakeek Creek which became known as Locust Hill. The exact boundaries of the grant are unknown; the original patent disappeared years ago and the grant's existence is proved only by mention of it in several deeds. The property was predominantly on the north side of Accakeek Creek, and followed the ridge that runs parallel with Brooke Road (State Route 608) for a distance of nearly two miles. The remains of two Mountjoy cemeteries are located .7 and 1.2 miles southeast, respectively, of the railroad underpass on the north side of State Route 608. The first cemetery (.7 mile from the underpass) contains the grave of Mary Crosby Mountjoy Mauzy Waugh, and probably marks the location of the old Locust Hill site.

John Mountjoy (c.1659-1741) also patented land on Accakeek Creek near that of his brother, though the exact location of the property is unclear. From 1723 to 1741 he was listed in the Quit Rent Rolls as owner of 100 acres. John married Anne Thornton around 1698 and the couple had two children, Sarah and Thomas. Thomas (c.1698-1769), who is probably the Thomas Sr. referred to in William Allason's Falmouth mercantile records, paid taxes on the 100 acres from 1742 to 1776, after which it was inherited by his son Edward (1728-1806). The tract was then inherited by Edward's son, "Blind" Thomas Mountjoy, so named because he was indeed blind.

At about the same time he patented the Accakeek Creek property, Edward also patented another tract on the north fork of the Rappahannock River. In 1705 he built a tobacco warehouse at the mouth of Richland Run, where it flows into the river. This building had the distinction of being the first tobacco warehouse built above the falls of Falmouth. Apparently this was a private warehouse, as the House of Burgesses minutes do not mention the appointment of any official tobacco inspectors there.

In June 1705, Edward acted as attorney for Robert Carter of Lancaster County. Carter had purchased 391 acres on the north side of Potomac Run in March 1705 from Edward Hinson, and Mountjoy was given the job of settling the deal. This was Robert "King" Carter, who was amassing real estate in the backwoods of Virginia with the intention of establishing his sons as land barons on the Rappahannock and Potomac Rivers. He made numerous purchases in Stafford amounting to well over 30,000 acres.

In September of that same year, George Mason sold to Edward Mountjoy 800 acres "on or nigh the head of Accakeek Creek" for 26,000 pounds of tobacco. This land was part of Mason's 1694 grant of 1,150 acres and may have adjoined Locust Hill. Sometime during the early eighteenth century, the Mountjoys built a stone grist mill on the head of Accakeek Creek, the site of which may have been on their grant or on the Mason property; in either case, the two tracts were very close to one another.

Edward continued to serve as a lawyer and to buy and sell land along Potomac Creek. In 1706/7 he was appointed by Nathaniel Hedgman as his attorney, and in that same year he was listed as a vestryman of Overwharton Parish (Potomac Church). In November 1708, town trustees George Mason and William Fitzhugh sold to Edward Mountjoy one lot in the town of Marlborough. It is unknown if he made any use of the lot.

Before 1686/7 Edward Mountjoy married Elizabeth, widow of Major Andrew Monroe of Monroe Creek,

County. He married secondly c.1710 Mary Crosby (16??-1756), daughter of George Crosby of Stafford. Edward and Mary had one son, Captain William Mountjoy (1711-1777), who resided at Locust Hill and became very involved in the affairs of Stafford County.

Edward's will, dated September 6, 1712, ordered that a certain tract of land on Potomac Creek be sold and appointed Mary his executrix. That land, 246 acres of the original 940-acre grant, was sold in June 1723 to John Lomax of Essex County for £40, the money being used to pay Edward's debts. Left with Edward's infant son, Mary married secondly Peter Mauzy, by whom she had issue. Like Edward, Peter died soon after his marriage, leaving Mary with several small children. Mary married thirdly c.1720 the Reverend Joseph Waugh (d.1727) of Belle Plain. His first wife had been Rachel Gowry, daughter of John Gowry.

Captain William Mountjoy resided at Locust Hill and was a considerable land holder in Stafford and adjoining counties. He married Phillis Reilly (1717-1771), daughter of Thomas and Elizabeth Reilly of St. Paul's Parish. They had nine children who lived long enough to be included in their father's will. To son William (1737-1820), he left his dwelling plantation (Locust Hill). To son John (1741-1825), he left 160 acres including the mill (Millvale). To son Alvin (1745-1827), he left 150 acres. Son Thomas (b.1740) received 200 acres. The other children received land in Stafford and Fauquier Counties. Several of the captain's children appear in Stafford County records, including Thomas (b.1740), who acted as Presiding Justice in Stafford. He was still living in 1806, when a deposition given by him listed his age as sixty-six.

Captain William Mountjoy's daughter Elizabeth (b.1751) married James Garrard (1749-1822), son of William Garrard, county lieutenant and proprietor of Garrard's Ordinary (site of the old Stafford Middle School on U.S. Route 1 just north of the court house). James and Elizabeth moved in 1783 to Kentucky, where he later served as governor for two terms.

Captain William Mountjoy and sons Edward (b.1736), William, Thomas, and John appear frequently in the ledger and account books of William Allason, Scotch merchant of Falmouth. Allason, who kept meticulous records, was careful to distinguish between this family and that of a certain Thomas Mountjoy Sr. of Stafford, with whom he also had business transactions.

Captain Mountjoy also appears repeatedly in county records. In 1742 and again in 1750 he was appointed tobacco inspector at Cave's Warehouse near Belle Plain. He served as a vestryman of Overwharton Parish in 1745 and attended Potomac Church, just south of his plantation. He was still a vestryman in 1757.

The Mountjoy family was supportive of the American cause during the Revolution. In 1772 William, Edward, Thomas, and John signed their names to a roster of Virginia magistrates who swore to defy the Stamp Act. A copy of that resolution and the names of those who signed it hangs in the court house at Montross, Virginia.

Three of Captain Mountjoy's sons served in the Revolution as well as in the Stafford militia. Alvin served as a lieutenant in the 3rd Virginia Regiment. Thomas was referred to as "Col. Thomas Mountjoy of the 10th Virginia Regiment" in the pension petitions of war veterans living in Kentucky, but he was listed as a captain in the official register of Revolutionary War veterans. John attained the rank of captain with the 10th Virginia Regiment.

Thomas Mountjoy, son of the captain, and William Garrard were appointed official tobacco inspectors at Cave's Warehouse in 1772. In March of that same year, they petitioned the House of Burgesses stating "that the Quantity of Tobacco brought to the said Inspection is considerably greater than it was formerly; and therefore praying that their Salaries may be increased."

In April 1780 Thomas Mountjoy and Robert Brent were appointed to procure deeds for the new court house (present location). The old court house on Potomac Creek had burned and the county's population had shifted. A petition circulated requesting permission from the Assembly to build a new court house in a place more centrally located for the majority of county residents. This new building was completed in 1783 (see Chapter 7). After the Revolution, Thomas filled the position of Justice for Stafford County from 1782 to 1793. He was also appointed county coroner in 1783 and 1784.

In 1785 Thomas was a vestryman for Overwharton Parish. In that year the House of Burgesses ordered the vestry to inventory the real and personal estate of the parish. Thomas and

John Mountjoy served with Robert Buchan, rector, John R. Peyton, William Garrard, Moses Phillips, Elijah Threlkeld, George Burroughs, and James Withers to make the report. They found that the parish had "235 acres of land worth £15 per annum, 100 acres worth the same, Chalice and plate at Aquia and Potomac, 5½ shillings each."

For the next seven years Thomas Mountjoy served as appraiser, sheriff, court record inspector, road inspector, and election superintendent. The last mention of him in the county records is in July 1792, when he and others were appointed to determine the benefits of reconstructing the stage road so that it would cross Accakeek Creek in a different location.

In 1945 George H. S. King, noted genealogist, located the Locust Hill cemetery seven-tenths of a mile southeast of the railroad underpass at Brooke Station. That year he wrote, "By a large lone cedar in the cornfield of Mrs. Robinson near Brooke Station is the crumbling headstone of Mary Waugh." King notes that a Mountjoy descendent moved the headstone of Captain William Mountjoy and his wife, Phillis, from this same location to St. John's Episcopal Church at King George Court House in order to preserve it. The descendent apparently didn't realize that the field had once been a part of the Mountjoy estate, Locust Hill, or that Mary (Crosby Mountjoy Mauzy) Waugh was actually the mother of Captain William Mountjoy, or he might have moved her stone as well. Captain Mountjoy's stone reads:

To the Memory of
Capt. William Mountjoy
was born the 17 day of
April 1711 and died the
27 of Sept 1777 his
Age 66 Years.
Phillis Mountjoy wife
of William Mountjoy
was born the 15 day
of November 1717
and died the 4 day
of April 1771 hir
age 54 years.

A second Mountjoy cemetery is located one-half mile further east (also on the north side of Brooke Road) and contains among others not identified the remains of John and Thomas Mountjoy, young children of John and Mary Mountjoy. The stones read:

Thomas
son of John and Mary Mountjoy
born August 20, 1760
died December 15, 1767

John
son of John and Mary Mountjoy
born December 15, 1762
died June 29, 1778

These two little boys were the great-grandsons of John Mountjoy the immigrant, rather than of Edward of Locust Hill. John owned 100 acres adjoining his brother Edward's 940-acre grant. The lack of surviving records makes it impossible to know if John received this land as a grant in his own name or if Edward gave him 100 acres on which to live. In any event, it is possible that the cemetery containing the remains of the two children was near John's dwelling house.

The Mountjoys ceased to play a major role in Stafford government and politics after about 1792. Over the course of the eighteenth and nineteenth centuries, Edward Mountjoy's 940-acre grant was divided into numerous smaller tracts, either as a result of death and inheritance or for the purpose of selling parcels for profit. By the early nineteenth century, most of the original grant had been disposed of.

With the exception of William, who inherited the Locust Hill home, all of Captain Mountjoy's sons moved to Kentucky after the Revolution, their parcels of the original Locust Hill tract being sold to various individuals. William died in 1820 and the Locust Hill home passed to his wife. In 1836 the property left the Mountjoy family when it was sold to Charnock Cox. From then on, descendants of the Mountjoy family were concentrated along the north side of Aquia Creek. In 1943 the Quantico Marine Corps Base was expanded to include some 30,000 acres on the north side of the creek, forcing the family to move again, many to Prince William County.

Mill Vale

Mill Vale was part of Edward Mountjoy's (d.1712) grant of 1703 called Locust Hill (see preceding article). Locust Hill was inherited by Edward's son, Captain William Mountjoy (1711-1777) who, at his death, divided the property between his four sons. John (1741-1825) inherited the 160-acre Mill Vale tract which included Mountjoy's Mill. He married Mary Ann Garrard (1753-1823), sister of James Garrard (see "Hartwood Baptist Meeting House" in Chapter 11), who married John's sister, Elizabeth. During the American Revolution, John served as a captain with the 10th Virginia Regiment.

John moved to Kentucky after the Revolution, arriving there sometime before February 1799. Mill Vale was sold to John Taliaferro Brooke (1763-1821) and his wife, Ann Cary Selden, of Salvington. There is no surviving deed to provide any detail about this transaction; in fact, the only record of the sale is in a letter from Peter Vivian Daniel of Crow's Nest, dated November 12, 1855, in which he lists the land owners along Potomac Creek and mentions the sale of Mill Vale to Brooke.

Brooke was active in local and state affairs. He attained the rank of major during the Revolution and from 1793 to 1806 was several times a member of the Virginia House of Delegates and Senate. He also served as a Stafford County Justice.

John Brooke increased the acreage of his farm by purchasing other tracts which adjoined Mill Vale. A deed dated September 12, 1813 records Brooke's purchase of three tracts, the first consisting of 102 acres bought from James Holliday, who had acquired it from William Brown; a second parcel adjoining the first, consisting of 107 acres, also sold by Holliday, who had acquired it from Allen Jones; a third tract adjoining the first two which was one-tenth part of the land left by Peter Mauzy to his ten children. Brooke had previously purchased the other nine-tenths of the Mauzy land, which amounted to about 190 acres. Brooke's various purchases totaled about 400 acres.

Mill Vale

Wooden
Smoke
House
12' square

distance 56 feet

Wooden
Kitchen
16' by 12'

Cellar
6' by 4'

distance 58 feet

Wooden Dwelling House
one Story high
with a hipped roof,
underpinned with stone 2 ½ feet
above the surface of the ground,
with a Cellar under the whole
house. This part is 32' by 16 ½'

This part
is 1
story
high and
not hip
roofed.

This part is 1
story high with
a hipped roof,
all wood,
underpinned
with stone 2 ½
feet above the
surface of the
ground with a
Cellar. 26 ½'
long by 16'
wide.

Portico
26' long
by 7 ½'
wide.

From an 1805 Mutual Assurance policy

Brooke put himself deeply in debt purchasing the farm, mill, and adjoining property. He no doubt believed that the mill would pay for itself and crops produced on the farm would pay the mortgage. Unfortunately, he died just a few years after he established his farm and his creditors were left with no recourse but foreclosure.

In 1825 Mill Vale was sold at public auction on the steps of the court house to satisfy the debts of John Taliaferro Brooke. John's son, Samuel Selden Brooke Sr., was the highest bidder, paying $3,147.16 for the farm and mill.

Samuel apparently struggled with debt just as his father had done and he, too, died deeply in debt. After his death about 1870, his real estate was divided between his heirs, including a "Store House at Brooke's Station together with fifty acres of Land" which was left to Samuel Selden Brooke Jr., and the "old Homestead" which was allotted to daughter Louisa S. Brooke. Samuel and Louisa exchanged these parcels by deed, recorded in January 1871.

In May of that same year, the court appointed a commissioner to sell the mill and six acres belonging to the estate of Samuel Selden Brooke Sr., deceased. This property was sold at public auction on the steps of the court house, the highest bidder being Samuel Jr., who paid $1,820 for it.

Samuel Jr., like his father and grandfather before him, found himself overwhelmed with debt. The economic collapse which followed the Civil War made it impossible to earn enough money to pay bills incurred prior to the war. In May 1871, Samuel Jr. took out a deed of trust on the mill and six acres; unfortunately he was unable to repay it. In October of that same year, a New York land speculator named George Barker bought the mill for $1,500 from trustee A. W. Wallace. The deed stated that the sale of the mill was to satisfy debts still owed by the estate of Samuel Brooke Sr. Financial conditions in Stafford remained dismal. Unable to pay the mortgage on their farm, Samuel Jr. and his wife, Bettie, sold their home and 85 acres in June 1875. The purchaser was again George Barker and he paid Brooke $2,250 and assumed the debt of $5,114 remaining on the farm.

The grist mill and large rambling frame farmhouse at Mill Vale were undoubtedly built by the Mountjoys, though Brooke may have enlarged the house. An 1805 Mutual Assurance Society policy taken out by Brooke shows a substantial building that appears to have been constructed in stages. The home was located about 200 yards east of the old railroad station at Brooke, and on the south side of State Route 608. The mill was located just a few hundred yards east of the house and very close to the road. Judging from the tax records, by 1882 the house was gone, for no building value was listed. At that point, the 185-acre tract had changed hands again and belonged to A. B. Maxwin, a northern land speculator who owned several tracts along Potomac Creek.

The Colonial Silk Industry

Silk! The very word conjures up images of the Orient, of luxurious royal robes, of the shimmering, incomparable fabric that can only be made by little caterpillars. Silk was a highly-prized commodity in seventeenth-century Europe. France had been so successful in starting her own silk industry that within just fifty years silk had become a major source of wealth and power. Nothing would have delighted Charles II of England more than having a source of silk in his own colonies.

Experimentation with silkworm farming began in Virginia in the late 1630s. In 1661 the Governor and Council of Virginia sent the King a gift of silk. So delighted was Charles with this present that he sent to the colony silkworms from his own stock as well as eggs from France, Spain, and Italy. Unfortunately, the Virginia colonists were too concerned with day-to-day survival to put much effort into silkworm culture.

Virginia Ferrar of Huntingdonshire, England, was fascinated with silkworms and did numerous experiments which led to her publishing an article on silkworm culture. She was certain that silkworms could flourish in Virginia because of the abundance of mulberry trees there. It was Miss Ferrar who discovered that the worms did not have to be kept inside and fed on hand-picked leaves. She noticed that her eggs hatched in May, just as the mulberry tree outside her window was sprouting its first leaves. She carried a few of the worms to the tree and they immediately began feeding. After forty days, the worms on the tree were much larger than the ones she had fed in her bedroom.

The outside worms then spun their cocoons right on the tree. The implications of this for the colonies were tremendous. Theoretically, silkworms could be raised with nothing more than a few mulberry trees. The cover of Miss Ferrar's article read

> A speedy way, and easie means, found out by a young Lady in England she having made full proof thereof in May, Anno 1652. For the feeding of Silk-worms in the Woods, on the Mulberry-Tree-leaves in Virginia: Who after fourty dayes time, present their most rich golden-coloured silken Fleece, to the instant wonderful enriching of all the planters there, requiring from them neither cost, labour, or hindrance in any of their other employments whatsoever.

In the Virginia colony, silk production was encouraged by two Royal Governors. Sir William Berkeley (1606-1677) served four terms as Governor of Virginia between the years 1641 and 1677, though those terms were not consecutive. During his administrations, he sought to advance the economic welfare of Virginia by introducing the cultivation of a variety of new products, especially silk, which he hoped would displace the exclusive reliance of the colony on tobacco growing.

Edward Digges (1620-1675) served as Governor from 1655 to 1656. During his administration, he reported that he had produced seven or eight pounds of silk from 400 pounds of cocoons. In 1655 the Assembly passed a law requiring each planter in the colony to plant ten mulberry trees for every hundred acres he owned. Members of the Assembly saw a two-fold purpose in encouraging the production of silk. The first, obviously, was to produce for the mother country something that she could not produce in great quantities for herself and had to import from elsewhere. The second purpose was to try to become less dependent upon tobacco. The entire economy of the colony was based upon this one crop and the members recognized the danger in this: a bad year could be ruinous for the colony. A second major industry would lessen the effects of a bad tobacco year.

In 1858 the Assembly offered a bounty of 5,000 pounds of tobacco for the first person who produced 100 pounds of wound silk. No one seems to have claimed the prize, for the following year the Assembly offered 10,000 pounds of tobacco for the first person to produce fifty pounds of wound silk.

It was not until 1660 that the industry showed possibilities of success; it was in this season that a gift of silk was presented to Charles. In his letter of appreciation to the silk farmers, the King indicated that he would have the silk made into garments, and it is possible that he wore the silk at his coronation in April of 1661.

Governor Berkeley, seeing great possibilities in the silk industry, continued to encourage the Virginia planters to plant mulberry trees. He was so encouraged by the progress being made in that direction that in 1665 he predicted an annual output of 100,000 pounds of silk once the mulberry trees matured.

In 1666 the planters were able to send the King 300 pounds of silk, and the future of the industry seemed assured. Two years later they sent a similar amount. Digges, who had been away in England for some time, returned to the colony and was named Auditor General in recognition of his work encouraging the silk trade. Unfortunately, Digges died in 1675 and Bacon's Rebellion erupted the following year. Although the uprising ended in failure for the rebels, the result was Berkeley's recall to England. With the loss of both Digges and Berkeley, the industry began to decline. Tobacco again became the chief crop and by the end of the century, silk was all but forgotten.

The law requiring the planting of mulberry trees applied to the entire colony. In Stafford County, Thomas Ludwell Lee (1730-1798) attempted to produce silk on his plantation, called Berry Hill. The property had been acquired by purchase in 1741 by Thomas' father, Thomas Lee of Stratford Hall. George King wrote in his notes (available in the Virginia Historical Society library) that he had always heard that Berry Hill took its name from the fact that Thomas Ludwell had planted the entire property with mulberry trees upon which his silk worms fed, and that for years he had attempted to produce silk. Other planters dabbled in silk as well; William Fitzhugh of Chatham was very interested in experimental farming, including silk production. The Brents, Wallers, Withers, Fowkes, and Carters also tried their hands with silk worms. The silk worms did not flourish in Virginia, however, and despite years of dedicated effort, silk production never progressed beyond the experimental stage. The Potomac–Accakeek Creek area, however, still has quite a few mulberry trees, descendants of the Lee plantings!

Thomas Sr. did not live at Berry Hill; rather, he lived just across Potomac Creek at another plantation called Bellview. His son, Thomas Ludwell Lee Jr. (died c.1808), resided at Berry Hill for many years before moving to Fauquier County around 1796.

On 21 July 1806, Thomas Ludwell Lee Jr. and his wife Fanny Carter Lee of Coton, Loudoun County, sold 700 acres of Berry Hill to James Hore for $1,700, "being all that part of said tract of land that lies above what is called the neck road running through the said land."

The remaining 300 acres of Berry Hill left the Lee family on 20 September 1810. Fanny, acting as executrix of Thomas' estate, was authorized to sell certain lands "and particularly the remainder or residue of a tract of land...known by the name of Berry Hill." Thomas Fitzhugh of Boscobel paid Fanny $4,000 for the property.

Based upon county land tax records, Thomas F. Knox acquired Berry Hill sometime between 1810 and 1812. Knox died in 1839, and the 391-acre farm was sold to Potomac Silk and Agriculture Company of Fredericksburg. They did nothing in the way of new construction until 1854, when the value of Berry Hill buildings increased from $756.32 to $2,500. Something happened in 1860, most likely a fire, because the building value suddenly dropped to $150. We do not know who was involved in the Potomac Silk Company. George Gordon believes that there was a resurgence of interest in silk manufacture partly because the old planting of mulberry trees was likely still living. Unfortunately, no records of the company seem to remain and no mention of its activities or its farm appears in local newspapers.

Bellview

This historic though little-known plantation was on the south side of Potomac Creek adjoining the western edge of Belle Plain. Today, the property lies on the north (left) side of State

Route 604, on the hill overlooking the great flak fields of Bell Plain. A modern government communications installation has been built on the property and is visible from State Route 604.

Bellview was the residence of Thomas Ludwell Lee Sr. (1730-1798). Thomas was born at Stratford Hall in Westmoreland County, the son of Thomas (1690-1750) and Hannah Lee. His brothers were Francis Lightfoot and Richard Henry Lee, signers of the Declaration of Independence, and Philip Ludwell Lee, master of Stratford Hall.

As a young man, Thomas decided to pursue a career in law and he went to London, where he studied at the Inner Temple for five years. During this time, his father died, but Thomas did not return to American until about 1756. His inherited portion of his father's estate was property in Stafford, the Berry Hill and Bellview plantations. Upon his arrival in Virginia from England, Thomas promptly moved to Bellview. He married pretty Mary Aylett and quickly became a leader in Virginia politics, known for his commitment to American independence and personal liberty.

Thomas Ludwell Lee was a private person and preferred the solitude of backwoods Stafford County to the bustle of lower Northern Neck. As a result, his contributions to America's struggle for independence and to the organization of Virginia's new state government have been largely forgotten. Thomas was a contemporary of Patrick Henry, George Washington, George Mason, and John Mercer. Mason, Mercer, and Lee formed a brilliant trio which played a vital role in the shaping of our country during the turbulent Revolutionary period. Thomas was highly respected and admired by his contemporaries in all levels of politics and society. John Adams claimed that Thomas Ludwell Lee was "the most popular man in Virginia, and the delight of the eyes of every Virginian."

In 1758 Thomas represented Stafford in the House of Burgesses along with his brothers Richard Henry from Westmoreland and Frank from Loudoun. By 1775 tensions between the colonies and England were fast reaching a crisis stage. During the conventions of July and December of that year, Thomas used his influence to push the House of Burgesses to accept independence as the price for preserving liberty. According to Paul Nagel in his *The Lees of Virginia*, "Without Thomas Ludwell Lee's work the cautious majority of Virginia politicians might not have been held in line to support American independence, or to back a new constitution for Virginia and a declaration of human rights."

After the Revolution, Thomas was appointed one of five "revisers" charged with revising colonial laws and organizing the new Virginia state government. He was also one of five judges elected to sit on Virginia's supreme court.

Virginia lost a true statesman with Thomas Ludwell Lee's untimely death in 1798. He died at Bellview after suffering from rheumatic fever for six weeks.

The will of Thomas Ludwell Lee was recorded in Stafford in a now-lost will book. Reference to the will, however, is made in a deed between his widow, Mary Aylett Lee, and their son, Thomas Ludwell Jr. (died c.1808). According to the deed, Thomas left his landed estate to Mary and directed her to dispose of it as she saw fit. She deeded 450 acres of Bellview to Thomas Jr. "whereon the said Thomas Ludwell Lee formerly lived."

Little else is known about Bellview. Thomas Ludwell Lee Jr. sold his Stafford property and moved to Coton in Loudoun County. Both Bellview and Berry Hill were bought, sold, and divided many times and, over time, forgotten.

Boscobel

Owners:

1658 6,000 acres patented by Thomas Wilkinson

1668 Tract inherited by Wilkinson's wife, Anne, who later married James Goodall

1687 Inherited by William Thomas (husband of Hannah Goodall)

1692 Conveyed to William Fitzhugh (died c.1714)

1701 Inherited by Henry Fitzhugh (1686-1758) of Bedford, son of William the colonist (c.1651-1701)

1758 3,000 acres conveyed to Henry Fitzhugh's son, Henry, as a wedding gift, excepting 500 acres containing a house (Boscobel) belonging to Thomas Fitzhugh (1725-1788)

1768 Inherited by Thomas Fitzhugh (1760-1820)

1820 John R. Fitzhugh

Boscobel

1823 Charles E. S. Fitzhugh
1842 Sold to Sarah S., Catherine R., and Henrietta Fitzhugh for $5,600
1854 Sarah and Henrietta Fitzhugh sold the property to William Henry Fitzhugh, their brother. They held a life estate.
1866 William Fitzhugh Jr. and William Little, partners and brothers-in-law, divided the property (765 acres). The house and corn crib went to William and Louisa Little (400 acres). Mrs. Little was a Fitzhugh.
1898 Conveyed to William Little Jr. as a wedding gift
1900 Conveyed to Duff Green as trustee for Jessie Sharpe Little (520 acres)
1901 Sold to Charles A. Hurkamp

Thomas Fitzhugh built his large frame house on a high ridge between the Potomac and Rappahannock Rivers, a short distance from Fredericksburg. Boscobel was long known as one of the most gracious homes in Stafford County. The Fitzhughs had extensive land holdings throughout Virginia and their hospitality was known far and wide.

Boscobel

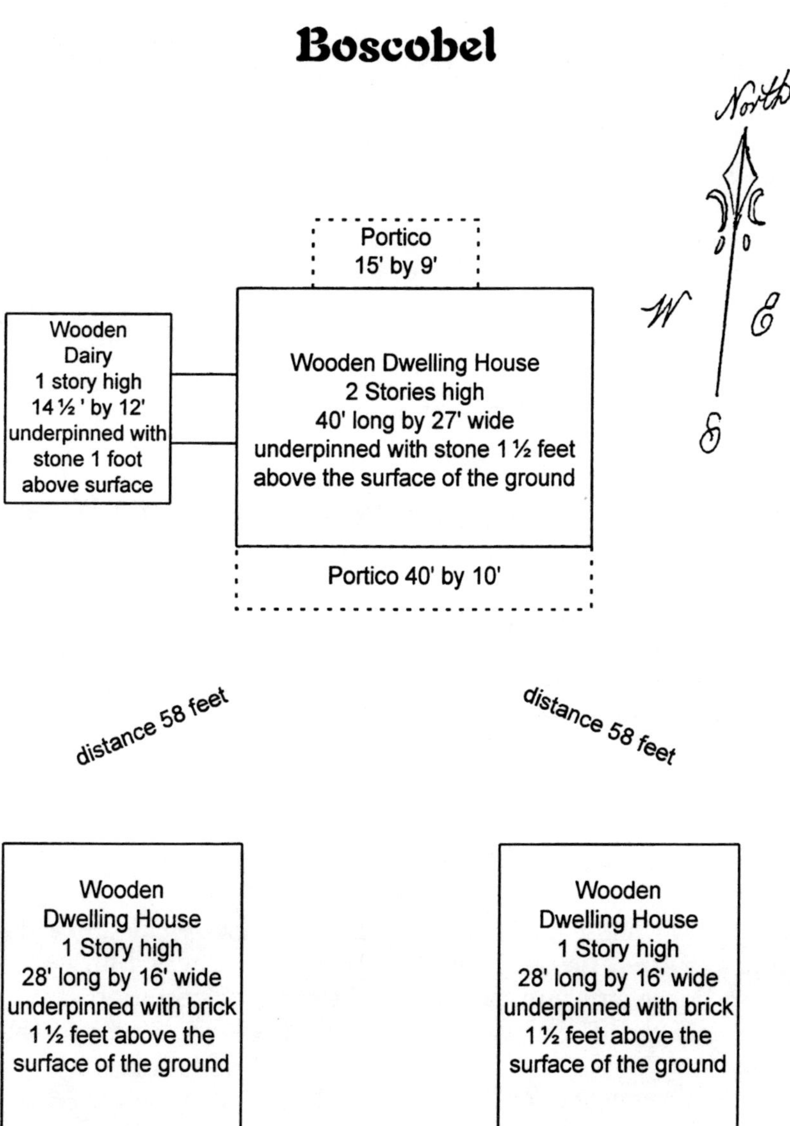

From an 1805 Mutual Assurance policy

The only remaining remnant of Boscobel is a fireback inscribed "T. F. 1752" which probably commemorates the date of building. There were eleven rooms in the house, seven on the first floor and four on the second. Nearby were large flower and fruit gardens supplying mint, berries, figs, and all sorts of stone fruits. The lawn was beautifully landscaped and included the formal gardens so popular in the eighteenth century.

Insurance policies often reveal a great deal about the activities on the old farms. An 1803 insurance policy from the Mutual Assurance Society of Virginia lists two dwelling houses and a kitchen at Boscobel. Two years later, a new policy shows two dwelling houses and a little wooden dairy to the west of the house. Oddly, the dairy was connected to the house's west chimney. Another unfinished dwelling house was located to the east of the main house. On a later policy, dated 1816, Fitzhugh insured a stone grist mill. Twenty-four by twenty feet, it was valued at $1,000. A mill house was located approximately thirty feet from the mill.

Boscobel managed to survive the Civil War, but burned in 1915. Until that time, the farm had the distinction of being one of the few homes in this part of Virginia to have remained in the hands of the descendants of the original builders, and for nearly a century and a half. The farm has now been subdivided and is known as Boscobel Farms.

Woodbourne

The house presently standing on this lovely old farm is the third built on the site. The first Woodbourne was a little two-story frame structure typical of late eighteenth-century homes in the county. The property was owned at that time by John Moncure IV.

Sometime prior to the Civil War, a larger two-story section was added to the east end of the original house. Overlooking beautiful fields, this addition was similar in design to The Fleurry's and was built at about the same time. There were three windows across the front on the second floor. Judging from a photograph in the possession of the owners, there may have been a half-story above the second floor; the gabled room was certainly steep enough to allow for such a half-story. A small porch at the front door added an air of hospitality.

Shortly after the war, the nineteenth-century addition burned. An almost identical replacement was built upon the same foundation. Photographs of both structures indicate that the major differences between the two were a slightly steeper roof on the original and two chimneys on the replacement as opposed to one on the original.

The present owners, Mr. and Mrs. Turner Ashby Blackburn, tell a story about his grandmother, who was faced with marauding Yankee soldiers. When Union troops marched onto Woodbourne, they spied the meathouse and decided to help themselves. She was just as decided that they should not take what did not belong to them. She barricaded the door to the meathouse with her own body. The soldiers were gentlemen enough not to hurt her. They simply began removing the weatherboarding from the building. In the end, she gave up and the soldiers took the meat.

The first meathouse deteriorated sometime along the way and another outbuilding nearer to the kitchen became the meathouse. This was a charming little frame building with a steeply-gabled, shingled roof. In the attic portion was a pigeon cote. Under the house was a little stone-walled cellar used as a dairy and accessed by way of about a half-dozen steep stone steps. The walls in the dairy had been constructed so that wooden shelves could be placed on stones protruding from each corner. The dairy was deep enough to remain cool even during the hottest summer. Being below the freeze line, vegetables could be stored there all winter without freezing.

The original eighteenth-century kitchen survived both house fires and is the oldest building still standing on the property. Unlike the house and other outbuildings which had been covered with horizontal weatherboarding, the kitchen is of vertical board and batten. This building continued to be used as a kitchen until the late 1940s when a modern kitchen was installed in the main house.

The quaint little building has only one room. There are two windows, one on the north side and one on the south. The north window was originally covered with oil cloth and had a single shutter to cover the entire window. Unlike many early kitchens which had huge fireplaces, this kitchen had a small fireplace and for many years the cooking was done on a wood stove which sat in front of the fireplace.

Valley View

Owners:

Thomas Seddon
The Green family
1880 Manuel Johnson
Inherited by his daughter, Sally Johnson Gray.

The original house at Valley View was replaced in 1850 by a one and one-half story log house that had a large stone chimney in the center. It was built on a rock outcropping. About twenty steps from the house was the kitchen, also made of logs. The house had only four windows and the interior walls were whitewashed.

Manuel Johnson's parents had been slaves of Charles Tackett. Manuel was born at the mill and was also a slave. He was not obedient and Tackett sold him at auction; he was sent south where he stayed until Emancipation. He returned to Stafford, lived near Brooke and, in 1880, bought the farm where he lived until his death.

Laurel Wood

Very little is known about this house which was located 1.5 miles west of the court house on State Route 630 and one-tenth of a mile south on a private road. The property was first owned by Thomas Gasconine, who changed his name to Thomas Gaskin. In 1850 the property was purchased by Armstead Nelson, who built a house there. This was a frame structure, one and one-half stories high with a shed room on the west side. A sandstone chimney was built on the south end. The house had four rooms with plastered walls.

Oakley

Located near Shackleford's Well, once a well-known Stafford landmark, Oakley was a lovely farm. The frame house boasted exceptionally beautiful wide wainscoting in some of the rooms, and the woodwork was of foxtail pine. Throughout the first half of the nineteenth century, the house was assessed at $2,000.

It is unknown how many houses preceded the present one at Oakley. During the eighteenth century, the land belonged to Robert "King" Carter, and his son Charles inherited it as part of 13,000 acres in Stafford. Sometime prior to 1776 Thomas Skinker (b.1729) bought 1,021 acres from Charles Carter which included Oakley. It is likely his grandson Samuel who is listed as owner when the surviving land tax records begin in 1782; this Samuel owned the property until 1856 when it was inherited by Margaret W. Skinker, who owned it until after the Civil War. The size of the farm remained 1,000 acres until Margaret's inheritance, at which point it was reduced to 650 acres. Today the gently rolling fields of Oakley provide pasturage for herds of cattle, much as they did 200 years ago. Sadly, the house has been allowed to decay and there is little hope of restoring it.

Shackleford's Well was located on the left side of Poplar Road (State Route 616) right in the corner created by the intersection of Shackleford's Well Road (State Route 754). Prior to the Civil War, Poplar Road was the major north–south route through the county and travelers could stop at "Shack's Well" to water their horses and mules.

Oakenwold

Owners:

1850 John Moncure
1858 William A. and Mary E. Nelson (she was the daughter of John Moncure)
1861 Willed back to John Moncure
1869 Purchased by Powhatan Moncure

1908 Willed to Powhatan's son, Frank D. Moncure
1936 Inherited by Hallie Chichester Moncure
1947 Deeded to McCarty Chichester Moncure

This quaint old farmhouse was built in 1850 in a beautiful grove of large oak trees. Mr. John Moncure, owner of Ravenswood (discussed later), built the house for his daughter and her husband on a tract of land which was originally a part of Chestnut Hill (discussed later). It is likely that he bought the land from the owners of Chestnut Hill in order to build the house.

The two and one-half story frame building was originally roofed with shingles but was later re-roofed with tin. There are two large brick chimneys with huge fireplaces, and the front entrance is through an unusually large door secured on the inside with a bar; this door also has a large iron lock with brass knob. There are six rooms with eight-foot ceilings. The stairway is attractive and each flight has a landing.

During the Civil War, a regiment of Federal troops camped on the lawn of Oakenwold. This was their headquarters for several weeks before and during the Battle of Fredericksburg. There is a large stone atop a hill near the house, and the soldiers carved their names and some graffiti in it.

Today, the house is in fine condition, though numerous additions have been built, dismantled, and rebuilt. Near the house are a corn crib, school house, and kitchen, an interesting feature of which is the chimney. The ground floor of the little building is divided into two rooms; the chimney divides the rooms and there is a fireplace on each side. On the second floor above the kitchen is a room used as a servants' quarters.

The beautiful flat fields of Oakenwold border Interstate 95 on the west side of the north-bound lanes.

Ravenswood

This old farm occupied the land between present-day U.S. Route 1 and Interstate 95 on the south side of Potomac Creek, and adjoined the east side of Oakenwold. The road back to the house is still visible on the west side of Route 1, two-tenths of a mile south of the bridge over Potomac Creek.

Ravenswood was one of the oldest homes in this part of Stafford and one of the loveliest. Very little is known about the farm and the only known description is from an 1854 advertisement for the sale of the property. The ad states that the farm consisted of 611 acres. The house and outbuildings were described as follows:

> Brick Dwelling House, and kitchen, overseer's house, Negro houses, ice house, barn, stables, carriage house, granary, and other outhouses; also a first-rate Grist Mill in complete order, and three dwelling houses...

Mr. McCarty Moncure, father of the present owner of Ravenswood and Oakenwold, remembered playing around the old house as a child. He said that it was three stories high and, in design, reminded him of Kenmore in Fredericksburg.

Mr. Moncure's grandfather, one of the John Moncures, lived at Ravenswood until the outbreak of the Civil War. Like most Stafford families, the Moncures left their home during the war. Union troops moved into the house and carried out all of the Moncure possessions (their piano was recently found in an old home in Pennsylvania). The house was heavily damaged and never reoccupied.

A unique feature of the Ravenswood house was that it had running water. The house was built at the foot of a hill and a pipe was run to the house from a spring flowing from the hill. No pump was needed as gravity served to move the water from the spring to the house.

The grist mill mentioned in the 1854 advertisement was built of stone quarried from the farm. There are several sandstone outcroppings on the tops of the numerous hills nearby (this same stone was used to build several of the newer stone buildings along present-day U.S. Route 1). Water to run the mill was diverted from Potomac Creek. A mill race nearly one mile long was dug by hand and is still visible today.

During the 1920s, when the National Cathedral in Washington was being built, men traveled to areas around the capitol city looking for brick and stone for use in the building. They found a ready supply in Stafford, and all of the brick from Ravenswood as well as the stone in the mill and ice house were sold and used in the Cathedral's construction.

Chestnut Hill

This odd old house was occupied by at least 1790 and the first documented owner was John Wallace, who served in the Revolution. The property stayed in the Wallace family for many generations before being purchased by Edgar Armstrong in 1930.

Chestnut Hill was to the west of Oakenwold and was an unusual stone structure with walls about three feet thick. The house was taller than it was wide or deep and seemed to explode out of the hill on which it was built. There were three floors above an English basement, so that on the downhill side it stood nearly four stories tall! Like Ravenswood, there was a good supply of sandstone on the property which provided building material. Family legend maintains that German stonemasons were hired to build the house.

The main entrance to the house was on the second floor, which was accessed via a massive sandstone stairway. The first floor of the house was slightly below the ground and to enter this level, one had to go down several stairs which were located underneath the main sandstone stairway.

The house's floor plan was simple. There were three large rooms, one right above the other. A tiny twisting interior stairway led from one floor to the next. There was a simple frame addition on the back.

One very unique feature of Chestnut Hill is that it housed Stafford County's first built-in bathtub with running water. People came from all around to see Mr. Armstrong's tub. A pipe ran directly from the tub to a spring on the side of a hill near the house. By simply turning a knob, water would flow into the tub. A plug in the bottom of the tub emptied the water, which was piped outside and then ran down the hill. Bathing would have been a chilling experience, no doubt, but that doesn't seem to have mattered, for the tub was the talk of the county.

George Gordon tells a story about John Wallace of Chestnut Hill at about the turn of the twentieth century. It seems that Mr. Wallace was out with some hired help working in his field one day. He looked down the hill and saw a large group of people dressed as though they were going to church. Curious as to why they were all dressed up on a weekday, he sent one of the field hands to ask them what was going on. The worker came running back to Mr. Wallace, obviously distressed. Panting, he reported, "Mr. Wallace, those folks are all dressed up because they're on their way to Aquia Church for your wedding! You're getting married today!"

John Wallace had been so intent upon his farming that he'd forgotten his own wedding. Panicked, he dropped his tools in the field and raced to the house to change. Although late, he made it to the church and the field work had to wait until another day.

After the sale of the Oakenwold tract in the 1850s, the owners of Chestnut Hill built an enormous stone addition on the front of the house. Unfortunately, the Civil War broke out shortly afterward and the owners had little time to enjoy their work. Union soldiers invaded the area and camped at Chestnut Hill as well as on most of the neighboring farms. Most male residents enlisted in the army and it was unsafe for the women, children, old, and infirm to remain in their homes, surrounded by enemy soldiers. Recently, a fire destroyed what little wood was left in the building, and today there is nothing remaining of Oakenwold but a shell.

Carmora

Carmora was a sizable plantation which bordered Oakenwold on the north and east. Very little is known about the farm except that it belonged to the Moncures for many years and was considered quite old at the time of the Civil War.

In 1860 John Moncure sold Carmora to Thomas Seddon for $6,000. Seddon was to pay $3,000 in cash, and the remaining $3,000 in three annual payments. This was an inopportune time to invest a large sum of money but, of course, during the early days of the war, no one expected it to last more than a few weeks.

Carmora

From an 1839 survey.

That same year Seddon sold the farm to Thomas Lee. In 1861 Carmora was purchased by Charles Herndon, who bought a great deal of acreage in Stafford County during the early years of the Civil War. Herndon seems to have been involved in the banking business in Fredericksburg and hoped to make money by purchasing cheap land in Stafford. Unfortunately, the Southern economy collapsed and Herndon lost everything. In November 1868 Carmora was sold at public auction. An advertisement for the sale describes the house as "a fine large Dwelling with good Out Houses."

Unlike many Stafford homes, Carmora was not destroyed during the war. However, during the 1920s vandals stripped out every piece of woodwork and carried it away. Quite a few houses suffered from this sort of vandalism because so many of them were never reoccupied after 1865.

The accompanying plat was copied from an 1839 survey completed for John Moncure.

The house site can still be seen today, though the last vestiges of the building are gone. Driving south on Interstate 95, the house was located to the west of the highway on the last hill before the land drops into the flats of Potomac Creek. The interstate was built right through the heart of the farm.

Fitzhugh's Accakeek Farm

Owners:

Parson John Waugh
Purchased by Richard Foote and others

1730 Purchased by Henry Fitzhugh of Bedford (1686-1758)

1755 Inherited by Henry Fitzhugh (1723-1783). His son, Henry (1750-1777) predeceased him and in 1783 the property was inherited by the grandson, Henry (1773-1850).

1800 Purchased by Joseph English of Fauquier County

c.1818 Sold to Hugh Atcheson who died c.1830. His wife, Sarah, had a life estate. At her death, the property went to Louisa Atcheson Stevens and her brother, Henry. Louisa was the mother of R. H. Stevens, who lived in the house until his death.

This property, located at the end of Jumping Branch Road, once extended all the way to Accakeek Creek. During the eighteenth century, the farm contained about 630 acres. Unlike many other Stafford homeplaces, this farm does not appear to have had a name. The various owners have simply referred to it as "the Accakeek farm" or "the Accakeek property."

Though located in a remote area of the county today, the farm was once in the mainstream of travel. The Potomac Church Road bisected the farm and served as the principle route to Fredericksburg.

For many years, the property was owned by the Fitzhughs. They owned many thousands of acres in Stafford, King George, Orange, Caroline, and Fauquier Counties. Two other Fitzhugh farms in Stafford were Chatham (discussed in Chapter 10) and Boscobel (discussed earlier).

There were a great number of Fitzhugh children, though it is not known if any Fitzhughs actually lived on the Accakeek farm. A common practice of the day was to own several farms and rent them out. Unfortunately, no records remain to indicate who actually lived on the property.

Judging from the construction, it is likely that the oldest part of the house is at least eighteenth century. There is, however, nothing to further indicate when the house was built or who built it.

During the Civil War, the house on this farm served as a Union hospital. Most likely, it was this occupation which preserved the old place, for most buildings not used by Federal troops were destroyed by them.

There is a cemetery near the house containing many graves; most have unmarked stones. Family tradition states that there are Union soldiers buried in the yard and, within this century, a very rainy spell exposed bones there.

Today, the house has been carefully restored. Far from the hustle of U.S. Route 1, the farm maintains an air of the past.

Hickory Hill

Owners:

	The first owner is not known.
1860 or '65	Owned by a Mrs. Turner

1865 or '66 Purchased by Mr. Monroe Stevens. He willed it to his grandson, John M. Stevens.

Hickory Hill is beautifully situated on a hill and surrounded by large weeping willow trees. At one time the house was shaded by hickory trees, hence the name. The construction is unusual for Stafford County; the house has three stories, a hip roof, and is rectangular. The roof was originally covered with cypress shingles, now with tin. There was a chimney at each end until the south chimney fell and was replaced with a flue.

Most of the timbers in the building are marked with Roman numerals. When there were not enough large trees suitable for constructing the framework for a house near the building site, the builders would find large timber elsewhere, cut and hew the logs, and drill them for the pegs. The frame would be assembled right there, where the trees were cut. Once the frame was completed, each timber would be inscribed with a number and the whole thing would be disassembled, moved to the building site, and reassembled using the numbers as guides.

The house has five rooms, including a small one over the hall called the office room. This room had shelving on the walls; the walls of the other rooms are plastered. The hall is eight feet wide and there is a three-flight stairway.

During the Civil War, a family by the name of Turner lived here. Union troops were camped on the adjacent farm and Mrs. Turner kept all her poultry and possessions hidden in the cellar. One day Mrs. Turner heard her geese making a commotion. Rushing to the door, she saw several soldiers coming out of the cellar carrying her geese. She grabbed her quilting frame and beat the soldiers saying, "Put them geese back in the cellar!" They obliged.

Park

Owners:

pre 1810-1819 John B. Cutting
1820 Landon Carter
1823 John T. Lomax

1836	Thomas Smith
1840	John T. Lomax
1841	Gould Phinney
1843	George Latham
1843	Thomas Seddon's Estate
1846	Joshua Reamy
1858	Fanny Reamy

Park, also known as Parke or Parke Quarter, was another tract of land belonging to the Carter family. In 1741 Landon Carter inherited the property from his brother George, who had inherited it from their father Robert. Landon frequently mentioned activities at "Parke Quarter" in his journals. A later descendant of Landon, also named Landon, owned the farm for a while.

A one and one-half story house was built about 1778 and had four large rooms, though it is unknown how many dwellings may have preceded it. A wide center hall divided the rooms. This building was torn down in 1912. Behind the house was a lovely park that had stone seats.

The "Parke Quarter" was roughly bounded by what is today State Route 612 on the west and State Route 662 on the south; its eastern edge nearly reached State Route 616 on the east. Potomac Run flowed through the farm.

By the time Joshua Reamy purchased Park in 1846, the farm consisted of 906 acres. After Reamy's death, the property was divided into numerous smaller parcels, though the general outline of the old farm can still be seen on the modern tax maps.

Additional Sites

Black Castle—probably adjoined Mount Pleasant. In 1861 the property was owned by Gus Wallace Jr.

Chadwell—at the intersection of State Route 628 (American Legion Road) and U.S. Route 1, on the south side of 628. Also known as the Embrey tract.

Cherry Hill—on the ridge on the north side of Brooke Road (State Route 608). This ridge runs parallel to the road nearly to Aquia Landing and had several farms which straddled it. The closest home to the modern railroad underpass was Locust Hill (see article this chapter). Adjoining Locust Hill to the east was Cherry Hill. It is likely that this was the old glebe for Potomac Church as it is here that Parson John Waugh was buried. The old house site is high upon the hill overlooking Accakeek Creek to the south and Aquia Creek to the north. To the south of the house, the land drops sharply towards Accakeek Creek. The land to the north, east, and west of the house, however, is relatively level.

Fairview

Ludlow—Landon Carter inherited this property from his father, Robert "King" Carter. Landon lived there for many years and often signed official documents "Landon Carter of Ludlow." The farm is today known as Enniskillen and lies on the northwest side of State Route 648 and the east side of State Route 616.

Oakland—on Potomac Run. Prior to the Civil War, this was owned by John Seddon.

Paint Ridge—near Accakeek Run. At the time of the Civil War, this tract belonged to Henry Conway.

Potomac Chapel—on the east side of State Route 616 at the intersection of State Route 662.

Ragged and Tough—the area on the south side of Potomac Run, part of which was inundated by Abel Reservoir.

Rose Hill—old Hedgman home. The original house was built on the ridge overlooking Accakeek Creek on the north and Potomac Creek on the south.

Salem—adjoined Cherry Hill on the east and occupied the area between State Routes 608 and 630.

Selwood—adjoined Crow's Nest to the west. It may have been a Hedgman home. An advertisement in the *Free Lance-Star* in 1888 described Selwood as "1,586 acres situated between Accakeek Creek on the north and Potomac Creek on the south, by the lands of Gus Wallace, deceased, on the east and the lands of P. V. D. Conway and others on the west...Some 1,000 acres in wood and timber convenient for transportation by water."

Shepherd's Green—during the nineteenth century, this property was owned by Henry S. Brooke.

Sherbourne—From the 1840s until the Civil War, this property belonged to John R. Fitzhugh, who also owned Ravenswood in the 1850s. After the war, Sherbourne became part of Glencairne. Later, Drew Middle School was built on part of the property, as well as Jefferson Town Houses and the old Brown's Motor Court across U.S. Route 1 from Drew School.

Windsor—adjoined Selwood to the west. It may also have been a Hedgman home.

Woodcutting—the area north and west of Ramoth Church. Cordwood was cut here from the mid-eighteenth century on.

Rappahannock

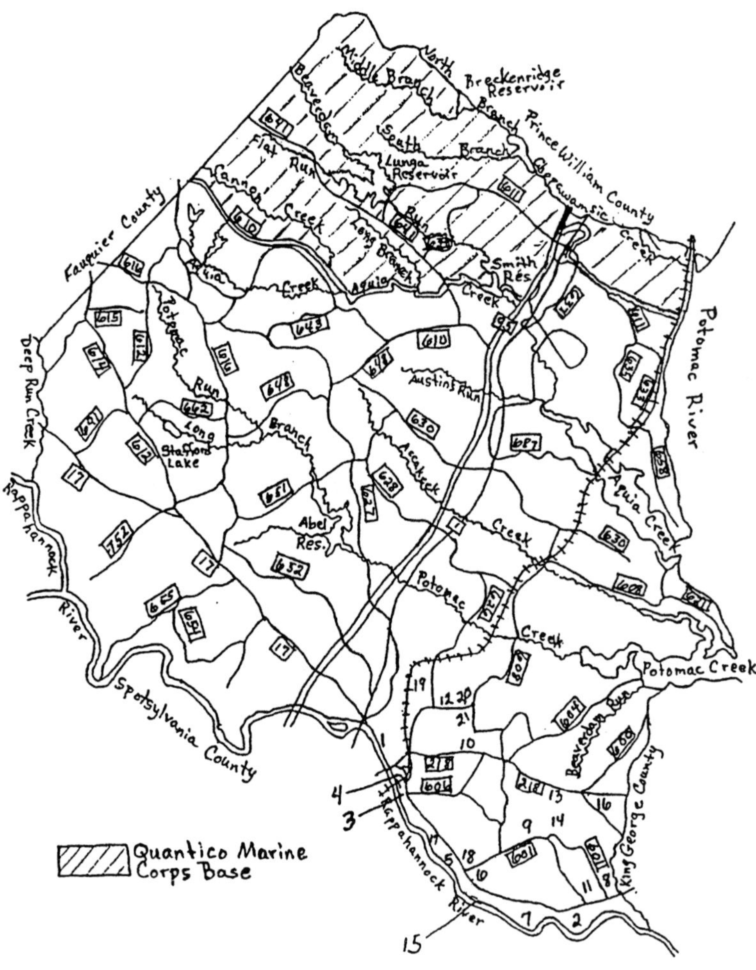

1 .. Chatham
2 .. Snowden
3 .. Ferry Farm
4 .. Pine Grove
5 .. Traveler's Rest
6 .. Sherwood Forest
7 .. Albion
8 .. Muddy Creek Church
9 .. Eastwood
10 .. Little Whim
11 .. Hollywood
12 .. Highland Home
13 .. White Oak Primitive Baptist Church
14 .. Monitieth Home
15 .. Little Falls
16 .. Chapel Green
17 .. Rumford
18 .. Little Falls Mill
19 .. Mount Pleasant

Chapter 10

The Rappahannock River East of Falmouth

🙜 🙞

The Rappahannock

There were many lovely homes built east of Falmouth along what is now State Route 3. We are fortunate that quite a few of these places have survived to the present day, among them Chatham, Sherwood Forest, Albion, and Eastwood. When these homes were first built, many had commanding views of the Rappahannock River. The land rises sharply from the river, providing lovely building sites. Sherwood Forest sits back from the river on the north side of the road, high upon a hill. From the front lawn one overlooks miles of countryside, the river, and Fredericksburg.

The road that we know today as State Route 3 east of Falmouth was, in George Washington's time, called the Great Road or "the road from King George Court House to Stafford." At intervals along the Great Road, smaller roads ran south to ferry landings on the Rappahannock. Two of these landings were at Albion and Ferry Farm, and they provided travelers with transportation from Stafford to Spotsylvania and Fredericksburg. The ferries were heavily used during the eighteenth and early nineteenth centuries, as the first bridge between Stafford and Fredericksburg wasn't completed until 1823.

Grants issued for land along the Rappahannock were some of the largest and the earliest in the county, predated only by patents on the Potomac River. Unfortunately, many of these grants have been lost or were so vaguely worded as to make it impossible to determine the exact boundaries of the tracts. Looking at a county road map, though, it is possible to still "see" the boundaries of some of these early grants. Several of the roads, including State Routes 601 and 603, run away from the river and outline the perimeters of ancient grants such as Sherwood Forest from which were cut Traveler's Rest, Eastwood, Little Falls, and other farms as well.

Most of those who settled along the Rappahannock were fairly wealthy and their plantations were large. Enormous brick homes were built at Chatham, Snowden, Hollywood, and Salvington, and even the less pretentious frame houses, were grand by comparison to the average dwelling in eighteenth-century Stafford.

Today, State Route 3 has been widened to four lanes from the Chatham Bridge over the Rappahannock and eastward, well into King George County. Yet, this part of Stafford retains a rural air and numerous large farms survive as remnants of the vast tracts patented in the seventeenth century. With the help of the Chesapeake Bay Act, which limits development in wetlands and along riverbanks, perhaps this historic corner of Stafford will survive into the twenty-first century largely unchanged.

Snowden

Owners:

1670	John and George Mott
1673	William Thornton
c.1677	Rowland Thornton
	Conveyed to grandson Rowland Thornton by will
	Inherited by Sarah Bruce Thornton Casson
	Inherited by daughter Sarah Bruce Casson Alexander
	Inherited by Ann Casson Alexander
	The property remained in the Alexander family until the death of Captain William Pearson Alexander in 1804.
1805-1824	Alexander Morson

1828-1844	Susan Morson
1845-1847	Arthur and Alexander Morson
1848-1849	Hugh Morson
1849-after the Civil War	John Seddon
1882	Purchased by William A. Little

Originally, Snowden was part of 15,654 acres granted to John and George Mott in 1670. In 1673 the Mott brothers sold 2,000 acres of their patent to William Thornton of Gloucester County. Two years later, Thornton divided the land equally between his two sons, Major Francis Thornton (1651-1726), whose half became Hollywood, and Rowland Thornton (1654-before 1701), whose half became Snowden. From this point on, the chain of ownership becomes confusing. Rowland's share descended to his grandson, also named Rowland. This Rowland married Sarah Bruce but died without male issue. Sarah inherited the property and married secondly Thomas Casson. No son survived this marriage so the 1,000-acre Snowden tract passed to their daughter, Sarah Bruce Casson, who married William Alexander. William was the son of John Alexander (1735-1775), who had married Lucy Thornton (17??-1781), the only daughter of William Thornton and great-granddaughter of Major Francis Thornton (of Hollywood), making William and Sarah cousins. By this marriage, Hollywood and Snowden were united.

In 1659 John Alexander came to Virginia from Scotland and quickly began acquiring land. By 1666 he was listed as a vestryman of Potomac Church, and by 1668 he owned over 6,400 acres in Stafford and Westmoreland Counties. It is unknown when John Alexander married Lucy Thornton.

The daughter of Sarah and William Alexander, Ann Casson Alexander (1781-1831), inherited the Snowden property after her brother's death in 1804. She married Alexander Morson (1759-1822), son of a wealthy Falmouth merchant. Alexander became master of Hollywood, though it is unclear if he purchased the property or if it passed to him by way of his marriage to Ann. Morson also bought several other large tracts of land in the same area, making him one of the larger land owners in Stafford.

Undoubtedly, there were houses on Snowden in the late seventeenth century, but the first one that we can document

Snowden

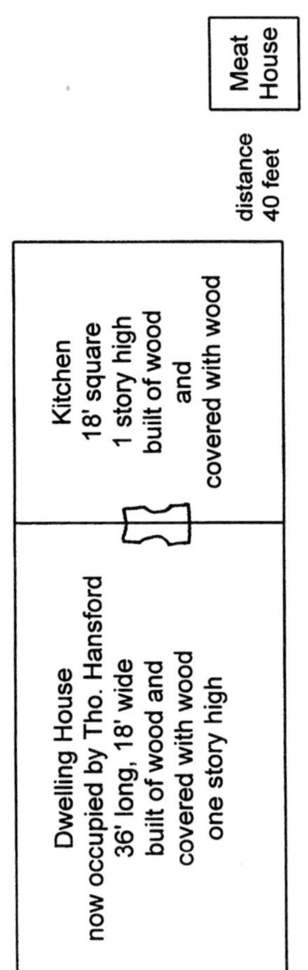

From a 1796 Mutual Assurance policy

appears on a 1796 insurance policy. This was not a large house in comparison to later homes in the area, but it must be remembered that early in the county's history, even wealthy people lived in simple homes. The 1796 Mutual Assurance Society of Virginia policy for this building shows a diagram of a basic one-story frame house. It is interesting to note that the diagram shows the kitchen attached to the house. At this time the house was valued at $700 and the meathouse at $200.

This building was destroyed and a second small house was built on the foundation. Succeeding owners made substantial additions to the house. By the time the tax records began listing building values in 1817, the house was worth $2,500. Alexander Morson added considerable acreage to the estate, increasing its size to 1,039 acres.

Susan Morson inherited the farm in 1828 and the house value declined (probably due to neglect or fire damage) until by 1845 it was assessed at only $756.

In 1849 the property was purchased by John Seddon, later a major in the Confederate Army. He enlarged the house dramatically, resulting in an increase in the building assessment from $800 to $5,000 in 1853. By 1857 the house was valued at $10,000. By the outbreak of the Civil War, Snowden and Chatham (also assessed at $10,000), were the two most valuable homes in Stafford County.

During the war, Union troops sailing up the river mistakenly believed Snowden to be the home of John's brother James Seddon (1815-1880), Secretary of War for the Confederacy. From the river, the ships opened fire on the house and the Seddons had only moments to get out. They took shelter in the laundry building, from where they watched their home burn to the foundation.

James Seddon resigned as Secretary of War in 1865. As the Confederacy fell, he was arrested and imprisoned by the Northern government, but quickly released. According to his son, Judge James A. Seddon Jr. of St. Louis, his father "was completely crushed by the collapse of the Southern Confederacy and considered his life to have been a complete failure." Seddon returned to his Goochland estate, Sabot Hill, where for many years before his death he was an invalid.

In 1882 the 397½-acre Snowden tract was purchased by William A. Little from John Seddon's estate. Tax records list a small house valued at $300.

Unfortunately, there are no known pictures of Snowden. The present house dates from the 1940s. It was the desire of the last owner, Katherine Gouldin Woods, a Gray descendant, that the Snowden property be given to a non-profit organization and not developed. Despite her wishes, the court overruled her will and, in 1996, this magnificent farm was sold at public auction to a developer.

Hollywood

Owners:

1670	John and George Mott
1673	William Thornton (born c.1620) of Gloucester County
1675	Major Francis Thornton
	William Thornton (1649-1727)
	Lucy Thornton Alexander
	John Alexander
	William Alexander
pre 1782-1822	Alexander Morson, who married Ann C. Alexander
1822-1827	Alexander Morson's heirs
1828-1851	Ann C. Morson's heirs
1852	Colonel Thomas Purkins
1937	Mr. N. S. Greenlaw, grandson of Colonel Purkins

Hollywood was a large tract of land which swept back from the Rappahannock on the far south-eastern corner of the county. The land was part of a 15,654-acre patent taken out by John and George Mott on October 17, 1670. In 1673 the Mott brothers sold 2,000 acres of their patent to William Thornton (born c.1620) of Gloucester County. Two years later, Thornton divided the 2,000 acres equally between his two youngest sons, Major Francis Thornton (1651-1726) and Rowland Thornton (1654-before 1701). Rowland's share became Snowden and Francis' share became Hollywood. The two tracts descended through the Thornton family for many generations.

An 1827 survey of Snowden and Hollywood

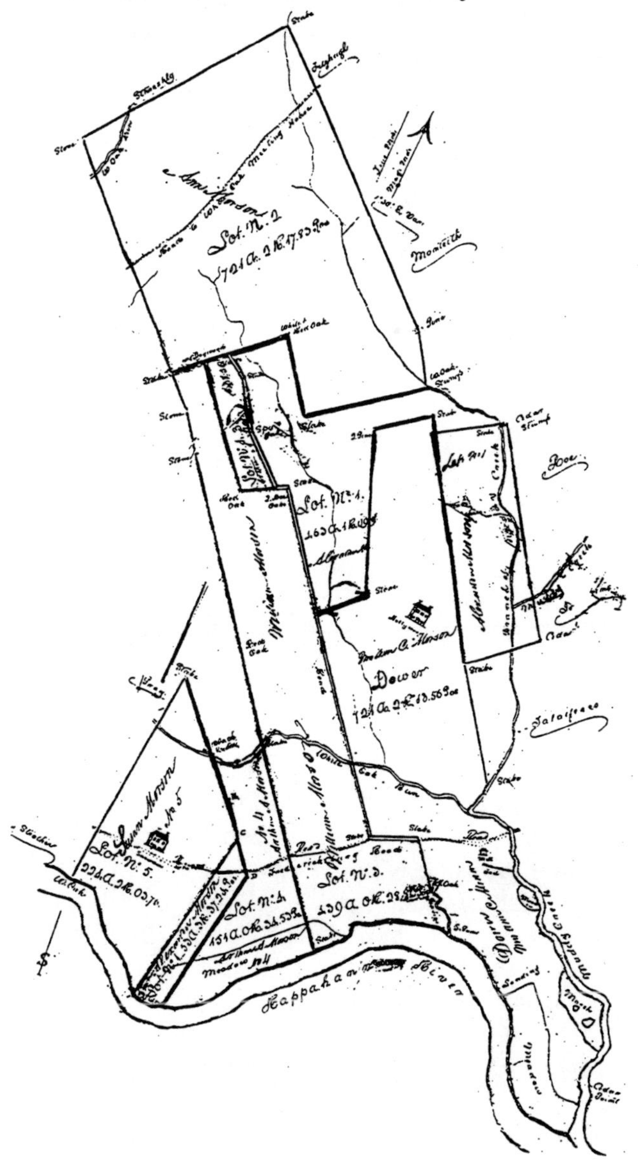

Francis Thornton's property descended to his grandson, William, who died without male issue, thereby passing the property in its entirety to his only daughter, Lucy (17??-1781), who married John Alexander (1735-1775). John was a major land owner in the colony and his land near Mount Vernon later became part of the city of Alexandria. After John's death, the property was inherited by William Alexander of Snowden, whose daughter, Ann Casson (1781-1831), married Alexander Morson in 1800. Due to a lack of records, it is impossible to determine if Morson became owner of Hollywood as a result of his marriage to Ann (a descendant of the Thorntons and John Alexander) or if he bought the property.

It was likely Alexander Morson (1759-1822) who built the house at Hollywood. This was an impressive structure, built of large, seven-pound bricks in the latter part of the eighteenth century, and was destroyed by fire in 1889. Larger than most houses in Stafford, it measured 54' by 36', just five feet shorter than Kenmore in Fredericksburg. The house was two stories high and had a basement beneath it. There were two brick and stone chimneys on the ends and from the southwest lawn there was a beautiful view of the Rappahannock River. A lane flanked by cedars led to the house.

Hollywood was a typical eighteenth-century Virginia plantation which featured a manor house flanked by dependencies. Today, only one of the dependencies remains. It may have originally been a laundry, kitchen, or office, but it was long ago converted into a dwelling and remains so today. This 19' by 36' brick building faced the side of the main house which stood about 100 feet away. There is a large brick chimney on each end and one door and one window on the front. The 13-inch thick walls are of Flemish bond brick work and probably matched the brick work of the main house. The original brick floor has been covered with wood. A dogleg stairway leads upstairs to what may have been living quarters for eighteenth-century domestic staff.

This must have been an impressive house, for in 1813 an insurance policy quoted its replacement value at $8,000. In 1817 when the first building values were listed in the tax records, the house was assessed at $6,000.

Alexander Morson was the son of Arthur Morson (1734/5-1798), a wealthy Scotch merchant in Falmouth. Alexander was a partner with his father in the mercantile business and was well-to-do in his own right, owning both Hollywood and Snowden. After his father's death in 1798, Alexander gave up the Falmouth store. Trade was declining in Falmouth as a result of silting of the seaport and depressed economic conditions of the early nineteenth century. After retiring from the mercantile business, Alexander turned his attentions to agriculture. Like his father, he was involved in county affairs, serving as High Sheriff of Stafford.

His extensive final inventory (recorded in Stafford County court records) of March 20, 1823, lists him as owning 51 slaves at Hollywood and 10 at Snowden. That same inventory provides us with a glimpse inside the old Hollywood house, as the inventory was listed room by room. The inventory includes a dining room and passage, a chamber, a drawing room, a small back room downstairs, a big room upstairs, a passage upstairs, a blue room upstairs, a boys' room, a library room, a cellar, and a kitchen. The inventory of the Morson library fills over two pages in the will book and includes books on astronomy, history, religion, grammar, chemistry, philosophy, medicine, geography, biography, farming, mathematics, gardening, Greek, French, law, Shakespeare, poetry, and surveying, as well as works of fiction. Also included on the Hollywood inventory were 12 oxen, 49 hogs, 9 horses, 14 sheep, and 43 cattle. Alexander also owned stock in the Bank of Virginia, the Farmers Bank of Virginia, the Union Manufacturing Company of Maryland, and the Rappahannock Bridge Company. The appraisers noted, however, that due to the depressed nature of the stocks at the time of the inventory, it was impossible to determine a value for them.

Ann Morson died in 1831. During the time Hollywood belonged to her heirs, it seems to have been sadly neglected; the 1840 reassessment lowered its value to $4,727. By 1851 the assessment had returned to $6,000, where it remained until the outbreak of the Civil War.

The Hollywood tract contained 1,137 acres when it was purchased by Colonel Purkins in 1852. The Purkins cemetery is located about twenty-five yards north of the house site. It was a large cemetery but as of January 1937, only ten of the graves were marked.

Albion

This home is located five and one-half miles east of Fredericksburg and is presently owned by Hunter Greenlaw Jr. Through the years, Albion has been a part of four counties: Old Rappahannock (1656-1692), Richmond (1692-1721), King George (1721-1777), and Stafford (1777-present).

The present house at Albion dates from the first half of the eighteenth century, though there was undoubtedly an earlier house on or near the present one. The present house began as a simple frame structure over a stone basement. A stairway leads from the basement to an upper room and a hall; beneath a steep roof with dormers is another small room. Carved into the bare wood of the stairway is the date, January 10, 1719.

Albion was part of a 1670 patent of over 15,000 acres to John and George Mott. The Motts divided their patent into numerous tracts, some of which they sold. The parcel which later became known as Albion was sold to the Kenyon family and from them it passed by way of marriage and inheritance to the Strothers. It is nearly impossible to track the Albion acreage accurately; the property was divided between daughters who intermarried and their portions were added to later purchases which adjoined previous divisions.

Abraham Kenyon (died 1750) inherited at least part of the tract bought from the Motts. He appears to have lived at Albion, though not necessarily on the part of the farm that includes the present house. Court records show that Kenyon was ordered to "keep the roads in repair" in 1724. Abraham and his wife, Elizabeth Waddington (whose parents also lived on part of the Mott-Kenyon purchase), had six daughters who each inherited one-sixth of the 300-acre farm. Daughter Elizabeth married Captain Anthony Strother (1736-1790), son of Anthony (1710-1765) and Behethland (Storke) Strother, who lived in the present house.

About 1739 William Thornton (who had inherited another parcel of the old Mott patent which adjoined the Kenyon property) conveyed to Anthony and Behethland Strother 259 acres below the falls of the Rappahannock. The property already included a small house (the oldest part of the present structure). Strother enlarged the house, adding a two-story wing. The addition included a central hall flanked up and down by a large room, each with its own fireplace. Outbuildings included a kitchen, smoke house, log barns, and slave quarters. The Strothers called their home Albion because the cliffs above the river reminded them of the white cliffs of England.

Anthony Strother (1710-1765) was the brother of Captain William Strother (c.1700-1732) of Pine Grove (see article this chapter) and was a Fredericksburg merchant. He was also a close friend of Augustine Washington and witnessed his will. Augustine added a codicil to the will, stating "and whereas, some proposals have been made by Mr. Anthony Strother for purchasing a piece of land...if my executors shall think it best for my son George, that I empower them to make conveyance of said land and promises to said Strother." As a result of the codicil, 134 acres were added to Albion.

During the time that Anthony lived at Albion, the main north–south road ran past his house to a ferry that transported travelers across the Rappahannock to Spotsylvania County. The next closest crossing was east of Albion at George Washington's Ferry Farm.

The Strother family occupied Albion from 1739 to at least the mid-1800s. The house and land sold at public auction in 1871 to Hanson Thomas, though several Strother sisters seem to have continued to live there after the sale. Albion was sold again in 1894. In 1907 the property was purchased by N. S. Greenlaw, who never lived there. In 1942 Hunter Greenlaw purchased Albion.

The house has been altered through the years but is still a weatherboarded farmhouse with a stone basement. As a note of interest, George Washington is said to have courted Mildred Strother of Albion. She refused his proposal of marriage because, like many other ladies of her day, she did not believe that a country surveyor would ever amount to much.

Muddy Creek Church

This was another very early church in the county. It was built ten miles east of Falmouth and west of Muddy Creek, about 200 feet north of King's Highway (State Route 3). It was a small frame building constructed between 1700 and 1745. It burned in 1748 or '50. Until the Stafford–King George boundary changes of 1777, this church was situated in King George County and was part of Brunswick Parish, as were Union Church in Falmouth and Yellow Chapel in the Hartwood area.

Several marked graves survive, though the church disappeared many years ago. Among the grave stones is the following:

> *Here lyieth the body of Mr. George Mayers, late of Whitehaven, who departed this life the 5th of October, 1755. Aged 42 years. "Waiting for a joyful resurrection."*

Others buried here include Ann Gailsrih (d.1749), Sarah Gailsrih (no date), Daniel Dickinson (d.1746), and the Reverend Daniel McDonald (d.1762).

Sherwood Forest

Owners:

1667 Grant to William Ball and Thomas Chetwood, 1,600 acres

1668 Thomas and Elizabeth Chetwood convey all their interests to William Ball

1680 William Ball divides the property in his will between his two sons, William and Joseph, each receiving 800 acres.

1711 Mary Ball inherits 400 acres from her father, Colonel Joseph Ball

1778 Mrs. Mary Ball Washington conveys the 400 acres to her son, John Augustine Washington

1787 John Augustine Washington wills the 400 acres to his son, Bushrod Washington

Sherwood Forest

1790 Bushrod and Ann Washington convey the property to Joseph Ball Downman
1800 Inherited by Jane E. Downman, daughter of Joseph Ball Downman
1867 Henry Fitzhugh and his wife, Jane E. Downman, convey the 400 acres to William S. Barton
1879 Conveyed to C. B. Morton
1881 Conveyed to William F. Hart
1900 William F. Hart wills the estate to his wife, Bernice, and their children. The Harts' daughter, Grace Hart Greenlaw, and her husband, Robert Hunter Greenlaw, lived there a short while before moving to Albion.
1928 Purchased by John Lee Pratt
1961 Purchased by Hunter and Mary Louise Greenlaw
1987 Sold to a developer

During the eighteenth century, Sherwood Forest was one of the largest tracts of land in the county and continues to hold that status today. The house is located on a lovely hill overlooking the Rappahannock River. The property is bordered on the lower side by what was known as the Judyville Farm, which was originally part of Traveler's Rest. Although the property changed hands some seven times before the nineteenth century, there does not seem to have been a house built until about 1810.

The house is a two-and-one-half story rectangular brick structure with a slate hip roof. Double brick chimneys grace each end of the house, impressing upon passersby the importance of the residents. There are eighteen windows, and porches on the south and west sides. Entrance is through a double door into a center hall which runs straight through the house. A large structure, it houses ten rooms with eight foot ceilings, plastered walls, random width floors, and large mantels. The cellar is divided into two rooms.

An interesting feature is the old kitchen with its huge double chimneys. The smokehouse and one slave cottage are still standing, as well.

Although the property was owned by Mary Ball Washington and later by her son, John, the Washingtons never lived there. George, however, mentions the property in his memoirs, commenting on the crops and financial status of the farm.

During the Civil War, Sherwood Forest was used as a lookout and hospital, accounting for its survival.

Traveler's Rest

Owners:

1700 Colonel James Ball

1754 Colonel Burgess Ball by will of his grandfather, Colonel James Ball

1800 Thomas Garnett's widow

1809 Purchased by John B. Gray from Richard and Margaret (Garnett) Tutt

1854 John B. Gray by will

1890 John Bowie Gray

1930 John Lee Pratt

Traveler's Rest

Around 1700 James Ball acquired part of the huge Sherwood Forest tract which had been granted in 1667 to William Ball and Thomas Chetwood. James Ball's grandson Burgess Ball (1749-1800) inherited the property and was likely the builder of the Traveler's Rest house. Burgess was an ardent supporter of the American cause during the Revolution. In 1776 he served as Captain in the 5th Regiment of Virginia. That same year he raised, clothed, and equipped a regiment of infantry for the Continental Line. He was commissioned Lieutenant Colonel of the 1st Virginia Regiment, Infantry of the Continental Army in 1777. His grandson later wrote of him, "At the close of the war, shattered in health and fortune, he returned to his old Homestead near Fredericksburg, Virginia, where in the exercise of the unbounded hospitality that had ever characterized the well-known and most appropriately named 'Traveler's Rest,' the remainder of his once princely fortune soon melted away." The government steadfastly refused to reimburse Colonel Ball for his economic and personal investment in the Revolution. Unable to maintain the property, Colonel Ball sold Traveler's Rest in the late 1780s and retired to a modest home in Loudoun County where he died.

The original house built by Burgess Ball was two stories high and had attic dormers. Chimneys were built so that the fireplaces were in the corners of the rooms.

John Gray was born in 1769 at Gartcraig, Scotland, and came to America in 1784, settling at Port Royal. Both his paternal and maternal grandfathers were substantial merchants in Glasgow and had traded extensively with Virginia before the Revolution. John was not the eldest son. His brother, William, inherited all of their father's estate as was customary at the time. Coming to Virginia was a sensible choice for John, who hoped to make his fortune there.

Gray purchased Traveler's Rest from Richard and Margaret Tutt in 1809. In 1815 he added a rectangular two-story wing on the east side. The addition had a long cellar, long hall, an entry, and three rooms on the first floor. The second floor contained a hall and two rooms, and eight "cuddies" or closets. The addition also had two doors, a porch, and a basement entrance.

In 1825 Gray bought a ten-acre mill tract from his Little Falls neighbor, Isaac Newton. Little Falls Mill soon became known as Gray's Mill. Tax records indicate that a replacement mill was built in 1827, suggesting that the old mill either burned or washed away in a flood. Gray's Mill was inherited by William Pollock in 1850 and sold to Oliver Watson in 1875. It is unknown when the mill ceased operating.

In addition to the purchase of Traveler's Rest in 1809, Gray also bought Wakefield in Westmoreland County, the birthplace of George Washington, from George C. Washington in 1813 and had his son, Atcheson, live there and operate the farm. Atcheson Gray married Catherine Willis of Fredericksburg. Atcheson died within a few months of their marriage and was buried at Traveler's Rest in 1822. After the death of his son, John Gray sold Wakefield and gave a substantial sum to Catherine who moved to Florida with her parents. There she met and married Achille Murat, son of the exiled King of Naples, and became Princess Catherine Murat. She died in Florida in 1867.

In 1854 John B. Gray inherited Traveler's Rest and began extensive renovations. He pulled down the old part of the house and built a new brick replacement attached to the wing his father had built. His new house was much grander than the first, being three stories above a cellar. Each floor had four rooms and was bisected by a long hall, except the ground floor which had a long parlor on the south side, with a large window overlooking the Rappahannock River. Gray added square porches to the front and back of his new house. County tax records of 1861 list the assessed value of Traveler's Rest at $2,500.

Unfortunately, Traveler's Rest was built on sand and by the time John Lee Pratt bought the estate in 1930, the house was cracking badly. There was no way of correcting the problem and Pratt had the house pulled down. Pratt, a King George and Stafford County native, had worked his way up to the position of vice president in the General Motors Corporation; he came home to Stafford and bought both Traveler's Rest and Chatham. His original intent was to live at Traveler's Rest but the house was so unsound as to be dangerous and he moved into Chatham instead.

The Gray cemetery, located to the south of the house site, dates from about 1848, and most of those buried there are members of that family. As of March 1937 there were eighteen graves, all but two with markers. Today, Fredericksburg Sand and Gravel Company occupies part of the farm.

Eastwood

Owners:

1748 Burgess Ball
1809 Purchased by John Gray
1848 Inherited by Miss Agnes Gray
1856 Purchased by Robert H. Gray, nephew of Agnes
Inherited by Katherine Gouldin Woods
Conveyed to Thomas McCarty Moncure

Burgess Ball, eighteenth-century owner of substantial land holdings along the Rappahannock (including the Eastwood tract), appears in the personal property tax records from 1783 to 1790. At his peak of wealth in 1783 he was taxed on 55 slaves, 21 horses, and 39 cattle.

In 1829 Eastwood was built on a hill overlooking expansive flat fields. The house consists of a large rectangular brick section with one brick wing. Bricks were made by slaves on the north side of the house. A slate roof, probably original, still protects this lovely building. The house is three stories on the east side and two and one-half on the west. There are six large rooms in the main part of the building. Each room is sixteen by twenty feet with ten-foot ceilings, and is accented by chair railing. The twenty-by-twenty-foot wing is attached to the north side. A porch extends the full length of the house on the third floor. Repairs have preserved the original design.

The Eastwood house was built on part of the Traveler's Rest tract. In 1809 the property was purchased by John Gray. At his death the property was divided, the house going to Agnes, his eldest daughter. About 1856 it was sold to Robert Hayman Gray, a nephew.

During the winters of 1862 and 1863, the house was occupied by Union soldiers primarily from the 88th and 136th Pennsylvania regiments. They left a wealth of graffiti on the walls, which was carefully preserved through the years. Two soldiers died at Eastwood and were buried in the lawn but were later removed.

Long unoccupied, this beautiful old home is being restored by the present owners.

Little Falls

Little Falls was a Ball and Newton plantation located about 2½ miles east of Fredericksburg on the south side of State Route 3.

Colonel Joseph Ball (1649-1711), grandfather of George Washington, held a grant of 1,600 acres along the Rappahannock River. In his will he left to his daughter, Mary, "four hundred acres of Land Lying in Richmond County in ye freshes of the Rappahannock..." Mary married Augustine Washington and became the mother of George, and part of the 400 acres became Little Falls. The Newtons acquired the property by purchase.

John Newton by will dated December 21, 1696, bequeathed to his son, Garrard Newton, 1,000 acres at the Little Falls of the Rappahannock with a mill thereon. Garrard, however, died underage in 1706 and his interest in the estate descended to his nephew, William (d.1722). When William came of age about 1741-42, he became owner of the 1,000 acres at Little Falls Run, then in King George County, in addition to other lands which had descended to him from other ancestors. The property at Little Falls became part of Stafford County when the Stafford–King George county boundary changes were made in 1777.

Major William Newton (c.1720-1789) was the eldest surviving son of William Newton and the eldest male representative of his great-grandfather, John Newton, who immigrated from Yorkshire, England, to Westmoreland County, Virginia. Major Newton was an influential man who in 1754 was appointed lieutenant of the Horse Troop. In 1761 he appears in the account books of William Allason, Falmouth merchant, as Capt. William Newton, inspector of tobacco at Dixon's Warehouse in Falmouth. By 1773, Allason's account books refer to him as "Major William Newton."

Little Falls adjoined the southeast side of Traveler's Rest, which was owned by Joseph Ball, son of Colonel Joseph Ball. In 1755 Major Newton brought suit against Joseph Ball for encroaching on his property. A survey of the property was made and, despite Ball's protests, Newton won the case.

During his lifetime, Major Newton amassed a considerable amount of property totaling nearly 2,000 acres in King George and Stafford Counties, as well as an estate in Yorkshire in the town of Hull which he had inherited from his great-grandfather. At his death, Major Newton divided his 1,112-acre Little Falls plantation between various sons and sons-in-law, though the boundaries of each tract were not clearly defined. The court appointed William Ball and Robert H. Hooe, commissioners, and James Leach, deputy surveyor of Stafford County, to survey and allot the tract. Isaac Newton (d.1838), his father's favorite, received the house and the riverfront property on the Rappahannock. By purchase he eventually acquired the remaining portion of his father's plantation.

On July 4, 1796, Isaac applied to the Mutual Assurance Society for insurance against fire on his buildings at Little Falls. Included in the policy were a "Dwelling House, 46 feet long and 18 feet wide, 1 story and half high; built of wood and covered with wood shingles," a "Kitchen 16 feet by 18 feet, 1 story high, all wood, which stands at a distance of forty feet from the house," a

"Mill House on Little Falls Run, 20 feet square, built of stone and covered with wood shingles, which stands at a distance of upwards of half-mile from the residence." The buildings were valued at $1,650 and insured for $1,325.

Isaac sold the mill and its ten-acre lot to John Gray of Traveler's Rest. This mill was built some time prior to 1696, making it one of the oldest grist mills in the county. A note in the 1827 tax records states that the mill was rebuilt that year, indicating that it had either burned or been washed away in a flood. The mill continued to operate after the Civil War though the exact date of its closure is unknown.

By 1942 the original house had been replaced with a brick home built on the old foundation; it is unknown when the old building was destroyed. Near State Route 601, on part of the land recovered by Major Newton from Joseph Ball, is a massive lone tombstone, badly defaced. By 1942 all that could be read of the inscription was:

In
Memory of
**artha Newton who*
parted this life* *
**** *1806 Aged* ****

Today, the riverfront portion of Little Falls is quarried for sand and gravel.

Rumford

Owners:

pre 1782-1830	George Thornton
1830	John Gray of Traveler's Rest
1832	Transferred to William Pollock
1868	1,006 acres divided into four parcels. Atchison Pollock retained the house.
1892	Sold to E. R. Weidman
1902	Sold to H. W. Willenbucher of Fredericksburg
1904	Sold to Herbert Harris of Michigan

1910	Sold to John H. Cassel
1911	Sold to Judge John L. Pancoast of Oklahoma
1932	Sold to Louis Schmied
c.1935	Purchased by Mrs. Rosa K. Graves

Rumford Farm, also known as the Pollock Place, Rumford Place, and Rumford Plantation, witnessed great prosperity as well as great hardship. In 1830 John Gray of Traveler's Rest bought 1,006 acres from the heirs of George Thornton. Shortly thereafter, Gray's nephew William Pollock (1797-1865) came from Scotland to visit his uncle. There he fell in love with his first cousin, Janet Gray, whom he married. Rumford may well have been a wedding present for the young couple. Judging from tax records, Rumford already had a house on it (valued at $1,500) when Gray purchased the property. The building date of the house is impossible to determine from tax records, though by 1815 when the value of buildings was listed separately, the house was worth $1,500. William and Janet moved into the house and, over the next twenty-eight years, established one of the most profitable farms in the county. They added outbuildings and enlarged the original brick house where they raised their five children, William Jr., John, Atchison, Hannah, and Matthew.

William Pollock seems to have been an excellent agriculturalist. By 1860 the farm was producing great quantities of hay, corn, wheat, oats, tobacco, peas, wool, potatoes, butter, orchard products, and livestock. Supporting the many activities of Rumford Farm were numerous dependencies including slave quarters and a large barn. An article in *The Virginia Herald* of June 21, 1834, lists William Pollock as an agent for and owner of a Douglass threshing machine, the only one of its type in Stafford. Clearly, the Pollocks were on the cutting edge of agricultural technology and enjoyed a lifestyle far above that of most Staffordians.

Pollock's wealth and agricultural base broadened in 1850 when he inherited his uncle's grist mill. Previously known as Gray's Mill or Little Falls Mill, it now became Pollock's Mill. By 1860 the tax records valued the 1,006 acres with its buildings at $22,635 and the mill and it ten-acre lot at $9,815, substantial sums for the period.

The Pollocks' comfortable life at Rumford came to a sudden end with the outbreak of the Civil War. Early in 1863 William Pollock made a major contribution to the Confederate cause. A surviving receipt from the Quartermaster of the Second Corps Artillery recorded his contribution of thirty-two horses, twelve mules, eleven four-horse wagons, twenty-two sets of lead harnesses, twenty-two sets of wheel harnesses, forty-four halters, ten curry combs, ten saddles, and six water buckets. Pollock's timing was excellent, for shortly thereafter Union soldiers overran his farm, broke into the occupied house, searched every room, cabinet, and drawer, and pillaged whatever they wanted. The intrusion didn't end there, however, as the soldiers, gathering for the Battle of Fredericksburg, stole much of the remaining livestock, chickens, and eggs. Unlike many besieged families, the Pollocks didn't flee their home and as a result, Mrs. Pollock, then fifty-two years old, was forced to cook for twenty to thirty Union soldiers every day.

Two of the Pollock children fought against the invading forces. In April 1861 the second eldest son, John, enlisted with the Fredericksburg Artillery. He was promoted to lieutenant and later to captain. He was wounded at the Battle of Chancellorsville but survived the war. The youngest son, Matthew, enlisted in the Ninth Virginia Cavalry in June 1863 and, miraculously, also survived.

Rumford was strategically located for the 1862 Union attack on Fredericksburg. A pontoon bridge was built from the property across the river to the town, and during December of that year the house served as a hospital for the First Corps' Second Division. Contemporary reports describe the grizzly scenes there as wounded soldiers were transported across the bridge for treatment. Hogs rooted through piles of amputated limbs. The unidentified dead were buried in the yard, three or four to a grave. Not until 1866-1868 were the graves opened and fifty-six Union bodies disinterred and moved to Fredericksburg National Cemetery.

William Pollock died in 1865, no doubt devastated by the stress of the war. Despite the devaluation experienced by most Southerners, William Pollock died a wealthy man. His inventory, on record in the Stafford County court house, included one carriage and harness, ten plows, two harrows, two two-horse wagons, one horse cart, one four-horse wagon, as well as over $25,000 in stocks and bonds in Farmer's Bank, the Bank of Commerce, Fauquier White Sulfur Springs, "State Stock," Fredericksburg Aqueduct Company, Richmond City Bonds, and James River and Kanawha Bonds.

In 1868 Rumford was divided into four parcels, Rumford, Argyle, Airdria, and an unnamed parcel. Atchison retained the original Rumford house and 310 acres. Matthew inherited 350 acres adjoining Atchison's land, and John received 388 acres adjoining Matthew's. A fourth parcel (known as Argyle) containing 344 acres was jointly owned by John and Matthew. This is now modern Argyle Heights Subdivision. The survey done of the time of this division does not specify which of the remaining two parcels became known as Airdria, and this is not a name which has survived to the twentieth century.

Captain John Pollock lived at Argyle until 1887 when he sold the property and moved to Hobson in King George County. There he married Estelle Lewis of Marmion, daughter of Fielding Lewis. John and his wife are buried at Marmion. The Argyle property later became Argyle Heights and Tylerton subdivisions.

The devastating economic effects of the war haunted Atchison Pollock long after the fighting ceased. He and his wife Hannah struggled to make a living at Rumford for twenty-four years but were unable to rebuild what William Pollock had created. Their difficulties were worsened in 1885 when the house burned. Atchison took out a loan for $1,500 and tried unsuccessfully over the next several years to repay it. He was unable to repay the debt or rebuild his house. In 1892 Rumford was sold at public auction for payment of Atchison's debt. Mr. E. R. Weidman bought the farm for $2,750.

Tax records suggest that it was the Weidmans who built the present house at Rumford sometime between 1892 and 1900. According to the records, there was no house on the property when they purchased it in 1892 but by 1900 one had been built. Mr. Weidman and his family lived at Rumford for ten years. In 1893 the Weidmans gave their son Frederick 149 of the 310 acres purchased from Atchison Pollock.

During the early part of the twentieth century, Rumford changed hands frequently. In 1902 Rumford was sold to H. W. Willenbucher of Fredericksburg. Just two years later the farm was bought by Herbert Harris of Michigan. In 1910 the property was sold to John H. Cassel who quickly resold it the following year to Judge John L. Pancoast of Oklahoma.

Judge Pancoast's will ordered that his wife and children live at Rumford until the youngest child attained the age of twenty-one. At that point the farm was to be sold. That event occurred in 1932, and the property was sold to Louis Schmied. Mr. Schmied seems to have had economic difficulties and the farm was taken over by a land bank. Around 1935 Mrs. Rosa K. Graves bought the farm and her relatives continue to live there.

Ferry Farm

Ferry Farm is best known as the childhood home of George Washington, though it has a history that predates the Washington occupancy.

Augustine Washington bought the property in 1738 from the heirs of William Strother (c.1700-1732). Strother had first lived at the family estate, Millbank, in King George County and served as a justice for that county. When Millbank burned, Strother bought 260 acres on the Rappahannock directly across from Fredericksburg. At that time the property was situated in King George County. Not until the King George–Stafford County boundary was changed to Muddy Creek in 1777 did the Strother farm become part of Stafford.

Strother died in 1732 and the farm was advertised for sale in *The Virginia Gazette* of April 21, 1738. The advertisement described the farm as "all that Messuage Tenement and Mansion House where the said William Strother lately Dwelt and all those several pieces of parcells of land thereunto adjoining and upon which the said Mansion stands containing together by Estimation Two Hundred and Eighty Acres...and all the Houses, out houses, Edifaces, etc." The plantation included "a very handsome Dwelling house, 3 Store houses, several other convenient Out-houses, and a Ferry belonging to it."

William Strother had amassed a sizable estate by the time he died in 1732. His inventory listed 22 slaves. After his death, his wife married John Grant.

At the time the Washingtons purchased the Strother farm, it consisted of two tracts, a 100-acre parcel which included the house site and a 180-acre "Quarter." Augustine purchased additional adjoining land to increase the size of his farm to 580 acres. He named the property Ferry Farm because of the ferry that operated on the shore below the house. The ferry had been authorized in 1728 to transport people from King George County to Fredericksburg.

Ferry Farm was the third Washington farm and the third home for George, then seven years old. George spent ten years at Ferry Farm; he didn't move away permanently until 1748 when he went to Mount Vernon with his brother, Lawrence. At the time of Augustine's death in 1743, an inventory listed 20 slaves, and horses, hogs, sheep, and cattle totaling 71 head at the 100-acre home site. The 180-acre "Quarter" had 7 more slaves and 40 head of livestock. The remaining 300 acres was composed of forest and open fields. Upon his father's death, George inherited Ferry Farm, ten slaves, and three lots in Fredericksburg. However, he did not take possession of the property until he came of age. His mother continued to live on the farm until 1772. George sold Ferry Farm sometime between 1772 and 1776.

While the dwelling may not quite have been the "Mansion House" mentioned in the Strother advertisement, it was nonetheless a substantial home for the period. There were at least seven rooms in the original house. The inventory made after the death of Augustine listed a "Hall," a "Hall Back Room," a "Parlour," a "Back Room," a "Passage," a "Hall Chamber," and the "Parlour Chamber." There were also several storehouses, a dairy, a kitchen, and a poultry house.

It is not known when or how the Ferry Farm house disappeared. It may have been destroyed or torn down in 1772. Washington advertised the property for sale in *The Virginia Gazette* on November 5, 1772, and the ad included no mention of a house. The advertisement noted that the tract had "one of the most agreeable Situations for a House that is to be Found on the whole River having a clear and distinct View of almost every House in town, and every Vessel that passes to and from it." Today all that is left of the old buildings is one small building, most likely the surveyor's office.

George was eleven years old when his father died and he remained at Ferry Farm for another five years, moving to Mount Vernon in February 1748 to live with his elder brother Lawrence. Upon the death of his sister-in-law in 1759, George inherited Mount Vernon. Sometime between 1772 and 1776, George sold the Ferry Farm (which he had inherited from his father) to Dr. Hugh Mercer of Fredericksburg. Mercer apparently purchased the property with the intention of starting a town there. He planned on calling the new settlement Mercer Town and hoped that some of the prosperous Falmouth merchants would open businesses in his new town.

Mercer served as a Brigadier General in the Revolutionary War and, unfortunately, was killed in January 1777, leaving his wife, Isabella, and five children. His will stated that all his property was to be inherited by his eldest son, William. In the event William died or was unable to manage the estate, the property was to go to the second eldest, George. Sadly, both William and George were deaf and dumb. Isabella and the executors of the estate, George Weedon and John Tennant, decided to petition George Washington, by then President, to have the land surveyed as Hugh Mercer had intended. The petition stated that the two sons, being deaf and "thereby rendered incapable of managing their Affairs," were not able to decide upon the best use of the farm. The property was surveyed in 1785 and the lots laid out, but there seems to have been some dispute as to William's abilities and limitations, for the town never came to fruition. The farm remained in the Mercer family until 1826.

On September 12, 1826, a notice appeared in *The Virginia Herald* advertising "Valuable Property for Sale: Mercer's Ferry and 500 Acres of Land Adjoining." The ad noted that "there are already commodious buildings for a plain family...with several beautiful and commanding eminences for a Dwelling upon a large scale, and one site in particular which is uncommonly fine." There was still no reference to a surviving Washington home. The farm seems to have been purchased at this point by Reverend Thomas C. Teasdale. After this, the property changed hands and was divided numerous times until by 1990 the total acreage was only sixty-eight acres. At this time the owners, Samuel and Irma

Warren, gave Stafford County the thirty-four acres which included the old house site.

During the Civil War, artillery was located on the higher ground (site of modern Ferry Farm Subdivision) overlooking the city of Fredericksburg. There were pontoon bridge crossings at the old ferry site. Maps of the period show a road leading to the home site. One map shows two building symbols and another map shows three, suggesting that farming continued at Ferry Farm until at least 1863.

Extensive archeological examinations are underway, the results of which will be used to plan a full restoration of the house and dependencies. In 1991 the 1726 cellar was opened and found to contain many artifacts.

In 1996, after a lengthy community-fired effort to prevent a Wal-Mart store from being built next to the Ferry Farm site, the Washington home and adjoining acreage was purchased by the Kenmore Association, operators of Kenmore House and Gardens in Fredericksburg. This was a fitting buyer for the Washington property, since Betty Lewis of Kenmore was George Washington's only sister. The Kenmore Association plans on completing extensive archaeological excavations and rebuilding the Washington home which will be open to visitors.

Pine Grove

Pine Grove was a Strother home on the Rappahannock which was part of the Washington Farm or Ferry Farm. An unpretentious frame house occupied the high ground on the edge of the river. Just prior to the Civil War, James McClure Scott bought several farms including Little Whim, Salvington, and Pine Grove, which he purchased from his friend, Henry Thompson. The old house at Pine Grove was in need of renovation and Scott and his wife rented Kenmore in Fredericksburg while waiting for repairs to be done on the house. The work was interrupted by the war and the house was destroyed during the Battle of Fredericksburg.

At the outset of the war, Scott invested most of his fortune in Confederate bonds. As a result, he lost everything but his lands which, after the war, nobody wanted to buy. Destitute, he and his wife returned to her ancestral home in Spotsylvania County.

The Richmond, Fredericksburg, and Potomac Railroad tracks were later built across the foundations of the house.

Chatham

For over 200 years Chatham has stood on the high ridge above the Rappahannock River, a serene sentinel watching over the city of Fredericksburg. The house and its occupants have been involved in most of the critical events of Virginia's history from the American Revolution through the War of 1812 and the Civil War. The design of the house bespeaks the elegance and dignity of the Virginia plantation era at its height. That dignity was sorely strained during the unwelcome Yankee intrusion of the Civil War; like the spirit of the war-ravaged Southerners, however, it emerged from the experience older, somewhat battered but none the less proud.

William Fitzhugh I (c.1651-1701) arrived in Virginia about 1670 and settled on the Potomac River in Stafford County (now King George County) on a plantation which he called Bedford. Fitzhugh was a planter, politician, attorney, and a very wealthy man. Although far removed geographically from others of his class at Jamestown, Fitzhugh managed his own estate, was a leading lawyer and Queen's Counsel, and a member of the House of Burgesses as well as Lieutenant Colonel of the Stafford militia. He maintained a sizable law practice and served as a justice of the Stafford Court, where he became a friend and law partner with George Brent of Woodstock on Aquia Creek.

By the time he died, William Fitzhugh had amassed some 54,000 acres in Virginia, including the Chatham property. This parcel had been part of a 6,000-acre patent taken out by Thomas Wilkinson (died c.1688) in 1658 and renewed in 1662. The Wilkinson patent was a huge tract, stretching back from the Rappahannock River north to Potomac Creek. During the early 1690s, Fitzhugh purchased the 6,000 acres from Wilkinson's heirs and others who had bought parcels from Wilkinson. Farms later cut from this tract included Boscobel, Bell Aire, Mount Pleasant, Highland Home, and Chatham.

On April 9, 1700 Fitzhugh, preparing to travel to England, wrote his will dividing his sizable land holdings between his sons. Fitzhugh owned several plantations in Stafford; the Quit Rent Rolls list him as holding some 17,630 acres in the county. To Henry (1686-1758) he left the 6,000-acre Wilkinson patent. Thomas was to inherit 400 acres on the Rappahannock and 1,090 acres bought from Parson Waugh "in the forest between the Rappahannock and Potomac Creek, nigh on the head thereof..." Finally, George was to receive 2,100 acres on Aquia and Chopawamsic Creeks. Fitzhugh didn't die during his voyage and his sons had to wait for their inheritance.

William I's tremendous land holdings eventually passed to his great-grandson, William, land holdings which included the acreage that would later become Chatham. Earlier generations of Fitzhughs had operated a plantation on the Chatham property and had built a grist mill on Claiborne Run about a mile east of the present house, but a sizable dwelling at Chatham did not arise until the time of William I's great-grandson, William (1741-1809), who for the sake of clarity is referred to as William of Chatham. This William was born at Eagle's Nest, the Fitzhugh estate in King George County, and was descended from William I's son Henry (1686-1758) and his grandson, Henry of Eagle's Nest (c.1705-1742). The wealthiest of the Fitzhugh clan, William of Chatham married Ann Randolph (1747-1805) of Henrico County.

The young couple were living at Somerset in King George County when Fitzhugh decided to seat the Rappahannock property across from the new town of Fredericksburg. Fitzhugh sold 10,000 acres to finance the building of the house which he named after William Pitt, Earl of Chatham. Construction began in 1768, and highly skilled craftsmen worked on the Georgian-style home until it was completed in 1771. Though quite long, the house was not wide. A two-story center section was flanked by two single-story wings built of Flemish bond brickwork with glazed headers.

The Virginia plantation era was at its height and the economy was strong. Fitzhugh continued to add to his land holdings until by 1768 the Quit Rent rolls list him as owning 23,975 acres, the total being comprised of numerous individual plantations. From 1783 to 1785 he was taxed on 105 slaves, 29 horses, and 28 cattle in Stafford County alone.

The Chatham plantation consisted of some seven hundred acres worked by a large number of slaves. Fitzhugh was keenly interested in experimental farming and planted a great variety of crops, testing their success in Virginia soil.

In 1771 Fitzhugh was elected to represent King George County in the House of Burgesses during the turbulent period preceding the Revolution. In 1775 he was present at the Second Virginia Convention and heard Patrick Henry make his fiery speech. A strong supporter of the American cause, he contributed substantial funds to help his friend and neighbor, James Hunter, manufacture guns and supplies for the Revolution.

In 1777 Fitzhugh became a Burgess of Stafford County. A redrawing of county lines earlier that same year had placed Chatham in Stafford rather than in King George. After the Revolution, Fitzhugh continued to farm at Chatham despite the financial and physical strain. The economy floundered after the war and he was no longer a young man. In his fifties, Fitzhugh found Chatham a burden and sold the house and 1,288 acres in 1806 to Major Churchill Jones for $20,000. At this time the house consisted of nine large rooms, a center entry hall, two pairs of stairs, and a cellar. There were numerous outbuildings including a meathouse, laundry, several offices, storehouses, stables for thirty horses, a carriage house, kitchen, servants' quarters for fifty, barns, granary, sheds, overseer's house, and a blacksmith shop. In the gardens grew all sorts of fruits and there were fields of clover and hay as well as open fields for planting all types of crops.

It was Churchill Jones who built the first bridge across the Rappahannock River to Fredericksburg. This marvel of engineering was a massive stone and timber structure that took one and one-half years to build but was washed away three years later in the flood of 1826.

Churchill died in 1822 and Chatham was inherited by his brother, William. Chatham was just one of several plantations belonging to William Jones, who was an astute businessman and something of a dandy. Despite the fact that they were no longer in style, he dressed in ruffled shirts and knee britches until he died. After over forty years of marriage, he became a widow in 1823 at the age of seventy-three. Apparently, single life didn't agree with him for five years later he shocked the community by marrying Lucy Gordon, his first wife's niece. Lucy was sixteen. This marriage lasted eighteen years and, in 1829, produced a daughter, Betty Churchill Jones.

William continued to live at his Spotsylvania home, Ellwood, but in 1825 deeded the Chatham farm to his son-in-law, John Coalter, and Hannah Jones Coalter, daughter by his first marriage. During the Coalter tenure, Chatham was known for its splendid hospitality and many dignitaries visited the plantation.

Betty Jones spent her childhood at Ellwood but was sent to Chatham to be educated. She spent several years there, enjoying the endless visitors and lovely parties. She felt at home at Chatham and came to love the beautiful plantation.

In time Betty was sent away to continue her education. She fell in love with her tutor, James Horace Lacy, the Missouri-born son of a Presbyterian minister and they were married at Ellwood in 1848.

In 1857 Betty's half-sister, Hannah Coalter, died. She left Chatham to her daughter, Janet, for her lifetime, then to Betty's children. Unfortunately, Janet was physically and mentally handicapped and unable to manage Chatham. Contrary to Hannah's wishes, the executors of the estate put Chatham up for sale. Betty, who had always loved Chatham, wanted to live there again so Horace bought it for her.

Chatham thrived under the Lacy tenure, producing bountiful crops and seven Lacy children. Several hundred slaves worked the fields, planted and tilled the gardens, maintained the magnificent brick home, and tended the endless domestic chores of a well-to-do Virginia plantation household.

Betty's comfortable life at Chatham was brought to a sudden, cruel end when, on April 22, 1862, Union general Irvin McDowell and his troops moved onto the estate. The Lacys were ordered to leave their home. McDowell had chosen Chatham as his headquarters because its position high above the Rappahannock provided a fine view of the town of Fredericksburg below. In some respects, this occupation may have been a blessing, for McDowell respected the property and took care to see that it was not totally destroyed. He even had two French chefs brought in to cook and he frequently entertained important guests at Chatham, including Abraham Lincoln.

During the Battle of Fredericksburg, Chatham served as a hospital and Clara Barton nursed the wounded on the lawn outside the house.

Horace joined the Confederate army and Betty and her young children left Chatham for a safer part of the state. Horace, with his connections to many influential Southern supporters, was considered "one of the most dangerous rebels" in this part of the state. He was with Robert E. Lee in Fredericksburg in 1862 and the two of them looked across the river at the Yankees occupying Chatham. Horace asked Lee to shell the house and the despised intruders, but Lee refused. He, too, had been a visitor in the fine old home and could not bear the responsibility for its destruction.

In November 1865, seven months after the war had ended, Betty and Horace and their seven children moved back to Chatham. There was little left that even resembled their once-lovely home. The house had been used by the Yankees as a field station, hospital, and troop headquarters. Fredericksburg had been shelled from cannon placed in the garden overlooking the town. Wagon wheels and thousands of marching feet had all but destroyed the lawns, which were also littered with the graves of Union soldiers and overgrown with briars and weeds. The great shade trees had all been cut to the ground. The interior floors had been damaged when soldiers had ridden their horses through the house. The banisters, doors, windows, and some of the paneling had been ripped out for firewood. Over 5,000 panes of glass were broken and the fields were overgrown.

Betty wept when she saw what had become of her home. She thought that she would at least still have her beautiful mahogany and walnut furniture, but much of that was lost, also. General Lee had managed to remove most of the valuable furnishings just prior to the Union occupation. He had had them transported across the James River for safekeeping, but on the way back to Chatham, the boat sank. After two months on the river bottom, some of the furniture was salvaged and dried out but much of it was ruined.

Even after the Lacys' return to Chatham, life was dangerous and difficult. The government Burial Corps dug up the lawn once again, exhuming the remains of the soldiers and reburying them at the cemetery in Fredericksburg. The children couldn't even play outside without risking being hit by stray bullets from occupation troops in Fredericksburg.

Betty and Horace struggled to return the plantation to a working farm, a difficult task with a labor force, a nearly impossible one without. Lacy had never been as wealthy as the previous Chatham owners and the economic depression that followed the war proved more than he could manage. The Lacys simply could not afford to keep their home and they sold it in 1872 to a Pennsylvania banker for $23,900, which was $12,000 less than they had paid for it fifteen years earlier. The Lacys moved into Fredericksburg and became active in town affairs.

After the war, Chatham exchanged hands several times before being purchased by Mr. and Mrs. John Lee Pratt in 1931. By this time, the estate consisted of 256 acres. Mrs. Pratt engaged the services of numerous gardeners to tend the flowers and grounds. Not only interested in gardening, she was also a collector of fine art and gave to the Virginia Museum in Richmond a priceless collection of Russian jeweled Easter eggs created by Peter Carl Fabergé.

The Pratts had no children and, at his death in 1975, the property was willed to the National Park Service. It is now open to the public, although the Pratts' exquisite furnishings were auctioned in 1976. The Park Service has undertaken extensive research into the history of this magnificent old home and has determined that most of what survived the Civil War is original to the Fitzhugh home. The focus of the Park Service interpretation is the role of Chatham during the Civil War.

Horse Racing in Stafford

William Fitzhugh was not just a man of law, a politician, and an experimental farmer. He was also a dedicated horse breeder and, like most gentlemen of his day, was passionately involved in racing. Only gentlemen (by the eighteenth-century definition of the word) were allowed to race their horses on the turf. During the early colonial period, races were included in county fairs. There were also many races run on private tracks and most of the larger plantations had tracks or racing fields.

Horse racing quickly became an extremely popular spectator sport. Races were advertised in the newspapers for the benefit of not only the owners, but the general public as well. *The Virginia Gazette* of July 22, 1773, advertised two days of racing to be held at Aquia. Gentlemen who intended to enter horses were requested to enter them the day before "with Charles Tyler, who keeps the tavern lately kept by Mr. Yelverton Peyton." This was most likely Peyton's Ordinary near Aquia Church.

Horses usually began running at the age of about six. The course was four miles long and three to five heats were frequently run at one event.

Seventeen-seventy-four was an especially good year for racing in Virginia. William Fitzhugh's fine horse, Regulus, who already had won many races, ran in the fall of that year. One particular race was held on Mr. Fitzhugh's racing field and was open only to members of the Fredericksburg Jockey Club. The first day's race was for the Jockey Club plate and one hundred guineas. Regulus won against a field including Eclipse, owned by Alexander Spotswood; Mann Page's Damon; Figure, owned by William Brent of Richland; William Fitzhugh's Master Stephen; and Moore Fauntleroy's Faithful Shepherdess.

Horses were not only run on local tracks, they were sometimes taken great distances to compete. Fitzhugh frequently sent his horses to run at Annapolis and in Upper Marlborough, Maryland.

Prior to the Revolution, most major towns had their own Jockey Clubs. In this part of Virginia there were Jockey Clubs in Fredericksburg, Dumfries, Portsmouth, Petersburg, Warwick, and Williamsburg. The earliest recorded race was held at Williamsburg in 1739 and the sport quickly gained popularity.

Fascination with the sport reached its pinnacle between 1745 and 1775. Nearly every town in Virginia, Maryland, and the Carolinas had a race course. Gentlemen of means spared no expense in the care of their animals. They also imported from Europe the finest breeding stock money could buy. Among the principal importers and breeders in Virginia were Theodorick Bland, William Brent, William Fitzhugh, Thomson Mason, and Colonel John Mercer, all of Stafford. Their breeding programs formed the foundation of the modern, internationally recognized Virginia Thoroughbred industry.

Horse breeding became a passion in Virginia, even in rural Stafford. A large proportion of advertisements in the newspapers were for horses standing at stud, and breeders sought to impress potential customers not only with their stallions, but with their facilities as well. *The Virginia Gazette* of March 12, 1779, contained an advertisement from James Mercer offering his father's great stallion Apollo at stud at Marlborough, "my late father's seat." He says, "Marlborough is one of the first pastures in America, a neck of upwards 2000 acres of high land, and 500 of marsh, occupied now by thirteen hands only, formerly seventy odd; this circumstance alone is sufficient to assure customers, that their mares will (contrary to custom) be returned in good order...."

The April 18, 1766, *Virginia Gazette* contained another ad for stud service at Marlborough. John Mercer was offering the stallion Ranter for stud for forty shillings per cover. A supplement to the advertisement mentioned a ferry owned by a Mr. Meeks, which was kept at Maryland Point in Charles County and could provide transportation for mares between Maryland and Marlborough.

Breeding Thoroughbred horses was a passion for men of means in the eighteenth century. No expense was spared to import the finest stock and careful breeding during this period ensured that only the finest traits were passed on. The exceptional bloodlines developed in eighteenth-century Virginia are still evident in the Thoroughbreds of today.

Chapel Green

This very old structure is located on the east side of State Route 602, one half-mile south of State Route 218. It is another house about which little is known. Chapel Green was built around 1723 by Colonel William Ball, first cousin of George Washington's mother.

While there have been changes made to the house over the years, much of the building seems to be as it was in the eighteenth century. There are three bedrooms, a full basement, and six fireplaces (the fireplace in the basement kitchen was covered by a previous owner).

William Ball built his plantation on a large tract of land known as the "Quarter Plantation." The house may have been a wedding gift to his son, Captain William Ball II, as he was married that same year to his cousin Margaret Ball. The property was inherited by their son, Aaron and, later, by his brother, Benjamin Ball. The Ball family lived there until 1919. By 1950 the house was abandoned, but was restored in the 1970s. The present owners, Mr. and Mrs. George Grimes, have lived there for about twenty years and have made Chapel Green one of the showplaces of Stafford County.

White Oak Primitive Baptist Church

This was originally known as White Oak Church of Christ. It was established on Saturday, October 31, 1789, and "declared independent of all others believing and holding forth the doctrine of election and the final perseverance of the saints to which covenant we all agree this 31st of October same date praying that God would preserve us and keep us from all evil. Amen."

In 1835 John Moncure gave the trustees of the church "the meeting house and one acre of land attached thereto." This building presently stands on the south side of White Oak Road (State Route 218) at the intersection of that road and Caisson Road (State Route 603).

Brother Andrew Leitch was the first pastor. Discipline was a major concern. Christ said, "withdraw from every brother that walks disorderly," and that philosophy was strictly followed.

The word "primitive" indicated the church's adherence to the original doctrines of Christ and the Apostles.

The church still meets twice each month, the worship services followed by a business meeting, much the same as in 1789.

Little Whim

This beautiful home is located approximately two miles east of Fredericksburg, on the north side of State Route 218. It was built sometime prior to the Civil War and miraculously survives today.

In 1852 James McClure Scott (1811-1893) and his wife, Sarah Travers Lewis (1813-1891) bought property on the north side of what is today State Route 218. Between that time and the Civil War, Scott purchased at least two other tracts in the county, among them Salvington (see Chapter 9) and Pine Grove (see article this chapter). Scott and his wife built the lovely frame house on the Route 218 property and she named it Little Whim.

In 1860 the Scotts sold Little Whim to Gustavus B. Wallace and rented Kenmore in Fredericksburg. James Scott lost his fortune during the Civil War (see "Pine Grove," this chapter) and the couple retired to Bell Aire, the Scott ancestral home in Spotsylvania County.

In 1863 Little Whim became General Burnside's command post. By this time, the home belonged to George Phillips King. On the eve on the Battle of Fredericksburg, Burnside moved his command post one-half mile east to the Phillips House. This beautiful brick home stood on Stafford Heights (also on the north side of State Route 218) and provided the general a better vantage point than Little Whim. The Phillips House became a focal point of the Union command and was finally burned to the ground.

After the war, Little Whim was owned by the Purvis family. It survives today, restored and cared for, one of the few frame homes in Stafford not used for Union firewood.

Monitieth Home

This home was located 1.5 miles southeast of Falmouth on State Route 607, then 5.3 miles east of State Route 218, four-tenths of a mile southeast on State Route 602, and half a mile south on a private road.

The first Monitieth to come to Stafford County was forced to flee Scotland. As a result of the religious upheaval under Charles I, Mr. Monitieth found himself in trouble with the authorities. Knowing he would not be allowed to leave the country, he hit upon a plan in which his friends sealed him inside an empty whiskey barrel. The barrel plug was left out so he wouldn't suffocate and he was loaded aboard a ship for America. He arrived at a dock on Potomac Creek and soon established himself there.

As was common at the time, the Monitieth house was first built on a low spot near the creek. The family soon found the area too swampy and, in 1812, moved the house to higher ground, replacing the original wooden chimney with a brick one. The modest building was moved three times from its original location. The first Monitieth child was born in 1812 while the house was being moved. The family had temporarily moved into the stable, and William always claimed that he was "born in a manger like the Savior." William Sr. died in 1894 and lived to be eighty-two years old.

Behind the house was a sulfur spring, the water from which was believed to have medicinal properties. People from all around would come to the spring to drink and would take water home with them.

The Civil War in Stafford

With the exception of the skirmishes at Aquia Landing and two minor battles at Hartwood Church, there was little actual fighting in Stafford during the Civil War. However, the county suffered more from the war than any other county in Virginia. With four major campaigns south of the Rappahannock, Stafford became a campground for the Army of the Potomac. Over 100,000 Union troops camped here for extended periods of time. These men had little with which to occupy themselves and so to keep discipline and to provide firewood for cooking and heat, the officers ordered the solders to cut wood. So well did they follow their orders that there are only about a dozen trees in the county which predate the war. Soldiers cut and burned every stick of wood, to the point that it eventually became necessary to ship in wood from outside sources. By war's end, every fence post and fence rail had been burned. Soldiers entered unoccupied homes and churches, ripped up flooring and removed paneling from walls. They even took the railings from the stairs to burn as firewood. What little was left of the home was usually then set ablaze. The same fate befell barns, kitchens, and other dependencies. Any buildings that were not being used for quarters, stables, or hospitals were dismantled for firewood, vandalized, or completely destroyed. The soldiers also killed or ran off livestock and stole anything they could carry, including court records, even massive deed and will books! As George Gordon aptly stated, "They proceeded to steal everything that wasn't nailed down, burned up a lot of houses and stole all the cattle—just picked the county clean." Many of the fine old homes in the county were lost to these marauders, and the total removal of the timber caused the topsoil to wash away, destroying the agricultural value of the land. Not until the turn of the century were the trees large enough to once again be cut for lumber. The county economy did not recover until the 1970s.

The war took a toll on Union troops as well. After a stunning Confederate victory at Fredericksburg on December 13, 1862, General Ambrose Burnside withdrew his forces back across the Rappahannock. There he worked to regain the confidence of his troops. The following month he decided to surprise the enemy by crossing the river above Falmouth at Banks' Ford (see "Greenbank" in Chapter 11) and on January 19, he ordered his troops to move back towards the town along the Warrenton Road (U.S. Route 17).

The day started out cloudy and cold, but dry. By midday a gentle rain began falling. This quickly turned to a downpour which continued all night and for two days following. With no sign of a let up, the troops slogged on, moving wagons, horses, mules, cannon, and supplies. Union soldier Dunn Browne wrote, "a driving rain...poached the ground into mud deeper than the New England mind can conceive of, and stickier than—well, I am at a loss for a similitude. Pitch, for cohesive attraction, is but sand compared with it." Another observer at the time described the miring of huge, wide-tired wagons loaded with pontoons intended for installation on the Rappahannock between Stafford and Fredericksburg. Six-mule teams on the wagons were doubled and then tripled but to no avail. The wagons were fitted with hand-holds enough for 150 men each and between the men and the mules, the wagons inched towards their destination, bogged down to their axles. The cannon proved even more difficult. The men dragged and hauled the massive guns until defeated by exhaustion. If they so much as stopped for a breather without putting brush or logs under the axle, the cannon quickly sank into the mud until only the muzzle remained above ground. It then had to be dug out of the mud with shovels and the process would begin anew.

Dunn Browne further described the scene: "all the roads and streams are full of dead horses and mules (I presume fifty are in sight from the top of the hill back of my tent), and pieces of wagons, and the way obstructed with caissons, and pieces of artillery, and pontoons, and all sorts of vehicles, fast in the mud." After two days of futile digging, pulling, and cursing, Burnside was forced to admit defeat. So exhausted were his troops that it took them a month to recover.

Burnside's effort to redeem himself with his men and his superiors evolved into a military fiasco remembered as the "Mud March" and cost him the command of the Army of the Potomac.

Stafford was a strong supporter of the Confederacy. Records indicate that there were about 1,000 county men in the Confederate service during the war. In 1861 the white population of Stafford was 4,918. Those over age 35 were exempted from service. Confederate soldiers from Stafford, then, represented 20.3% of the total white population. Many others, male and female, were involved in the Southern cause. At night older Stafford men formed raiding parties and harassed Union camps. Women spied on Federal soldiers and passed information to the Confederate side.

People returning home to Stafford after the war found it quite desolate and many moved away. The population dropped to about 6,000, less than it had been when George Washington had lived at Ferry Farm (see article this chapter). Those who decided to stay had a very difficult time. For four years the land had not been worked and had grown up in scrub trees and bushes which had to be grubbed out by hand. A man returning home from the war might have a cow or a horse, but usually not. He had no laborers. About the only thing he could grow without additional labor was corn. Corn could be planted by hand, worked by hand, and harvested by hand. County residents used to say that to make money on the farm you sold the corn and wheat, and what corn you couldn't sell, you fed to the hogs, and what the hogs didn't eat you ate yourself. Between corn and fish, somehow the hardy people of Stafford survived. Planting corn year after year on the same piece of land, however, will ruin the soil—soil already weakened by repeated planting of tobacco. As a result, Stafford became known as the poorest county in the state. Repeated plantings of corn and a loss of topsoil as a result of the cutting of most of the timber during the war earned the county that well-deserved reputation.

Many who attempted to rebuild their lives in Stafford had to admit defeat and leave. Yet even that proved difficult. There were few buyers interested in purchasing Stafford real estate. Some of the remaining large tracts were bought by Northern land speculators, but by the end of the war, most of the farms had been divided into smaller parcels and distributed between family members. For those who managed to find buyers for their land, they often couldn't complete the deal because Yankee troops had stolen or destroyed so many of the court records and it was impossible to prove ownership of the property. These cases clogged the court system for years afterward and many of those unfortunate enough to have lost their deeds simply moved west with what they could carry.

The days of Reconstruction were nearly as heartbreaking as the war itself. Betty Lacy of Chatham wrote, "I shall not attempt to describe the dreary and disheartening struggle of Reconstruction days. My older children remember that time that tried men's souls even more severely than the four long years of conflict, and to the younger ones it has become familiar by frequent repetition. I sincerely hope that none of them may ever be called upon to pass through the fiery ordeal to which their parents were subjected, and that never again will our dear old State be so bowed in the dust with trouble and humiliation as in those dark days."

After the war, the county recovered very slowly. Not until the 1950s did the population exceed what it had been in the 1790s. The Rappahannock River flowed along the county's south side and the Chopawamsic Swamp bordered the north, effectively eliminating most north–south travel through the county. The swamp had been a nightmare to cross since the earliest settlement in that area. It was nearly impossible to get a horse and an empty wagon through, much less a load. An eighteenth-century mail route which provided north–south communications between the colonies was often delayed for weeks because of this notorious swamp. In fact, conditions in Chopawamsic Swamp prevented Union troops from descending on Fredericksburg from the north and forced them to use the Warrenton Road, adding miles to their trip.

A good road through the swamp was not built until 1920. Miss Anne E. Moncure used to tell a story about the two enterprising Mahoney brothers who, early in the twentieth century, found the swamp to be of some economic value. Each morning they would go down to the swamp and cut a few drainage ditches to drain the water out of the enormous pot holes in the road. Then they would sit down and wait. Before too long, a wagon or perhaps even one of those newfangled automobiles would come along. When the vehicle became stuck in a hole, which was inevitable, the "helpful" brothers would be right there with a mule or two to drag out the hapless driver (for a small fee, of course). At night they diverted the water back into the road in preparation for the next business day.

Additional Sites

Bell Aire—Adjoined the eastern side of Highland Home and was owned by John Fitzhugh. The Wheeler family lived at Bell Aire during the Civil War and used the property as a Union campground. Today, Bell Aire is best known as the "Walnut Farm" because of the hundreds of black walnut trees planted there in the twentieth century. At one time, Bell Aire adjoined Thomas Fitzhugh's Boscobel. Today, the property is bounded be Leeland Road (State Route 626) and Grafton Village to the east and the Richmond, Fredericksburg, and Potomac Railroad tracks to the west. A new subdivision is planned for this property.

The Glebe—A large farm belonging to the Episcopal Church during the late eighteenth and early nineteenth centuries. This property was bounded by State Routes 600 and 674, and Muddy Creek. Today, the road to The Glebe turns north off of State Route 208, very near the King George County line and is marked "The Glebe Road." The glebe house was very near State Route

600. At the time of the Civil War, the property belonged to Hugh Scott.

Grafton—The old Deacon farm. It is now the site of Grafton Elementary School. The house was built c.1840 and the property originally belonged to the Fitzhugh family. In 1895 George R. Fitzhugh sold Grafton to Henry W. Edwards who willed it to his daughter, Minnie Edwards Deacon. The Streshley family lived there during the Civil War. The two-story house was built of logs covered with weatherboard.

Highland Home—an old Lee farm on the west side of Deacon Road. The property was owned by Captain Daniel M. Lee (1843-1917), son of Sidney Smith Lee and nephew of Robert E. Lee. In 1875 Daniel married Nannie E. Ficklen of Belmont. He built Highland Home around 1880 on 135 acres of land. The twentieth-century subdivision built there retains the name.

Inglewood—on Claiborne Run. At the time of the Civil War, this farm belonged to Margaret A. Washington.

Mount Holly—on or very near the Rappahannock. In 1860 it belonged to William Brown.

Mount Pleasant—an old Bradshaw family farm that was between Highland Home and U.S. Route 1. The old house there was built c.1811. Mount Pleasant subdivision now occupies the land.

Mulberry Hill—Near the Rappahannock; was the home of Benjamin Broughton from the 1830s to c.1842. In 1860 the farm belonged to Alexander K. Phillips.

Wildwood—on Claiborne Run.

Falmouth & U.S. Route 17

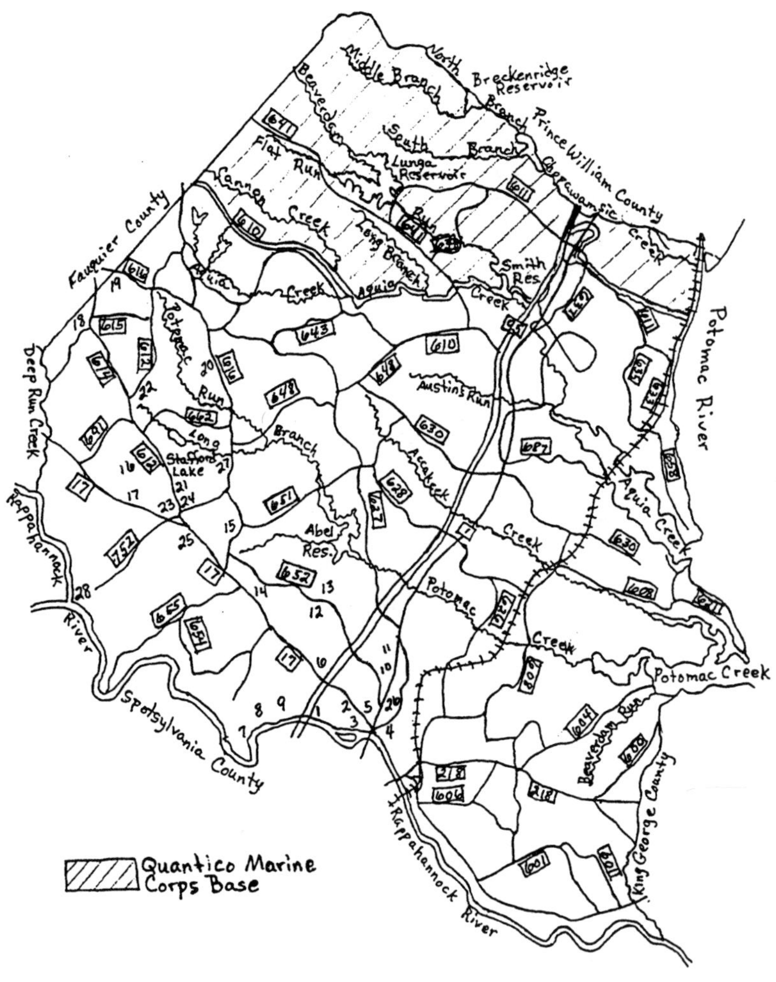

1 .. Hunter's Iron Works
2 .. Prospect Hill
3 .. Belmont
4 .. Clearview
5 .. Carlton
6 .. Stanstead
7 .. Greenbank
8 .. Greaves' House
9 .. Harwood Branch
10 .. Glencairne
11 .. Mont Anna
12 .. Ellerslie
13 .. Liberty Hall
14 .. Hammet Place
15 .. Locust Grove
16 .. Marsh Home
17 .. Old Stone House
18 .. Petmouth Grove
19 .. Poplar Hill
20 .. Scotland
21 .. Spotted Tavern
22 .. Stony Hill
23 .. Hartwood Presbyterian Church
24 .. Yellow Chapel
25 .. Hartwood
26 .. Inglewood
27 .. Cedar Ridge
28 .. Richard's Ferry
29 .. Grafton

Chapter 11

Falmouth Town and the Rappahannock West of Falmouth

Falmouth

In the beginning, Stafford County was predominately agricultural, and crops were shipped from here to England. The continuing influx of new colonists, however, encouraged the development of interests other than farming. Colonists began to build mills and develop small industries. Falmouth, built on fifty acres belonging to William Todd on the fall line of the Rappahannock River, was named for the seaport of Falmouth in Cornwall, England, and was incorporated in 1727.

The first town government was in the hands of seven trustees appointed by the House of Burgesses. These trustees, some of the most respected men in the area, were Robert Carter (president), Nicholas Smith, John Fitzhugh, Charles Carter, Henry Fitzhugh, John Warner, and William Thornton. By 1773 the town charter had been amended so that the trustees were elected and the president served as mayor.

Although a small town, Falmouth was one of the most important business centers in Virginia during the eighteenth and early nineteenth centuries. Business here began to grow as that at Marlborough faded. The town, however, had been a prosperous business center prior to its incorporation in 1727. A tobacco warehouse was built at Falmouth in 1730 and ships carried not only tobacco but also grain and cotton raised to the west of the town.

An influx of Scotsmen to Stafford during the first half of the eighteenth century contributed to Falmouth's early success. The Scots were merchants who took over most of the businesses, bringing about widespread prosperity to the area.

Falmouth was an ideal place for business in the eighteenth and early nineteenth centuries because of its location and water power. Factories were built along the Rappahannock, and sailing vessels could come right up the river.

On October 14, 1839, a group of citizens organized a company which they called the Falmouth Manufacturing Company. They hoped to interest people in becoming stockholders. Shares were sold for $100 each and soon quite a few people in the Falmouth and Stafford areas were stockholders, including Basil Gordon, John O'Bannon, and John Green. Among the factories in Falmouth were a flour mill owned by George Kirge and a nail factory. A visitor to the town in 1845 described it as having "1 free church, 6 or 7 mercantile stores, 2 extensive flouring mills, and 1 large cotton factory, and a population of about 500."

Raw materials from all around were brought to the plants. Grain was brought by wagon load from the surrounding farms. Manufactured products were sent to Scotland, England, and other world ports.

By the late 1840s, silting of the river caused by poor farming techniques brought an end to shipping activities in Falmouth, and the town's business boom quietly died. Silting was a common problem in this type of port town because, typically, they were built as far inland as possible. This shortened the distance that inland farmers had to haul their products. Falmouth, and Dumfries to the north, were built as far upstream as ships could possibly travel. The filling of the channel with silt was inevitable and usually occurred within fifty years of the building of shallow-water port towns.

Today, Falmouth has a number of charming little buildings. Among the old buildings remaining are Union Church, the surveyor's office, a workman's cottage, the Temperance Hotel, two warehouses, the counting house, several shop buildings, and a few residences.

One of the quaint little homes is the Barnes' House. Built around 1780, this frame house was purchased by Gari Melchers of

Belmont. Very little is known about the house. It is one and one-half stories above a stone foundation and has a quaint Dutch-style room. There are three dormers on the front but on the back there is just one tiny window located in the center of the roof.

The surveyor's office or Customs House was built around 1790. A tiny one and one-half story building with a wood-shingled roof, it was probably first used as an office for the Trustees of Falmouth Towne. Later, it became a port of delivery office. Here customs were collected on goods being shipped from Falmouth. For a time, it also served as an office for the local surveyors. In 1786 the Continental Congress designated Falmouth port of delivery to receive goods from foreign countries. In more recent years, this building has been used as a Magistrate Court, Falmouth Towne office, council meeting house, and polling place for the town. Although unoccupied at this time, it is still a Stafford County government building. For a while it was used as a county museum but proved to be far too small to accommodate artifacts and visitors simultaneously.

The old cotton warehouse at 201 Cambridge Street has also survived into the twentieth century. Built around 1780, this is a two-story frame building, the wooden roof of which was later replaced with tin. Dependencies including a meat house, stable, kitchen, and milk house complemented the building. None of these survive today.

The structure has had many uses over the last two hundred years. During the eighteenth century, the building was used as a cotton warehouse, probably by Basil Gordon. It may also have served as an early Masonic Lodge prior to the building of a lodge in Fredericksburg.

After the Civil War, the warehouse became a residence for the Duff Green family. In 1885 Mr. and Mrs. Edwin Brooks bought the property. Their family lived in the building until 1987. Recently, the warehouse was renovated and presently serves as a real estate office.

The old counting house is at 103 Gordon Street and was built about 1800. It is a frame one and one-half story building over a stone foundation. It has the unusual steep roof frequently seen on the old buildings of Falmouth.

The Master Hobby school has long been a part of Falmouth, though not at its present location. Several years ago, it was moved to its new home near Union Church. This charming little one-room building dates from about 1740 and is built of logs and brick. Local legend says that George Washington attended school in this building, though it is more likely that he was tutored at Ferry Farm.

The Shelton cottage, overlooking the Rappahannock from River Road, is one of the few old buildings in Falmouth to be properly restored. This is a typical workman's cottage and one of the few to have survived in the state of Virginia. It seems to date from about 1770. Many of the timbers show evidence of having been pit sawed. That is, a log was laid across a pit deep enough for a man to stand up in. A second man stood on top of the log. Each man held an end of a long saw which was drawn up and down through the log until it was cut in two. Pit sawed timbers which have not been planed have straight marks left from the vertical action of the saw. Timbers which have been cut in a sawmill have curved marks from the circular saw.

Originally located several hundred yards west of its present location, the Shelton cottage was moved about ten years ago. There are two rooms, one up and one down. The beams in the house are quite large and hand-hewn, and the cottage sits upon a stone foundation.

Long unoccupied, the Moncure Conway house at 305 King Street (River Road) is one of Falmouth's handsomest buildings. The exact date of construction is unknown. James Vass bought this home from the William Cunningham Company of Glasgow, Scotland, and it is known to have been standing as early as 1807.

At the time this house was built, business in Falmouth was at its peak. Ocean-going sailing ships laden with merchandise and slaves docked within one hundred yards of the front door. Passengers and cargo moved in a steady, constant flow past the house and onto ships destined for distant ports. During the day, vendors sold their wares to merchants, residents, and travelers drawn by the presence of the ships. Slaves were bought and sold at the docks, as Falmouth was the official port of entry for slaves coming to this part of Virginia. Activity on the Falmouth docks began well before first light in the morning and lasted long into the night as sailors finished their duties and noisily headed up King Street towards the Eagle Tavern.

The builder of this fine home sought to express in his dwelling the prosperity that was Falmouth at the turn of the nineteenth century. He was likely a well-to-do businessman who had not quite reached the peak of his earning power but expected to become wealthier soon. Though it does not appear so at first look, the builder only constructed *half* of his house! This style of building is known as a "flounder house." Viewed from the front, the house appears to be a complete two-story Federal-style brick dwelling with a central hall. Viewed from the east end, however, it is evident that only the front half of the house was completed. Frequently, flounder houses had the back half added at a later date when money was available. In this case, however, the back half was never added, perhaps due to the decline in shipping and business in Falmouth which occurred by 1850 and was a result of silting of the Rappahannock River.

In 1838 Moncure Conway and his family moved into the home. Conway was a nineteenth-century author, lecturer, clergyman, and abolitionist. During Conway's residence, the hill behind the house was terraced and the dining room wall paper had a scene of Rotterdam which continued all the way around the room.

The interior of the house is exceptionally fine. The first floor has an enormous central hall suitable for dancing and gracious entertainment. A wide stairway leads to the second floor. On each side of the hall is a large, airy room. Beneath the house is an English basement which frequently floods when the rain-swollen Rappahannock overflows its nearby banks. As a note of interest, severe flooding occasionally reveals the stone abutments of the eighteenth-century docks which once stood in front of the Conway house. Abandoned for many years, this historic home has recently been purchased and is being lovingly restored.

Standing above the little town of Falmouth is picturesque old Union Church. As part of the town charter in 1727, the trustees were ordered to set aside two acres for a church and cemetery. Upon this land a frame sanctuary was constructed slightly behind the site of the present building. This Episcopalian church was in the shape of a cross, similar to Aquia Church, and was used for some time before being abandoned between 1755 and 1760. A replacement brick church was built on the site of the present facade but burned about 1818.

Local residents decided to rebuild the church, but because of the proliferation of religious denominations after the Revolution, it was decided to make the new church a "union church." The new building was used by Episcopalian, Presbyterian, Baptist, and Methodist congregations on revolving Sundays. This church remained in use until 1950, when a violent storm destroyed all but the facade. Behind the church is a cemetery; the oldest surviving marker is dated 1738.

By this time America had broken free from England and the Episcopal Church was no longer the official church. People of varying denominations resided in and around Falmouth and a new brick multi-denominational church was built upon the foundation of the destroyed church.

In an effort to preserve what was left of the venerable old building, Historic Falmouth Towne took over its care. Today the church is a part of the Falmouth Historic District and is designated a historic landmark by the state. St. Luke's Anglican Church plans to rebuild the body of the church for use as a house of worship.

Warrenton Road

With few exceptions, the homes to the west of Falmouth were very simple in design prior to the Civil War. Most were made of logs, and few of frame. Most were fastened together with wooden pegs, a few with nails. This is not surprising because up until the war, this area was considered a wilderness. Colonial settlement always began along the rivers and moved up the creeks. The earliest homes were nearly always of log, as such were quick and easy to build. There being few, if any, roads, travel by water was often the only means of getting around. Once all the land along the rivers and creeks was claimed, settlers had to push further and further westward into the wilderness. So it was that while people along the Warrenton Road were living in rough log cabins, the Fitzhughs were comfortably established in

Chatham cultivating berries and breeding fine horses and the Wallaces were entertaining well-to-do visitors at Clearview.

Nearly all the homes along the Warrenton Road were basic farmhouses, normally one and one-half stories with one or two chimneys, and two to four rooms. As the families became established and prospered, they covered their houses with frame or built new ones of brick or stone. Stafford County sits on an enormous quantity of sand and gravel, and the fall line runs through the county, providing plenty of building stone. Stafford's red clay makes very attractive bricks, and people of some means could have their slaves dig the clay and burn the bricks right next to the house site.

Few of the old homes on the Warrenton Road survive today, victims of the Civil War, termites, fire, and general neglect. Log houses do not weather as well as stone or brick, and the people who lived in these little cottages rarely had the means to preserve them. Many burned, fire being a constant hazard prior to the development of central heating. Many early homes were actually built with wooden chimneys. The insides of the chimneys were lined with mud, which baked as the chimney was used. However, over time the chimney could settle, causing cracks to form in the mud. Sparks would slip through the cracks, setting the dry wood frame afire. Poor farmers who lost their log homes to fire could hardly afford to replace the buildings with anything other than something similar to what they had. So while many of the farms can still be seen today as one travels out the Warrenton Road, few of the old buildings remain.

Industries In Stafford

By the eighteenth century, there were numerous industries in Stafford—quarries, iron works, grist mills, fisheries, and several small mines. A geologic fault runs diagonally through the county from about Garrisonville to the Rappahannock River. Along this fault are mineral outcroppings including gold, iron, copper, graphite, mica, and silver which were mined intermittently throughout the county's history. Only the sandstone quarries along Aquia Creek, the fishery at Clifton, and the iron works at

Accakeek and Falmouth became major commercial operations; by and large, the mills and mines provided services and raw materials for the local population only. Water-powered saw mills came into use, thus beginning a lumber business that would last until the region's loss of timber during the Civil War. That lumber business didn't resume until about 1900.

One of the earliest industrial efforts in the Virginia colony was weaving. In October 1666 the House of Burgesses sought to encourage manufacturing: "the nakednes of the country doe suffitiently evidence the necessity of provideing supply of our wants…five women or children of 12 or 13 years of age may with much ease provide suffitient cloathing for thirty persons." Within two years of this act each county court was to set up a loom and weaver paid from public funds. The existence of private weavers did not fulfill this requirement. Stafford, however, "who by the newness of [its] ground pretend themselves incapable of makeing provision for the soe soone imployment of a weaver," was granted a four-year extension.

Gold was discovered in Stafford during the eighteenth century. In 1787 Thomas Jefferson wrote in his *Notes on Virginia,* "I know a single instance of gold found in this state. It was interspersed in small specks through a lump of ore, of about four pounds weight, which yielded seventeen pennyweight [1/20 ounce] of gold, of extraordinary ductility." This gold was found in Stafford about four miles below Fredericksburg on the north side of the Rappahannock.

"Gold fever" struck the area around 1829. From then until 1900 gold was mined at several locations in the county. Hopeful gold-seekers ranged through Stafford, Orange, Culpeper, Fluvanna, Goochland, and Louisa Counties following the Rappahannock, Rapidan, and their tributaries. This gold belt extended from the Potomac to the James Rivers and was part of a larger deposit which extended through the Carolinas and into Georgia.

Panning was the most frequently used method of separating the precious metal from creek or river deposits. This method was later used by California prospectors. While primitive, panning in Stafford was successful enough to encourage other more elaborate methods of mining.

Working Gold Mines
1836-1850

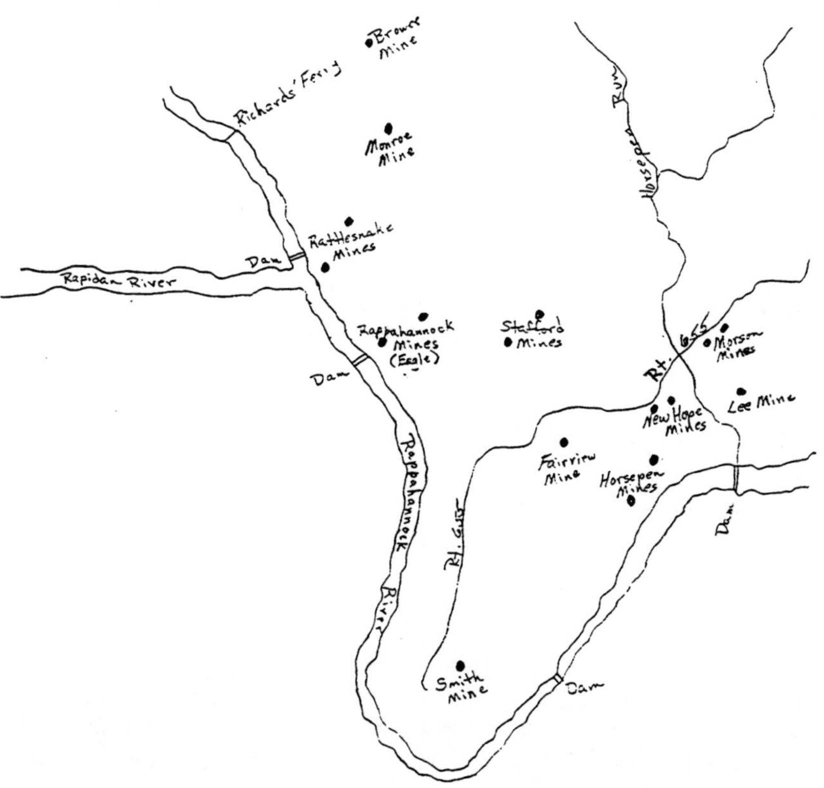

In Stafford, most of the gold mines were in the vicinity of present-day U.S. Route 17. Gold and graphite are present in the rock outcroppings of the Rappahannock River. Those deposits follow the river bed into Fauquier County. There were other gold mines in this part of the county, including Prospect Mine, Three Sisters Mine, New Hope, Monroe Mine, King Mine, Rattlesnake Mine, Horsepen Run Mine, Eliot Farm, and Wise Farm.

The old Eagle Mine near the Fauquier County line had its own stamping mill. The Eagle, like most local gold mines, was a shaft mine. Ore was dug from the hole and crushed. The gold was extracted from the rock and stamped into usable lumps. The machinery used at the Eagle operation was expensive, indicating the presence of high-quality ore. Unfortunately, shaft mines had a tendency to fill up with water. The pumping equipment didn't work well, which made the extraction of ore unprofitable after the discovery of gold in California. Panning for small quantities of gold, however, continues today. The area known as Gold Vein was named because of mining operations there. Even after the Civil War, when the land had become poor from overwork and much of the population had moved west to Kentucky, land around the mines brought prices almost as high as today.

The Iron Works

Iron was discovered in the Stafford County by John Smith, who in 1608 sent two barrels of the ore to England for analysis. After the first permanent settlement in Virginia, a group of English merchants sponsored the building of a furnace at Jamestown. An Indian massacre ended this endeavor soon after it started.

The first successful furnace operation in Virginia was the Tubal Furnace built in 1715 at Germanna in Spotsylvania County. This was a large and rather productive venture that set the stage for the iron works near Falmouth.

In 1725 the Principio Company of Maryland decided to expand its already sizable operation into Virginia and leased a ridge of high grade ore-bearing land on Accakeek Run near Potomac Creek. Principio was an English company whose only non-English partner was Augustine Washington. Principio leased this land for one thousand years and gave Washington a one-sixth interest in the total production from the furnace and a tonnage fee for the ore that Washington's workers dug from the mines. Principio also had the right to build and use any necessary improvements and to take from the site all timber necessary to run the operation. Washington, then, was given a stock interest in the company and was paid for every ton of pig (rough iron bars ready for manufacture into usable products) produced from ore taken from his mines.

Principio was the largest iron exporter in the colonies. Prior to 1720, the company had built a bloomery or small crude forge at the head of the Chesapeake Bay which produced low-grade wrought iron. Bloomeries were common along the Atlantic coast, though more so in New England. From this modest beginning Principio became one of the largest iron producers in the colonies with blast furnaces and mills for making high-grade iron products.

The man behind the growth of Principio in Virginia was John England, an ironmaster from Staffordshire, England. Although he never learned to read or write, he designed and built the Accakeek Furnace. This sizable industrial complex was situated on the south side of the creek approximately two and one-half miles west of Stafford Court House. The plant began operations in 1728 and for many years the Accakeek Furnace was a profitable venture, producing fire backs, nails, latches, and assorted small farming implements.

The process used to make the iron was fairly simple. The ore from the mines was first broken into small pieces. These pieces were then placed in a stone cone-shaped furnace which was open at both the top and the bottom. Often, these furnaces were built against a hill so that a bridge could be built from the top of the hill to the top of the furnace, allowing quantities of ore, limestone or oyster shells, and charcoal to be dumped into the top. This mixture was fanned by a water-driven bellows and produced intense heat which separated the metal from its rock matrix. A crucible in the bottom of the furnace collected the molten metal which was then poured into molds making "pigs." The pigs were then moved to the forge where they might be refined into wrought iron. Blacksmiths used the wrought iron for making all types of tools and ironware.

It appears that a dam was built on Accakeek Creek to provide water power to run the bellows. Remains of a silted-in pond appear on the northeast side of the creek. More than likely, the water level in the creek was higher than it is now. A raceway, or channel, approximately ninety feet long was excavated directly into the bedrock. Four to five feet deep, it probably carried the water back to the creek after it had provided head (power) for the bellows. Immediately south of the raceway is an elevated berm about thirty feet wide and eighty feet long. The remains of a stone wall or foundation are still visible on top of the berm and may mark the location of the old furnace.

The Accakeek Furnace is on the National Register of Historic Places. The site is in good condition for archaeological study as it has remained largely undisturbed since the furnace was dismantled. The furnace is the second oldest iron works identified in Virginia, predated only by the Tubal Furnace mentioned earlier. The Accakeek operation included a store, warehouse, forge, and mill. Most likely, there would also have been living quarters for a large assortment of laborers including miners, millers, agricultural workers, blacksmiths, and charcoal makers.

The only visible remains of this once-sizable operation are the pond site, two mine pits, raceway, possible furnace location, mill wheel pit, a retaining wall, and a slag dump. One mine pit is on the southwest side of the creek and one is on the northeast side.

A description of the operation was written in 1732 by William Byrd II of Westover:

> England's Iron Mines, called so from the chief manager of them, belongs to Mr. Washington. He raises the ore, and carts it thither for 20 s. the ton that it yields. The furnace is on a run which discharges into the Potomac. And when the iron is cast, they cart it about 6 miles to a landing on that river. Besides Mr. Washington and Mr. England there are several persons in England concerned in these works. Matters are very well

> handled there, and no expense is spared to make them profitable, which is not the case in the other works I have mentioned.

Accakeek served for a time as Principio's headquarters in Virginia. Pig iron was produced here and sent on to the company forge or loaded onto company ships for export or for processing elsewhere in the Chesapeake region. Much of it was carted to major river ports where it was loaded on tobacco ships for ballast. The cost for transporting it in this manner was one-third that for regular cargo.

John England died in 1734 and the Washington family moved to Ferry Farm so Augustine could be closer to the business. In 1737 Augustine became a full partner in the Principio Company and served as the company's representative in America. At his death, Augustine's shares were worth £1,200. He also owned Wakefield, Ferry Farm, and several lots in Fredericksburg. When Augustine died in 1743, his son Lawrence inherited the entire interest in Principio and became a partner in the company. Lawrence died in 1752 and left his shares to his brother Augustine. They were finally inherited by William Augustine Washington.

In 1756 Principio decided to abandon the Accakeek Furnace. They had stripped the surrounding area of all available wood and the soil had eroded away. Although there was still sufficient iron to mine, it was too costly to ship it to Maryland for processing. Further, by 1771 Principio was feeling the effects of the colonial distrust of the mother country and business was on the wane. Principio ended their business venture in Virginia and withdrew to Maryland.

The Virginia Assembly, well aware of the importance of the iron manufactory, passed an act for the encouragement of iron works. By this time, James Hunter (1721-1784) was already manufacturing iron products on the Rappahannock, just outside of Falmouth, but he was unable to obtain enough ore to keep his furnace operating at capacity. According to *Hening's Statutes*, on May 1, 1777, the owners of the Accakeek property were given thirty days to "begin and within six months thereon, a furnace and other necessary works on a scale equal to or larger than the former one, and prosecute the same for making pig iron and other castings" and if they did not do so, Hunter could "enter upon and locate two hundred acres of the said tract, including the old furnace seat and dam...and pay a sum for the property as determined by the court." Hunter produced a letter from Principio stating that they had no intention of reopening the Accakeek furnace. Hunter paid Principio for two hundred acres of ore bearing land and commenced mining for his own furnace.

After the Revolution, William Augustine Washington and several partners in the Principio Company petitioned the Virginia legislature to revoke Hunter's grant, claiming that Hunter had not built anything upon the property. This remained an issue until the end of the century and was never resolved.

James Hunter (1721-1784) was the son of James Hunter, merchant of Duns, Scotland. His uncle, William Hunter, settled in Virginia in the 1730s and was one of the first Scottish merchants to settle in the Fredericksburg area. James was brought up in the mercantile business and soon began making business trips to Virginia during which time he also bought property here. By 1749 he had settled permanently in Virginia becoming a junior partner in his uncle's Fredericksburg store and a trader of slaves. Owing to the failing health of the elder Hunter, James was soon carrying out most of the daily activities of the store.

In 1754 William died, leaving three young children as orphans. James was left to administer the property and carry out the provisions of the will. William had stipulated that proceeds from the sale of goods in the store and income from his real estate was to be used to educate his two sons at William and Mary. Under James Hunter's administration, this stipulation was never carried out. His handling of the estate and his failure to provide financial support to several debt-ridden family members resulted in family dissention which continued long after his death.

The exact date of James Hunter's earliest involvement in the iron industry is uncertain. By the mid-1750s Hunter was branching out of the mercantile business and developing planting and industrial interests. He was making extensive land purchases in Fredericksburg and in the surrounding counties. By 1761 he was shipping tobacco and pig iron to Liverpool which indicates that sometime shortly prior to that time he had at least developed the rudimentary processing of iron.

The foundry produced supplies for the military as well as commonplace items such as hinges, bridle bits, curry combs, kitchen implements, traveling forges and the famous Farmer's Friend plow. This was a single horse plow with a replaceable wooden beam that was light and easily disassembled for carrying in a wagon. Much of the prairie was plowed with the "Farmer's Friend" and it was said that the West could not have been settled without it.

Very often other industries and shops were associated with an iron works. Since the site already provided water power, it was usual to find a grist mill as a part of the forge complex. Hunter's foundry also included a store, counting house, smith's shop, tannery, grist mill, sawmill, forge mill, and merchant mill. The grist mill ground grain brought by local farmers and also provided flour for the iron workers. A merchant mill, on the other hand, handled huge quantities of flour and meal and shipped the finished products to distant ports. The sawmill cut logs into boards and the forge mill powered huge hammers that shaped the steel. Other businesses associated with the iron works included blacksmith shops, a tannery, loom, and small general stores. By the time of the Revolution, Hunter's iron works was one of the largest single industries in the New World and from about 1775 to 1781, it was the largest iron works in the colonies. At one time, in fact, the government owed Mr. Hunter some $930,000 for items made at his foundry.

It is unknown how much of the foundry's success was a result of Hunter's involvement or of the abilities of his manager, John Strode. Strode was a Pennsylvania Quaker who was originally hired as a plantation overseer for one of Hunter's Stafford plantations. Contemporary Henry Banks described Strode as "farmer, mechanic, [and] skilful and accurate accountant." Sometime prior to the Revolution, Strode became manager of the iron works. At the outbreak of the war, he returned to Pennsylvania and recruited mechanics of many vocations. Under his management, the foundry was soon producing muskets, pistols, carbines, camp kettles, spades, shovels, and any other iron objects required for the war effort.

James Mercer wrote to Thomas Jefferson on April 14, 1781, describing the importance of the iron works:

> It is from Mr. Hunter's Works that every camp kettle has been supplied for the continental and all other troops employed in this State, and to the southward. All the anchors for this State and Maryland and some for the continent have been produced from the same works; that without the assistance of the bar iron made there, even the planters hereabouts and to the southward...would not be able to make bread to eat.

In June of 1776 Hunter showed a sample musket with bayonet, sheath, and steel ramrod to the Revolutionary convention. The members were so pleased that they made the gun standard and asked him to make as many as possible within the next twelve months.

In addition to the musket, Hunter was producing three other types of guns at his foundry—a .69 caliber, 9-inch, smooth bore pistol; a .65 caliber, 8.75-inch smooth bore pistol; and an unusual weapon called a "wall gun" or "amusette." Essentially a large musket, it filled the gap between a shoulder arm and a cannon. The wall gun was semi-portable, though not easily handled from the shoulder due to its 53.5-pound weight, and could propel a large ball for a long distance. The barrel was rifled and the stock was manufactured with a swivel rod to support the barrel from a fixed position such as the top of a wall.

That same year, William Fitzhugh of Chatham advanced money to help pay for the muskets produced by Hunter's forge. The following year Fitzhugh was appointed commissioner to encourage the expansion of the operation to furnish materials for the army and navy.

Patrick Henry was also impressed with the works and, in 1777, he put before the General Assembly an Act for the encouragement of the Iron Works.

Britain recognized the importance of the iron works, also, and attempted to take them on two occasions, in February and again in June of 1781. General Weedon's job was to protect the iron works and in this endeavor he was successful. The Revolution caused little damage in Stafford.

It is highly doubtful that the Accakeek mines produced adequate iron for the Rappahannock Foundry. Hunter was also shipping iron from Principio in Maryland and Jefferson's *Notes on Virginia* states that in 1781 Hunter was annually processing three hundred tons of bar iron from Maryland pig. He was almost certainly shipping ore down the Rappahannock from mines in Spotsylvania, also.

Early in the war, Hunter had made an agreement with the General Assembly that his artisans would not be drafted and sent to fight. The Assembly broke that promise in February 1781, thereby causing Hunter to close his small arms factory. The state was already deep in debt to Hunter. In an effort to raise money, he allowed the state to take over his stock of coarse woolens, enough to clothe from one hundred fifty to two hundred men. For these goods the state might pay him in tobacco at fifty pounds per hundredweight of wool. In March the legislators attempted to correct their mistake by passing an act to exempt iron work artisans from military service, but the damage to Hunter's operations had already been done. Hunter's workers were in the army.

Later in 1781, Hunter managed to procure more artisans and he put himself in debt to expand his works. He began producing traveling forges in October. The war was over after Yorktown, however, and the Assembly, eager to encourage him before and during the war, now would not pay him the heavy debts they had incurred. A true patriot, he had invested much of his own fortune in the forge but was forced for lack of funds to dismiss all his workers in December 1782, ending foundry operations.

James Hunter died in 1784. Unfortunately, his record books, ledgers, and personal papers were lost and there is little that sheds light on the career or personal life of this fascinating individual. In his will of November 18, 1784, James left the bulk of his estate to his brother, Adam, who spent many years disposing of the property. In 1794 Adam advertised in *The Virginia Herald* the sale of James' plantation, Stanstead (see article this chapter):

> ...his late Mansion House, in Stafford county, containing near four hundred acres of Land, lying on Rappahannock river, opposite the town of Fredericksburg, of which it commands a complete

> view: There is on the Plantation about thirty acres of valuable meadow, and a large peach and apple orchard; the Ferry Landing on the north side of the river and Boats will be sold with this tract. This seat, in point of elegance, beauty, and many other advantages, is equal, no: superior, to any in this part of the country.

An additional 385 acres adjoining the plantation was offered for sale, also. Of this property, forty acres of meadow was suitable for corn or wheat. Money from the sale was to be applied to paying the debts of the testator.

An advertisement for the sale of Hunter's forge complex appeared in the May 18, 1798 *Fredericksburg Herald.* From the description in the advertisement we are given an idea of the impressive size of his operation:

> The Iron Works and Mills...consisting of a Forge 128 feet by 51 feet, eight fires and 4 hammers, a coal house 80 by 40 feet, a merchant mill 70 feet by 36 feet with two pairs of French burnstones [burstones]...a grist mill 20 feet by 18 feet...a saw mill 55 feet by 11 feet...Contiguous thereto are a stable 54 feet by 27 feet...a nailery, a tanyard, coopers, carpenters, and wheelwright shops...and houses for the managers and workmen.

The forge didn't sell until the first quarter of the nineteenth century when it was bought by Joseph Ficklen. The operation never again produced as it had in Hunter's time; in fact, it is uncertain if it was ever used as a forge at all after Ficklen's purchase. Tax records after the Civil War are scant but by 1870 the property is listed as 371½ acres with no buildings. It is unknown what happened to so many buildings; they may have just collapsed from neglect.

Hunter invested much of his fortune in his iron works and seems never to have received full compensation from the government. Contrary to local legend, however, James Hunter was not destitute when he died. His will provided £1,000 legacies to cousins on the condition that they not bring suit against his estate because of disputes over his father's estate or that of his brother, William. The stipulations attached to the gifts suggest that family dissention had never been resolved to everyone's satisfaction. Hunter was buried behind old Union Church in Falmouth.

Belmont

I have long believed that Belmont is one of the most beautiful homes in Virginia. It is a large, white, rambling frame building with several porches and sits high on a terraced hill overlooking Falmouth and the Rappahannock River.

The house was built in several stages over the last two centuries. The original tract was granted to the Reverend Thomas Vicaris in 1678 for transporting twenty-seven settlers to Virginia. Three hundred acres of this patent were lost to overlapping grants in 1727. In 1748 Martha Todd conveyed a piece of this property just west of Falmouth to John Dixon. Recent research has shown that the oldest part of the present structure dates from 1761, during the Dixon ownership. In 1779 Dixon sold this same tract to John Richards. The land was divided between his heirs and one acre was given to Richards' daughter, Patty, and her husband, John Horner. By 1807, however, when Alexander Voss sold the property to Thomas Knox, the deed included "all houses, outhouses, buildings, garden monuments and Hereditaments whatsoever to the said acre of land." Knox purchased the property for his mother, Susannah Fitzhugh Knox, formerly of Boscobel (see Chapter 9). An insurance policy purchased by Knox described the house as a "modest two story, 32 by 32 foot wooden dwelling located on the hill near Falmouth." This probably describes the part of the house which presently includes the central halls and the library, dining room, and bedrooms. In 1823 and 1824 Knox's sons advertised the sale of the property in the newspaper. This is the first recorded instance of the house being called Belmont.

A flour mill operator from Culpeper, Joseph Burwell Ficklen bought Belmont in 1824. The 1834 insurance policy held by Ficklen lists the dimensions of the house as thirty-nine by thirty-four feet with an addition which, for some unknown reason, was not covered by the policy.

Ficklen married Ellen McGhee in 1843 but she died just two years later. He then married Ann Eliza Fitzhugh and they raised a family of six children at Belmont. The house remained in the Ficklen family for ninety-two years.

Gari and Corinne Melchers bought Belmont in 1916 and, by that time, the house was in need of repair. The Melcherses added the sun porch to the south end and installed two bathrooms in the Ficklens' bedrooms. They also built a second story on the rear portico. They re-floored the east and west porticoes and probably added the two third-floor rooms in the service wing.

Much of the furnishings in the house were collected by the couple during their world-wide travels. Melchers, already a well-known artist, continued to paint in his studio at Belmont for the last sixteen years of his life. Melchers was chiefly known for his portraits of famous people such as Theodore Roosevelt. His paintings decorate the Library of Congress, and he chaired the Smithsonian Commission to Establish a National Gallery of Art.

He also served on the Virginia Arts Commission and helped to plan the Virginia Museum of Fine Arts.

At the death of Corinne Melchers, the property was deeded to the state of Virginia and is administered by Mary Washington College. Visitors are welcome to come and enjoy the lovely home and gardens as well as Melchers' studio and paintings.

Clearview

The second of the "hilltop houses," Clearview was built circa 1740. It is a fine example of a lesser plantation house in Virginia. The land was first patented by Thomas Vicaris in 1707. In 1720, fifty acres were taken to build the town of Falmouth. The property was later owned by the Dodd, Dixon, and Lawson families. In 1786 the property was sold to Andrew Buchanan, who probably built the house. Buchanan was a major in the Caroline County militia and served on Washington's staff during the Revolution. Buchanan died sometime before 1805, and the property changed hands several times. By 1814 the house belonged to William James and was valued at $3,500. In 1822 the property was in the possession of Alexander Walker. An 1836 insurance policy for Clearview was issued to John C. Scott, and it appears to have remained in the Scott family for some time, as maps made during the Civil War show the area as Scott property. The Wallace family obtained the farm from the Scotts.

This is a hip-roofed, two-story frame house; one wing was added to the west end in 1918-19. Two brick and stone chimneys grace the east and west ends of the house. Plain weatherboarding is accented by ornate cornices below the roof.

The front porch is Tuscan in style and probably dates from the same period as the wing. The back of the house has a three-bay facade with double raised-panel doors. Mutual Assurance policies dating from 1796 to 1839 list three outbuildings associated with the house, namely a twelve-by-sixteen-foot study, a thirty-by-sixteen-foot kitchen, and a twelve-foot-square meathouse. The meathouse disappeared from the records by 1836. Today, none of the original outbuildings survive.

The interior of the house was designed for gracious living. A beautiful circular stairway is the focal point in the center hall. The house contains seven rooms; the cornices deserve special notice. The dining room has two corner fireplaces accented by fine Federal woodwork.

The Wallace family owned Clearview until very recently. The first member of the Wallace family to live at Clearview was Mary Wallace, daughter of Dr. Michael Wallace of Scotland. Mary married the previously-mentioned Dr. Andrew Buchanan and went to Clearview to live.

Despite its proximity to Fredericksburg, Clearview survived the Civil War. General Burnside camped there, and while the house was extensively damaged, it did not burn.

By the time of the war, the Misses Mary and Fanny Scott and their aunt, Mrs. McNeil, were living at Clearview. Ten thousand Federal troops were camped on the hill, and some soldiers decided to place a cannon next to one of the chimneys. From this position they had a clear shot at Fredericksburg. Miss Fanny chastised the soldiers, saying that firing the cannon from that location would surely kill her aunt who was ill and confined to the house. It is unknown whether it was her caustic tongue or her ability to persuade, but the cannon was not fired from that location.

Repairs to the house have preserved the original design and much of the fine Federal trim remains. Although the house was allowed to run down in later years, it has since been purchased by Mr. and Mrs. William P. Sale, who have beautifully restored it.

Carlton

Another of Stafford's beautiful homes, Carlton stands high above the Rappahannock River overlooking the little town of Falmouth. Georgian in design, the house is a forty-eight by twenty-six foot frame, two-story, hip-roofed structure built above an English basement. A tiny slant-roofed wing graces the north end of the house and now serves as a mud room. In earlier days, food was brought from the outside kitchen and placed on shelves built against the chimney to keep it warm.

Much of the interior of the house is original. The dining room is especially fine. The corner fireplace is accented by a mantel. Most of the north wall is occupied by an exceptional four-section, built-in cupboard. Originally, all four sections had glass-paneled doors. Recently, the two outer glass-paneled doors were replaced by raised-panel wood doors.

It is unknown who built Carlton or even when it was built. It seems probable, however, that it was built by one John Short, a merchant in Falmouth, sometime between his marriage in 1785 and his death in 1794. Short purchased the property from William Richards though no deed seems to have been recorded. John Short was the third son of John and Theodosia Mathews Short of St. Paul's Parish, Stafford County (now King George County). On June 17, 1796, John's wife, Judith Ball Short, took out a fire insurance policy to insure "five buildings on the hill near the town of Falmouth consisting of a dwelling house, dairy, kitchen, meathouse and stable." The kitchen, dairy, and meathouse survive today.

In 1837 the property (some 4,000 acres) was purchased by John M. O'Bannon. A slave owner, O'Bannon provided slave labor to Falmouth when the town was a very busy shipping port. O'Bannon's two daughters, Lillie and Nanny, lived at Carlton for many years. They owned several small houses at the foot of the hill which they rented and each month they would go from house to house in a wagon collecting the rents.

During the Battle of Fredericksburg, Carlton was out of the line of fire and was undamaged by the fighting. No battles were fought on the property and no gun emplacements were built there.

Dr. and Mrs. E. Boyd Graves purchased the house in 1941. By that time, it had seen many years of neglect and abuse and, when purchased by the Graveses, it was little more than a shell. Dr. Graves and his wife had to replace all of the plaster in the house as well as undertake other major repair work, which took several years to complete. Fortunately, the home still has all of its original latches, H and L hinges, and large brass locks. Each first-floor room has a fireplace and the banister in the entry hall is unique in that it ends in a ram's horn design.

Gordon Green Terrace

Owners:
1783 Land bought by Samuel Gordon who built the house
c.1800 Purchased by a Mr. Green
1858 C. Jones
1900 John Humphrey
1909 Mr. and Mrs. Clarence Wheeler

Samuel Gordon (1759-1843), brother of Basil, built the brick portion of this home about 1784 on the hill overlooking the Rappahannock. The middle frame portion was built during the mid-nineteenth century. The end wing on the south side of the house was added later. The land was terraced down to the road until the new road (U.S. Route 1) was built, taking almost all of the lawn. The frame portion of the house is two stories above a cellar. The brick section is one and one-half stories. The roof was originally finished with cedar shakes but is now covered with shingles. There are two brick chimneys, beaded weatherboarding, and elaborate cornices under the roof. Green shutters flank the twenty-five windows. Inside, there are six large rooms that were originally plastered and painted; the walls have since been papered. A lovely stairway is decorated with elaborate carvings at the end of each step. The living room mantel is very elaborate, having three bouquets of beautifully-carved flowers.

The cellar is divided into two rooms with pink sandstone floors. The basement fireplace had a crane and a Dutch oven. When the present Falmouth bridge was erected, the new road was built through the lovely terraces, taking all but a few feet of the front yard.

Samuel and Basil Gordon were born in Scotland. Like a great number of Scots, they settled in Falmouth around 1786 and became engaged in the grain and cotton exchange. Business in Falmouth at that time was very good, due to a shortage of flour in Europe caused by the French Revolution and the Napoleonic Wars. By 1813 Falmouth boasted five flour mills, four of which were capable of producing 15,000 barrels of flour per year. In addition to their milling interests, the Gordon brothers also operated several stores in and near Falmouth. Thanks to this period of economic prosperity, Basil became the first millionaire in America. Samuel's son, Samuel, bought a Fredericksburg home from Colonel Fielding Lewis and named it Kenmore after an old castle in Scotland that he admired. There he retired.

Prospect Hill

This old farm has been known by various names through the years, including Richards' Hill, Ingleside and, more recently, Pill Hill. Long before becoming a farm, this property was a trading post for the Native Americans, who preferred trading on a hill rather than on the riverbank.

Shortly before the Revolution, Captain John Richards (1734-1785) came to Falmouth from King and Queen County. He was a merchant who acquired a great deal of property in and around Falmouth. In 1754 he married Susannah Coleman. Richards built his home just one-tenth of a mile northwest of Falmouth.

The house was built on a rock foundation in 1750. Through the years, there were three houses built on this foundation, all being of different design and all destroyed at different periods.

In 1796 a Mutual Assurance Society policy was purchased by William Richards insuring a dwelling house "52 feet long by 18 feet wide, one story high, built of wood and covered with wood." A shed or porch was attached to the rear of the house. Another shed, a lumber house, stable, and kitchen were also insured. For insurance purposes, one and one-half story buildings were called one story. It is likely, therefore, that the house was actually one and one-half stories.

William Richards sold the property to his brother-in-law, William S. Stone (1764-1827), who served as Mayor of Fredericksburg for a time.

A later Mutual Assurance Society policy, issued in 1811, lists the owner of the property as Walter Graham (who married Sarah Richards, daughter of Captain John Richards). The 150-acre farm left the Richards family in 1816, when it was sold.

During the Civil War, the house and grounds were used as a headquarters for Union forces engaged in the Battle of Fredericksburg. A fort was built on the hill in front of the house.

At the foot of the hill was a little spring walled with flat stones known as Richards Spring.

Barnes' House

Falmouth has a number of charming little buildings, one of which is the Barnes' House, located across the street from the Temperance Hotel. Built around 1780, this frame house was purchased by Gari Melchers of Belmont.

Differences in roofline and interior woodwork indicate that the house was built in stages. The west end probably dates from the late-eighteenth century when Falmouth was a very busy port town. This part of the house is one and one-half stories, with a room and hall on the first floor and a single room above. A single chimney served both levels.

The east end may have been built as late as 1800. The house sits upon a stone foundation and has a quaint Dutch-style room. There are three dormers on the front, but on the back there is just one tiny window located in the center of the roof.

The early history of the house is unknown. Joseph Ficklen, owner of Belmont, bought the house sometime prior to 1850. Ficklen sold the building in 1850 to Harrison Barnes who lived there with his sisters. When the last sister died in 1890, a life tenancy was given to "an old and faithful friend," Annie Duncan Lucas, and her husband, Daniel. Annie had been a servant in the Barnes household for many years and it is quite possible that she had been their slave prior to the war. Daniel and Annie were both born around 1834 and Daniel may have been a Barnes slave or perhaps a slave from a neighboring farm. He held a position of importance in Falmouth, however, serving as the mail carrier between Fredericksburg and Falmouth.

Apparently a school for black students operated for a time in the house. Very little is known about the school but it most likely was in existence after the Civil War because of the strict laws forbidding the education of blacks before the war. Because of complaints from white residents, the school was short-lived.

Taverns In Colonial Life

Taverns, also known as ordinaries, were located about every fifteen miles along the road. Ordinaries were so named because they served ordinary people. Anyone having a little money could stop and get a meal and lodging for the night. Some ordinaries had a special dining room where, for an extra fee, gentlemen could have their meals in private. Inns served meals and drinks, and provided accommodations for weary travelers. They also were little centers of social activity. About 1780 the Marquis de Chastellux described a cock fight held at one ordinary to which men gathered from as far away as forty miles. He was amazed that they would be aware of the event as there was no mail service. He spoke of the food as frugal but wholesome and the accommodations clean. "For lodging there is one large room for all the company. A pallet brought in and laid on the floor for each guest suffices for these country folk."

All ordinaries had to be licensed and the county courts were required to see that these licenses were issued only to men of substance, that "the Petitioner is of Ability to provide Travelers with Lodging, Diet, Provender, Pasturage and other Necessaries; but must not grant License to poor Persons under pretense of charity, but to such only who are able to keep good Houses and a constant supply of all necessary Entertainments." The tavern keeper had to renew his license annually with the county court "having given bond and security according to law." The court could refuse to renew the license if it believed the owner of the ordinary had not operated his business according to law.

Of course, in the days before newspapers, the innkeepers were a source of news and information, and usually were ardent politicians and patriots.

Many innkeepers went on to hold high public office or military rank. One local example of this was George Weedon, an able soldier who won his position with the Revolutionary army having been "zealous in blowing the flames of sedition" in his ordinary.

Temperance Hotel

The Temperance Hotel was originally built as a warehouse sometime between 1813 and 1815. While the primary entrance appears to be on Washington Street, the original main entrance was actually on the east side of the building. A large door on the second floor of the Washington Street side opened to allow the loading and unloading of merchandise. The old brick floor was laid in a herringbone pattern and random width planks were used for the floor upstairs. A heavy oak wall divided the upstairs in half. The north half, today the back half, contained the owner's living quarters. A separate stairway provided access to these rooms.

The building continued to be used as a warehouse until business declined in Falmouth as a result of silting in the river. Sometime between 1835 and 1840 the building was converted to a stage inn and tavern. The two large arched warehouse doors on the east side were bricked in and the Washington Street side became the front, welcoming stage travelers along the busy thoroughfare. Two chimneys were added to the building, each providing flues for double fireplaces. The large chimney on the north side served two corner fireplaces on the ground floor, one in the kitchen and one in an adjoining sitting room. A fireplace on the same flue heated the large bedroom upstairs. A smaller interior chimney on the east side served two fireplaces at the front of the building. At this same time the windows were enlarged and new sandstone sills were installed under the doors. Partitions were built upstairs, creating two large bedrooms for travelers. The old stairway which had provided access to second-floor warehouse storage was removed and the opening in the floor closed.

Flooding of the ground floor was always a problem due to a stream that flows along the north and east sides of the building. Part of the c.1840 renovation included filling the interior with about two feet of river sand and placing a plank floor over the sand. While this did nothing to prevent flooding, at least the travelers' feet stayed dry. A similar depth of sand was also dumped around the outside of the building in an attempt to thwart the advance of the water.

The first indication of the name of Temperance Hotel appears in an 1884 deed in which the building is called the "Falls Temperance House."

The property was purchased in 1886 by the Brown family, who used it as a residence. They made several changes to the building, primarily the addition of indoor plumbing, dormers on the second floor which improved ventilation, and the opening of an interior wall.

The building has changed hands numerous times since 1966, but little had been done in the way of renovation or preservation and it was on the verge of collapse when new owners purchased it in 1990. Present renovation has included the removal of the sand from the interior of the building as well as on the outside. The lovely terraced gardens are being restored and their stone retaining walls are being rebuilt. After years of neglect, the Temperance Hotel will once again be a living part of the old Falmouth landscape.

Basil Gordon House

At 303 King Street (River Road) stands the Basil Gordon house. Built in the 1830s, it was the home of Basil Gordon, who is best remembered as one of America's early millionaires. Basil (1768-1847) and his brother, Samuel (1759-1843), were prominent Falmouth businessmen during the early nineteenth century and were involved in the shipping and sales of tobacco, cotton, and general merchandise.

Samuel came to America in 1780, where he successfully pursued the mercantile business. In 1798 he married Susan F. Knox (1775-1869). His younger brother, Basil, settled in Falmouth in 1783 and, in 1814, married Anna Campbell Knox (1784-1867), younger sister of Susan and daughter of William and Susannah Fitzhugh Knox of Windsor Lodge, Culpeper. (After William's death, Susannah returned to her family estate, Belmont, on the hill overlooking Falmouth.) Basil and Anna had seven children, four of whom lived to adulthood.

Basil owned other buildings in Falmouth, including several warehouses located across the street from present-day Waterfront Park and what is now known as Lightner's Store at 104 West Cambridge Street and the Cotton Warehouse (now Simpson and Associates Realty) at 201 West Cambridge. Lightner's Store was built in the 1830s and used as a warehouse. The warehouses which once stood across from the park are now gone, perhaps victims of the frequent flooding that occurs along this low area by the river.

Since its construction, the Gordon house has undergone major structural changes. The building may have started out as a warehouse. In the present basement are warehouse-style doors with heavy lintels. These doors are unusable now because they are underground. Excavations have shown that the original walking level in the yard concurs with the walking level in the basement, suggesting that the present basement was once above ground and simply the first story of a three- or four-story warehouse. Siltation from repeated flooding has all but buried the lower level.

In later years, the top story of the building was removed as well as a wing, evidence of which can still be seen in the back yard. The front porch was a later addition, making the present building far different from the house Basil Gordon lived in.

When Basil Gordon died in 1847, he left his heirs one of the largest fortunes in the state, accumulated through endless energy and the strictest integrity.

Glencairne

Owners:

pre-1811	Landon Carter
1812-1816	Thomas Seddon
1817-1818	Robert Finnall
1819-1825	William and Sarah Langfit
1825	Sold to Richard Cassius Lee Moncure (later Chief Justice of the Virginia Supreme Court)

Glencairne

1882 Judge Moncure died and his daughter, Agnes Robinson Moncure Chichester, wife of Judge Daniel McCarty Chichester of Fairfax, inherited the property

1919 Inherited by her son, Judge Richard Henry Lee Chichester

1930 Inherited by Daniel McCarty Chichester

1938 North wing restored

1957 House completely restored

1987 Inherited by Daniel McCarty Chichester

This magnificent two-story home stands on a hill just north of Falmouth on the west side of U.S. Route 1 and overlooks great rolling green fields. Judging from county tax records, there has been a house on the property since at least 1804, though major construction on the present building seems to have been done by R. C. L. Moncure. Like many old homes, Glencairne was built in stages, a room here, a wing there, and until the early to mid nineteenth century was quite unpretentious.

The house is topped with a gabled tin roof, though the original roof would have been of wood. There are two brick and stone chimneys, twenty-three windows, and a cellar. The perfectly symmetrical design is complemented by plain weatherboarding.

Glencairne has been in the Chichester family for four generations and has been the home of two Supreme Court Justices and three members of the General Assembly of Virginia. The Honorable Richard Cassius Lee Moncure (1805-1882) was the son of John Moncure (born 1772). He was President of the Supreme Court of Appeals of Virginia from 1852 to 1864. Lovingly restored and maintained, Glencairne retains the peaceful and genteel atmosphere of a Southern plantation. During the ownership of R. C. L. Moncure, Glencairne was a much larger farm than it is today and most of the property was on the east side of U.S. Route 1. At one time, the farm stretched north and east to include what is now Dogwood Air Park and east to include Jefferson Place Townhouses, Falmouth Elementary School, and what is now known as "the old walnut farm" near Highland Homes subdivision on Deacon Road (State Route 607). Through the years, the acreage was gradually sold and, today, the farm is restricted to the west side of U.S. Route 1. In the twentieth century Daniel M. Chichester gave the county land to the south of the house on which was built Drew Middle School.

There is a second house on the Glencairne property know as Mont Anna. Though built after the close of the Civil War, Mont Anna bears mentioning because it is representative of the close family ties which allowed people to survive in what little was left of Stafford County after the war. Stafford was devastated by five years of encampment, and many of its former inhabitants moved elsewhere. A few, though, did come home and struggled to eke out a living from the exhausted clay soil. Family members looked out for each other as a matter of survival and shared what little they had.

After the war, Judge John Conway Moncure, oldest of the fourteen Moncure children, obtained a portion of Glencairne, on which he built a modest home—Mont Anna—for the parents of his sister's husband, the Hulls. Anna Jane Moncure, sixth of the fourteen children, had married her second cousin, John Moncure Hull, in 1834. Like most genteel Southerners after the war, the Hulls were financially devastated.

The exterior of the two-story house is of wood siding painted white. The windows are flanked by green shutters and the roof was at one time painted red. The interior walls were originally rough, unpainted plaster, and the floors are still tongue and groove wood. The front hall is unusual in that it runs across the width of the house, rather than down through the center. The hall served as a parlor or living room for family gatherings on wet or cold evenings. The front porch was a place for socializing when the weather was good.

Edgar Marburg, a cousin, spent quite a bit of time at Mont Anna from 1900 to 1907. He remembered the front hall as having "a horse hair lounge, maybe two rocking chairs, several straight chairs, and the only pictures in the house that I can remember. There were two large oil paintings of a man and a woman, I believe, Hull relatives. There was a large portrait of Landon Carter, son of old Robert 'King' Carter...an ancestor of ours.

"Of course there were pictures of the two leading Confederate generals, Robert E. Lee and Thomas J. 'Stonewall' Jackson."

Mr. Marburg recalled, "I remember Grandma Hull (Anne Moncure Hull who was then about seventy), sitting in a rocking chair on the back porch, and, between naps, peeling apples or shucking corn, while yellow jackets swarmed all around her. Grandpa Moncure would take a walk every day, usually up the front road and into the corn field beyond the gate. He would have a mint julep in a tall glass each afternoon. As he would stir the sugar in the glass this would, like as not, be accompanied by a discourse on the virtue of temperance."

The road from Mont Anna to Fredericksburg was nothing like it is today. The main road was of red clay, full of ruts and pot holes. On the worst sections people would lay wooden poles, four to five inches in diameter, side by side, forming what was known as a corduroy road. The bridge at Falmouth was a two-lane, overhead truss bridge with a wooden floor.

After the deaths of the Hulls, Mont Anna was inherited jointly by Frances Marburg, eldest of that family and niece of Anna Jane Moncure Hull, and John Conway, eldest member of the Conway branch of the family. Frances bought John's share and used Mont Anna as a vacation home for some years before selling it back to Dan Chichester, owner of Glencairne.

Today, Glencairne is owned by Mr. Chichester's nephew, Daniel Chichester. The Mont Anna house is being restored and is inhabited again.

Ellerslie

Ellerslie is located on the south side of the intersection of State Routes 652 and 654.

In 1734 Michael Wallace was indentured by his uncles Thomas and Michael, merchants of Glasgow, to Dr. Gustavus Brown of Maryland. The term of the indenture was six years, during which time Wallace was to learn "Physick, Surgery, and Pharmacy." While studying with Dr. Brown, he secretly fell in love with Elizabeth, one of Dr. Brown's many daughters. At the age of twenty-one Michael and Elizabeth eloped (via a ladder held by his fellow medical students to a second-story window). As she was one of nine daughters, Dr. Brown saw no practical reason to retrieve Elizabeth. Michael assumed the title of Doctor and by 1746 the couple were settled in Falmouth. He provided medical care to patients in Falmouth and Culpeper, Loudoun, and Fauquier Counties for many years.

In 1748 Dr. Wallace bought a large tract of land from William and Margaret Waugh, part of a 1691 patent to Parson John Waugh. Dr. Wallace named his plantation Ellerslie after his ancestral estate in Renfrewshire, Scotland.

The first Ellerslie house was built shortly after Dr. Wallace purchased the property. Fire destroyed most of this house in 1754, and the Wallaces immediately rebuilt the house. Burned timbers in the basement of the present house suggest that this second dwelling may have incorporated part of the original.

Ellerslie's most famous resident was Dr. Michael Wallace's son, Lt. Col. Gustavus Brown Wallace (1751-1802). After attending school in Fredericksburg, he began studying law in 1774. His studies were interrupted by the death of his aunt in Scotland, necessitating a trip abroad in 1775. That same year he returned to Virginia and enlisted in the continental army as a captain. In the fall of 1777 he was promoted to major and served

Ellerslie

Dwelling House
all wood 1 Story high
with a hipped roof
24' long by 30' wide
underpinned with
Brick 3 feet above the
surface of the ground,
with a Cellar

distance 70 feet

Wooden
Smoke
House
10' square

distance 83 feet

Wooden
Kitchen
20' by 16'

From an 1805 Mutual Assurance policy

under Colonel Daniel Morgan. Major Wallace spent the terrible winter with his men at Valley Forge.

He was transferred from the 3rd to the 25th Virginia Regiment and, finally, to the 2nd Virginia Regiment. During the late 1770s he was captured by the British at Charleston. At the request of Governor Thomas Nelson, Lord Cornwallis released him on parole so that he could return to Virginia. There he was to make arrangements for officers of the Virginia Line to pay the debts they had incurred at Charleston.

After the Revolution, Wallace was given 7,000 acres of land in Virginia for his services during the war. He was also given an additional 960 acres for special services.

In 1802 Colonel Wallace made a business trip to Scotland. On the return voyage he contracted typhus. Upon reaching Potomac Creek the ship captain put Wallace off the boat. Fortunately, he was put ashore on property belonging to his cousin, Mrs. Travers Daniel of Crow's Nest (see Chapter 9). Servants found Colonel Wallace and notified Mrs. Daniel. She sent a cart for him and had him taken to Fredericksburg where there was a doctor. Several days later, he died there and was buried at the Masonic Cemetery in Fredericksburg. He died unmarried.

A Mutual Assurance Society policy dated 1805 provides a description of the house and two outbuildings. Ellerslie is a two-story frame house with a hip roof. This was an exceptionally fine house in its day, for the Wallaces were quite well off. Over time, however, the house was neglected. The 1805 policy insured the house for only $1,200. Near the house were the wooden kitchen and smokehouse. It is interesting to note that the owner, Captain William Brown Wallace, spelled the name of his home Eldersley.

Captain Wallace was the son of Dr. Wallace and he also served during the Revolution. He inherited Ellerslie but sold the property for $3,022 to his brother Gustavus in 1817 and moved to Kentucky.

Ellerslie has been lived in throughout the twentieth century, though it has suffered from periods of abandonment and neglect. Today the house has been restored and is occupied, though the house tract contains only four acres. The remaining acreage has been purchased by a developer and will soon be yet another high-density housing project.

Stanstead

Owners:

1703/4	Robert Carter of Carter's Grove
1732	Charles Carter, by will
After 1746	James Hunter
1784	Adam Hunter, by will
1804	Joseph Enniver
1849	Lucy Enniver, by will
1884	Enniver Lucas and Maria C. Lucas, by will
1912	Lilly O'Bannon Barber, niece of Enniver Lucas, by will
1926	N. N. Berry and George Wyne

Today, nothing remains of the Stanstead farm or house. It is likely that those who once lived there would be horrified to see their farm transformed into Servicetown Truck Stop, a McDonald's, and acres of commercial development on both sides of busy U.S. Route 17.

This farm was part of four grants to James Innes in March 1703/4. Totaling 2,331 acres, the land was on and immediately above the falls of the Rappahannock River; twenty-five years later, the town of Falmouth would be established on part of the property. A few months after the March grant, Innes received 11,115 acres "in Richmond and Stafford Counties in the forests above the falls of Rappahannock River, upon the branches of the Run called Potowmack Run, falling into Potowmack Creek and upon the Run called Deep Run, falling into Rappahannock River about ten miles above the falls thereof." Innes was acting as an agent for Robert Carter (1663-1732) and the grants were immediately transferred to Carter's name. For years, Robert purchased land along the Potomac and Rappahannock Rivers with the intention of establishing his sons, Charles and John, as land barons in that region.

After his father's death, Charles Carter (1707-1764) inherited 13,000 acres in Stafford; Stanstead was a part of that inheritance and was listed in Robert Carter's 1732 inventory. The property likely included all of what is now the truck stop, south to border on the Rappahannock, and east to at least U.S. Route 1 (Carlton and Belmont would have been a part of this, also).

After Robert Carter's death in 1732, Charles moved from his Urbanna plantation to the land he had inherited in what was then King George County. By 1737 Stanstead was the well-known and no doubt elegant residence of the Charles Carter family and contained some 500 acres. Sometime thereafter, he purchased of Ralph Wormely a plantation known as Cleve where, by 1750, he had completed a gracious brick mansion. Upon removing to King George, Charles sold much of his property in Stafford, including Stanstead. Unfortunately, lost court records make it impossible to determine how or when he disposed of the farm. By 1746, however, James Hunter was in possession of the property, though Carter seems to have retained ownership of the family cemetery.

In his will, Charles ordered that the bodies of his family be removed from the cemetery at Stanstead and moved to Cleve, where he himself was to be buried in a vault. He also willed that the remains of Joseph Enniver be interred at Cleve. Enniver came to America from Dunkurque, French Flanders, when he was seventeen years old. He was a bookkeeper and scribe who seems to have worked for Carter at Stanstead. After Charles moved to King George, Enniver was apparently employed by James Hunter, who built Rappahannock Forge on the river edge of the farm. By 1804, Joseph Enniver is recorded as the owner of Stanstead, though this was likely the son or grandson of the Joseph who had worked for Carter.

While a resident of Stafford, Charles was one of the trustees appointed to lay out the town of Falmouth in 1728. After leaving Stafford, he was also a justice of King George County as well as County Lieutenant. In August of 1736 he became a burgess for King George County and held that position for the next twenty-eight years.

James Hunter settled in Falmouth sometime around 1746 and died there, unmarried, in 1784. He appears in the 1773 and 1776 Quit Rent Rolls and was charged in those years for 1,176 acres. In 1783 he is listed twice in the personal property tax records, once for his plantation and once for the forge (mentioned earlier in this chapter). Between the two, he owned 260 slaves, 94 horses, and 30 cattle. He seems to have been the largest single slave owner in Stafford's history. The inventory of James

Hunter's estate, recorded in Stafford County court in November 1785, includes the "Stanstead Plantation...AKA Furnace." Hunter's inventory fills several pages in the deed and will book and includes "8 Buckskins, 44 pair Negroe Shoes, 264 Soldier's Coats at 12/2, 172 pr overhauls."

The inventory also lists the contents of Adam Hunter's room, indicating that he lived with his brother, James. As primary heir to James' estate, Adam advertised the plantation for sale in 1794, part of 4,976 acres amassed by James prior to his death. The forge was advertised in 1798 but did not sell until the first quarter of the nineteenth century, when it was purchased by Joseph Ficklen. The forge was located on the river just below what is now Old Forge townhouses. James also owned considerable acreage in Culpeper and Fauquier Counties, property which Adam inherited.

Adam Hunter apparently continued to operate the forge after his brother's death. Tax records from 1789 and 1790 for Adam list slaves, horses, and cattle for his plantation as well as for the forge.

Little is known about the houses at Stanstead. Charles Carter and James and Adam Hunter surely lived in a fine house. However, building values are not reflected in the tax records until 1817, and by that time the house was assessed at only $500. The "Mansion House" mentioned in James Hunter's will likely burned sometime after his death and a second frame building was erected nearby. Spencer Berry, owner of the property in the 1950s, found the foundations of what he believed to be the original house near the nineteenth-century house in which he lived.

The house listed in the 1817 tax records depreciated during the ownership of Joseph Enniver until by 1840 it was worth only $378. Lucy Enniver seems to have made some improvements, for it had returned to $500 by 1851 and the value remained the same until the outbreak of the Civil War. The house stood well behind what is now the truck stop just to the west of Interstate 95 and the lane leading to the house was the road now dividing Servicetown and the McDonald's restaurant.

During the Civil War, every acre of Stanstead was part of the vast encampment of Union forces before, during, and after the Battle of Fredericksburg. Northern soldiers with their wagons, horses, cannon, and supplies became bogged down in the muddy road that ran past the house towards Falmouth and Fredericksburg (now U.S. Route 17). Troops marching to Fredericksburg from the north had to approach from the west by way of the Warrenton Road to avoid the notoriously boggy conditions of Chopawamsic Swamp along the Stafford–Prince William border. While this was the most direct north–south route, it was impossible to move wagons, horses, mules, and supplies through the swamp. Winter travel on the Warrenton Road, however, was only slightly better than contending with the swamp.

Until the pull out from Fredericksburg in 1863 (which evolved into the Battle of Chancellorsville), Union General French maintained his headquarters at Stanstead. Because of its abundant water supply, all of the butchering of meat to feed the soldiers involved in the Fredericksburg campaign was carried out at Stanstead. Cattle and hogs were brought in from the surrounding area and butchered; the meat was then loaded into wagons and delivered to encampments all around the battle area.

When the troops finally left the area, the once-stately Stanstead farm was in shambles. Every tree and fence post had been removed and used for firewood. The topsoil had all washed away. Hundreds of wagon wheels had cut deep ruts in the lawn, fields, and lane. It was a picture of total devastation.

A little-known fact about Stanstead is that the property contained a stone quarry. While most stone quarrying was done along Aquia Creek in the northern part of the county, there was a quarry about one-half mile from the house at Stanstead. Here stones were cut and shaped for local grist mills and stone was quarried for building foundations. Unlike the Aquia stone which is light in color, the Stanstead stone is a dark gray.

Greaves' House

The Greaves' house was built around 1790 by a Reverend Greaves. Typical of building techniques in this wilderness area, the original house was constructed of logs and stones. The farm was located two miles from Falmouth on U.S. Route 17. The house was one mile from the road, behind Harwood Branch farm.

The Reverend Nathaniel Greaves was a Northern Methodist preacher. In 1840 he owned about four hundred acres off of the Warrenton Road. He gave two acres for the building of a Northern Methodist Church. This first building was frame and was destroyed by fire. He then had a little brick church built on the site. Called Greaves' Chapel, this building was destroyed by Union soldiers during the war. Greaves left the property to his nephew, Nathaniel Sanford. Sanford had no heirs and he sold the property in four portions.

The Greaves family cemetery was also located on this property.

Greenbank

Throughout Stafford's history, Greenbank has been one of the most productive and fertile farms in the county, yet relatively little is known about it or the people who lived there. Greenbank was always a large tract of land and remains so today. Only in the last ten years has farming declined on the property and today, Greenbank stands poised to become an industrial, business, or residential development.

Greenbank is located on the south side of U.S. Route 17 and forms a broad, Texas-shaped peninsula bounded by the Rappahannock River. The old road into the farm is now State Route 656, both sides of which are in the process of being developed. At the end of this road is the old farm.

This property was part of 733 acres purchased by Adam Banks in 1674. Adam died intestate sometime between 1674 and 1690 and the property descended to his only son, Gerard (born c.1672).

Greenbank remained in the Banks family until it was inherited by George Banks, probably the grandson of Gerard. George was a student at the College of William and Mary in 1798, and the Register of the General Assembly lists him as representing Stafford County in the House of Delegates from 1817 to 1818. George married Jemima Ann Overton of Louisa County in 1806.

George Banks increased the acreage of Greenbank from the 768 acres he inherited to 1,300. This 1,300 acres, described in tax records as "the family residence," was valued at $12.50 per acre, totaling $16,250. After George's death, family fortunes declined. There are no surviving county records which detail the division of the estate; George's widow mortgaged Greenbank and in 1851 it passed out of the family when it was purchased by William S. Scott.

There was a mill on the eastern side of Greenbank built by the Banks family. Long known as Banks' Mill, it later became known as Scott's Mill and operated as such until the Civil War. The mill ground grain for Greenbank and other nearby farms and a ferry provided transportation across the Rappahannock to Spotsylvania County.

Nothing is known of the house or houses on this property.

Harwood Branch

Primitive conditions in the western part of Stafford County were reflected in simple lifestyles and basic building techniques. Few early dwellings were built of frame or brick. Most were constructed of logs and Harwood Branch was typical of these. Located two miles from Falmouth on the Warrenton Road, this farmhouse was built of logs and had several log additions made through the years. All the timber was hand-hewn and the frame of the house was put together with pegs.

The land was granted to Thomas Harwood in 1740 and remained in the family until well into the twentieth century. In 1936 the property was in the possession of Mrs. James Simpson, a great-granddaughter of the original owner.

Thomas Harwood served in the Revolution but was too old to fight in the Civil War. Union soldiers moved onto the farm in the fall of 1860. The family was at dinner when the soldiers overran the farm. The Federals began slaughtering hens, hogs, and cows. The children had a horse and they rushed out to protect it. Far too valuable to slaughter, the animal was being led by a soldier across the field; the children grabbed the soldier and horse and, finally, the man gave up and released the animal to them. Their father placed the horse in the hands of the Confederates, who kept it for them.

With the exception of two teaspoons and the family Bible, all of the Harwoods' possessions were destroyed by the marauding soldiers. The house was used as a headquarters by General Stimson. Just across the road were the headquarters of Grant and Burnside.

All of the timber on the place was cut for huts and houses for the Union Army, which remained camped there until after the Battle of Fredericksburg in 1863.

The story of Harwood Branch illustrates that while there was little actual fighting in Stafford during the Civil War, the county suffered more devastation than localities which endured battles. So much damage was done by camping Union soldiers that there was little or nothing for residents to return to after the war. Houses were vandalized or razed, livestock was stolen, eaten, stampeded, or slaughtered. The destruction of acres of timber resulted in an almost complete loss of topsoil. By the end of the war, returning residents were so disheartened that most moved out of the county. Only now is Stafford recovering from that agonizing experience.

Hammet Place

Owners:

1726 Abben Randolph of New Jersey

1860 Purchased by Louis Hammet and Sally Chichester Hammet. At the deaths of Mr. and Mrs. Hammet, the farm was willed to the Misses Hattie and Jennie Hammet

This farm was located 5.5 miles northwest of Falmouth on the Warrenton Road. The house was built during the eighteenth century of logs and was two stories with a large attic. The logs were hewn by hand and the doors were plain with heavy iron locks. The interior was plastered and contained only two rooms besides the attic. The original wooden roof was later replaced with tin and there was one stone chimney on the east end. There was a porch on the front.

The Hammet sisters lived to be very old (Miss Jennie was ninety-seven when she died). After the deaths of Misses Jennie and Hattie early in the twentieth century, the house was inherited by a nephew who would not allow anything to be moved. The furniture and all of the possessions of the sisters were kept just as they had left them and a man was paid to stay in the house at night.

By the middle of the twentieth century, the house fell victim to neglect and nothing remains of it today.

Locust Grove

Owners:
1843 Mrs. James Robinson
1870 Purchased by Mr. William Beale
1887 Inherited by John Beale

This house was located six miles northwest of Falmouth on the Warrenton Road, 1.2 miles north on State Route 616, and then six-tenths of a mile west on a private road. It was built in the early eighteenth century in a grove of locust trees, hence the name. The structure was rectangular, one and one-half stories, and built of logs with a gabled roof. There was one brick and stone chimney. The house had only two large rooms and the entrance was a plain handmade door. The walls were plastered and accented with a chair rail. Wide planks were used for the floor and a simple mantel decorated the fireplace.

Marsh Home

This was another simple log home, located 8.9 miles from Falmouth between the Warrenton Road and State Route 612. Like Locust Grove, the house was built in the early eighteenth century and reflected the wilderness which surrounded it. The Marsh family constructed a two-story log house with a lean-to roof. The bricks for the large chimney were made on the site and as of the Works Progress Administration report of 1936, the old brick kiln pit was still visible.

Present-day State Route 612 was part of the route of the "Mud March" of the Northern soldiers who camped near the house, making this an altogether unpleasant place.

Old Stone House

This home was located 13.3 miles from Falmouth on the Warrenton Road and 1 mile west of State Route 612 on a private road.

The house was built around 1800 by the Cropp family but was torn down early in this century. Again, it was typical of homes in the area, being one and one-half stories above a cellar. The half-story upstairs had some small hidden closets. Family legend says that these little closets were used to conceal Bushwhackers during the Civil War. Bushwhackers were Confederate men who would sneak out at night, go into the Union camps and cause as much mischief as possible.

Around 1862 a man named George Heflin lived on the property. He thought the Union troops had left the area for a while and decided to hold a dance in his house, a rare treat for war-weary neighbors. During the dancing, Union soldiers came in and captured some of the men including Tom Courtney, Buck Embrey, and Jessie Anderson. One man hid under a bed, another under the large hoop skirt of one of the ladies, and thus these men avoided capture by the soldiers.

Petmouth Grove

This old home was on the left side of State Route 615, about one mile from the Cropp Post Office. The house was built around 1760 by a Captain Hill. It was one and one-half stories and built of hand-hewn logs fastened together with pegs. There was a hip roof, and a chimney was at each end. The house has long ago disappeared and the graveyard nearby has lost all of its markers.

Captain Hill served in the Revolution and commanded a troop of men from Stafford. He died before the Civil War. His farm was used as a scouting ground by both Northern and Southern soldiers. The original house burned early in this century.

Poplar Hill

The home on this property dates from around 1850, and was a large frame structure above a brick-walled basement. There was a very large brick chimney on each end of the house. Eight rooms and large halls made for a comfortable residence when compared to other dwellings in the area. The walls were plastered and accented with chair rail. By the time of the Works Progress Administration report of 1937, the house had almost collapsed.

Miss Nannie Tackett, daughter of Charles Tackett, taught school at Poplar Hill. People who could afford to pay for their children's education did so; poor children were taught for free. Miss Tackett also taught Sunday school in the same building, known as Tackett's Mill School. The Tacketts were Huguenots who had come to Virginia to escape persecution in France.

Scotland

Owners:

pre 1790-1791	Part of 1,400 acres owned by Hancock Lee
1791-c.1804	Part of 903 acres owned by Gavin Lawson
1805-1832	397 acres owned by William Briggs (or Bridges)
1833-beyond 1860	Inherited by Andrew Briggs (or Bridges)

Scotland is a very old farm located 12.1 miles northwest of Falmouth. The house site, on which only a small brick building survives, is situated on the north side of Stony Hill Road (State Route 662) very near where this road intersects with Poplar Road (State Route 616). The surviving structure is visible from Route 662. Scotland was a large tract through which flowed both Potomac Run and Long Branch, and the western edge of this farm

Scotland

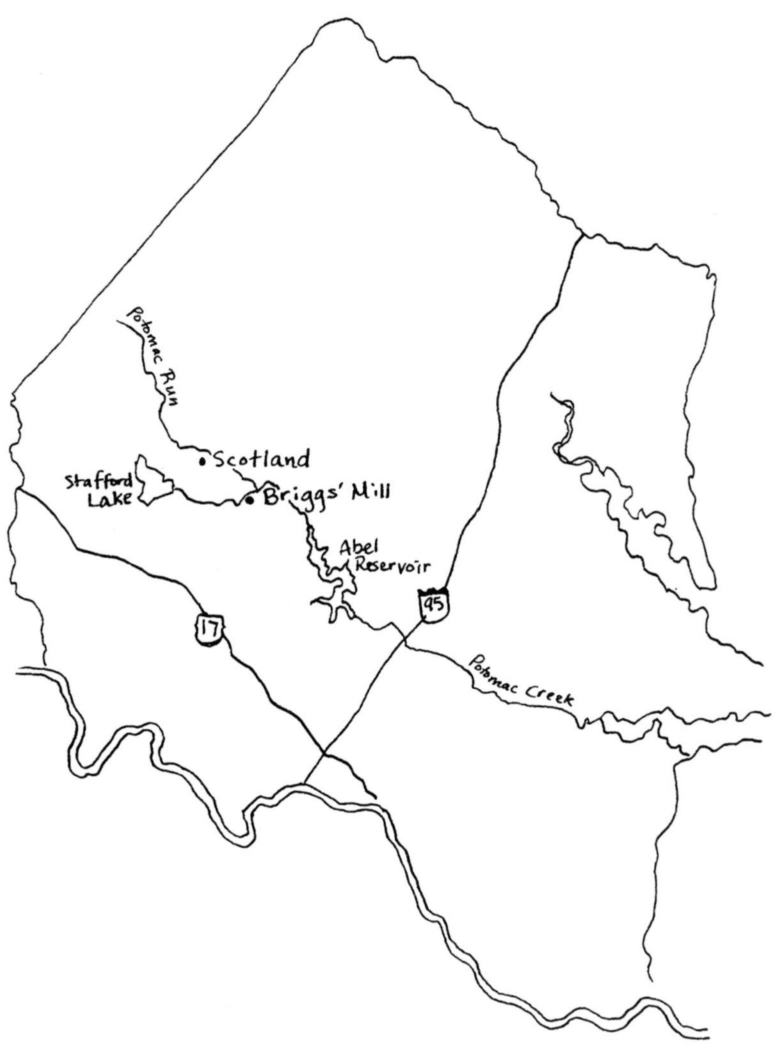

Potomac Run
Scotland
Stafford Lake
Briggs' Mill
Abel Reservoir
95
17
Potomac Creek

may well have adjoined Stony Hill (see article this chapter). The farm stretched southward along Poplar Road and the southern edge may have adjoined Oakley (see Chapter 9).

Originally, Scotland was part of two massive grants to Robert "King" Carter, which were inherited by his son, Charles. These grants gave the Carter family control of all lands between the Rappahannock River and Potomac Creek Run, and from roughly present-day Falmouth to the modern Fauquier County line.

William Briggs (or Bridges) immigrated from Scotland and purchased 261 acres from Gavin Lawson. Briggs named his new plantation Scotland. Tax records from the early nineteenth century and before do not list a separate value for buildings, so it is impossible to determine when the house was built.

The James Briggs family lived at Stony Hill, very near Scotland, yet they claimed to be unrelated. There seems to be some reason to believe that this is true. In the tax records William's and Andrew's last names are given as Briggs and Bridges with equal frequency while the last name of the Stony Hill Briggs was never subjected to alternate spelling.

Scotland was never a large farm, though in 1807 or 1808 William Briggs bought an adjoining 136 acres from a Mr. Buckner to increase the size of his farm to 397 acres. Despite its relatively limited acreage, however, Scotland boasted a comfortable brick house which was quite superior to the log or clapboard dwellings nearby. The two-story house had a gabled tin roof and one brick chimney on the east side. There were nine windows without shutters. The front entrance was highlighted by pine double doors. There were four rooms, with a stairway in the center of the house. The walls were plastered, and random width planks were used for flooring. Plain oak mantels topped the fireplaces.

By the time building values were listed separately in the tax records (1810), the house at Scotland was assessed at $700 which was four to five times what most houses of the day were worth. The building value remained at $700 until 1840 when it suddenly dropped to $378 (this may reflect damage to the house or simply a drop in area property values). A reassessment was conducted in 1851 and the building values were increased to $1,200. Another increase occurred in 1857 when they were listed at $2,000.

Building a brick house required a good deal of money and labor. The property owner needed enough slaves to not only dig foundations, cut lumber, and make bricks and mortar, but to clear and cultivate the land. It seems likely, therefore, that William Briggs was a Falmouth merchant and thus wealthier than his neighbors. Whatever his source of income, he does not appear in local newspaper accounts and it is difficult to know much about him.

The brick house burned at an unknown time and the kitchen was converted into a dwelling. Within recent years, the occupants left the renovated kitchen and the property was abandoned and sold.

The Briggs cemetery is near the house on a hill overlooking a small creek and is enclosed by a brick wall. One stone predates the Civil War. Unusual in its beauty, it is a tall stone with a bouquet of carved roses above the inscription:

> *Sacred to the memory of Betsy Briggs, wife of Andrew Briggs, born August 13, 1800 and departed this life October 20, 1858, aged 58 years. "One who made home happy, and now she rests at Good's right hand before her Father's throne."*

Long associated with Scotland and the Briggs or Bridges family was a grist mill most commonly known as Briggs' Mill. This structure was located on Long Branch on the east side of Poplar Road (State Route 616) and the south side of Stefaniga Road (State Route 648) near where Long Branch and Potomac Run converge. The mill lot had been part of the 1,000-acre Oakley tract owned by Thomas Skinker and his son Samuel from late in the eighteenth century until around 1820. The mill was built sometime prior to 1817, when it was valued in the tax records at $1,000. At this point the tract contained 851 acres. From 1821 to 1823 William Briggs (Bridges) of Scotland owned the mill lot, which by then had been reduced to 151 acres. In 1824 Andrew W. Briggs (Bridges) was listed as owner of the mill. The assessed value of the mill remained the same until 1839, when Fountain H. Lane bought the building and 15 acres. The deed recorded at the time of this purchase mentions that the grist mill was accompanied by a cotton gin. Age and neglect were likely responsible for a $200 reduction in the assessed value. Fountain Lane sold the property in 1852 to Andrew Briggs (Bridges) of Scotland, who appears to be the son of Andrew W. Briggs (Bridges) who had owned it previously. In 1856 Andrew sold the mill and 15 acres to James M. Briggs of Stony Hill. The following year a reassessment placed a value of $400 on the structure. The mill continued to operate until at least the 1940s, though by that time it was powered by a kerosene engine rather than by water.

Stony Hill

There were two homes in Stafford with the name of Stony Hill. This farm was located 8 miles northwest of Falmouth on the west side of State Route 622. The other Stony Hill was located in the northern part of the county and is now a part of Aquia Harbor.

Owners:

pre 1782-1813	David Briggs Sr.
1814-1843	James Briggs
1844-post Civil War	James Briggs' estate
1890	Purchased from other heirs by Mollie Briggs Cosby

David Briggs (1730-1813) came to Stafford from Fifeshire, Scotland, at the age of twenty-two. He settled at Stony Hill and operated a successful import business in Falmouth for many years.

As early as 1782 when the surviving tax records begin, Stony Hill was comprised of two tracts, 464 acres and 216 acres, totaling 680 acres. In 1824 James Briggs sold 102 acres to William Briggs (or Bridges) of Scotland, a nearby farm. In 1851, 27½ acres were sold to George Curtis, reducing the size of the farm to 550½ acres. That acreage remained constant until the Civil War, when the records gap.

Stony Hill was built on a terraced hill. It was one and one-half stories high and had dormers. Around 1840, the original house was torn down and a two-story frame house built on the site. This house had two large stone chimneys, four rooms, and a center hall. The walls were plastered. The gabled roof was covered with shingles and there were ten windows. In addition to the house, there was a small school on the farm where Briggs' children were educated by a tutor.

Building values were not listed in the tax records until 1817, when the house was assessed at $1,000, a considerable amount for the period. David Briggs died in 1813 and the property was inherited by his son James. The Briggses apparently did little to maintain or improve the house and it quickly lost value. By the time James Briggs died in 1843 the house was valued at only $661. By the time the Civil War broke out, the farm contained 550½ acres, with a dwelling valued at only $400. The Briggs heirs continued to live on the farm until well into the twentieth century. Stony Hill burned in the 1960s, the victim of an apparent Halloween prank.

Spotted Tavern Farm

Owners:

c.1780	Thomas Hopwood
c.1789-1800	James Dowdall (also spelled Dowdle)
1801-1839	Thomas and Ann Alcock
1840-1852	George Latham and heirs
1853-1899	Francis Forbes
1900-1942	William Huffman

Spotted Tavern stood just off U.S. Route 17 on the west side of State Route 612 near the old Hartwood Post Office. The history of the tavern is vague and descriptions of its construction vary considerably. Civil War accounts describe the tavern as being built of logs or of frame. There were three rooms on the first floor and two small rooms in the half-story. A porch ran the length of the building, and a very large chimney was built on the west end. There were three entrances, one to each room, with bars to fasten the doors. The interior walls were whitewashed in the simple fashion of the time, and the floors were made of wide planks.

The building was used as a tavern during the colonial days. The owners also farmed the 264-acre tract; an 1813 notation in the tax records states, "Spotted Tavern [is] good farming land."

During the eighteenth century the tavern was situated in a very remote part of the county. It provided necessary services, however, as covered wagons hauling goods from Fauquier and other northern counties stopped overnight on their way to Falmouth, yet another day's journey.

Exactly when the tavern was built is uncertain. Around 1789 James Dowdall bought the property from Thomas Hopwood. It is likely that Dowdall bought an established tavern, perhaps built by Hopwood. He was obviously operating a tavern for in 1790 and again in 1792 Dowdall was charged with "retailing spiritious Liquors without a license." Dowdall apparently didn't want to be bothered with applying for his annual license. This would not have been much of a bother; despite his remote location, he often had business at the court house. On several occasions he was appointed to do official inventories and even to report on the conditions of the roads. Court records show that in 1791 he did manage to apply to the court for a license to keep his ordinary. In April 1793 the court granted him leave "to erect a water grist mill on his own land."

Assessed property values often reveal a great deal about a farm or building. By following a tract through the tax records, one is able to determine dates of fires or other destructive forces, periods of ambitious building, and years of neglect. Building values were not included in the land tax records until 1817 and judging from those figures, Spotted Tavern's brightest days seem to have been from the mid-eighteenth century (when we know from court records that business was being conducted there) until the early 1820s. During that period the tavern was valued at $2,000, typical of most commercial properties such as taverns and mills. In 1825 the assessment dropped to $1,700 and by 1840 the value was listed as $945. By the time of the Civil War, the tavern, which by then had become a residence, was worth only $200. This substantiates the observation of one Union soldier, who noted that the building appeared well past its prime.

Since the earliest days of the colonies, taverns had served as post offices. Spotted Tavern continued that tradition by being the area's official post office from 1805 to 1825 and again briefly in 1835.

Spotted Tavern farm was an unwilling host to the Union Army on several occasions. Mr. Eli Embrey, who lived on the farm as an overseer, was too old to serve in the army and on one occasion when the Federals came onto the farm, he was away. His two daughters ran to warn a neighbor, leaving their mother and her sister-in-law alone in the house. Mrs. Embrey was so terrified of the soldiers that she raced all about the house praying. Amazed at her bizarre behavior, one of the soldiers asked, "Lord, Missus, haven't you ever prayed before?" The officer in charge put a man near the house to guard it and Mrs. Embrey was finally reconciled about the soldiers' camping there. However, she was only allowed to remain in her home if she took an oath of allegiance to the Union. It read:

> Headquarters 5th A.C.A.B.
> February 5, 1864
>
> I certify that I have this day administered the oath of allegiance to Kitty Embrey of Stafford County, Virginia.
>
> J. E. Holland
> 1st Lieutenant, F.F.
> U.S.A.

Hartwood Baptist Meeting House

Long ago destroyed by Federal troops, Hartwood Baptist Meeting House dated from 1776, when members of the Old School Order of the Baptist Church established themselves in Hartwood. Followers of the Old School adhered to a rigid code of behavior and worship, disciplined errant members, and interpreted the Bible literally.

Hartwood began as an extension of Chopawamsic Baptist Church (see "Chopawamsic Creek" in Chapter 7). Founded in 1768 by Elder Davis Thomas, Chopawamsic Baptist Church was one of the earliest Baptist Churches in this part of Virginia, meeting well before the Revolution which made denominations other than Church of England legally permissible. In 1771, thirty-six members of Chopawamsic were dismissed to form Potomac Baptist Church (probably located somewhere between Chopawamsic and Aquia Creeks). Potomac Church moved to Hartwood in 1776 where members erected a small frame or log sanctuary and changed the name to Hartwood Baptist Meeting House.

According to Robert B. Semple in *A History of the Rise and Progression of the Baptists in Virginia,* Potomac Baptist was organized under the pastorage of Elder William Fristoe, who had been ordained at Chopawamsic Baptist. Semple was highly critical of the lapse in obedience to the strict discipline code of the Old Order and praised Fristoe for his leadership in reviving the traditional tenets. After Fristoe ceased to be pastor, Elder John Hickerson was called as pastor. Following his death, Ephraim Abel attended the Hartwood Baptists though he may not have been an ordained minister.

From time to time, Hartwood would hold its business meetings in Fauquier County. In 1811 Robert Latham, George Sedwick, and fifty-five members from Hartwood were dismissed to form Grove Baptist Church in Fauquier. After the Civil War, a group from Grove returned to Stafford to organize Richland Baptist Church just off of U.S. Route 17.

Hartwood remained in continuous use until its destruction by Federal troops during the infamous "Mud March" of 1863 (see "The Civil War in Stafford" in Chapter 10). The precise location of the church is unknown. Cursory searches on both sides of Shackleford's Well Road (State Route 754) have failed to find so much as a foundation stone. Two maps from 1827 and the Civil War both show the building on the northwest side of Route 754, which was then known as Courthouse Road. The cemetery is on the southeast side of Route 754, directly behind Hartwood Elementary School.

In this church arose James Garrard (1749-1822), the son of William Garrard, who was an official tobacco inspector, county lieutenant, and proprietor of Garrard's Ordinary (site of the old Stafford Middle School on U.S. Route 1 just north of the court house). In 1769 James married Elizabeth Mountjoy, daughter of

Captain William Mountjoy (see "Locust Hill" in Chapter 9). In 1781 James held the rank of colonel in the Virginia militia. How much fighting he actually saw during the Revolution is open to speculation; his military career was interrupted by a year in the House of Delegates in 1779, when he represented Stafford County.

In 1783, accompanied by his wife and seven children, he removed to Kentucky. There he settled on Stoner Creek in present-day Bourbon County (then Fayette) which was still part of Virginia, Kentucky not yet being a state. Upon his arrival in Kentucky, he began preaching where, according to Semple, he "was thought to possess talents for the pulpit." For many years after his removal to Kentucky, his interests vacillated between religion and politics and, in 1787, he helped organize Cooper's Run Church near his home. Here he preached for the next sixteen years. In 1785 he was elected to represent Fayette County, a position which he used to work for Kentucky statehood.

In 1796 James was elected governor of Kentucky, an office he held until 1804. During his tenure as governor, he continued to preach at Cooper's Run but was very much influenced by his secretary, Harry Toulmin who, according to Semple, "was said to be a transatlantic Socinian preacher, but a man of talent." Toulmin was actually a Unitarian who interpreted the Bible as a collection of human experience and who disavowed the traditional Christian belief in the Trinity and the divinity of Jesus. Garrard espoused Toulmin's Unitarian views, totally contrary to the Baptist teachings, and succeeded in spreading those ideas in his own congregation at Cooper's Run. The resulting church schism caused James' removal as pastor of Cooper's Run and he was dropped from the Baptist Association, thus ending his ministry in 1803.

James never preached again and, after his term as governor expired in 1804, he never again ran for public office. However, his popularity with the population as a whole and with the legislature was attested to by the fact that his name was given to a newly created county in Kentucky.

The cemetery at Hartwood contains just .613 acre. There were at least 70 graves, all or most of which were marked with plain field stones, only a few of which survive. According to Mr. W. F. Monroe, former postmaster of Hartwood, the last interment was that of Aunt Puss King (probably a slave) around 1900. Over time, the cemetery was obliterated by dense undergrowth and trees. In more recent years, the site became a popular place for people to dump their trash. In 1990 the Citizens to Serve Stafford, a civic organization, removed some 18,000 pounds of trash, bedsprings, tires, and such. They marked the corners of the cemetery and placed plain white wooden markers on all of the discernible graves.

In 1910, John C. Stewart and his wife, Nannie, deeded the cemetery to Dr. H. W. Patton, B. B. Patton, and Suzie A. Monroe, trustees for Hartwood Baptist Church. They have long since died and work is being done to determine who presently owns the land and find a group or individual willing to maintain it.

Hartwood

The earliest known resident of the Hartwood plantation was Arthur Morson (1734/5-1798). Born in County Renfrew, Scotland, he settled in Virginia in 1752 and became involved in the mercantile business in Falmouth where he prospered. He seems to have been a man of some means before coming to Virginia, for as soon as he arrived here, he began purchasing numerous large tracts of land in King George, Stafford, and Fauquier Counties, including the Hartwood property and Hollywood (see Chapter 10), both of which were then situated in King George County. Within a few years of his arrival in Virginia, he was styled in King George County records as "Arthur Morson, Gentleman." Active in county affairs, he served as Sheriff of King George and in 1770 was one of the presiding Justices for that county. After the King George–Stafford boundary changes of 1777 placed most of Morson's landed estate in Stafford, he served as a Stafford County Justice. He was also a trustee of the town of Falmouth.

Morson acquired the Hartwood property shortly after his arrival in Falmouth, though it is unknown exactly when he built his home, or what became of it. The house was still standing in 1827 when the 3,677-acre plantation was surveyed but it was either gone or beyond occupation by the 1840s, when the Irvine family purchased the property.

Hartwood

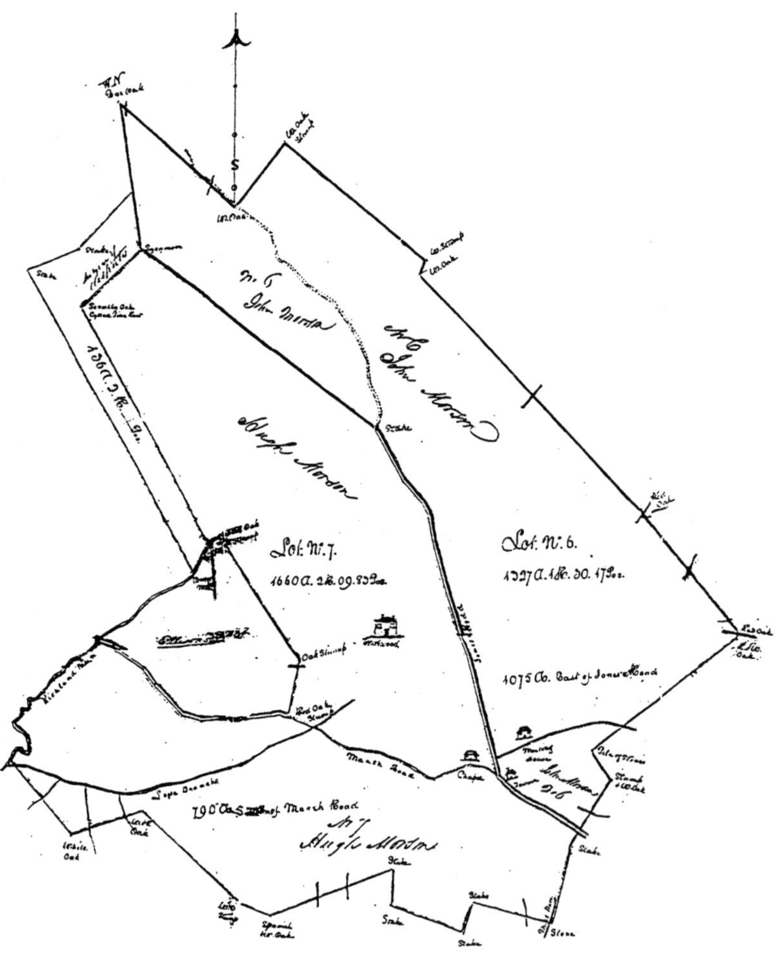

Lot: No. 7.
Lot: No. 6.
Hugh Morton
John Morton
March Road
Chapel
Hartwood
Stake

Sometime before the 1777 county boundary changes, Morson donated land on the corner of his Hartwood estate for the building of a chapel. Records refer to this house of worship as a "chapel of ease," apparently indicating that it was easier to get there than to get to churches in Falmouth or Fredericksburg. Morson's chapel soon became known as the Yellow Chapel because the outside of the building was covered with poplar siding which had a yellow hue. At the time of its establishment, Yellow Chapel was Anglican and was a part of Brunswick Parish whose lines were coterminous with King George's county lines. Other local churches that were originally part of Brunswick Parish included Union Church in Falmouth and Muddy Creek Church on Muddy Creek (the present-day boundary between Stafford and King George). Later on, Yellow Chapel (and Hartwood Church which followed it) became Presbyterian. Arthur Morson died in 1798 and was buried in the cemetery at Yellow Chapel, now the cemetery of Hartwood Presbyterian Church.

After Morson's death, Hartwood and Hollywood were inherited by Arthur's eldest son, Alexander (1759-1822) who had been a partner with his father in the Morsons' Falmouth store. Alexander resided at Hollywood and soon after his father's death gave up the store in town. Trade in Falmouth was declining as a result of poor economic conditions early in the nineteenth century and silting of the seaport. Once free of the business, Alexander devoted his attentions to agriculture.

Alexander Morson married Ann Casson Alexander (1781-1831) of Snowden (see Chapter 10), and they had nine children. Alexander's sons John and Hugh inherited Hartwood. The accompanying plat of 1827 illustrates the division of the Hartwood estate and is especially interesting because it shows the house as well as Hartwood Baptist Meeting House, Yellow Chapel, and Spotted Tavern.

On July 25, 1848, Hugh Morson sold to John and William Irvine 790 acres of the Hartwood tract for $2 per acre. The present Hartwood house was built soon after by William and his wife, Sarah. Something must have happened to the old Morson house between the survey of 1827 and the purchase of the property by the Irvine family, for the Irvines lived in a log house across the Marsh Road (U.S. Route 17) while waiting for their new house to be built.

Irvine's house was impressed in its day as this part of Stafford was still largely wilderness and most of the Irvines' neighbors lived in log houses. Hartwood was built near a crossroads, however; just to the east of Hartwood, the Marsh Road took a turn to the south (modern State Route 752), leading travelers to a ferry which would carry them across the Rappahannock to Spotsylvania. Earlier in the eighteenth century, this same road had led to Mountjoy's tobacco warehouse built at the mouth of Richland Run. On the north side of the Marsh Road was the Courthouse Road (now Shackleford's Well Road, State Route 754) which connected with Poplar Road (State Route 616), the main north–south route through the county. Straight beyond Hartwood, the road led to another ferry that transported travelers across the Rappahannock to Fauquier County. At the intersection of Marsh Road and Courthouse Road stood Spotted Tavern, the Yellow Chapel, and Hartwood Baptist Meeting House.

Irvine was a successful merchant who amassed a considerable estate in Stafford. He was eighty-four years old when the 1850 census was taken, at which time he was listed as owning 5,000 acres and 125 slaves. His land was not in one contiguous piece but, rather, in several farms each having its own labor force. At Hartwood, the slave quarters were located down by the run below the house. They disappeared long ago.

Hartwood is Federalist in design and has unusually fine brickwork and structural detail not normally found in houses of its era. Over time, the area around the Irvine farm came to be known as Hartwood, and this name may have been derived from the many deer, or hart, that lived there.

The house escaped the destruction that befell so many Stafford homes during the Civil War. Interestingly, the only real fighting in Stafford occurred near the house and Hartwood Church, but the two minor skirmishes resulted in little local damage. The Hartwood barn was used as a hospital for troops wounded at the Battles of Wilderness and Chancellorsville; it survived and has been restored.

The Irvine family were still living at Hartwood at the time of the war, and from October 1862 until May 1863 they were forced to share their house with Colonel William Averell's 3rd Pennsylvania Cavalry. The Union soldiers took over the ground floor of the house and the owners were allowed the upstairs.

In the fall of 1862, Irvine's eighteen-year-old grandson, Confederate private John William Irvine, attempted to return home for a fresh horse. Unknown to him, his home was now behind enemy lines. Dressed in civilian clothes, young Irvine was arrested by Union troops, tried, convicted as a spy, and sentenced to hang on December 21. He was held prisoner at Hartwood Church to await his execution. Letters from his family and girlfriend failed to convince General Burnside to pardon the boy. Only a last-minute appeal by General Robert E. Lee prevented the hanging. Lee explained to Burnside that young Irvine had been ordered by his commanding officer to procure a fresh horse from home—a typical order which the private was obeying. Neither the officer nor John had any way of knowing that the Irvine house had been commandeered by enemy troops. Burnside agreed with Lee's argument and just two days before his scheduled execution, John's sentence was commuted. He was released and allowed to return to his unit, in which he served the Confederacy for the remainder of the war.

Shortly thereafter, Confederate Colonel Fitzhugh Lee's troops seized the house and nearby Hartwood Church, killing nine and taking 125 Union prisoners. Lee retreated back across the river four days later, taking his prisoners with him and Union forces quickly moved back into the house. Five months later in March 1863, Confederate Cavalry Colonel Wade Hampton repeated Lee's earlier success by capturing and reoccupying the house for a short time.

The house was largely unoccupied during the mid-twentieth century and all but collapsed from neglect. Had it not been for the efforts of members of Historic Falmouth Towne, the building would have been demolished in 1972 by the Highway Department for the widening of U.S. Route 17. Fortunately, the highway planners were convinced to build the road around the house rather than through it.

In 1975 Charles Hudson bought the very dilapidated property and began restoring the fine old house. By the time Hudson found Hartwood, thick undergrowth had nearly hidden the house from sight. Termites had eaten so much of the beams and joists that the walls and floors sagged. Jacks were used to raise the floors and steel beams added support. All six fireplaces were repaired and reopened. In 1985 Hudson completed a new kitchen and family room. To the roof he added two dormers that balance beautifully with the stately brick chimneys.

Today, Hartwood again stands majestically. Most of the original farm has been sold but the nearby barn and a few surrounding acres provide a beautiful backdrop to this gem of Stafford's history.

Hartwood Presbyterian Church

William Irvine left his native Ireland in 1803 to escape religious persecution and settled in the Hartwood area of Stafford County, building a new home on the old Hartwood tract he had purchased from Hugh Morson. Irvine was a Presbyterian and, like his Presbyterian neighbors, had to travel to Fredericksburg each Sunday to worship as there was no church of their denomination nearby. Arthur Morson's Yellow Chapel had apparently been abandoned, for on July 22, 1825, the Winchester Presbytery organized a new Presbyterian congregation of about forty members. The group met in the little eighteenth-century Anglican chapel and from that time on, Presbyterian services were held there.

Around 1858 a red brick sanctuary was built near the early frame chapel at a cost of $2,000. This was quite inexpensive as most of the work was done by the parishioners, including the firing and hauling of bricks and the actual construction. The church was then renamed Hartwood Presbyterian Church.

During the Civil War, troops from both North and South vied for the use of the building. Union soldiers finally gained control and used it as a camp. During their stay, they burned every piece of wood flooring as well as all of the timbers in the church, resulting in massive damage to the building.

After the war, everyone in Stafford County was poverty-stricken, but the Hartwood Presbyterian parishioners managed to raise enough money to repair their beloved church. Donations ranged from $1 to as much as $10, and between 1868 and 1872 the church was repaired. Modernizations added at the time included a wood stove and two chandeliers with kerosene lamps.

In 1872 William, Sarah, and Rebekah Irvine deeded the church with one acre, along with the Hartwood manse and twenty-five acres, to the trustees of the church. Not until 1950 were major changes made to the building to allow for expansion. Today the manse belongs to a private owner.

Additional Sites

Berea Baptist Church—This church, founded in 1852, was located on the northeast side of U.S. Route 17 and on the north side of State Route 654. Donations of land and money enabled the congregation to build a brick church at a total cost of between $600 and $700. The church suffered major damage during the "Mud March" of January 1863. Union soldiers used the building as a stable, tore out the gallery and pews, and broke windows. After the war, the building was repaired and the U.S. government made restitution for the damages. The present walls are original.

Cedar Ridge

Eastern View—The house was built in 1742 by the Cropp family. It was later the home of the Sherman family. This farm was on the west side of State Route 614 almost on the Fauquier County line.

Inglewood

Liberty Hall—Near Berea. It was first acquired by Dr. Michael Wallace, who gave it to his son, John. The house was a two-story L-shaped log structure. The Wallace cemetery is northwest of the house site. By 1988 the farm still consisted of 518 acres stretching from Truslow Road (State Route 652) near Enon Community Center to Potomac Run near Abel Lake.

Mountjoy's Warehouse—Around 1703, Edward Mountjoy received a patent on the north fork of the Rappahannock. Two years later at the mouth of Richland Run where it flows into the Rappahannock, he built the first tobacco warehouse to be located above the falls of Falmouth. Nothing remains of the warehouse today.

Mount Olive Baptist Church—located on the north side of Kellogg Mill Road (State Route 650). This is the oldest black church in Stafford and was organized in 1818. The building began as a slab wood shelter which was later replaced by a more comfortable church.

Oak Grove—on Deep Run. In 1858 this was home to the Hill family.

Poor House Farm—2.4 miles northwest of Falmouth on U.S. Route 17 and very near the present-day truck stop. In 1835 the farm was bought by John Coleman, a slave trader. In 1840 it was sold to Willie Bond. General Burnside's troops camped here on the "Mud March" to Fredericksburg. After the Civil War, the county bought the farm and built several buildings to house the poor. There was one group of buildings for blacks and another for whites. The property was used as a county poor house until the first quarter of the twentieth century. Each of Stafford's two districts had a poor house; an "old poor house" was located just south of the court house on Accakeek Creek and another on the "Aquia Road" near Garrisonville.

Potomac Chapel—A small Episcopal chapel used from the late eighteenth century through the Civil War. It was on the east side of State Route 616 near the intersection with State Route 662. The bell from Potomac Chapel now rings in Hartwood Presbyterian Church.

Richard's Ferry—north on U.S. Route 17, west on State Route 649 to the end. This ferry transported people across the Rappahannock to Spotsylvania County.

Stringfellow's Mill—on Deep Run.

Chapter 12

Women of Note

&

Women of Stafford

It is obvious that the self-sufficient, independent woman was the norm for rural areas such as Stafford County. Only in developed areas could women afford the luxury of being pampered—only in areas where basic survival was not an everyday concern. Because Stafford hasn't seen much development until the last fifteen or twenty years, that strength and resiliency continued to be passed from mother to daughter and can still be found in the local population. Yet, one has only to drive a short distance now to see the conveniences that will bring an end to the conditions which produce this type of female.

A sense of business and management is not something new to women. It is something we had and then let go of and now we are trying to regain it, imagining all the while that this is some great and novel step forward. During the days before the Civil War, the wife of a planter was responsible for the operation of the entire household. This included directing numerous servants, managing household finances, educating or overseeing the education of the children, tending to the medical care of all of the workers and the family, training servants, overseeing the feeding of all the people living and working on the farm, and being the perfect hostess at any given moment for frequent but unannounced guests.

A newspaper article written by John Goolrick which appeared in *The Free Lance-Star* extolled the virtues of Stafford's women with great finesse:

> This narrative would be both imperfect and incomplete did I not include some reference to [Stafford's] women. 'I attribute all my success in life to the moral, intellectual and physical education which I received from my mother,' said Washington. I hazard nothing in declaring that this could be written of Stafford womanhood in general, especially as is it applicable to the success in life of its best and most distinguished citizens. The type, character and kind of its women 'of ye olden days' can never exist again, for the reason that the conditions, circumstances and environments under which they were born and in which they were reared can never return. They willingly, reverently and lovingly dedicated their unselfish lives to the uplifting and upbuilding of all who came within the sphere of their high and holy influence. A vast majority of these of whom I write sleep in the silent places of the dead. The world was made better and brighter that they lived, and heaven more beautiful when they died. To those of that era who linger among us, we pay tribute in admiration and devotion.

Indeed, there were many exceptional women who called Stafford home. They were the "Superwomen" of their day who had a profound influence on local affairs and in some instances, international affairs, as well.

Margaret Brent

Margaret Brent was born around 1600, one of thirteen children of Richard Brent, Lord of Admington and Stoke and his wife, Elizabeth Reed, of Gloucester, England. Margaret was the first woman in America to own vast tracts of land, to have business interests, to govern a manorial estate, to be appointed an executrix by a colonial governor, and to ask for a vote in the colonial assembly.

Margaret arrived in St. Mary's, Maryland, in November 1638 with her brothers Giles and Foulke and her sister Mary. With them came four maidservants and five male servants. Margaret also brought with her letters from Lord Baltimore advising the officials of St. Mary's to grant her "as much land in about the towne of St. Maries and elsewhere in that Province in as ample manner and with as large Priviledges as any of the first Adventurers." Margaret was the first woman in Maryland to own land in her own right and the Maryland officials, somewhat unsure how to address her, listed her in the deed books as "Margaret Brent, gentleman." Apparently, she had to repeatedly petition for additional land but by 1650, she controlled her own property, Sister's Freehold, the estates of Trinity and St. Gabriel, and Fort Kent which her brother Giles had deeded to her in 1642. These extensive holdings made her the largest land owner and, therefore, the most influential resident in Maryland.

Governor Leonard Calvert was undeniably impressed with Margaret's managerial abilities. During Calvert's temporary absence, she assembled a group of armed volunteers to help put down the Claiborne Rebellion of 1646 and managed to keep disgruntled soldiers from rioting until Calvert returned to pay them. The following year he appointed her executrix of his estate, and the Provincial court appointed her attorney for Lord Baltimore so she could handle both estates.

Two years after Calvert's death, Cecilius Calvert complained to the court about Margaret's handling of the estate. He claimed that she had used money from the estate to pay soldiers. The Maryland Assembly wrote a most remarkable answer to the allegations:

> As for Mrs. Brent's undertaking and meddling with your Lordship's estate here (whether she procured with her own or others importunity or not) we do verily Believe and in Conscience report that it was better for the Colony in her hands than in any man's else the whole Province after your Brother's death, for the soldiers would never have treated any other with that civility and respect, and though they were even ready at several times to run to mutiny, yet

> she still pacified them until at last things were brought to the Strait that she must be admitted and declared your Lordship's Attorney by an order of the Court (the copy where-of is herewith enclosed) or else all must go to ruin again, and then the second mischief were far greater than the former...We do conceive from that time she rather deserved favour and thanks from your Lordship for her so much concurring to the public safety than to be justly liable to those better invectives you have been Pleased to express against her.

Because she felt that she was assuming a man's responsibilities and, therefore, should be entitled to the same privileges, on January 21, 1648, Margaret appealed to the Assembly asking for a voice in their proceedings as well as two votes—one for herself as a landowner and one for her function as Lord Baltimore's attorney. Maryland authorities had been uncommonly permissive in their handling of Margaret but at this they drew the line. Her demand for voting rights was resoundingly denied.

In the meantime, Giles had moved across the Potomac River and settled in what was then Westmoreland County (now Widewater). Margaret joined him two years later, maintaining her land holdings in Maryland and acquiring yet more land in Virginia. Within a couple of years Giles built himself another home not too far from his Aquia Creek plantation, Peace, which he called Retirement.

Margaret and Mary continued to live at Peace and build their land holdings in Virginia. Although she left Maryland, Margaret did not give up her vast landholdings there. What is more, she greatly increased her holdings after arriving in Virginia. Land record books indicate that she held some 2,700 acres in Virginia, including the sites of present-day cities Alexandria and Fredericksburg.

Margaret died in 1671, leaving vast landholdings in Maryland and Virginia. Below is the will of Margaret Brent:

> In the name of God, Amen. I Margaret Brent of Peace in the County of Westmoreland in

Virginia, considering the casualtys of human life do therefore make this my last Will and Testament as followeth: my Soul, I do bequeath to the mercies of my Savior Jesus Christ, and my worldly estate to be disposed of by my Executors as followeth:—

To my nephew George Brent, I give all my rights to take up land in Maryland except those already assigned to my cousin James Clifton. To my niece Clifton I give a cow; to my niece Elizabeth Brent I give a heifer. To Ann Vandan I give a cow calf. To my niece Mary Brent, daughter of my Brother Giles Brent, I give all my silver spoons, which are six. To my nephew Richard Brent son of my brother Giles Brent, I give my patent of land at the Falls of Rappahannock River, also my lease of Kent Fort Manor in Maryland, saving yet power to his Father my brother Giles Brent that if he should like to do so he may sell said lease and satisfye to his son otherwhere as he shall think fit in lands goods or money, and in case of my said nephew Richard Brent's death under age and without heirs of his body lawfully begotten, his legacy thereto to go to his brother Giles Brent or his sister Mary Brent or to the heirs of my brother Giles Brent or otherwise as my said brother shall dispose it by his Deed or last Will.

To my brother Giles Brent and to his heirs forever I give all my lands, goods and chattels, and by estate real and personal and all that is or may be due to me in England, Virginia, Maryland or elsewhere still excepting the before disposed of in this my last Will and Testament.

In witness whereof I have hereunto set my hand and seal this 26th Day of December, Anno Domini, 1663.

Margaret Brent (Seal)

Probated
19 May 1671

Ann Thomson Mason, Wife of George Mason III

Ann Thomson was not a native of Stafford. She came to the county as a result of marriage into one of the most important families in the colony, the Masons. Regardless of this, she is well worth remembering, for her dedication to her family, her ability to handle tragedy, and her natural sense of business no doubt helped her son, George Mason (IV), become one of the great powers in eighteenth-century America. Ann was the daughter of Stevens Thomson, an Attorney General of Virginia. The Thomsons had several children all of whom, except Ann, died before their father. She inherited all of her father's substantial estate, making her a wealthy woman in her own right. In 1721 she married Colonel George Mason (III).

The Mason family had immigrated to Virginia from Staffordshire, England, in the 1650s and had settled on Accakeek Creek in what was then Westmoreland County. Soon thereafter, new county boundaries were drawn and the area became known as Stafford County, the name said to have been suggested by George Mason. George Mason (II) sold the Accakeek property after his father's death and moved to another tract on Chopawamsic Creek which he called Chopawamsic Farm (see Chapter 7). He built a fine stone house on a hill above the creek where he lived for a time. He continued to purchase property in northern Virginia and Maryland, as did his son, George Mason (III).

Ann's life in the Mason household seems to have been pleasant, and she bore her husband three children. Unfortunately, tragedy struck and Ann was forced to make decisions that she had never dreamed of. In 1735 George Mason was traveling by sail-powered ferry from his home on Chickamuxon Creek in Maryland to Quantico Creek. A sudden squall capsized the boat in the Potomac River and Mason drowned. After her husband's death, Ann returned to her parents' Maryland plantation with her children, where she remained until the settlement of her husband's estate. Of his numerous properties, Ann chose Chopawamsic Farm in Stafford

County as her dower; she moved there with her three children, George, 10, Mary, 4, and Thomson, 2, and began her new life.

Unlike most widows of her day, she did not re-marry. Ann was still a young and beautiful woman when her husband died. It is said that she had many suitors but she chose to remain a widow. She lived on the dower plantation for the next twenty-seven years, dedicating her life to her children and their futures. During this time, she developed a reputation for her intelligence, personal charm, and domestic disposition.

Mrs. Mason showed a remarkable sense of business, selling and leasing property and successfully handling all of her husband's business affairs. She kept meticulous ledgers, including child care expenses amounting to one thousand pounds of tobacco per child per year. She also entered minor expenses for the children including the cost of petticoats (regular and hoop), wooden-heeled shoes, and linen for Mary, and ruffled linen shirts for George and Thomson.

Two years after her husband's death, she leased to John Mercer the Occoquan plantation. This actually appears to have been a small settlement with several houses, a court house, prison, and ferry. The lease agreement was careful to stipulate that a room in the mansion house was reserved for her use any time she was traveling in the area. This is the property which later became known as Woodbridge.

John Mercer of Marlborough was guardian to the children and no doubt had a tremendous influence on them, especially George, who spent a great deal of time with him. Mercer's extensive law library and knowledge of that subject was freely available to the child. But George was also growing up in a household where responsibility, careful accounting, prudent financial management, and love were the priorities. This combination of influences created a man whom Ann was no doubt extremely proud of.

Under the English law of primogeniture, young George would inherit all of his father's estate. Like many other people of her day, Ann was adamantly opposed to this system because she felt it manifestly unjust to the younger children in the family who would be left penniless. Ann could not change the law but she could ensure that Mary and Thomson were provided for. Mrs. Mason spent years accumulating money with which to buy property for the two youngest children. By prudent economy she gathered enough money to buy 10,000 acres of "wild lands" in Loudoun County. Even though she paid only a few shillings per acre, this purchase was huge by contemporary standards. Rather than wait until her death to convey this property to Mary and Thomson as was customary, she did it immediately after purchasing. She said she did this so her children would not grow up feeling any sense of inequality between them. This greatly increased Mary's dowry and provided Thomson with land upon which he later built his home, Raspberry Plain. Unknowingly, by this wise investment Ann actually made Mary and Thomson wealthier than George.

Ann died on November 13, 1762. By this time, her son George was living at Gunston Hall. The loss of a mother is always one of the most heartfelt burdens for a man, and the loss of this mother must have been nearly unbearable. She had a reputation for great prudence, strong business sense, and an amiable and charming disposition. John Moncure, rector of Overwharton Parish and long-time family friend, described her as "a good woman, a great woman, and a lovely woman."

Anne Eliza Stribling Waller

Anne Eliza Stribling was born at Mountain View in Fauquier County on January 14, 1832. She married Withers Waller of Clifton on February 28, 1855. The couple had ten children, eight of whom (all girls) reached adulthood. The oldest of the girls was Kate Waller Barrett, one of the most influential people of her day.

Withers Waller owned and operated the nation's largest seine fishery at Clifton, and his wife assisted with the business (see "Waller Fishing Shore" in Chapter 6). The fishery shut down during the Civil War and Mrs. Waller and her small children followed Colonel Waller from camp to camp, a common practice. At one point during the war, she found herself and her children without food. Although she hated the Yankees, she walked right into General Grant's camp demanding to see the general himself. She had to settle for a member of his staff instead, but as luck would have it, the officer was the son of a man whom her father, Dr. Stribling, had treated. The man had died and the doctor had taken in the child and provided for him for three years. So thankful was he that not only did he provide her with food, but, sometime later, he also helped Mrs. Waller find transportation for her family from Appomattox to Fredericksburg.

After the war, the Wallers reopened the fishing shore. Colonel Waller died on January 14, 1900, leaving the operation to his wife and she continued to run the business until her death on April 13, 1903. She was seventy-one.

Kate Waller Barrett

Katherine Harwood Waller Barrett was the eldest of eight daughters born to Withers and Anne Eliza Stribling Waller of Clifton, Stafford County, Virginia. Born on January 24, 1857, her early education was by governess at Clifton, as her mother believed that girls should learn housekeeping skills along with other studies. Later, she attended the Arlington Institute in Alexandria.

During the Civil War, Kate's father joined the company headed by Fitzhugh Lee. The family followed him as closely as they dared, traveling to Fredericksburg, Bowling Green, Tomahawk, Petersburg, Burkeville, and Richmond. They struggled with chicken pox, measles, pneumonia, and childbirth.

A gift from her grandmother on her eighth birthday taught Kate a valuable lesson about human nature. Mrs. Stribling gave her as slaves two little black girls whom she had often played with (as was typical in those days). They ceased to be her friends, and Kate was not always kind to them. Yet, after Emancipation, Lucy and Jane remained, proving to Kate that people, once in unfortunate situations, often refuse to change, even if given the opportunity.

At Aquia Episcopal Church in Stafford she met the man with whom she could share her dreams for an education and an opportunity to serve all mankind, the Reverend Robert South Barrett. They were married in 1876 in the parlor at Clifton. Robert was then assigned to Christ Church in Richmond. The couple moved into a house in the midst of their congregation—in a very poor section of town. They were surrounded by poverty, drunkenness, slums, and factories.

Kate was most horrified by the countless number of abandoned children. One night, a very dirty girl appeared at their door carrying a baby. They took in the girl and her child, fed them and gave them clothes. Kate later made the observation:

> My boy with every door open to him, with every hand stretched out to aid him; her boy with every door closed to him, with every agency of society against his future progress. And when I realized that...good men and bad men, good women and bad women stood shoulder to shoulder to keep her down and out...that...society denied to her the right to redeem the mistakes of the past by an unblemished future—my very blood boiled within me....'Seest thou this woman?'

She promised herself then and there to help society's outcasts. With Robert's help, she completed the nursing program at the Florence Nightingale Training School and St. Thomas' Hospital in London. In 1892 she received her medical degree from the Medical College of Georgia, a rare feat for a woman of her day. Her husband died in 1896, leaving her with three sons and three daughters.

While her parents were quite proud of her accomplishments, her ideas and activities sometimes shocked them. Her father had told her that when passing some waif on the street, she should gather her skirts and pass quickly. Instead, she would hold open her arms and embrace the child. On the streets, Kate was known as "Mother Barrett."

Dr. Barrett was keenly interested in social work and from 1909 until her death sixteen years later was president of the National Florence Crittenton Mission for wayward girls (unwed mothers). In 1899 she served on the board of the National Council of Women and directed the American delegation of the Quinquennial of the International Council of Women in London. She also held numerous offices in connection with the Conference for the Care of Delinquent Children, the National and

International Councils of Women, the National Congress of Mothers, the Parent-Teacher Association, the Commission of Training Camp Activities during World War I, and other organizations. Her involvement with the Virginia Committee on Training Camp Activities revolved around her concern for the girls who flocked to the encampments. During a single war year, some 9,000 girls in the United States required care, more that twice the peacetime average.

In 1907 she represented both the National Council and the Florence Crittenton Mission at conferences in Jamestown, and in 1909 was a delegate to the International Council of Women at Toronto. That same year she also attended the Conference on the Care of Delinquent Children and spoke on this topic at meetings of the National Congress of Mothers and Parent-Teacher Associations. She was elected president of the National Council in 1911. In 1912, Kate served on a United States commission to study "the girl problem." She also served as a delegate on the International Conference of Abolition of White Slave Traffic in London. She also became a delegate in the conventions of the Women's Christian Temperance Union, the King's Daughters, and the State Conference of Charities.

In 1913 Kate attended the International Executive Council of Women at The Hague. Before leaving for Rome, she promoted two conferences. One dealt with an international agreement on white slavery and industrial employment, and the second with immigration and laws to protect children. Her reputation as an orator and an expert in these areas drew Washington legislators and foreign dignitaries. She was also appointed as a special agent of the Bureau of Immigration and the Department of Labor and sent to Europe to discuss immigration problems. After World War I, she was appointed by President Wilson as one of ten women to attend the Versailles Conference. Driven by her son, Major Charles Barrett, she took a 500-mile tour of the battlefields, stopping along the way to talk to the soldiers. To one group she said, "Young men of today up to the age of thirty and even beyond, are nearer perfection in conduct, morals and ideals than any similar generation of young men in the history of the world." Needless to say, she was a great favorite among the soldiers.

In 1914 and 1919 the United States government sent Dr. Barrett to Europe to discuss immigration problems.

She wrote several books, including *Some Practical Suggestions on the Conduct of a Rescue Home* (before 1904). A chapter in *Fourteen Years' Work Among Street Girls as Conducted by the National Florence Crittenton Mission* (1897) illustrated her belief that the chief influences in a rescue home were friendship, work, and religion. The girls who stayed in her shelters lived there for many years. She did not believe in separating infants from their unmarried mothers. A gentle person, she spent a good deal of time with the girls, offering advice and support.

Kate Waller Barrett was a remarkable woman who was many years ahead of her time. She died at her home in Alexandria of diabetes on February 23, 1925. She is buried at Aquia Church.

Dr. Barrett touched thousands of lives and had an immense influence over local, national, and international affairs. In tribute to her selfless work, the flag over the Virginia state capitol was flown at half mast to mark her death. She was the first woman to be so honored.

Her daughter later said of her, "If one wishes to know what a woman of national patriotism can do in the public service while standing for all that is noblest in the relations of public life, let one consult the record of Mrs. Barrett. It would be difficult to name any woman or even man that could match Dr. Barrett's public service for good in this generation."

Agnes Waller Moncure

Agnes left an indelible mark on Stafford County as did her daughter, Anne Eliza Stribling Moncure. Born on January 25, 1864, Agnes was a tiny woman. For a great many years, she was the backbone of Aquia Church. Her niece remembers that every Sunday would find her stationed in the corner of her church pew, and a family joke quipped that were it not for Aunt Ag sitting there, that corner of the church would collapse.

Agnes married Robert Ambler "Cappy" Moncure at Clifton Chapel on December 7, 1887. Typhoid fever was a terrible problem at that time and claimed many lives. There were no medical facilities in Stafford and few doctors, so members of the community had to look out for each other. Agnes and "Cappy" traveled about the area nursing people with typhoid and, in the process, risking their own lives. After attending a patient, they would stop off at the barn, bathe, and change clothes so as not to bring the disease into their own home.

Agnes adopted Aquia Church as her own as did many other members of the Moncure family. Had it not been for the devotion of this family, Aquia would probably have suffered the same fate as Potomac Church. Agnes Moncure founded the Aquia Church Association to assure a future for this venerable old structure. Her brother-in-law, Alfred Joseph Pyke, was the first president of the Association that continues to support the preservation and restoration of Aquia Church.

Agnes died on October 22, 1951, at the age of eighty-seven.

Miss Anne E. Moncure

Stafford has produced quite a few remarkable women and I have been truly blessed to have grown up around several of them. One who had a profound influence on my life was Anne Eliza Stribling Moncure, or Miss Anne E. as most of the county knew her. I am not alone in saying that she had an influence on my life. Any number of people in this country knew and loved Miss Anne E. as a teacher and friend. I knew her for almost thirty years and yet even in my earliest remembrances she was an old woman. She was one of those magical people who never changed, who was always there when I needed her, who was a "constant" in my life. I suppose the fact that she never changed made it that much harder for me to accept her death. She was eighty-nine when she died, and for several years prior I had intentions of writing down the multitude of stories she used to tell. Then one day, she was gone.

There is an unexplainable emptiness when someone who has been an integral part of your life since the beginning of memory suddenly leaves. But as I drive past the site of The Fleurry's, as I walk over what is left of rural Stafford, I realize that she is not gone. Miss Anne E. left an indelible mark on Stafford

County. I feel her presence everywhere and I know that I have been truly blessed to have been touched by her.

While growing up, I spent many a summer evening on the porch of the home of George and Louise Moncure. Miss Anne E., who lived alone a short distance from these, her cousins, would drive out several times a week to visit. We would all sit on the porch shelling peas or beans and sipping iced tea while her cousin Scott would encourage her to "tell us again about the time you..." and we would listen and laugh and enjoy. Much of my knowledge of Stafford and of life itself, I believe, had its roots in these evening sessions of story telling.

For those who didn't know Miss Anne E., seeing her drive was a bit startling. She had a severe congenital hip deformity that left her only about four and one-half feet tall. She had a huge green car and when she sat behind the wheel, she was all but invisible. In fact, in order to see where she was going, she had to look through the steering wheel and over the dash. To see her on the road, one had the distinct impression that the car was driving itself. Despite this, however, she drove anywhere and everywhere.

Teaching Days

Miss Anne E. worked in the Stafford schools for forty-three years, most of it spent as an elementary teacher. Upon graduating from the Normal School in Fredericksburg, she accepted the position of first grade teacher in Stafford. Her first class consisted of over thirty children ranging in age from six to sixteen, all of whom were in the first grade. This was in the 1920s when authorities set out to enforce compulsory school laws. One morning, a very large woman threw open the classroom door and stormed into the room with a nine-year-old boy slung over her hip. The child had never seen a schoolroom and was screaming and clawing madly. His mother tossed him towards Anne E. and said, "You want him? Well, here he is." On that note she turned on her heel and left. For several weeks he was deposited in much the same manner and in order to prevent his running away, Anne E. had to barricade the door with her body.

In addition to reading, writing, and arithmetic, Anne E. taught her students basic living skills such as ordering from the Sears' catalog, making change, and using indoor plumbing. For many of these children, running water and the toilet were things at which to marvel. There was a bathroom in the back of the classroom and Miss Anne E. took each child and taught him or her how to turn on and off the water and how to flush. Often, she would realize that one of her charges had vanished and she would know exactly where to look. The little one would be in the bathroom flushing and flushing, puzzling over the disappearing water.

Miss Anne E. had been teaching for several years when, one day, the superintendent came to her most agitated. He had just talked to the only teacher from the one-room school at Brooke, about five miles from the court house. She had had her hands full with some very rowdy children and had finally given up. In fact, right in the middle of the day she had walked out. In desperation, the superintendent asked Anne E. if she would take the class and try to restore order. Anne E. accepted the challenge and drove to Brooke. There she found a very disgruntled seventeen-year-old who was only in the third grade. Anne E. took him aside and he told her that life hadn't been very fair to him and he just didn't see much point in staying in school. His new teacher agreed that it certainly wasn't fair that he had been in school for so long and had only made to the third grade. If he would promise to stay in school, she would work with him and help him get into the proper grade. This young man went on to hold a very important position in government but she would never tell me who he was.

Many of our most influential citizens had Miss Anne E. for a teacher. Hence, she could tell stories about her experiences as a teacher for hours on end. But she never identified the characters in her stories. She said that we would recognize the names and she didn't think it was right to be telling tales. And so, the children that I feel I know personally will forever remain anonymous.

~ The First Field Trip ~

Anne E. worked with children who had never seen anything beyond Stafford. Their parents had never been beyond the county line nor had their parents before them. Miss Anne E. decided to take her students on a field trip to Mount Vernon, which had recently been opened to the public. She spent weeks preparing the children for the trip by teaching them about the British coming to America, about the Revolution and George Washington. They studied a world map and learned where America, Virginia, the Atlantic Ocean, and England were located. She told the children that they would be doing a great deal of walking and to wear comfortable shoes (many of the students had only one pair of shoes during warm weather and they were stiff fancy shoes for going to church).

Some of the children were to travel in Anne E.'s big station wagon and the rest in another car. Finally, the group set out on their first trip out of Stafford. Everything was fine until they reached the Occoquan River above Woodbridge. Upon seeing the bridge spanning the rock cliffs high above the river, one little boy began screaming in terror. They weren't taking HIM across that thing! He knew it would collapse and they would all fall into the river and drown! The little caravan came to a halt as Anne E. tried to explain about the bridge and how it was built to let cars get from one side of the river to the other. The little boy would not be swayed, however. He was not going across. There being little traffic in those days, the class sat for some while before a large truck came lumbering along and crossed the bridge. Anne E. pointed out to the child that the truck was much larger and heavier than their car and that it had made it across without the bridge giving a single shake. If that big truck could get across, couldn't a car? Finally, the child agreed to go and the group set out.

They arrived at Mount Vernon and had a wonderful time. The children had never seen so fine a house, and they told stories about George and Martha Washington and the Revolution. Out on the lawn the children enjoyed the beauty of the buildings and landscaping. One child, noticing the vast stretch of water below the house, pointed to the opposite shore and shouted, "Look, Miss Moncure, there's England!" Well, his sense of direction was fine but he was a few miles off, for he was looking across the Potomac River at the Maryland shore. When the only flowing water he had ever seen was narrow enough to hop across, the Potomac seemed like an ocean indeed!

Stafford's First Library

These Stafford children had critical educational needs and Anne E. knew that access to books played a vital role in education. Since there were no libraries in Stafford, she put one together and ran an early type of "Bookmobile." She owned a very large station wagon at the time and she managed to procure a number of books that she packed into the back of her car. She would drive to each school within the county once a week and the children could select a book to read. The following week she would return and the students could exchange their books for different ones. She ran her mobile library for quite a few years and brought a world of literature to children who might not otherwise have ever experienced it.

Mary Cary Expresses Her Regrets

In the living room of The Fleurry's hung a large oil painting of Mary Cary Ambler, a distant Moncure relative. Miss Anne E. always enjoyed telling the tale of how the painting came to have a tear over her heart. It seems that George Washington had been one of Mary Cary's suitors (actually, George had tried to marry a number of Stafford women but none would have him) and she had rejected him because he was just a surveyor and she didn't believe he would ever amount to anything. George ended up doing better than many people expected and, supposedly, Mary Cary had some regrets about her decision. She apparently carried those regrets with her into the next world.

Mary Cary's portrait had hung on the parlor wall above a chair for many years when, in 1931, Mount Vernon was opened to the public. This was quite an occasion indeed, because few former residents of Stafford have ever been honored in such a way. Miss Anne E. and all her family traveled north for the opening but when they returned home that evening, they found that Mary Cary had fallen off the wall and the corner of the chair had pierced her through the heart. The Moncures had her repaired and returned her to the wall, where she remained until the house was torn down.

Oh, Horsefeathers!

Although she was tiny in stature, Anne E. was always feisty. As a young woman, her father sent her to Brooke Station to meet visitors who were arriving by train. She drove the horse and wagon from The Fleurry's to Brooke with no problem. When the train arrived, however, the horse became terrified and began rearing and bolting. Anne E. ran to the animal's head and took hold of the bridle just as he reared straight into the air. Holding tight, with long skirts flying, she went right up with the horse. She came down with the horse, straightened her skirt, picked up her guests and took them home. The poor station attendant was so distraught that he called her father and asked that she never again be sent alone to meet a train.

Bibliography

Albaugh, William A. and Edward N. Simmons, *Confederate Arms*. NY: Bonanza Books, n.d.

The Alexandria Gazette, September 1769, Advertisement for sale of Chopawamsic Farm.

Allard, Dean C. "The Potomac Navy of 1776." *Virginia Magazine of History and Biography*. October 1976, vol. 84, no. 4, pp. 411-430.

Anderson, Sarah Travers Lewis. *Lewises, Meriwethers, and Their Kin*. Richmond: Dietz Press, 1938.

Barrett, Kate Waller. "Some Reminiscences," *The Florence Crittenton Magazine*. March 1899.

Berry, Spencer. "In Stafford county: Memories of Stanstead." *Fredericksburg Times*. June 1990, 46-48.

Binford, Elizabeth R. "Four George Masons of Stafford." *Northern Neck Historical Magazine*. December 1951, vol. 1, no. 1, pp. 56-65.

Boye Map of Stafford County, Virginia, c.1820.

Brent's Mill Ledger Books, 2 volumes, 1804-1806, University of Virginia.

Brent, Chester Horton. *The Descendants of Coll. Giles Brent, Capt. George Brent, and Robert Brent, Gentleman, Immigrants to Maryland and Virginia*. Vermont: Tuttle Publishing Co., 1946.

"The Brent Family," *Virginia Magazine of History and Biography*. vol. XVII, no. 3, Richmond, House of the Society, July 1909, pp. 308-311.

"British Mercantile Claims: 1775-1803." *Virginia Genealogist*. July-September 1970, vol. 14, no. 3, pp. 129-134.

Brooke, St. George Tucker. *Autobiography of St. George Tucker Brooke*. Virginia Historical Society.

Brown, Kathi Ann. "House of Another Chance: Kate Waller Barrett's Ivakota," *Northern Virginia Heritage*. Reston VA: Better Impressions, Inc., vol. 10, no. 3, October 1988, pp. 3-6, 19-20.

Bruce, Kathleen. *Virginia Iron Manufacture in the Slave Era*. NY: Century Co., 1931.

Bruce, Philip A. *Virginia: Rebirth of the Old Dominion*. Lewis Co., 1929.

Carter, Edward C., John C. Van Horne, and Lee W. Formwalt, ed. *The Journals of Benjamin Henry Latrobe, 1799-1820: From Philadelphia to New Orleans*. vol. 3, New Haven: Yale University Press, 1980.

"Carter Papers." *The Virginia Magazine of History and Biography*. vol. 5, Richmond: House of the Society, 1898, 408-428.

Chastellex, Marquis de. *Travels in North America, 1780-1782*. vol. 11, p. 420.

Chilton, W.B. "The Brent Family." *Genealogies of Virginia Families: from Tyler's Quarterly Historical and Genealogical Magazine*. vol. 1, Baltimore: Genealogical Publishing Co., Inc., 1981, pp. 233-428.

Choppawamsic Baptist Church Records, 1776-1919, Rappahannock Regional Library.

Coakley, R. Walter. "The Two James Hunters of Fredericksburg: Patriots Among the Virginia Scotch Merchants." *Virginia Magazine of History and Biography*. vol. 56, no. 1, January 1948, 3-21.

Commager, Henry Steele, ed. *The Blue and Gray: The Story of the Civil War as Told by the Participants*. "The Mud Campaign" by Dunn Browne. NY: Bobbs-Merrill Co., Inc., 1950, 320-321.

Culver, Francis Barnum. *Blooded Horses of Colonial Days*. Baltimore: Kohn and Pollock, Inc., 1922.

Darter, Oscar H. "A Glimpse of the Background and Early History of Stafford County," *Northern Neck Historical Magazine*. December 1958, vol. VII, no. 1, pp. 704-709.

Darter, Oscar H. *Colonial Fredericksburg*.

Davis, Vernon Perdue and James Scott Rawlings. *The Colonial Churches of Virginia, Maryland, and North Carolina: Their Interiors and Worship*. Richmond: Dietz Press, 1985.

Dictionary of American Biography. vol. I, NY: Scribners, 1964, pp. 645-646.

Edrington and Moncure Company Account Book, Virginia Historical Society.

Embry, Alvin T. *History of Fredericksburg, Virginia*. Richmond: Old Dominion Press, 1937.

Embrey, Ida J. "History of Grove Baptist Church." 1945.

Foote, A. Edward. *Chotankers: a Family History*. Florence, Alabama: Thornwood Book Publishers, 1982.

Foote, Shelby. *The Civil War, a Narrative: Fredericksburg to Meridian*. NY: Vintage Books, 1986, 129.

Free Lance-Star. July 13, 1888, advertisement for the sale of Selwood.

French, David M. *The Brent Family*. Alexandria, VA, 1977.

Friends Historical Association, Barbara L. Curtis, President, Haverford College Library, Haverford, Penn., 1941.

Gaines, William H. *Virginia Cavalcade*. vol. XVI, no. 4, Spring 1967, pp. 32-37.

"Genealogy: the Ancestors and Descendants of John Rolfe, with Notices of Some Connected Families," *Virginia Magazine of History and Biography*. vol. XXIII, no. 2, April 1915, pp. 214-216.

General Index of Stafford County Court Records, Stafford County Court House.

Gordon, George L., Jr. "History of Aquia Church," (transcribed speech), June 1985.

Gordon, George L., Jr. *Highlights of Stafford County History.* Historic Falmouth Towne and Stafford County, Inc., 1973.

Griffin, William E., Jr. *One Hundred Fifty Years of History Along the Richmond, Fredericksburg, and Potomac Railroad.* Richmond: Whitter and Shepperson, 1984.

Grigsby, Hugh Blair. *The Virginia Convention of 1776.* Richmond: 1855, pp. 162-165.

Hageman, James. *The Heritage of Virginia.* Norfolk: Donning Co., 1986.

Hall, Virginius Cornick. "Virginia Post Offices, 1798-1859." *Virginia Magazine of History and Biography.* January 1973, vol. 81, no. 1, pp. 49-97.

Happel, Ralph. *Chatham, the Life of a House.* Philadelphia: Eastern National Park and Monument Assn., 1984.

Harrison, Fairfax. *Landmarks of Old Prince William.* Berryville VA: Chesapeake Book Co., 1964.

Harrison, Fairfax. "The Will of Charles Carter of Cleve." *The Virginia Magazine of History and Biography.* vol. 31, December 31, 1923, Richmond VA: House of the Society, 39-69.

Harrison, Noel G. "Rumford." *Fredericksburg Civil War Sites.* Lynchburg VA: H.E. Howard, Inc., 1995, pp. 109-114.

Hayden, Rev. Horace E. *Virginia Genealogies.* Baltimore: Genealogical Publishing Company, 1979.

Heite, Edward F. "Markets and Ports." *Virginia Cavalcade.* vol. 16, Autumn 1966, 29-41.

Hening, William Waller, ed. *Hening's Statutes at Large.* Richmond VA, 1821.

Historical and Archaeological Committee, Citizens to Serve Stafford. *Foundation Stones of Stafford County, Virginia.* 1991.

"James Alexander Seddon." *Dictionary of American Biography.* vol. 8, NY: Scribners, 1964, 545-546.

"James Garrard." *Dictionary of American Biography.* vol. 8, NY: Scribners, 1964, 159-160.

Jett, Dora Chinn. *In Tidewater Virginia.* Whittet, 1924.

"Kate Waller Barrett." *Dictionary of American Biography.* vol. 8, NY: Scribners, 1964, 645-646.

King, George H.S. "Notes from the Journal of John Mercer, Esquire (1704/5-1768) of Marlborough, Stafford County, Virginia," *Virginia Genealogist.* vol. IV, no. 3, July-September 1960, pp. 99-110.

King, George H.S. "Notes from the Journal of John Mercer, Esquire (1704/5-1768) of Marlborough, Stafford County, Virginia," *Virginia Genealogist.* vol. IV, no. 4, October-December 1960, p. 153.

King, George H.S. "Notes on Stafford Springs." June 4, 1992.

King, George H.S. *Register of Overwharton Parish Stafford County, Virginia, 1723-1758.* Easley, S.C.: Southern Historical Press, 1986.

King, George H.S. "The Will of Capt. William Mountjoy of Stafford County." *Tyler's Quarterly Historical and Genealogical Magazine*. vol. 26, January 1945, 99-104.

King, George H.S. "The Will of Maj. William Newton of Stafford County." *Tyler's Quarterly Historical and Genealogical Magazine*. vol. 23, January 1942, 222-234.

Lacy, Bettie Churchill. "Memories of a Long Life." 1903, Rappahannock Regional Library.

Lee, Margaret DuPont. *Virginia Ghosts*. Berryville VA: Virginia Book Co., 1930.

Lemay, J.A. Leonard. "John Mercer and the Stamp Act in Virginia, 1764-1765." *Virginia Magazine of History and Biography*. January 1983, vol. 91, no. 1, pp. 3-38.

"Letters of William Fitzhugh," *Virginia Magazine of History and Biography*. vol. III, 1895-96, Richmond: House of the Society, p. 255.

"Local Notices from the Virginia Independent Chronicle, Richmond, 1787," *Virginia Genealogist*. vol. 37, no. 2, April-June 1993.

Longmore, Paul K. "From Supplicants to Constituents: Petitioning by Virginia Parishioners, 1701-1775." *Virginia Magazine of History and Biography*. October 1995, vol. 103, no. 4, pp. 407-442.

McIlwaine, H.R., ed. *Journals of the Council of the State of Virginia*. vol. I, July 12, 1776-October 2, 1777, Richmond: Virginia State Library, 1931.

McIlwaine, H.R., ed. *Journals of the Council of the State of Virginia*. vol. II, October 6, 1777-November 30, 1781, Richmond: Virginia State Library, 1931.

McIlwaine, H.R., ed. *Journals of the Council of the State of Virginia*. vol. III, December 1, 1781-November 29, 1786, Richmond: Virginia State Library, 1931.

McIlwaine, H.R., ed. *Journals of the Council of the State of Virginia*. vol. IV, December 1, 1786-November 10, 1788, Richmond: Virginia State Library, 1931.

McIlwaine, H.R., ed. *Journals of the Council of the State of Virginia*. vol. V, November 13, 1788-November 29, 1791, Richmond: Virginia State Library, 1931.

McIlwaine, H.R., ed. *Executive Journals of the Council of Colonial Virginia*. vol. IV, October 25, 1721-October 28, 1739. Richmond: Virginia State Library, 1930.

McIlwaine, H.R., ed. *Executive Journals of the Council of Colonial Virginia*. vol. V, November 1, 1739-May 7, 1754. Richmond: Virginia State Library, 1930.

McIlwaine, H.R., ed. *Executive Journals of the Council of Colonial Virginia*. vol. VI, June 20, 1754-May 3, 1755. Richmond: Virginia State Library, 1930.

McIlwaine, H.R., ed. *Journals of the House of Burgesses of Virginia, 1619-1658/59*. Richmond: Virginia State Library, 1915.

McIlwaine, H.R., ed. *Journals of the House of Burgesses of Virginia, 1659/60-1693*. Richmond: Virginia State Library, 1915.

McIlwaine, H.R., ed. *Journals of the House of Burgesses of Virginia, 1695-1696, 1696-1697, 1698, 1699, 1700-1702.* Richmond: Virginia State Library, 1915.

McIlwaine, H.R., ed. *Journals of the House of Burgesses of Virginia, 1702/3-1705, 1705-1706, 1710-1712.* Richmond: Virginia State Library, 1915.

McIlwaine, H.R., ed. *Journals of the House of Burgesses of Virginia, 1712-1714, 1715, 1718, 1720-22,1723-1726.* Richmond: Colonial Press, 1915.

McIlwaine, H.R., ed. *Journals of the House of Burgesses of Virginia, 1727-1734, 1736-1740.* Richmond: Colonial Press, 1915.

McIlwaine, H.R., ed. *Journals of the House of Burgesses of Virginia, 1742-1749.* Richmond: Colonial Press, 1915.

McIlwaine, H.R., ed. *Journals of the House of Burgesses of Virginia, 1752-1755, 1756-1758.* Richmond: Colonial Press, 1915.

McIlwaine, H.R., ed. *Journals of the House of Burgesses of Virginia, 1758-1761.* Richmond: Colonial Press, 1915.

McIlwaine, H.R., ed. *Journals of the House of Burgesses of Virginia, 1761-1765.* Richmond: Colonial Press, 1915.

McIlwaine, H.R., ed. *Minutes of the Council and General Court of Colonial Virginia, 1622-1632, 1670-1676.* Richmond: Virginia State Library, 1924.

"Mercer Land Book," *William and Mary College Quarterly.* vol. XIII, no. 3, January 1905, p. 167.

The Miller in Eighteenth-Century Virginia. Williamsburg: Colonial Williamsburg, 1978.

Moncure, Thomas M., Jr., and Molly A. Pynn. *The Story of Aquia Church.* Fredericksburg: Cardinal Press, 1987.

Musselman, Homer D. *47th Virginia Infantry.* Lynchburg VA: H.E. Howard, Inc., 1991.

Musselman, Homer D. *Stafford County in the Civil War.* Lynchburg VA: H.E. Howard, Inc., 1995.

Musselman, Homer D. *Stafford County, Virginia, Veterans and Cemeteries.* Fredericksburg VA: Bookcrafters, 1994.

Mutual Assurance Society of Virginia Policies, 1803-1816.

Nagel, Paul C. *The Lees of Virginia: Seven Generations of an American Family.* NY: Oxford University Press, 1990.

Neumann, George C. *The History of Weapons of the American Revolution.* NY: Bonanza Books, n.d.

Northumberland/Westmoreland County Court Records.

Nugent, Nell Marion. *Cavaliers and Pioneers: Abstracts of Virginia Land Patents and Grants.* vol. I-III, Richmond: Virginia State Library, 1979.

Palmer, William P., ed. *Calendar of Virginia State Papers and Other Manuscripts.* Richmond, VA, 1875.

"Peter Vivian Daniel." *Dictionary of American Biography.* vol. 3, NY: Scribners, 1964, 69-70.

Peters, Margaret T. *Guidebook to Virginia's Historical Markers.* Charlottesville: University of Virginia Press, 1985.

Peyton, John Lewis. *The Adventures of My Grandfather.* London: John Wilson Pub., 1867.

Powell, Lewis F. "Supreme Court Justices from Virginia." *Virginia Magazine of History and Biography.* April 1976, vol. 84, no. 2, pp. 131-141.

Prince William: The Story of its People and its Places. Manassas: Bethlehem Good Housekeeping Club, 1961.

Quantico Condemnations Book, Stafford Court House.

Rawlings, James Scott. *Virginia's colonial Churches: an Architectural Guide.* Richmond: Garrett and Massie, 1963.

Readnour, Harry Warren. *General Fitzhugh Lee, 1835-1905, a Biographical Study.* Ann Arbor: University Microfilms, 1971.

Records of Dettingen Parish: Prince William County, Virginia. Dumfries VA: Historic Dumfries, Virginia, Inc., 1976.

Round, Harold F. "Aquia Creek," *Virginia Cavalcade.* XIII, Summer 1963.

Rowland, Kate Mason. *Life of George Mason: 1725-1792.* vols. I & II, NY: Russell and Russell, Inc., 1964.

Schriner-Yantis, Netti and Florene Speakman Love. *The 1787 Census of Virginia.* Springfield VA: Genealogical Books in Print, 1987.

Semple, Robert B. *A History of the Rise and Progression of the Baptists in Virginia (revised and extended by Rev. G.W. Beale).* Richmond VA: Pitt and Dickinsons Publishers, 1894.

Sparacio, Ruth and Sam. *Stafford County Deed and Will Abstracts 1686-1689.* McLean, VA, n.d.

Sparacio, Ruth and Sam. *Stafford County Deed and Will Abstracts 1689-1693.* McLean, VA, n.d.

Sparacio, Ruth and Sam. *Stafford County Deed and Will Abstracts 1699-1709.* McLean, VA, n.d.

Sparacio, Ruth and Sam. *Stafford County Deed and Will Abstracts 1722-1728.* McLean, VA, n.d.

Sparacio, Ruth and Sam. *Stafford County Deed and Will Abstracts 1748-1767.* McLean, VA, n.d.

Sparacio, Ruth and Sam. *Stafford County Deed and Will Abstracts 1780-1786.* McLean, VA, n.d.

Sparacio, Ruth and Sam. *Stafford County Deed and Will Abstracts 1809-1810.* McLean, VA, n.d.

Sparacio, Ruth and Sam. *Stafford County Deed and Will Abstracts 1810-1813.* McLean, VA, n.d.

Sparacio, Ruth and Sam. *Stafford County Deed and Will Abstracts 1825-1826*. McLean, VA, n.d.

Sparacio, Ruth and Sam. *Stafford County Order Book Abstracts 1689-1692*. McLean, VA, n.d.

Sparacio, Ruth and Sam. *Stafford County Order Book Abstracts 1692-1693*. McLean, VA, n.d.

Sparacio, Ruth and Sam. *Stafford County Will Book Abstracts 1729-1748*. McLean, VA, n.d.

Sparacio, Ruth and Sam. *Stafford County Will Book Abstracts 1749-1767*. McLean, VA, n.d.

Stafford County Circuit Court Records, Henry Moore vs. Withers Waller, 1868.

Stafford County Court Records, Deed and Will Books.

Stafford County Land Tax Records, 1782-1861, Virginia State Library, Richmond.

Stafford County Land Tax Records, 1880-1900, Stafford County Court House.

"Stafford County Legislative Petitions, 1776-1781," *Virginia Genealogist*. vol. 31, no. 1, January-March 1988, pp. 62-71.

"Stafford County Legislative Petitions, 1776-1781," *Virginia Genealogist*. vol. 31, no. 4, October-December 1987, pp. 306-310.

Stafford County Mines (Maps) 1836 and 1850, Virginia Historical Society, Richmond VA.

Stafford County Personal Property Tax Records, 1812 and 1817, Stafford County Court House.

Stanard, W.G. "The Thornton Family." *Genealogies of Virginia Families*. vol. V, Baltimore: Genealogical Publishing Co., 1982, pp. 19-64.

"Stanstead Farm." *The Spur*. September 1955, 2-3.

Strother Family Reunion Booklet, August 1992, pp. 25-31.

Swen, E.G. "The Disqualifications of Ministers in State Constitutions." *William and Mary Quarterly*. vol. XXVI, p. 75.

Tilp, Frederick. *This was Potomac River*.

"Virginia Council Journals," *Virginia Magazine of History and Biography*. Richmond: Virginia Historical Society, vol. XIV, no. 3, January 1907, p. 236.

The Virginia Gazette, April 21, 1738, Sale of Strother farm.

The Virginia Gazette, November 5, 1772, Sale of Ferry Farm.

The Virginia Gazette, September 27, 1776, Court-martial of Capt. James.

The Virginia Gazette, January 8, 1780, Notice of closing of Cave's Warehouse.

The Virginia Gazette, June 6, 1751, Advertisement for undertakers for new church at Aquia.

The Virginia Gazette, May 1773, Advertisement for sale of Chopawamsic property.

The Virginia Gazette, September 27, 1776, Notice of the burning of Brent's Richland by the British.

The Virginia Herald, December 13, 1792, advertisement for the sale of Bellview.

The Virginia Herald, November 9, 1808, Duel between Peter Vivian Daniel and Capt. John Seddon.

The Virginia Herald, June 21, 1834, William Pollock owner of Douglass threshing machine.

The Virginia Herald, September 12, 1826, Sale of Mercer's Ferry.

The Virginia Herald. July 31, 1794, Advertisement for sale of James Hunter's home and land.

Virginia Historic Landmarks Commission Staff Report: Accakeek Iron Works, February 1984, Richmond VA.

Virginia Historic Landmarks Commission Staff Report: Aquia Church, Richmond VA.

Virginia Historic Landmarks Commission Staff Report: Clearview, Richmond VA.

Virginia Historic Landmarks Commission Staff Report: Falmouth Preservation Zone, Richmond VA.

Virkus, Frederick A., ed. *Abridged Compendium of American Genealogy.* vol. III, Chicago: F.A. Virkus, and Company, 1928.

Vogt, John and T. William Kethlely. *Stafford County, Virginia Tithables: Quit Rents, Personal Property Taxes and Related Lists and Petitions, 1723-1790.* Athens, GA: Iberian Publishing Co., 1990.

Wertenbaker, Thomas J. *Planters of Colonial Virginia.* Princeton University Press, 1922.

Whitton, Amy H. "Silk-masters of Virginia," *Virginia Cavalcade.* Spring 1964, pp. 42-47.

"Will of William Fitzhugh," *Virginia Magazine of History and Biography, vol. II, 1894-1895.* Richmond: House of the Society, pp. 276-278.

Works Progress Administration Historical Inventory, Stafford County. Virginia Conservation Commission, 1936-38, Rappahannock Regional Library.

Index